MW00787763

Alias Jack the Ripper

Alias
Jack the Ripper

Beyond the Usual Whitechapel Suspects

by

R. MICHAEL GORDON

McFarland & Company, Inc., Publishers
Jefferson, North Carolina, and London

Photographs from the Public Record Office (London) © the
Metropolitan Police. They are reproduced by permission of
the Commissioner of Police of the Metropolis.

Library of Congress Cataloguing-in-Publication Data

Gordon, R. Michael.
　　Alias Jack the Ripper : beyond the usual Whitechapel
suspects / by R. Michael Gordon.
　　　　p.　　cm.
　　Includes bibliographical references and index. ∞
　　ISBN 0-7864-0898-7 (softcover : 50# alkaline paper)
　　1. Jack, the Ripper.　2. Serial murders — England —
London — History — 19th century.　3. Serial murderers —
England — London — History — 19th century.　4. Whitechapel
(London, England) — History — 19th century.　I. Title.
HV6535.G6L65348　　2001
364.15'23'092 — dc21　　　　　　　　　　　　　　　　00-46458

British Library cataloguing data are available

Cover image © 2001 Image Club.

©2001 R. Michael Gordon. All rights reserved

*No part of this book may be reproduced or transmitted in
any form or by any means, electronic or mechanical, including
photocopying or recording, or by any information storage and
retrieval system, without permission in writing from the publisher.*

Manufactured in the United States of America

McFarland & Company, Inc., Publishers
　Box 611, Jefferson, North Carolina 28640
　　www.mcfarlandpub.com

For the Ladies of Victorian London's East End,
who so long ago walked into history.
Rest well.
The darkness is over.

I have been so struck with the remarkable coincidences in the two series of murders that I have not been able to think of anything else for several days past ... not, in fact, since the Attorney-General made his opening statement at the recent trial, and traced the antecedents of Chapman before he came to this country in 1888. Since then the idea has taken full possession of me, and everything fits in and dovetails so well that I cannot help feeling that this is the man we struggled so hard to capture fifteen years ago...

Inspector Frederick George Abberline, March 1903

Acknowledgments

No work on the Whitechapel murders, popularly known as the Jack the Ripper series, stands alone, as there are many references published which allow interested readers and researchers the opportunity to discover the known facts of the case. There is indeed much written on the subject. There are two monumental works, however, which stand above most in compiling and presenting the facts of the case in an intelligent and thoughtful manner. It is to these two giants that I am most grateful, and I readily acknowledge their overwhelming usefulness in my researching and understanding the subject of "Jack the Ripper."

The first is *The Jack the Ripper A to Z*, by Paul Begg, Martin Fido and Keith Skinner. This is easily one of the best reference works on the subject of Jack the Ripper and is highly recommended to anyone with an interest in the subject.

The second of these two giants is *The Complete History of Jack the Ripper*, by Philip Sugden. This detailed work fully and colorfully unfolds the Ripper case, step by step, and brings the reader along for an entertaining and fact filled ride. It is indeed a complete and vital reference of the known facts.

There is one additional source which has proven to be of great help in understanding the history and background of the Whitechapel murders and that is the Ripper *Casebook* found on the internet at HTTP://RIPPER.WILDNET.CO.UK/MAIN.HTM. This electronic source is extremely complete, referencing nearly every aspect of the Ripper case. It is well worth the effort to search its dusty electronic files.

We should not forget the investigators such as Inspectors Godley and Abberline who, so many years ago, fought so hard to uncover the identity of the man who brought to the East End of London an Autumn of Terror.

I want to thank my friend Robert Urquidez for his help in preparing the graphics found in this book. Finally, my thanks to the officers at Southwark Police Station and especially Debra Gosling of the Crime Desk whose assistance in researching the background of the Borough Poisoning case was invaluable in helping me understand that portion of the Ripper's life of crime.

Cheers to all, as we continue the hunt!

R. Michael Gordon
Los Angeles, Fall 2000

Table of Contents

Introduction
to a Serial Killer

He became known as the first sexual serial killer of the modern age and he would hold a nation's primal fears in his bloody hands. He had above average intelligence and moved with unusually good luck through his chosen area. He was never officially accused, and would never stand trial for the series of crimes which for months terrorized London. He was educated and skilled in his profession but would choose not to fully participate in that demanding occupation. He would, however, learn to kill, after his first attempts had failed, and he would perfect his craft with speed. He was an Eastern European white male with considerable physical strength, seemingly increased by the very act of murder, and he was a sadist. In his early twenties during the late 1880s, he became a predatory animal in the well stocked East End London hunting ground known as Whitechapel.

The area he selected was one of high rates of infant mortality, suicide, and prostitution, of widespread alcoholism, and of daily street crimes including even the occasional murder. This backdrop was as commonplace in the East End as the filth which spawned the deadly cholera, another ever present danger. His chosen killing ground was at times fully shrouded in thick, black tar smoke, from thousands of soft coal fires and local factories which covered the area. Hell indeed was this, as burnt flakes fell throughout the area days at a time.

His victims were of the lowest class: plentiful, weak, accessible, and mostly in the grip of alcohol when they were dispatched by his ever ready blade, and for reasons unknown, very willing to go along with him to their deaths. They were also, in the mind of the killer, disposable. These women

1

moved constantly from one doss house to another or slept "rough" on the ground, but rarely left the killing grounds for any length of time. His targets lived in wretched housing, in mostly dilapidated dirty buildings where they were little able to sustain life and never able to acquire much more than the merest of necessities. They were, for the most part, apparently chosen at random — victims of opportunity on a schedule of death known only to the killer himself. He was literally feeding a deep anger and a *need* to kill.

At the time of the major killing spree he was single, living alone, and may not have been married before he began his murder spree, which made him accountable only to himself and the demons which drove him. This freedom allowed him to make as many trips as necessary, stalking in and around the area at night to familiarize himself with the territory and future escape routes. How long he sat alone before starting out we cannot know. When he interacted with other people in his daily life it was with repressed difficulty, as most people, especially women, tended to make him uncomfortable. Only on a surface level did he interact with people but at those times he would have seemed quite normal. He was the friendly barber next door who was known by all and trusted by the women of the area. But normal socializing with women would have been difficult, if not impossible, on a long term basis. Indeed, he both feared and hated women. Deep within he was greatly intimidated by them, yet he needed to always have them near. He needed to kill his chosen victims with great speed to remove the power he felt they held over him. But speed was also required because of the great risk he took during each and every event. Discovery was always a distinct possibility, but the potential for it was something he also fed on.

The killing, however, was only a prelude to the real need held deep within. He needed to remove the physical reminders that his victims had once been women. The most important aspect of his crimes was the removal of the women's organs, followed by the distraction of the mutilations, and this is the key to the killer himself. To be sure, he despised women and set out to completely destroy them, yet he needed women to admire and care for him, which must have confused and finally torn his mind to shreds. He could only have hated himself for the needs he could not escape and knew he must serve. The only way these women would no longer be able to control him was if they were de-sexed. Only then, by these acts of mutilation, would his fear of women, and his demented sexuality, be satisfied, but only for a short period of time. It was a form of temporary release.

He was also a collector, taking trophies he could go to again and again to relive the excitement and power of each individual event. When he was interrupted during one murder, he was not satisfied until he had acquired that night's trophy, and for that he would seek out a new victim. It would be a double event, which has yet to be fully explained.

As he moved about his favorite hunting grounds at night, his behavior may have been noticed as different or strange, but in those dirty coal choked slums of London, where over 90,000 people crowded the streets and back alleys, attention must not have been drawn too closely to him. There was, after all, much to be concerned about on those evil 19th century streets. If he had been noticed at all it would have been for his late evening habits as well as his many walks through the dimly lit filth covered streets of a London now vanished. Yet his disguised disheveled looks and poor personal hygiene would have caused few to look twice, as there were many daily distractions in the slums of the East End. This was a well chosen area in which crime was everywhere. He was rarely far away from his victims during the Ripper period, as he lived very close to where they were killed and even closer to where they lived. He began his "work" only yards from his own front door. It is possible that he may have followed his victims for some time before he moved in for the kill, or perhaps he simply waited for his prey to come to him. He may have even escorted them home night after night for safety, until it was their turn. Although he may not have been in the area a great deal of time before he began to kill, his nightly walks would have made him familiar with the killing grounds. Perhaps he even knew the routes his victims would take on their last long walks, as they moved past his home and workplace.

His regular job was not of great value, certainly well below what he was capable of, and not in an area he had trained in for years. But normal work, of an expected variety, was not what most concerned this insane and tormented soul. It was the killing fields that most preyed on his mind, and his ability to continue his "work" without being discovered. The people at his job would have been of little interest to him: they were not part of his real work; not part of his need or his plan.

Early in his life he would have generally failed to receive any nurturing experience when he most needed it and may even have been abandoned, or at least he may have felt he was. This early experience produced an identity problem as well as a gender disorder which overwhelmed him, pushing him towards revenge and hate. It was a painful hate, so deep and overpowering that he would never be able to defeat it. It is possible that as a child he grew to hate his mother who must have dominated and may well have abused him, mentally and perhaps sexually. These feelings would later rise to the surface again and again as the driving force behind his very real need to kill. But when he killed, in his mind, who was this serial killer really killing? Who was his real victim? History gives no answer, only more questions.

We only know that the Ripper was, to be sure, sexually insane and that he would go to great lengths to satisfy his sexual needs.

He may not have gotten much recognition as a child for his accomplishments, but the fact that he left most of his victims out in the open, for all the world to see, must have given him tremendous inner satisfaction at the time. When someone else attempted to take credit for his "work," and give him a false name, he would communicate directly with those who sought him so desperately. Even while he was trying so hard to hide his identity he was not about to let others take credit for his "work." It was yet another example of risky actions taken by this tormented individual.

We all hold within the dark uncharted recesses of our minds the impulse to kill. It may even be part of our general survival makeup. For most of us however, it is an area we shall never visit. For the serial killer, it is *the* world in which he lives on a daily basis. It should be remembered that the Ripper was married towards the end of the series and had a daughter; he also had a second child with another woman. It is a very distinct possibility that a direct Ripper descendant is walking the streets of London today. Does this individual have the same impulses as his ancestor? Only time will tell. We can however, see that serial killers continue to this day to prey on their targets of opportunity.

When he arrived in London the killing began, and when he left to find other hunting grounds the series of death he had brought to the East End came to an end. But that terror would forever be linked to a small slum area of London known as Whitechapel. Even though he would move around and successfully hide his true identity during his short lifetime, the world would never forget the name he was given by a press just beginning to feel the power of words. And the world would never forget one of the most notorious serial killers of all time — alias Jack the Ripper.

An Overview of Terror

Over a century ago, in the late 1880s, a depraved sexual serial killer stalked the back alleys and crowded streets of a small slum section of London's East End. Centered on Whitechapel, this killer, given the name "Jack the Ripper," hunted down and killed at least six, probably more, prostitutes who lived in an area of less than 260 square yards. Their murders occurred, for the most part, within a single square mile comprising the districts of Whitechapel, Spitalfields, Aldgate, St George-in-the-East, and the eastern edge of the City of London. These murders would unleash the largest and most detailed manhunt in British history.

The number of victims is understandably unclear. The killer was never officially captured for this series of crimes so the authorities have no confession on which to base a fixed number. Even the officers and doctors on the case disagreed as to how many were his alone. However, there was a closely grouped series which comprise the central killing spree. Within a 13 week period the Ripper killed at least:

1. Martha Tabram on August 7, 1888
2. Mary Ann Nichols on August 31, 1888
3. Annie Chapman on September 8, 1888
4. Elizabeth Stride on September 30, 1888
5. Catherine Eddowes on September 30, 1888
6. Mary Jane Kelly on November 9, 1888

Although he was not the first serial killer, and certainly would not be the last, or most "successful," he has become the best known in the field. At a time of political tensions, great poverty and social change, the newspapers were starting to feel their ability to shape the public's opinions. The inability of the police authorities to end the killings of a single madman electrified the population through daily press coverage of the chase. It is possible that the coverage may have even aided the Ripper in his quest for victims. Eventually, the world press would cover the events as they unfolded on the streets of London's East End.

The name Jack the Ripper was never used by the killer. In fact it has come to be accepted that the name and the original letters signed as Jack the Ripper were devised by a news reporter to increase the interest in the murders and thereby increase newspaper sales. (A newly discovered document names Tom Bulling, from the Central News Agency, as the author of the most well known Ripper notes.) The real killer was not a man who would have left a lot of clues for the police, and toying with them was simply not his style. However, serious consideration must be given to at least one letter. George Lusk, who had been elected to head the Mile End Vigilance Committee, received, in the mail, a small package which contained half a human kidney and a letter "from hell." The organ could very well have come from Catherine Eddowes' body. It was reported to have shown signs of Bright's disease, an ailment Eddowes suffered from. So it is possible that there was at least one true example of the killer's handwriting, although the original note to Lusk has now been lost.

For most individuals who are aware of the Ripper series of crimes, the victims' dying by cut throat is the best remembered facet of the murders. But in point of fact many of his victims were first strangled before tasting his blade. After the victims were at least unconscious the Ripper quickly slashed their throats. It is also interesting to note that most of his victims were not thrown to the ground but lowered with care, as there was generally no bruising on the back of their heads. This seeming care is in contrast to the mutilations which occurred after death and the collecting of body parts, usually from the viscera. His "work" on the bodies, given the low light or almost complete darkness, coupled with the need to keep an eye out for intruders, shows a good deal of surgical skill in the killer. There is no doubt that he had medical training, and later wholesale mutilations were an attempt to cover up that skill and background.

As for suspects there are many. Most prominent are the three men named in Chief Constable Melville Macnaghten's confidential report written in 1894. In that report he named M. J. Druitt, whom he described as a 41 year old doctor who committed suicide immediately after Mary Kelly's murder. In point of fact Druitt was 31 when he died, had no medical experience and killed himself a full month after Kelly's death. The second suspect was described as a Polish Jew and resident of Whitechapel. Later, it was discovered the man's name was Aaron Kosminski, a lunatic who heard voices in his head which told him to eat from the gutter. The last suspect was Michael Ostrog who turned out to be a mad con man who was investigated on no real evidence that he was the killer or for that matter even in the area at the time of the murders. In fact, there is no evidence whatsoever which points to any of these so called main suspects being Jack the Ripper. They were simply not the killer.

In *Alias Jack the Ripper*, we shall endeavor to show that there was, however, one man who was never on the official suspect lists, at least at the time, who nevertheless had the training, the skills and the murderous intent. He lived as well as worked in the heart of the hunting ground and as such *had access to each and every victim.* After all, the police never captured the Ripper, not officially, so not being on a suspect list is a major plus in favor of his being the murderer. He was hanged in 1903 for other crimes as a serial killer and was named, at that time, as the best suspect for Jack the Ripper ever to come to light by the police Inspector who was in charge of the Ripper investigations at the street level. This other serial killer was also suspected of being the Ripper by the man who arrested him.

It was 1888, in a small area of one of the world's greatest cities. A madman was about to unleash a murder spree on the people of London's East End. It would be a series of atrocities to which he would never confess and for which he would never be required to pay the price. This deadly rampage in London had its earliest beginnings 23 years before, in central eastern Europe.

SECTION I—GENESIS OF A KILLER

Chapter One

A Student from Warsaw

I was born in 1865, in the village of Nagornak, district of Kolo, Government of Kalish. I lived with my parents until the age of 15, attending at the same time, the primary school.

Yours Faithfully, S. Klosowski

During a period of 14 years at least 16 women would die at his hand.

When death becomes a way of life the price is cheap and the product is plentiful. He came into an abused world he could not control, but soon learned to understand. Thus began the tormented life of an individual who was destined to bring to mankind a terror so devastating and violent that history would long remember his sensationally vicious deeds, yet fail to grasp his true identity. He would do much to cover his past as he moved from place to place searching for more and more victims. But was he insane?

On the morning of December 14, 1865, 29-year-old Emilie Klosowski (nee Ulatowski) gave birth to a son who bore the name of Severino Antonovich. The next day, before the Clerical Registrar of Kolo, the child's father, Antonio Klosowski, a hard working 30-year-old carpenter from the tiny village of Nagornak, along with two witnesses, Ludwika Zywanski and Jacob Rozinski, delivered the news of the birth of his son to the proper authorities in order to acquire a birth certificate for this newest Polish subject. The certificate would attest to the fact that Severin's godfather, Ludwig

9

Zyanski and godmother, Marianna Colimowski, were present at the birth and that they had signed to that effect on the document. The Ripper was alive.

At the time of his birth, Poland was under full occupation by Imperial Russian forces. Bloody insurrection had once again broken out in 1863–64, as it had done in 1830, 1846 and 1848, and once again it had been brutality suppressed by the Russian military. Brutality, by the state, was a way of life for many in Europe. The Polish provinces had become administrative areas of the Russian Empire, and with that control, the Polish people had no access to the political process which gave rise to much unrest among the population. It was not a secure or easy time to grow up in Nagornak. Later in the decade, some local control of administrations and courts would become entirely Polish, but unrest and violence would continue to rule the land. In Prussia, during 1886, Bismarck expelled alien Poles from his nation increasing the reasons many would leave for the slums of London and other nations. Can anyone wonder that an individual would be seriously affected by this environment of death and constant terror?

Very little is known of his early years other than where he attended school and what type of student he was. He was Roman Catholic by birth, but would learn Yiddish, and at times would attempt to pass himself off as being Jewish. It was a deceptive skill which would serve him well in the future. Later, he would tell those around him that he was an American as he displayed the banner of that nation, but those close to him would not believe this false trail. It would be one of many lies formed on a daily basis to help cover the acts of a madman, who, for some as yet unknown reason, would be driven to kill again and again.

From October 1873 to June 1880, Severin attended a rural public school in Krasseminsk. His teacher, Mr. Merkish, would write that he "completed the full term of studies of the first department, and his conduct throughout his attendance at the school was very good." Yet, there must have been something about this deeply troubled and secretive individual which drove him to levels of personal, bloodthirsty violence, rarely achieved in human beings. Perhaps it was a sense of being somehow abandoned early in his life or simply a feeling that he did not belong. Many killers, as studies have shown, are products of broken homes. Perhaps this was so with Severin. Whatever the cause, he developed a deep and very powerful hatred of women at an early age, even as he needed them always near. Indeed, he felt an overwhelming need to control and then finally destroy them. And ironically, their deaths finally destroyed him.

A common theme in the backgrounds of serial killers is abuse at an early age, often abuse of a sexual nature. Many are raised in violent households in which they have little or no control. This lack of control, coupled with confused directions, helps to create a very angry child, one which has no real outlet for its rage within the household. However, they rarely attack the individuals who abused them and will, in many cases, go to great lengths to defend those people. It is also possible that the abused child may push aside all memories of the abuse, but that the rage, which it created, will remain. In Severin's case, it is that deep seated rage which, displaced, would explode upon his random victims. His acts would be direct attacks on the very nature of his victims' being. He was not destroying single lives but the lives of all women when he attacked, again and again and again.

Modern psychiatrists would point to a possible love-hate relationship with his mother as a possible driving force. Perhaps. It is possible that she was able to dominate him so completely that eventually he erupted in a rage which could barely be imagined. Or was it that he knew his mother walked the streets? Whatever the source of his demons, for Severin, they were very real and would need to be crushed with the brutal speed and crystal clear determination of a madman.

In December 1880, he began his professional studies as an apprenticed surgical student under the guidance of Senior Surgeon Moshko Rappaport in the town of Zvolen. At the age of 15, Severin found himself away from his familiar surroundings, possibly for the first time in his life. Working for a man he probably knew little about, it is possible that he felt abandoned by his parents and truly alone. He was no longer living with his family and in his papers, found years later, there was no mention of them other than in a short biographical review of his life. "In 1880 my parents apprenticed me for the purpose of studying surgery to Moshko Rappaport," he wrote. This must have been a dramatic turning point in his life, but was it "the" event which drove him to personally destroy so many lives? There is no way, this far distant in time to know. We are only allowed to wonder, and remember the results.

Severin studied the art of surgery for four and a half years under Doctor Rappaport who would pay for Severin's membership in the Society of Surgeons. In November 1882 Severin became a registered student of surgery, along with others, under Moshko Rappaport, in the town of Radom, 60 miles south of Warsaw. During this training period, the 16-year-old student would acquire a most curious document. From a Mr. Dushevitch, who was at the time the Magistrate of the County in the village of Zvolen, he received written confirmation that he was not a criminal! In part the document reported that "Severin Klosowski, resident of the village Zvolen, is a well-behaved man, and was never found guilty of any crime whatever." The document is dated November 16, 1882.

History does not record the events which made the issuance of this extraordinary document necessary. However, the wording would, on its surface, seem to suggest that an incident had occurred in which young Severin was, at the very least, suspected. Serial killers are known to begin with lesser crimes against animals or perhaps petty theft. There is no known record of that incident but it is interesting to note that Klosowski retained and guarded that document, with the official Magistrate's seal, for the rest of his life, even while he denied being himself. A pattern was beginning to form. Severin needed to prove himself and he collected the documents and other items to document that proof. He was very proud of his skills and wanted to show them off.

Upon completion of his apprenticeship in surgery, on June 1, 1885, the 19-year-old Klosowski received the first of two official documents which he hoped would further his efforts to become a certified junior surgeon. The first was a certificate issued by Senior Surgeon Moshko Rappaport to the effect that his student had studied the art of surgery from December 1, 1880, until June 1, 1885. The doctor reported that Severin had "discharged accurately all duties." It was also noted that Severin, "was diligent, of exemplary conduct, and studied with zeal the sciences of surgery." Certainly this was a young man who had worked hard for four and a half years under the close supervision of his instructor and had earned the older man's trust. Dr. Rappaport signed the certificate as "Senior Surgeon and proprietor of the surgery in the village Zvolen," on June 1, 1885. It is clear that his student was now ready to continue his career. There was much more to learn in the art of "cutting," and Severin was a more than willing student.

Perhaps this was when he first began to fantasize about killing? Before he became a serial killer the thoughts of murder must have flooded his mind. As he possibly remembered past or imagined abuses, was it now that he decided that he would strike back at those who had taken part of his soul? Or did he wait until later when he was in a different hunting ground? The answers are unknown, but he may have committed earlier crimes as yet undiscovered or at least unassigned.

The second document concerning Klosowski's studies came from O. P. Olstelski, who was reportedly a "medical practitioner" in the village of Zvolen. The certificate, issued in October 1885, restated that Klosowski had studied under surgeon Rappaport for four and a half years. It relates that he had, "in the capacity of a practicing surgery pupil, and under the doctor's instruction rendered very skilful assistance to patients...." It is interesting to note that this assistance included, according to the testimony of the "medical practitioner," many now seemingly ridiculous practices such as, "in cupping by means of glasses, leeches, and other assistance comprised in the science of surgery." (Although it must be said that leeches do seem to be making a comeback in some quarters.) This eyewitness account does not elaborate further. However, it is again clear that Klosowski did make a favorable impression on those in the surgical profession, as he became more skilled, and collected more documentation.

He then traveled the short distance north to Warsaw where he enrolled at the Hospital of Praga for a three month course in practical surgery. Warsaw has a rich history since its beginning in the 12th century as a small village ruled by the princes of Masovia. It was occupied by the Swedes and Russians in the 17th and 18th centuries and was given to Prussia in 1795. It was captured by Napoleon in 1806, but once again recaptured by Russia in 1813. From 1832 to 1882 its population grew from 127,000 to 383,000 becoming a major industrial center as well as a learning center focused on the University of Warsaw, which had been founded in 1816. Severin found himself in one of the great cities of old Europe — and, he was alone.

Certifying his instruction from October 1, 1885, through January 1, 1886, was Senior Surgeon Krynick. The certificate of training stated an interesting fact that Klosowski, "…while residing in Warsaw was not observed by the police to be concerned in any improper conduct whatsoever." That statement was, "in consequence of inquires ordered to be made, [therefore] the present certificate is issued from the office of the Chief of Police of Warsaw." To say the least this is an interesting statement to be made on the conduct of this 20-year-old student of surgery. The purpose of the certificate seems to have been to allow Klosowski the opportunity to attend the Imperial University of Warsaw. It was dated April 29, 1886, by Deputy Chief of the Department, Mr. A. Darenskov. No other explanation was given.

August 1885 also found Severin employed part time in the town of Praga as an assistant surgeon to C. F. Olshanski. His certificate from November 1886 stated that from August 20, 1885 until February 1, 1886, he had, "during the whole of the time he fulfilled the whole of his duties with zeal, and was of good behavior." He noted in his short biography that he had been employed by Mr. V. Olshanski. Again this young assistant was able to impress those he worked for with his "good behavior." Klosowski wrote, "I came to Warsaw, and whilst employed by Mr. V. Olshanski I also attended a practical course of surgery at the Praga Hospital. Upon the termination of my hospital practice I entered the service of Mr. D. Moshkovski … S. K."

By January 20, 1886, Severin had found employment as a surgeon's assistant under D. Moshkovski in the city of Warsaw. He would continue in this position until November 15, 1886, with the report that he had "performed his surgical functions with a full knowledge of the subject and his conduct was good." Certainly by this time he was well on his way to becoming a junior surgeon with "full knowledge of the subject."

On November 24, 1886, at the age of 20, he was issued a passport under the name Severin Antonovich Klosowski which he still had with him upon his arrest in 1902, despite the fact that he was calling himself George Chapman and denied being Klosowski. This document described him as: "height, medium; hair, of a dark shade; eyes, blue; nose and mouth, medium; chin and face, longish; birthmarks, none." It has been suggested that the passport was issued at the time Klosowski was recruited into the Russian military forces for a period of 18 months, but there are no surviving records to attest to that claim. It is difficult, however, to find 18 months in his early life in which to place him in a military uniform, unless one has him serving while he was training in the surgical skills. None of his documents appear to be of a purely military nature. For the time being the story of military service must rest there. Before his passport expired, in November 1887, Klosowski would find himself in the center of one of the most crowded, filthy and dangerous areas of east London known as Whitechapel. It was an area, according to Inspector Dew, which "...had a reputation for vice and villainy unequalled anywhere in the British Isles."

There was another incident, recorded in November of 1886, which should be mentioned in the context of future events. During that month, a young woman's dismembered body was found left in front of Montrouge Church in Paris, France. Her legs, right arm and head had been cut off, very similar to the Torso murders which would occur in London in 1887–89, and again in 1902. As later, the target was a suspected prostitute. The killer had also removed, and gone off with, her right breast and uterus. This could very easily be a crime performed by a different killer, but the question should be asked whether or not Klosowski had gone on a vacation to Paris just after he received his new passport. The timing would have been very close, but it would have been possible! Dr. Thomas Dutton's *Chronicles of Crime* reported that, "I have learned from a French doctor of a Russian junior surgeon, or feldscher, who was known to him in Paris about 1885–88. He was suspected of having killed and mutilated a 'grisette' in Montmartre, but he left Paris before he could be arrested." Colin Wilson in his *Encyclopedia of Murder* reports that, "Another chronicler declares positively that Chapman had decapitated a woman before he left Poland...." But Wilson then states a lack of evidence is provided and does not name the chronicler. The question must be asked, though, just how many Russian–Polish junior surgeons, who were also serial killers, were active at the time.

However, leaving Warsaw and Poland was apparently not on his mind in December of 1886. From his home at Number 16 Muranovskaja Street,

Klosowski, then 21 years of age, petitioned the dean of the medical faculty of the Imperial University of Warsaw for an examination which would have advanced his surgical career. He wrote, "I have the honor to request your Excellency to grant me permission to undergo the examination for the purpose of receiving the degree of Junior Surgeon.—Yours faithfully, Severin Klosowski."

The record does not show the results of the "examination," which seems to have occurred, but a document does survive from the Ministry of Interior, Medical Administration of Warsaw, dated December 5, 1886. This document, which required a duty stamp, was signed by the Collegiate Councillor and Inspector, a Dr. M. Oreszaief and by the Secretary, A. Pominski. It states that, "In consequence of the application presented by Severin Klosowski, surgical pupil, the Medical Administration hereby testify to the effect that they do not see any reason to oppose his receiving the degree of a Junior Surgeon." Considering his background and this documentation it would seem clear, on the surface at least, that he did indeed acquire the title of junior surgeon. There is no documentation to show otherwise. He had the background, the intelligence and the training to do the job.

Much noise has been made over the years concerning the lack of "real" surgical training and skills of this individual, and yet there is much documented proof of not only his education but of his abilities as well. No matter what our later opinions are of his capacities, it is evident *from the record* that Severin Klosowski did indeed acquire the skills and training to successfully kill an individual the way he did and remove parts of the victim's body. That much at least is very clear, and cannot be disputed by any post-period writer. This man knew how to use a knife and use it expertly.

Despite the lack of documented evidence of his new status as a junior surgeon, he was a member of the hospital staff in February of 1887. There survives a record of fees being paid and thus his membership is confirmed. "Severin Klosowski has paid to the Treasury of the Warsaw Society of Assistant Surgeons, hospital fees four rubles per month.—Warsaw, February 28, 1887. Cobalski Senior Surgeon. Paid up till March 3, 1887." He was actively engaged in the profession. Klosowski would later tell his sister-in-law, Mrs. Stanislaus Rauch, that he worked as a feldscher (assistant surgeon) at the Hospital of the Infant Jesus in the city of Praga just outside of Warsaw, in 1887. This would have been just before he applied for junior surgeon status. Years later, while being interviewed by police in London under an assumed name, Klosowski would inform his interrogator that he had trained at this hospital but a check of hospital records showed that he had never been registered there. Perhaps he used an alias even before he left Poland. Was he really named Klosowski? Documentation says yes, but...

It was also in early 1887, while still in Warsaw, that Klosowski first met a man named Wolff Levisohn, a travelling hairdresser salesman. He would later come in contact with Levisohn in London, which would become a key to what the assistant surgeon was capable of and what he was planning. However, at this time no such deadly plan appears to be evident, at least on the surface. It is interesting to note that Mr. Levisohn seemed, as the years went on, always to be in just the right places at just the right times to peer into the world of Klosowski. It is at this point, on February 28, 1887, the record of Severin Klosowski in Poland comes to an abrupt end. The record would soon begin again in the City of London.

It is not known what event caused this advancing medical student to cut short his burgeoning career as a surgeon and find his way to a foreign country in which he reportedly spoke little of the language. Perhaps the marriage he is said to have entered into went wrong or maybe he was rejected in his attempt to become a junior surgeon. The record is silent on this matter, but it seems unlikely that these types of events would cause such a disruptive change in this young man's life. Rather, it would seem that this wholesale flight from his motherland, this complete change of direction in his life, must have been in response to a much graver matter. Could it be that Klosowski was involved in a murder or other high criminal act which forced him to flee for his freedom or his very life? Was his mother alive at the time? Hargrave L. Adam, in his work, *The Trial of George Chapman*, published in 1930 wrote, "It would be interesting to discover when the idea of murder for gross personal gratification first germinated in the brain of this unscrupulous Polish adventurer. Probably it occurred to him when he commenced to acquire knowledge of the power that lies dormant in the various poisons to which his medical duties in Zvolen gave him access. It is possible that he may have committed murder before he left Poland; his good-conduct certificates, which he seems to have collected fervently, certainly do not prove otherwise."

Only silence remains from that period, but what was about to occur in London is a matter of record. Whatever the cause of his flight from Poland, even in his haste he did not forget to take with him his medical books including one on poisons. There is also no evidence that he ever tried to contact anyone in Poland after he left. Certainly he was hiding from something or someone. In Poland he was educated to a level much above the average citizen in an occupation which, if followed, would have given him esteem and respect. Yet he left it all behind at the drop of a hat to live in a London slum.

Alone in London

Half a mile away from the central killing fields of Whitechapel and 150 yards south of where Mary Ann (Polly) Nichols' mutilated body was found, sat London Hospital. The hospital was within easy walking distance of Severin Klosowski's lodgings and workplace and yet he may never have applied for any position at that medical facility. Why? It would seem, at least on the surface, that he did not want anyone to be able to easily track him through his medical training. If he was wanted for a crime in Poland perhaps he felt it would be too easy to find him in a hospital. Indeed, during the Ripper murders the hospital staff was closely questioned by the police as they desperately attempted to locate the killer. It could very well be that Klosowski did apply at the London hospital, and possibly because he was a foreigner, was not accepted into the close knit professional community of British doctors and surgeons. As a new Polish immigrant, posing as a Jew, he would not have been one of the select individuals allowed to join the "club." Perhaps this triggered a resentment in the young junior surgeon who then sought revenge on a population who had refused him an equal position. If this is correct he may have taken his skills with a knife to the streets to simply prove to those in authority that indeed he did have the same power they possessed — the power of life and death.

He arrived in the densely populated East End of London as early as March 1887. There is no surviving record of how he travelled or what route he took which finally led him to the dark back streets of London. However, it must be remembered that his newly acquired passport expired in November 1887, so time would have been critical. He was alone, a stranger in a strange land, 21 years old, speaking little or no English and with very little money. He did speak Yiddish, which must have served him well in the mostly Jewish areas of Whitechapel and Spitalfields. This section of the East End was one of the most crowded and crime ridden areas of London and it was full of newly arrived immigrants, legal or otherwise, from many other European nations. Fifteen thousand people were homeless and over 100,000 were living in workhouses. As many as 90 percent of all immigrants to England at the time had come from Europe. Since 1881, a vast migration of Jewish peoples had crowded into the area, many from Poland and Russia where they had been persecuted. It would have been a perfect place to hide, and prepare for the "work" ahead. It was a target rich environment for a serial killer.

It was a confusing, and at times dangerous, period to be in London. There was much unrest in the great city. On November 13, 1887, a mass demonstration of mostly unemployed had occurred in Trafalgar Square, and troops had to be called in to quell the violence. The event was long remembered as "Bloody Sunday" and it ended with at least 300 people being injured and one man killed. The overcrowded city was beginning to lose its way.

The Whitechapel area of London's East End alone was crowded with over 90,000 people living closely together in dirt and filth just north of the busy docks which lined the historic Thames River. It was also the home of at least 60 brothels and hundreds of low class prostitutes (estimated at around 1,200 by the police), many of whom had fallen into the profession simply to survive in an area where high unemployment and low wages prevailed. Some worked at it full time while many others did so to help make ends meet. Not surprisingly, suicide was not uncommon, with mind numbing poverty so much a way of life. It seemed to offer some the only release. Basically described, the East End was *the* skid row human dumping ground of London with as many as 230 vermin infested common lodging houses in Whitechapel alone. Some lodging house rooms bedded upwards of 70 or more sleeping wall-to-wall.

In the late 1700s, Whitechapel had been a prosperous area, with the homes of successful merchants located throughout the section. By the late 19th century the area had become a filthy deathtrap. It was a society in which the age of consent was 13, but that had been raised from 12 only in 1875. Incest was also an all too common event between brothers and sisters or fathers and daughters. This was what "Victorian Age" meant to the people of the long forgotten East End. Death was not the enemy—it was an escape.

The Church of St. Mary Matfellon, on Whitechapel Road, gave the area its name: it was literally the "White Chapel." It would later be destroyed in 1941 by an enemy air raid during World War II. Whitechapel Road could boast of 48 pubs along its length to service the many denizens of its long dark nights. The area, during the late 1800s, mixed a large transient population, workers from the docks and the many tradesmen, with prostitutes and street gangs who controlled some of the local areas. Poverty and drunkenness were rife, and the many homeless who slept "raw" in the streets and back allies lived daily with assaults and robbery. A cry of murder could easily have been ignored by the residents who were themselves desperately concerned with staying alive.

Whitechapel and Spitalfields were also the central Jewish business areas of London. It was a good place to hide if you spoke the language. It was a part of the great city that author Jack London termed the "abyss." In his 1903 groundbreaking work, *The People of the Abyss*, he vividly described the intense poverty of the area only a short ride from the overwhelming wealth and power of royalty, crowded with common lodging houses in which a bed or a woman could be had for four pence a night. Indeed, many who were forced into this abyss were not in any way living; they were simply existing. London wrote, "My first discovery was that empty houses were few and far between. Not one empty house could I find — a conclusive proof that the district was 'saturated!' ... True, the sanitation of the places I visited was wretched. From the imperfect sewage and drainage, defective traps, poor ventilation, dampness, and general foulness, I might expect my wife and babies speedily to be attacked by diphtheria, croup, typhoid, erysipelas, blood poisoning, bronchitis, pneumonia, consumption, and various kindred disorders. Certainly the death rate would be exceedingly high. So one is forced to conclude that the Abyss is literally a huge man-killing machine...." In fact, for small children there was a 55 percent chance they would not make it to their fifth birthday. The East End was a world unto itself, but it was about to become famous all over the larger world. The atrocities of Jack the Ripper would expose the daily horrors of life in the East End to shocked masses everywhere.

As for the average people who lived and worked in the area Detective Inspector Edmund Reid, who was active during the Ripper investigation, would write, "Whitechapel has an evil reputation, and one that it does not deserve. During the whole time that I had charge there I never saw a drunken Jew. I always found them industrious, and good fellows to live among."

Greater London itself was, at the time, deeply in the grip of change and transition. Queen Victoria had reigned for more than fifty years and central London was being converted from a residential area to one of commercial and political usage. This rapid change had cut the central city's population from 124,000 in 1841 to less than 60,000 by 1881. The sudden depopulation helped balloon the population of the inner London boroughs which surrounded the central city. From 1841 to 1901 the inner boroughs' population went from 1.8 to 4.5 million while outer London boomed from 286,000 to 2 million residents. There were at the time scattered throughout the city an estimated 80,000 women who made their way in life on the edge, with prostitution as their only way to survive. These women could surely fall no further in life.

Earlier, in 1829, the ancient British system of local watchmen and parish constables was replaced by a centralized Metropolitan Police Force. The force, under Sir Robert Peel, became known as "bobbies" after their leader. It was still a force in transition in the late 1880s with much to learn and little time to adjust to the populational forces pushing to overwhelm places like the East End. At the time of the Ripper murders the force had some 13,000 men on duty and not well enough distributed to guard against crime in the East End. The force had been placed directly under the Home Secretary, which was a political position, and this led to the Metropolitan Police being subject to considerable political pressure. It was this political pressure which would in some ways hinder the investigation of the Ripper murders.

The Metropolitan Board of Works had been set up in 1855, as an elected body, to take charge of public works such as London's sewers and developing infrastructure. Later, the board would be replaced by an elected London City Council in 1888. Political and social changes were all around. Many changes in communications and transportation were being developed throughout the city in the late 19th century. New roads were being built through some of the most blighted areas of London, including the East End. Along with new subways and tramway systems came railways, which connected central London with its crowded suburbs. The city at large, during this period, was literally reinventing itself for the new century.

Although many changes were upon this great metropolis, poverty and disparity would long continue to walk its East End streets. During the Ripper series, the *Weekly Herald* of October 5, 1888, would report that, "The East End of London with its slums, its rookeries, its gin-palaces, its crowded population living in poverty, and not knowing where its tomorrow's dinner will come from, has claims of the most pressing kind on the West End, where idleness and luxury are the temptations that assail virtue and charity, where in the gilded saloons, at the gaudy parties, in the ballroom and the theatre are wasted in empty show or worse, that wealth which is entrusted to those who have it for dispensation of mercy, for feeding the hungry, clothing the naked and spreading truth where error holds sway." Social unrest between the haves and have-nots was also a part of the colorful backdrop of Victorian England. Less than three miles from the East End, a Queen sat on her throne. Eighteen eighty-seven had been Victoria's Golden Jubilee year.

Again from Jack London we are shown a first hand account of life in the East End. "From the slimy sidewalk, they were picking up bits of orange peel, apple skin, and grape stems, and they were eating them. The pits of green gage plums they cracked between their teeth for the kernels inside. They picked up stray crumbs of bread the size of peas, apple cores so black and dirty one would not take them to be apple cores, and these things these two men took into their mouths, and chewed them, and swallowed them...." Life in the East End was very cheap indeed before the Ripper arrived, but it was about to become even cheaper. The East End was a place to be feared and avoided.

The streets central to this overcrowded London slum were Flower and

Dean, Thrawl, George and Dorset. Dorset Street alone could boast, if that is the correct term, some 1,200 residents. Inspector Walter Dew wrote, "So bad was the reputation of Flower and Dean Street that it was always 'double-patrolled' by the police. A single constable would have been lucky to reach the other end unscathed.... Life for the police officer in Whitechapel in those days was one long nightmare." It was within these crowded streets, barely 250 yards in a single direction, that the Ripper would find most of his victims. The actual perpetrator would never be far away from this area and yet his real name would not appear on any surviving police reports in connection with these crimes. Only much later would he become a suspect in the Ripper killings, and then, only after he was convicted of an unconnected series of murders, committed on women of different means. These would be his last atrocities. But in the 1800s, he was alone with time on his hands to think of deeds soon to come. His fantasies were about to become reality.

By early 1887, or possibly the fall at the latest, Klosowski surfaced in England after months of undocumented travel and activity. It is possible that he made his way directly to the East End of London, but there is no conclusive evidence to show this. He would have probably travelled through Germany and France before arriving in England, or perhaps by ship directly to London. However, it should be recalled that during this unaccounted for time period, a prostitute was reported to have been murdered in Paris, in 1887, and mutilated in a manner similar to that of the later Ripper and Torso series. Without proof, though, the Paris matter is simply left as an interesting historical speculation on yet another death by person or persons unknown. Or maybe it was by serial killer — unknown. As for when Klosowski actually arrived in London the only base of information we have is the last documented proof of his being in Poland which is the receipt he received for dues paid, in February 1887.

The First Torso — The Rainham Mystery

In May 1887, a series of murders began which would become almost overlooked in the minds of the residents of London owing in part to the sweeping and sensational press coverage of the upcoming Ripper murders. Certainly the press itself paid less attention to the Torso murders because they could not be readily linked to the Ripper crimes — a link which was effectively played down by the government officials. They were as brutal as the Ripper series, but perhaps the fact that the five murders were spread over a 15 year period, and the police did not want to place them at the hands of one serial killer, helped deflate the effect on the much stressed East End inhabitants. Maybe without a fancy and chilling catch name there was little reason to become alarmed. It would be a series of murders begun around the time a young man named Klosowski arrived in London and would end only months before he would no longer be able to walk the dark streets of the East End. Between those two events five women would lose their lives to a vicious, sexual serial killer working the same streets as Jack the Ripper. Was he the same man or another unknown and crazed medical student? Unlike the Ripper murders, neither the police nor the press were willing to link this set of murders to a single madman.

Two workmen standing near the ferry at Rainham in Essex made the first discovery. They noticed a curious large bundle floating on the River Thames. They retrieved it and proceeded to investigate their find. To their horror, they discovered that they had found the torso of a woman, without arms, legs and head. It had been wrapped in a piece of coarse canvas for transportation to the river, and simply dumped in, to be taken down stream by the current.

The police, upon being informed, began an immediate search of the river and river banks, as well as the local Rainham area in a vain attempt to locate the missing body parts. It would prove to be a fruitless effort as no other remains were located and the search was soon called off. The authorities also requested from the general public to come forward and identify the victim. Although there were people who did come forward, none were able to positively identify the Thames Rainham Torso.

The authorities would have to wait until June 8 for their next clue. On that day, a second bundle containing limbs was found floating on the Thames near Temple Stairs. The new find was taken to Dr. Calloway, a local police surgeon, who concluded that they did indeed belong to the torso found the month before. He further stated that the killer was "someone skilled in surgery," as the body parts had been removed with expertise, not simply ripped off. In July the final remains were recovered by a laborer named William Gate. While walking near the Thames, at Regent's Canal, Chalk Farm, he located the final bundle floating in the canal. Due to the condition of this latest find it was felt that a new crime had occurred, as the remains appeared to be from a much older woman. This was an error. It was soon discovered that the misunderstanding was due to the time the remains had spent in the water. There was no second murder — not yet.

The inquest into the Rainham Torso murder was begun on August 13, 1887, at the Crowndale Hall in Camden Town. Coroner, Dr. G. Danford Thomas, for Central Middlesex, was in charge. Representing the Home Office was Dr. Thomas Bond, Divisional Police Surgeon for A Division of the Metropolitan Police. (He would later become deeply involved in the Ripper investigation.) Bond had examined the remains and concluded that they were of a young woman in her twenties, five feet four inches in height, who had never given birth. He also testified that the arms and legs had been removed by someone "with a knowledge of anatomy." But he also felt that the removal was not for anatomical study. Dr. Bond determined that the removal was done for the purpose of covering up a murder. In the end, a cause of death could not be discovered, but it was clearly, "death at the hands of person or persons unknown."

His First Job?

By late 1887 or very early 1888, Klosowski could be found working as an assistant hairdresser in a shop owned by Abraham Radin, located at 70 West India Dock Road in Poplar, two miles east of Whitechapel in the East End. The *Post Office London Directory* shows the Radins at that address for 1888 only, but the listing was probably confirmed in late 1887. There is no evidence to show that this was his first job, however. He held the position for at least five months and it was reported that he helped nurse Mrs. Radin's oldest son during the time he spent at the hairdresser's. Ethel Radin would later testify that Klosowski had shown her some of his personal papers which he said showed that he had studied medicine. He was obviously very proud of his abilities and of who he was. But the papers were in Russian and Polish so she could only report what he said they represented. She also testified that he had helped nurse her son during an illness which could very well point to him living with the Radins while he worked in their shop. It would not have been a good place to use as a base for murder. Far too many potential witnesses were close at hand and his late night movements would not have gone unnoticed. Her testimony does show, though, that Klosowski not only began activities in the medical field upon arriving in London, but that he was proud of his earlier training. Nonetheless he was unwilling or unable to continue in that field.

It was also during this period that he once again ran into the hairdresser supplier Wolff Levisohn, at times described as a Jewish commercial traveller. As reported in Jay Robert Nash's *Almanac of World Crime*, "...he [Klosowski] was secretly trying to obtain poison from under-world sources in Whitechapel at the very time of the Ripper murders." Perhaps that was the reason Levisohn said nothing to the authorities at the time. He later reported that Klosowski was using the name Ludwig Zagowski and speaking Yiddish when he met him in London. (Could Klosowski have been using his godfather's name, Ludwig Zyanski, and Levisohn simply remembered incorrectly some 15 years later?) And why would this recent young immigrant to London need to hide his identity, unless he was already running away from the authorities? There can be little doubt that at this meeting Klosowski attempted to purchase poison from the good Mr. Levisohn. But Levisohn's response must have been less than satisfactory for the new hairdresser. "I talked to the accused about medicines," Levisohn later told the authorities, "and he asked me for a certain medicine, but I said no, I did not want to get twelve years." He could not have meant any drugs, as they had not been declared illegal in 1888. Perhaps he was unwilling to supply poison to a man he probably knew to be hiding and using an assumed name. For Levisohn almost certainly knew Klosowski's real name. But perhaps Klosowski felt he could take no chances and had to use a false name with someone who could have remembered an old Polish crime as yet unpaid for. Or was it possible that the man history knows as Klosowski was in reality Ludwig Zagowski, known to Levisohn as such in the old country? In that case, what of Severin Klosowski? Whatever the reason for Klosowski using the name Ludwig Zagowski, it was the only time he did use it, as far as is known.

It is interesting to note that Mr. Levisohn, while on business in Whitechapel on November 15, 1888, at the height of the Ripper scare, was himself accosted by two prostitutes and accused by them of being "Jack the Ripper." When he failed to accept the services of the two women, named Johnson and DeGrasse, they shouted, "You are Jack the Ripper!" They would later report that they accused him because he looked like the Ripper with his "shiny black bag." It has also been reported that Levisohn went to the trouble of informing Inspector Fred Abberline that Klosowski was not Jack the Ripper, but the question must be asked as to why he would feel the need to do such a thing? Did he know much more than he was willing to talk about or testify to? Certainly Levisohn knew two critical facts about Klosowski: first, that he was using an assumed name; and second, that he had left Poland in haste. Did he know a great deal more?

At this point in his travels Klosowski was unable to obtain the deadly poison he needed. Later, this would not be the case, as a person he befriended would be all to happy to supply the substance to his "barber." For now, other means would have to be found to quench a thirst for death growing deep inside. He would turn to a method he knew so very well. Klosowski was trained in the ancient art of blood-letting, which was a part of his surgical background. He would turn to his blade. He was an expert in its use. And in any case, perhaps he needed more study of poison before that would serve him just as well.

> *Obviously the work was that of an expert; of one, at least, who had*
> *such knowledge of anatomical or pathological examinations as to*
> *be enabled to secure the pelvic organs with one sweep of the knife,*
> *which must therefore have at least 5 or 6 inches in length, proba-*
> *bly more. The mode in which the knife had been used seemed to*
> *indicate great anatomical knowledge.*
>
> Dr. George Bagster Phillips
> Testimony on Annie Chapman's postmortem

Thanks to the historical work *The Trial of George Chapman*, edited by Hargrave L. Adam in the *Notable British Trials* series, April 1930, we are left with the text of a series of documents which were confiscated from Klosowski by the police upon his arrest in 1902. It would be this, his own collection of papers, which would conclusively identify George Chapman as Severin Klosowski. These documents, in Polish and Russian, were translated by Joseph Betrikowski for Klosowski's 1903 trial and were published by Adams. They are reproduced below as reference material from the early life of a serial killer.

1. **Extract from birth certificate**
   On the 15th day of December, 1865, at ten o'clock in the morning, there appeared Antonio Klosowski, 30 years of age, a carpenter by trade, native of the village of Nagornak, together with two witnesses, Ludwika Zywanski, aged 32, and Jacob Rozinski, aged 56, both of Nagornak, and employed there. They stated that Emilie, the wife of Antonio Klosowski, nee Ulatowski, age 29, had given birth to a child the previous morning. The child was named Severin and that his parents are Polish subjects. The godfather of the child was Ludwig Zyanski and the godmother's name was Marianna Colimowski. That they were present at the birth and that they affixed their signatures hereto in testimony thereof.—(Then follow the signatures of the Clerical Registrar of Kolo, the Chief of the Parochial Registry of Kolo, and a magistrate of Kolo.)

2. **Primary school**
   This is given by the teacher of the Krasseminsk rural public primary school, consisting of one Standard, to the effect that Severin Klosowski, son of Antonio, attended the Krasseminsk School from October 17–29, 1873, till June 6–13, 1880, and completed the full term of studies of the first department, and that his conduct throughout his attendance at the school was very good.— In witness thereof I affix my own signature, Merkish, teacher, village of Krassenin, December 7–19, 1880.—(The authenticity of the signature of Merkish is attested by two witnesses.)

3. Society of Surgeons

Receipt for one ruble, paid by Rappaport to the Treasury of the Society of Surgeons of the town of Radom on behalf of the surgical apprentice, Severin Klosowski. Radom, October 23–November 5, 1882.— N. Brodnitski, Senior Surgeon.

4. Well behaved

The magistrate of the County of Zvolen hereby certifies that Severin Klosowski, resident of the village Zvolen, is a well-behaved man, and was never found guilty of any crime whatever. To which effect he bears testimony by his own signature and official seal.— Dushevitch, Magistrate of the County, Village Zvolen, November 16, 1882.

5. Registry of Surgical Pupils

October 23–November 4, 1885.— The Radom Surgical Society, of the town of Radom, hereby certifies that the surgical pupil, Severin Klosowski, was entered at the registry of surgical pupils by the Senior Surgeon, Moshko Rappaport, in the town of Radom, November 22–December 3, 1882. Subject No. 8, and in accordance with Article 17, letter b, of the Surgical Society. One ruble in silver was paid by him into the Treasury of the said Society.— In witness whereof, Brodinski, the Chief of the Society, testifies by affixing his signature and the seal of the Surgical Society.

6. Apprentice Certificate

Certificate issued to the surgical apprentice, Severin Antonio Klosowski, to the effect that he, Severin Klosowski, was in my surgery for the purpose of studying surgery from December 1, 1880, till June 1, 1885, and during the whole of the time he, Severin Klosowski, discharged accurately all his duties. He was diligent, of exemplary conduct, and studied with zeal the science of surgery.— In testimony thereof I affix my signature, Moshko Rappaport, Senior Surgeon and proprietor of the surgery in the village Zvolen, June 1, 1885.

7. Certificate of Employment

Certificate issued to Severin Klosowski, resident in the village of Tyminitsa, county of Nodga, district of Iltetsk, Government of Radom, to the effect that he was employed for a period of four-and-a-half years by the local surgeon, Moshko Rappaport, in the capacity of a practicing surgery pupil, and under the doctor's instructions rendered very skilful assistance to patients — i.e., in cupping by means of glasses, leeches, and other assistance comprised in the science of surgery. To all the above I am able to testify as an eyewitness.— [Signed] O. P. Olstetski, medical practitioner in village of Zvolen, October 10–22, 1885.

8. **Instruction Certificate**

This is given to Severin Klosowski, surgery pupil, to the effect that from October 1, 1885, till January 1, 1886, he received instructions in practical surgery at the Hospital of Praga, Warsaw, and his general conduct was good. — [Signed] Krynick, Senior Surgeon.

In accordance with the application of Severin Klosowski, and in consequence of inquiries ordered to be made, the present certificate is issued from the office of the Chief of Police of Warsaw to the effect that the applicant while residing in Warsaw was not observed by the police to be concerned in any improper conduct whatsoever. The present certificate is given to Mr. Klosowski under the proper signature and government seal for the purpose of submitting the same to the Imperial University of Warsaw. Stamp duties have been collected. — Warsaw, April 29, 1886. Kasievitz, Deputy Chief of the Department. [Seal] A. Darenskov, Manager.

9. **Employment Certificate**

Warsaw, November 15, 1886. — This is to certify that Severin Klosowski has been employed by me as surgeon assistant from January 20, 1886, up to the present time, and during the whole of that period he performed his surgical functions with a full knowledge of the subject, and his conduct was good. To this fact I testify with my own signature, and affix my stamp. — [Signed] D. Moshkovski.

10. **Employment Certificate**

Town of Praga, November 24 to December 6, 1886. — I hereby certify that Severin Klosowski was employed by me in the capacity of an assistant surgeon from August 20, 1885, till February 1, 1886, and during the whole of the time he fulfilled the whole of his duties with zeal, and was of good behavior. In witness whereof I have affixed my own signature. — [Signed] C. F. Olshanski.

11. **Biography**

I was born in 1865, in the village of Nagornak, district of Kolo, Government of Kalish. I lived with my parents until the age of 15, attending at the same time the primary school. In 1880 my parents apprenticed me for the purpose of studying surgery to Moshko Rappaport, senior surgeon of the town of Zvolen. Having served my term of apprenticeship till 1885, I came to Warsaw, and whilst employed by Mr. V. Olshanski I also attended a practical course of surgery at the Praga Hospital. Upon the termination of my hospital practice I entered the service of Mr. D. Moshkovski, by whom I am still employed. I present herewith all my documents. — Yours faithfully, Severin Klosowski, Warsaw, November 15, 1886.

12. Passport

Passport, given on November 24, 1886, to Severin Antonovich Klosowski, residing in the Radom Government, district of Ilshetsk, county of Khotche, village of Tyshenitsa, Nova Nil to travel to the city of Warsaw from the above date till November 1–13, 1887, upon the expiration of which the said document shall be returned to me. The civil and military authorities shall allow the bearer a free passage, and if necessary render him legal assistance. Given in Khotche, November 24, 1886. Physical description. Age, 21; born in 1865; height, medium; hair, of a dark shade; eyes, blue; nose and mouth, medium; chin and face, longish; birthmarks, none. Passport within the limits and the Kingdom of Poland. Free.—[Signed] Mazur, Magistrate of the County of Khotche. [Seal] Godlevski, County Clerk.

13. Petition for Junior Surgeon Degree

Warsaw, December, 1886.—His Excellency, the Dean of the Medical Faculty of the Imperial University of Warsaw. Petition from Severin Klosowski, surgical pupil, residing at No. 16 Muranovskaja Street.

I have the honor to request your Excellency to grant me permission to undergo the examination for the purpose of receiving the degree of Junior Surgeon. I enclose herewith the required documents.—Yours faithfully, Severin Klosowski.

14. Acceptance for Junior Surgeon Degree

Ministry of Interior, Medical Administration of Warsaw, December 5, 1886.—In consequence of the application presented by Severin Klosowski, surgical pupil, the Medical Administration hereby testify to the effect that they do not see any reason to oppose his receiving the degree of a Junior Surgeon. The required stamp duties have been paid.—[Signed] Dr. M. Oreszaief, Collegiate Councillor and Inspector. A. Pominski, Secretary.

15. Hospital Fees

Severin Klosowski has paid to the Treasury of the Warsaw Society of Assistant Surgeons, Hospital fees four rubles per month.—Warsaw. February 28, 1887. Cobalski, Senior Surgeon. Paid up till March 3, 1887.

Chapter Two

A Shadow Falls
Over Whitechapel

"They can take my life, but they cannot kil my soul and take it from
me. God is my Judge and I Pray to have Mercy on my soul, for my
sins which I have dun durin my Life."

Severin Antonovich Klosowski

It began slowly, and indeed would hardly have been noticed at all in the dirty, crime ridden back streets and alleys of London's East End, if it were not for the spectacular press coverage soon to unfold. Assaults and murder were common enough in 1888, especially in the crowded East End, but the savage methods used by this killer, his extraordinary good luck during the hunt, and the press coverage marked this series of crimes as emotionally unforgettable. It would be long remembered as the "Autumn of Terror." H Division of the Metropolitan Police, serving Whitechapel, were in for one hell of a ride.

Years would pass before the full scope of his deeds could begin to come to the fore, and even now, after more than a century has passed, there is disagreement as to exactly how many women met their ends at the hands of the Whitechapel Killer. However, a pattern does emerge which shows a process of learned technique and tested methodology. It is of a young man, who in the act of defining himself, learns how to kill with speed and efficiency. But there must first be practice and failure, though there was little of either.

A pattern of earlier crimes is common to serial killers. Among such

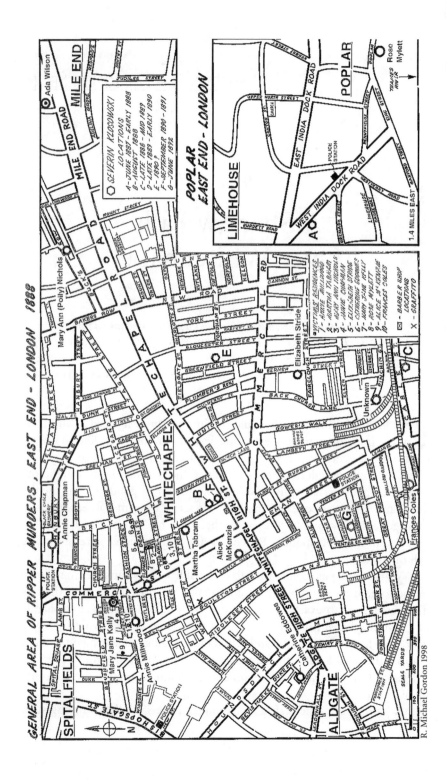

GENERAL AREA OF RIPPER MURDERS, EAST END - LONDON 1888

SEVERIN KLOSOWSKI
LOCATIONS
A – JUNE 1887 – EARLY 1888
B – AUGUST 1888
C – LATE 1888 – MID 1889
D – LATE 1889 – EARLY 1890
E – 1890 ? EARLY 1890
F – SEPTEMBER 1890 – 1891
G – JUNE 1892

POPLAR
EAST END - LONDON

LIMEHOUSE

POPLAR

Rose
Mylett

1.4 MILES EAST

Ada Wilson

Mary Ann (Polly) Nichols

Annie Chapman

Elizabeth Stride

Annie Millwood

Martha Tabram

Alice McKenzie

Mary Jane Kelly

Catherine Eddowes

Frances Coles

Unknown

VICTIMS/RESIDENCES
1 – ADA WILSON
2 – MARTHA TABRAM
3 – MARY ANN NICHOLS
4 – ANNIE CHAPMAN
5 – ELIZABETH STRIDE
6 – CATHERINE EDDOWES
7 – MARY JANE KELLY
8 – ROSE MYLETT
9 – ALICE McKENZIE
10 – FRANCES COLES

☐ – BARBER SHOP
○ – LOCATIONS
X – GRAFFITO

SPITALFIELDS

WHITECHAPEL

ALDGATE

SCALE YARDS

R. Michael Gordon 1998

crimes are rapes or at least rape attempts. Petty theft is also a common ear-lier crime. But certainly it is one of the keys to the behavior of serial killers that violent acts in the past become the best predictors of future violence. They will make mistakes in their earlier crimes, but many are also intelli-gent and very resourceful, and they will learn from those mistakes. It surely takes time for a fully developed technique to be settled on. So it is unreal-istic to believe that a serial killer would murder six women in 13 weeks and simply have come from nowhere and vanish just as fast, never committing any crimes again. Yet in the end, it would appear that's what happened. He would succeed completely and then seemingly walk into the dark back pages of history, never officially identified, and never paying for the crimes he committed. Or did he pay?

The first to taste his blade lived delightfully close by.

Her name was Annie Millwood. She was the 38-year-old widow of one of the Queen's soldiers, Richard Millwood. Her general occupation is not really known, although it is possible that she, at least partially, supported herself through the ancient art of prostitution, but this is purely specula-tion. What is known, is that she lived at 8 White's Row, Spitalfields, in the very heart of the Ripper's hunting ground, only 300 or so yards away from the cheap rundown lodgings of a man named Klosowski. It would seem that attacks began almost as soon as Klosowski moved into the heart of Whitechapel and Spitalfields. At the time Spitalfields was known locally by the colorful name "Thieves Kitchen."

So hers was the address from which the first of his many known vic-tims would come. Three years later, almost to the day, the final killing in the London series would end with a victim who lived at that *very same* address! By then the killer had come full circle in this deadly series. He would find a new hunting ground; later a new type of victim and a new form of murder. Was there some type of message he was sending by start-ing and finishing at the very same house? Was he playing a game? After all, there were literally thousands of houses and hundreds of lodging houses in the general area. Whitechapel alone had 233 common lodging houses, hous-ing thousands of the poorest of the poor. Or was the message simply one of death?

On Saturday, February 25, 1888, a man whom she had never seen before attacked her, with what Annie described as "a clasp knife which he had taken from his pocket." He stabbed her numerous times on her legs and lower torso. But the attack was far from skilled, even clumsy. And the vic-tim survived. She was admitted to the Whitechapel Infirmary at 5 p.m. reporting that "the man was a stranger." The records simply recorded "stabs." There were no other witnesses to the attack, and no description of the man with the clasp knife has been found. His street work had begun with a failure. That he was a stranger, and possibly new to the area, was the only clue to his identity. The attack must have occurred during the daylight hours based on the time she was admitted to the infirmary. In point of fact there were dozens of murders the year before in the general area including many infanticides of which only eight ended in conviction.

Crime levels being what they were at the time, it is interesting to note that the events were actually reported in the *Eastern Post*. It must surely have been a slow local news day, as a stabbing in the East End was nothing new. Daily criminal activity was to be expected in this vicious London ghetto.

Despite the attack, Annie would recover and was soon released from the infirmary, on March 21. She was sent to work at the South Grove Workhouse, Mile End Road, where she would collapse and die only 10 days later, on March 31. It was reported that while she was "engaged in some occupation" in the backyard of the workhouse she collapsed due to, according to Coroner Wynne Baxter's inquest, "sudden effusion into the pericardium from the rupture of the left pulmonary artery through ulceration." It would not be the Ripper who ended the life of Annie Millwood, despite the clumsy attempt; it would be by natural causes completely unrelated to the knife attack. Perhaps it was time for him to choose a more vulnerable part of the body to attack, to be certain of causing death. It would also be advisable for him to work in the darkness of night. It would be much easier to escape through the night fog of a London spring.

As for Coroner Baxter, he would soon find himself deeply involved in the Ripper murder series. He fought to discover the Ripper's identity, while fighting the very authorities who were actively hunting the killer. Politics would play a part in this investigation. As for the many local inquests into the many deaths common to the East End, it is of historical interest to note that many of them were held in the local pubs or saloon bars so as not to keep the jurors too far away from a fast drink after the inquires were completed.

She was a 39-year-old "seamstress" who lived at 19 Maidman Street, Mile End. Her name was Ada Wilson. She called herself a seamstress, but in that era this was a self-description used by prostitutes who were perhaps unable to admit, even to themselves, what their occupations truly were. Records of serial killers show that prostitutes are high on their list of most common targets. Prostitutes were always the target of choice for the Ripper, at least during this phase of his career.

On March 28, 1888, Ada was home at 12:30 in the morning, when a man appeared at her door whom she had never seen before. Overpowering her, he forced his way into her home and demanded that she give him money, or "she would not have long to live." When Ada refused, possibly because she had no money to give, the intruder stabbed her twice in the throat expecting this work to be sufficient to kill her. The attacker was wrong and Ada was still able to scream. He had made a tactical mistake which almost ended his murderous career very early. Not spending any time looking for money, he immediately ran, which was a lucky response, for it was not long before Mrs. Wilson's neighbors were on the scene and took up the chase. But he soon made his escape in the darkness, only to later learn that his victim was indeed still alive. Again, he had failed, and this time the individual was able to describe her attacker. She told the authorities that he was a man of around 30 years of age with a sunburnt face, fair moustache, standing 5 feet 6 inches in height. It was a crude word picture of Klosowski, now on the verge of becoming a serial killer. Next time he would need to find a much easier target, and in a better place. As for Ada, she would spend the next 30 days in London Hospital after which she would go home and fade from Ripper history.

Her attacker learned two valuable lessons with this venture. The first lesson was that, in case he was chased, it was best to have a hideaway close by in order to effect his escape. He would learn from this oversight and would make his future attacks nearer his home and workplace. The second lesson was to ensure that his victims would never be allowed to scream. He would also learn this lesson very well, as no one would ever again hear a single scream from a Ripper victim. He would also look for victims who had drunk too much and could not put up a fight like these two women had.

Some researchers would look at the demand for money as a way of excluding this attack from the Ripper series. However, it must be remembered that nothing was actually taken, and the demand may have only been a ruse to gain the upper hand while he positioned himself for his vicious attack. He was, after all, perfecting his method. Then again, Klosowski would in the future be shown to have been a thief and a conman so perhaps money was part of the plan. This time the knife would find the throat and although the assault was not a success he was now closing in on the "proper technique." If the police forces at the time had been able to connect this attack with the other later killings, perhaps the description of Wilson's assailant would have led them to the killer. Perhaps. By this time, though, the man had failed twice in his efforts to take a life. It would not happen a third time. After this attack there would not be another, on a woman, which was unsuccessful.

To add to the general confusion and terror of the period there was a murder that occurred in Whitechapel which reflected the overall lawlessness of the area, and the general danger to be found in the East End. There was real fear here. It was not a fear one could read about, or see — it was the deep seated fear of people truly not knowing, from one day to the next, if they would survive to see the sun rise the following day. For a time, after he became "successful," this attack would also be credited to the Ripper by the press, but it was clearly a crime of a different nature.

The victim was a common prostitute named Emma Elizabeth Smith, who had lived at 18 George Street, Spitalfields, for the previous 18 months, which was the address of a crowded common lodging house well beyond its prime. The 45-year-old widow, who was reported to have had a son and daughter living in Finsbury Park, had been out late once again on April 2. While she was walking home from her night of soliciting, along Whitechapel Road at around 1:30 a.m., she passed St. Mary Matfellon Church. At that point she noticed three men coming directly towards her from the opposite direction. She crossed the street to avoid them, but they turned and followed her after she had passed them. As she went into Osborn Street, at a faster pace, the three men overtook and attacked her, then brutally raped her in front of the Taylor Bros. cocoa factory. They then took the small amount of money she possessed, and went on their way.

After this vicious and bloody attack, Emma somehow, slowly and painfully, made her way back to her lodging house where she told the deputy keeper, Mrs. Mary Russell, what had happened. Mrs. Russell took her to London Hospital where, two days later, she died of a ruptured perineum due to the blunt instrument which had been forced into her by one of her attackers. It was a most heinous street crime indeed, but not the work of Jack the Ripper. The men, who were never captured, were probably members of one of the many gangs which had infected the area. As for the local response to her murder, there would be the usual street corner gossip but not much more than that. Brutality was a way of life and it was not yet time to panic. Even without the Ripper working the streets of the East End, it was a very dangerous place to call home. The newspapers did not even bother to report Emma's death. The Ripper had chosen his area well.

A Successful Venture

Martha Tabram, who at times used the name "Emma," did not have a great deal of beauty, and life had not been particularly kind to this 39-year-old occasional prostitute. Her last short day of life would prove to be typical. At the inquest into her murder she would be described as, "a plump middle-aged woman, dark hair and complexion, about 5'3" tall."

She was the youngest of five children born to Charles Samuel White and his wife Elizabeth (Dowsett) on May 10, 1849. At the time, Martha White and her family lived at 17 Marshall Street, London Road, Southwark. Her father, when he found work, was employed as a warehousemen while her mother stayed home with the children. When Martha was 16 her parents separated, for reasons which have long been forgotten, but it may have been because of her father's inability to work due to what was referred to as his "weak back." However, his wife and children continued to keep in touch with him up until the time of his sudden death, said to have been from natural causes, at the age of 59, in 1865.

A few years after her father died Martha began living with the foreman of a local furniture packing company, Henry Samuel Tabram. He was said to be "not tall" but he dressed well, and sported a mustache and iron gray hair. They were married on December 25, 1869, at Trinity Church in St. Mary's Parish, Newington, and eventually moved to 20 Marshall Street in February 1871. And it was in February 1871 that she had her first child, Frederick John. Her second, Charles Henry, arrived in December 1872.

It would not be long, though, before problems developed in the marriage, apparently brought on by Martha's heavy drinking. In 1875 the union ended when Henry walked out, leaving her a weekly allowance of 12 shillings. He would later reduce this to only two shillings and six pence because of the many times she came up to him on the streets demanding money. Even this small amount was cut off when her husband learned that she had moved in with another man by the name of Henry Turner. (At times Martha is referred to in published sources as Martha Turner, but since she never married Henry this is an incorrect name.)

Turner was a local carpenter who would at times share a home with Martha over the next 12 years. This off and on relationship would be accented by Martha's drinking and continuous habit of staying out late, going from pub to pub. At times she would stay out all night. As reported in the London *Times* of August 24, 1888, "While living with witness, deceased's usual time for coming home was about 11 o'clock. As far as he knew she had no regular companion and he did not know that she walked the streets. As a rule he was a man of sober habits, and when the deceased was sober they usually got on well together." At the time Turner was living at the Victoria Working Men's Home on Commercial Street, Spitalfields.

During the inquest into her death Turner testified, "Since she has been living with me, her character for sobriety was not good. If I give her money she generally spent it in drink. In fact it was always drink.... When she took to drink, however, I usually left her to her own resources, and I can't answer to her conduct then." By July of 1888, Turner had had enough of Martha and her many problems brought on by alcohol. She was on her own to make a meager living selling cheap trinkets, as well as herself. Turner would later recall last seeing her on August 4, 1888. By then she was destitute, walking along Leadenhall Street, possibly looking for another customer. He gave her one shilling and six pence so that she could purchase more trinkets to sell, but as was her habit she more than likely went to get drunk. Three weeks before her death Martha had left her rooms at 4 Star Street because she had not paid her rent. Her last lodging house address was 19 George Street, Satchell's Lodging House, about 100 yards north of Klosowski's room at George Yard Buildings (actually named George Yard Dwellings), Whitechapel. These were relatively new buildings, having been constructed in 1875 as cheap single rooms for the very poorest of the area's working class.

Martha Tabram was the perfect subject for the Whitechapel Killer. She was out late, drunk, and many times wandered alone through the dangerous, narrow, dark streets and back alleys of the East End. She would be on her own, unprotected, unwanted, and the Ripper would be close — very close.

On her last full day Martha, who at times used the name Emma Turner, went, as was her habit, from pub to pub during the evening with her friend Mary Ann Connolly, nicknamed "Pearly Poll." Martha had for the past two nights lived at one of the lodging houses on Dorset Street, Spitalfields. The London *Times* would later report that, "A visit to Dorset Street, which runs parallel with Spitalfields Market from Commercial Street, reveals the fact that nearly every house in the street is a common lodging house, in which wretched human beings are, at certain seasons of the year, crammed from cellar to roof." As described by Jack London, "The little private doss-houses, as a rule, are unmitigated horrors. I have slept in them, and I know.... A feeling of gloom pervaded the ill-lighted place. Many of them sat and brooded over the crumbs of their repast, and made me wonder ... what evil they had done that they should be punished so."

Martha and her friend were, for a portion of that evening, in the company of two soldiers. In the Two Brewers public house the pair had connected with two guardsmen: a corporal and a private. Later, they all found themselves in the White Swan on Whitechapel High Street. Martha was seen among them in the White Swan at 11 p.m. by her widowed sister-in-law Ann Morris. They would end their drinking at the Blue Anchor at 67A Whitechapel Road. It was an area well known to the Ripper.

Around 11:45 in the evening, on that warm Monday, the August 6 Bank Holiday, Martha and Mary Ann separated and paired with their gentlemen friends. Martha went with the private into George Yard while Mary Ann took her corporal into Angel Alley, with the objective probably being a

Martha Tabram - August 7, 1888

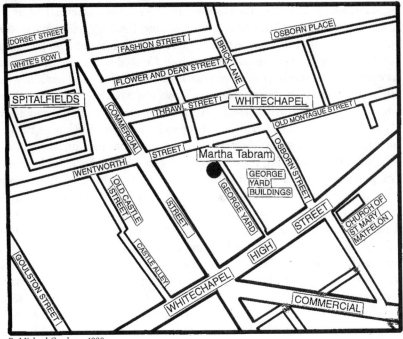

R. Michael Gordon   1998

Martha Tabram was the first generally accepted Ripper victim. She was found by cab driver George Crow at 3:30 a.m. August 7, 1888.

sexual encounter. The time may have been a little earlier or later, however, because keeping time was not on the minds of the individuals involved. This was the last recorded sighting of Martha Tabram alive, save by her killer. After the soldier, there would still be plenty of time for one last customer; one more chance to earn her doss money, or more likely one last drink.

Closer to the critical time, Mrs. Elizabeth Mahoney, aged 25, who made her home at No. 47 George Yard Buildings with her husband Joseph, reported seeing nothing unusual when she arrived back home after purchasing supper at 1:50 a.m. She normally worked in a match factory at Stratford from 9 a.m. until 7 p.m. but because it was a bank holiday she had been out all day with her husband. The Mahoneys lived in a block of what has been referred to as "model dwellings," but only the poorest of the poor lived in George Yard Buildings, and many of them were criminals. Her path took her to the first floor landing and up the very stairs which, in short order, would hold the remains of Martha Tabram. But there was no one there.

At 2:00 that morning, the local police constable, by the name of Thomas Barrett, No. 226 H Division, saw and questioned a young Grenadier Guardsman as he waited on Wentworth Street. These men stood at the north end of George Yard effectively blocking the alley from any unseen approach. When questioned as to why he was standing around on that warm early morning the young Guardsman told Constable Barrett that he was waiting for a "chum who went off with a girl." If Martha and her killer had entered George Yard during that time, it would have been from the south end, off Whitechapel High Street. That was irrelevant, though, because Severin Klosowski lived in one of the cheap lodging rooms in George Yard on the east side of the alley. Martha would have walked past his very rooms. When Benjamin Charles, former police sergeant, wrote his autobiography, *Lost London*, he reported that, "Chapman lived in Whitechapel, where he carried on a hairdresser's business in a sort of 'dive' under a public-house at the corner of George Yard and Whitechapel High Street." While Richard Altick in *Victorian Studies in Scarlet* reported that Chapman was, "For a time ... a floating barber in the East End and elsewhere in London." From Martin Fido in his *Murder Guide to London* we learn that, "...Severin Klosowski was working as a hairdresser's assistant in or around the White Hart, Whitechapel High Street, right in the Ripper territory throughout 1888." And finally, Donald McCormick writes that Klosowski "...had a barber's shop in the basement of George Yard Buildings at the time...."

It is not known exactly how and when Martha met her killer. She may have met him in one of the pubs after she departed from the guardsman, but that is unlikely. This was not a man who would have wanted to be seen with his victim in a public place. It is also possible that two men either working together or separately came upon and attacked her. Indeed, when she was examined by Dr. Timothy Robert Killeen at the postmortem, it was found that one wound had been deeply inflicted by a left handed attacker, while the rest were shallow by a right handed person using an "ordinary penknife." Dr. Killeen, who was the first doctor to examine the body, stated that, "One of the wounds might have been made by a left-handed person, but the rest appeared to have been inflicted by a right-handed person. And two different weapons had been used."

It is also possible that the woman, most likely drunk, was killed on the staircase with a single blow from a dagger or bayonet to the sternum, then left for dead. Was she killed by the young guardsman and left for someone else to mutilate? With the Whitechapel Killer roaming around, it is conceivable that he came across the dead or dying woman as he returned home to his lodgings in the very same building, and either finished her off or simply stabbed the body with his penknife 38 more times. Did he find that he enjoyed pushing his knife into her? It is a possibility which cannot be discounted. If so, this would have been a truly unique event in the series and one which would have shown the killer that a longer bladed knife would do a much better job than a small thin penknife. It would all be part of the learning process which he appears to have taken one bloody step at a time. Klosowski was, after all, a very good student and a quick learner, and he is the closest suspect ever placed next to a murdered Ripper victim, and more than just once. No other suspect ever lived in the same building as a Ripper victim —*none*. And serial killers like to begin their work very close to home.

As reported by the *Daily Chronicle* on March 23, 1903, "The police have found that at the time of the first two murders *Klosowski was undoubtedly occupying a lodging in George Yard, Whitechapel Road, where the first murder was committed*." This report relied on information about Chapman found in the Metropolitan Police file which has regrettably not survived the bombings of World War II. However, it is known that Inspector, then Sergeant, Godley, who was responsible for that file, did at least suspect that Chapman and the Ripper were one and the same. Can there be any more credible source for Chapman's location at the time of the murders than the officers who personally investigated the case so many years ago? The answer must indeed be no. It is possible that Klosowski moved into the area twice. He may have moved there once in 1888 into George Yard, and a second time in 1890 when he is said to have worked in a barber shop at the southern end of George Yard on Whitechapel Road.

When interviewed in 1903 by the *Pall Mall Gazette*, Inspector Abberline stated, "There are many other things extremely remarkable. The fact that Klosowski, when he came to reside in this country, occupied a lodging in George Yard, Whitechapel Road, where the first murder was committed, is very curious, and the height of the man and the peaked cap he is said to have worn quite tallies with the descriptions I got of him." A further investigation of the Ripper murders, with a view towards Klosowski, would have revealed that Mary Jane Kelly had lived in the George Yard Buildings up until March 1888, very possibly at the exact time Klosowski had lived there. They could easily have known each other. She would then move to Miller's Court, an address which could have also been easily known to Klosowski. At the very least he must have known the area very well indeed. If he knew Kelly from the time at the George Yard Buildings, her murder a few months later would be unique in that she would have been possibly the only victim he personally knew, and he may well have specifically targeted her for death.

By the time Tabram's body was discovered the killer was long gone. At

‿ was no longer on the staircase. When George Crow, a 35-year-old licensed cabdriver, returned home to his rooms, number 35, in George Yard Buildings, it was 3:30 in the morning. Arriving, he saw, on the first floor landing, what appeared to be one of the many homeless individuals sleeping near the stairs. In the dark, crowded days of London's East End of the 1880's, this was not a singular event, so he went to his room and simply went to bed. As reported in the *Times* of London, "He took no notice, as he was accustomed to seeing people lying about there. He did not know whether the person was alive or dead." Even if he had stopped there was nothing he could have done. But there is a clue which may be gained from George Crow's brief encounter.

It was, of course, dark in that first floor landing, but would anyone have missed an individual who was lying on her back with her clothes pushed up exposing her lower body with her legs open? Even in the dark, this position would not have appeared to be natural for a sleeping individual. If he noticed this was a person, he would have at least seen that. It is not something that is likely to be missed *unless Martha was not in that position* when he passed her by. And Crow, who had good eyesight, would not have missed it. By 3:30 a.m. she was most certainly dead, as indicated by the later inquest, but was she mutilated? There is reason to believe that both sets of wounds (one from a long blade, many from a short blade) came at separate times. Is this evidence of two separate crimes? It must also be noted that George Crow did not step in any blood and did not track any up the staircase when he walked past. This was checked by the police and would certainly have been noticed by Crow.

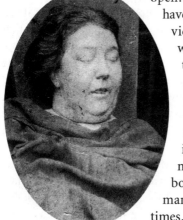

Martha Tabram — August 7, 1888. Stabbed 39 times: five wounds to the left lung, two to the right lung, five stabs to the liver, two stabs to the spleen, six stabs to the stomach, and stabs in the throat, and one fatal stab wound to the heart. (Public Record Office.)

The "effective" discovery was left to John Saunders Reeves, a 37-year-old dockside laborer, who lived in a lodging, number 37, in the George Yard Buildings. Reeves was described as being short with a pale face and full beard and mustache, and sporting earrings! The time was 4:45 a.m. as he left his room for work, and the lighting was probably better in the landing at that time, 1 hour and 15 minutes after

Crow had passed by. The body was easy enough to identify at this point as Mr. Reeves walked down the stairs and noticed that she was lying on her back in a "pool of blood." He actually stepped in and slipped on the blood. All he was able to do, because of his shock, was summon the local constable and he did not spend any time to check to see if she was dead. The killer or killers had made sure that he did not track any blood from the location. Perhaps he did not want to lead anyone up the stairs to his room.

It was not long before Police Constable Thomas Barrett arrived to take charge of the body. Examining Martha Tabram he quickly found how extensive the attack had been. She had been stabbed 39 times, focusing on the breasts, groin and belly. She was lying on her back with the fingers of each hand tightly clenched. At Martha's post-mortem Dr. Killeen reported that she was mutilated well beyond what would be needed to kill her. This was a frenzy. Her clothes had also been damaged by the killer's blade as her petticoat had been ripped open by the knife and pulled upwards with great force. Her clothes "were turned up as far as the center of the body, leaving the lower part of the body exposed; the legs were open, and altogether her position was such as to suggest in my mind that recent intimacy had taken place." This was according to Deputy Coroner George Collier working for the South Eastern Division of Middlesex. But could she have been placed in that position to, as the deputy coroner stated, "suggest" intimacy? When interviewed by the police no one in the building could identify the woman. Klosowski must have been interviewed. The police had come face-to-face with Jack the Ripper after the very first murder!

> The *Star*— August 7, 1888
> A Whitechapel Horror
> A woman, now lying unidentified at the mortuary, Whitechapel, was ferociously stabbed to death this morning, between two and four o'clock, on the landing of a stone staircase in George's — Buildings, Whitechapel.

There are aspects of this killing which appear to be a mix of or transition into later murders. However, the multiple wounds and the pulled up clothes clearly place this attack within the Ripper's modus operandi. The sexual nature of the attack is beyond question, as shown by the areas of the body the attacker focused on. This was not an assault for robbery or defense. This was a violent and senseless, predatory start to a long string of similar murders. On August 14, the body of Martha Tabram was identified by her husband Henry Tabram after he had read reports of her death in the newspapers. He had not been with her for 13 years.

East London Advertiser— August 11, 1888
The circumstances of this awful tragedy are not only surrounded with
the deepest mystery, but there is also a feeling of insecurity to think
that in a great city like London, the streets of which are continually
patrolled by police, a woman can be (locally) and horribly killed almost
next to the citizens peacefully sleeping in their beds without a trace or
clue being left of the villain who did the deed.

One of the local responses to this seemingly senseless and brutal murder was the formation of a Vigilance Committee. It would be the first of
several such civilian activist and patrol groups looking for the killer. Only
a few days after the murder, the St. Judes Vigilance Committee was formed
consisting of 70 local working men as well as students from Toynbee Hall.
Out of that group 12 were selected to patrol and keep watch over selected
streets, mainly from 11 p.m. until 1 a.m. the next morning. Mr. Thomas H.
Nunn was selected as honorary secretary of the group which continued
their watch until February 1889, when the students no longer participated.
It has been reported that the long hours and bad weather forced them off
the streets but perhaps by then they felt that the job had been completed.

Despite the dangerous daily living conditions in the East End slums it
is interesting to note that brutal, sadistic murders were not as common as
one might expect. Certainly there were people killed, but the senseless brutality of the Tabram murder, coming so closely after the non–Ripper related
murder of Emma Smith, seems to have shocked the local residents. They
responded very quickly with vigilance committees. Their speed was in direct
contrast to the slower moving wheels of government in recognizing a new,
much greater terror. But was the Ripper using one of the vigilance committees as cover to search for himself while he selected his targets? What
better way could he have found to get his "work" done? Perhaps he even
escorted a few women home, night after night, before he killed. If he had
escorted them they would have been very comfortable going with him along
the dark back streets of the East End of 1888.

East London Advertiser— August 18, 1888
The police seem to be as far from solving the mystery as they were on
the morning the crime was committed.

In the same issue the *East London Advertiser* reported that the
Whitechapel Board of Works had approved that "lamps with double the
illuminating power be fixed at the corner of the following streets, viz —
Wentworth Street west corner, Thrawl Street, Flower and Dean Street, Vine
Court, Quaker Street, Worship Square..." It would, however, be too late

for Martha Tabram. As for the murder site it became an area of great interest to the locals. As reported in the *Weekly Herald*, "There have been many visitors to George Yard Buildings with the rather morbid purpose of seeing the place where the deceased was discovered. Here there is still a large surface of the stone flags crimson stained."

The First Inquest

With this death coming so early in the series, it gave the authorities no idea of what was to come. There would be no clue to the type of individual they were dealing with until later in the year. With murder not uncommon in London's back alleys, a case of this sort would not have been that different from many others except for the multiple wounds inflicted on the victim. That was unusual. But if many more killings had not occurred subsequent to this one, the case would have long since faded from view. The inquest was handled by Deputy Coroner George Collier, as the Coroner, Mr. Baxter, was on vacation in continental Europe at the time.

At the inquest, begun on the afternoon of August 9, in the Alexandra Room, actually the library, at the Working Lads' Institute on Whitechapel Road, Police Constable Barrett described to a hushed and crowded room what he saw as he investigated the early morning crime scene. He stated that it was clear the victim had been killed where she was discovered, but no evidence could be found of a struggle. Only her clenched fists held against the sides of her body indicated some type of response. There was no blood trail. And, her hair was not out of place.

The superintendent of the George Yard Buildings, Francis Hewitt, and his wife, lived only 12 feet from where the crime had been committed , yet they had heard no sound. It is entirely possible that Martha was simply passed out, due to the night's drinking, and may never have even seen her killer or killers. Inspector Edmund John Reid, as quoted in the London *Times* of August 24, stated that, "Deceased would rather have a glass of ale than a cup of tea, but she was not a woman who got continually drunk, and she never brought home any companions with her." Hewitt testified that his wife had heard a cry of "murder," which she said had echoed throughout the building, but it was much earlier than the time of this crime and was said to have originated outside the George Yard Buildings. Later, in an interview conducted by the *Times*, Mr. Hewitt recalled that Tabram had been seen in a pub with two soldiers the evening of her death.

Dr. Timothy Robert Killeen, who lived at 68 Brick Lane, was called to testify about his postmortem examination of Tabram. He had conducted the examination at 5:30 a.m., on the morning of August 7. He estimated that she had been killed around three hours before he examined her. That would put the time of death at around 2:30 a.m. He further reported that she had been stabbed 39 times, all to the front of the body. He recorded that she had five wounds to the left lung and two to the right lung; five wounds to the liver; two wounds to the spleen; six wounds to the stomach; and, finally, one wound, fatal, to the heart. Dr. Killeen stated that, "The wounds generally might have been inflicted with a knife, but such an instrument could not have inflicted one of the wounds, which went through the chest-bone."

The London *Times* reported that, "His opinion was that one of the wounds was inflicted by some kind of dagger, and that all of them had been caused during life." And yet, if true, why was there no struggle suggested at the murder scene? It seems more likely to be the case that the deep mortal wound to the chest, which penetrated the heart, would have been delivered first, with the rest of the wounds coming later. This could have been easily settled if a more detailed report of the knife marks on the clothing were available, but alas… It would appear that the attacker was in a rage at the time of the murder and used Martha Tabram as the object of exorcising his personal demons.

Later, the police, under the watchful eye of Detective Inspector Reid from H Division, CID (Criminal Investigation Department), would locate Mary Ann Connolly who had been with Martha the night of her death. At first they found it difficult to find "Pearly Poll" because she had disappeared shortly after the murder. It is quite likely that she may have feared for her own life. She could, after all, identify the two guardsmen who had been out with her and Martha. Even if they had not committed the murder they would have been suspects and may have been looking for her. When found, she was interviewed by Sergeant Caunter. A lineup was conducted at Wellington Barracks, Birdcage Walk, to identify the guardsmen, but she picked the wrong two men. The soldiers she identified had airtight alibis and could not have been with the women on the night in question. In the end the police realized that Martha's companion on that fateful night was not going to help the police in any way. Could she have known the killer, who lived very close, or was she simply not one to give a lot of information to "Johnny Law"?

Echo— August 20, 1888
Inspector Reid, Detective Sergeant Goadby (Godley) and other officers then worked on a slight clue given them by "Pearly Poll." It was not thought much of at the time; but what was gleaned from her and other statements given by Elizabeth Allen and Eliza Cooper of 35 Dorset

Street, Spitalfields, certain of the authorities have had cause to suspect a man actually living not far from Buck's Row. At present, however, there is only suspicion against him.

The record of the suspect has been lost, but it is doubtful any information given by Pearly Poll would have led to the actual killer or killers. When she was finally located by the police, she threatened to drown herself, but would later state that, "It was for a lark." Did she know more than she was willing to tell the police? Probably, but if the information was of value we shall never know. The record of Pearly Poll fades from the scene, but the area near Buck's Row would soon become one of horror as the pace of death began to increase. Is it possible that the Ripper viewed the area of Buck's Row as a way to throw suspicion away from the central Whitechapel area?

One historical note of interest may be found in the fact that 14 years later Sergeant, then Inspector, Godley would arrest Severin Klosowski for murder. He was very close to the Ripper in George Yard but he did not know it. History no longer records whether or not he interviewed Klosowski, in reference to this first successful Ripper killing, but someone in the police department must have. It would be to Godley that Hargrave Adam would turn to detail the movements of Klosowski for his 1930 work *The Trial of George Chapman*. In that work Adam would present his suspicions, based on the police investigation, that the Ripper and Klosowski were one and the same.

The London *Times*—August 24, 1888
The police would be pleased if anyone would give them information of having seen anyone with the deceased on the night of Bank Holiday. The Coroner having summed up, the jury returned a verdict to the effect that the deceased had been murdered by some person or persons unknown.

The work of the Whitechapel Killer had begun, but the sleeping city did not yet know it.

Chapter Three

A Dark Night
Down Buck's Row

"…But as to crime I am innocent and I have clear conscious of it."

Ludwig Zagowski

It had already been a cool and wet summer during that dismal year of 1888. In fact, Londoners had experienced one of the worst seasons on record. As summer moved towards an early fall, frequent thunder storms, with heavy rains, made life in the East End ever more difficult. It was on such a vile night, with thunder and flashes of lighting, that Mary Ann (Polly) Nichols once again moved through those dark streets in search of a customer. She would, instead, soon meet a monster and become the first victim to be purposely mutilated by the man the press named Jack the Ripper.

Polly was an alcoholic and a prostitute. Even her father would later state that she was "not a particularly sober woman." She was described as "nearly 44 years of age," 5'2" tall, with brown eyes, dark complexion and brown hair, which had begun to turn gray. She had several front teeth missing, but she was also said to be small and delicate with high cheekbones. Her friend, Emily Holland, probably a fellow prostitute, said she was "a very clean woman who always seemed to keep to herself."

She was born Mary Ann Walker, on August 26, 1845, to Edward and Caroline Walker of Shoe Lane, off the well known Fleet Street in London. At age 19 (some reports say 12) on January 16, 1864, she was married to a printer's machinist named William Nichols at Saint Brides Parish Church on Fleet Street by the Vicar, Charles Marshall. Together the Nicholses had five children. In 1866 Edward John was born, followed by Percy George in 1868, Alice Esther in 1870, Eliza Sarah in 1877 and finally Henry Alfred in 1879.

The marriage was not an altogether good one for Polly and her husband. There is some dispute as to who was to blame for its eventual failure. Indeed, at Polly's funeral, her oldest son Edward, who had left home at age 14 to live with Polly's family, would have nothing to do with his own father. Perhaps he blamed him for Polly's death at the hands of a madman. The record is silent on that issue. Certainly, if the family had stayed together she would not have been on the streets. After 17 years of marriage, in 1881, they were separated for possibly the sixth, but certainly the last time. This final separation would be due to William's affair with a nurse who had taken care of Polly during an illness. The story, which was confirmed by William, was told by Polly's father. Her husband would only say that it had occurred after Polly had left him and that, "The woman [Polly] left me four or five times, if not six." When he was interviewed he attempted to clarify the situation. "I did not leave my wife during her confinement and go away with a nurse-girl. The dead woman deserted me four or five times, if not six. The last time she left me without any home, and with five children, the youngest one year and four months. I kept myself with the children where I was living for two and a half years before I took on with anybody, and not till after it was proved at Lambeth Police Court that she had misconducted herself."

Her husband continued support payments until 1882, when he found that she was living with another man and selling herself on the streets. Local Parish officials attempted to press William for continued support but ended their objections when they learned how Polly was living, and supporting herself.

From April 1882 through March 1883, Polly lived for the most part in Lambeth Workhouse before moving in with her father for two months. He would later describe her as "a dissolute character and drunkard whom he knew would come to a bad end." He also stated, however, that she was not in the habit of staying out all night.

After leaving her father's home she stayed briefly, once again, at the Lambeth Workhouse, but soon began living with a blacksmith named Thomas Dew. She lived with him in Walworth from June 1883 through October 1887. This period of her life may have been better than the years previous, as witnessed by her attendance at her brother's funeral. He had been burned to death by the not uncommon explosion of a paraffin lamp, and Polly was said, by her family, to have been "respectably dressed." However, the relationship with Dew eventually ended and Polly would once again find her way to the workhouses of London's East End. It would be in the Lambeth Workhouse where Mary Ann Monk would meet and befriend her. This young woman would later be called upon to identify Polly's body for police officials at the morgue.

On April 12, 1888, Polly left the Lambeth Workhouse to accept a position as domestic servant for Samuel and Sarah Cowdry who lived on Rose Hill Road, Wandsworth. (The well known prison at Wandsworth is nearby.) Samuel worked as the "clerk of works" for the local police department. Polly's job, which she would hold for only two months, had been found for her by the workhouse, which was a common practice at the time. While employed, she wrote what was to become her last letter, to her father, on April 17, 1888.

> I just write to say you will be glad to know that I am settled in my new place, and going all right up to now. My people went out yesterday and have not returned, so I am left in charge. They are teetotalers and religious so I ought to get on. They are very nice people, and I have not too much to do. I hope you are all right and the boy has work. So goodbye for the present.
>
> > From Yours Truly
> >
> > Polly
>
> Answer soon, please, and let me know how you are.

Her father's return letter to Polly was never answered, and Polly would soon leave her modest job after she had taken clothing from her new employers. It would seem that an easy life was just not what she was looking for. What she would find instead was an early death at the hands of a madman.

After her employment had been abandoned she was once again to be found in the center of the East End, living in the common lodging house located at 18 Thrawl Street, Spitalfields. In the house she shared a four pence per night room with three other women, including her friend, 50-year-old Emily Holland. From Thrawl Street on August 24, 1888, Polly moved to a doss house named the "White House." In this building, at 56 Flower and Dean Street, one block north of Thrawl Street, men and women were allowed to share a bed. Many of the women who resided in these doss houses were prostitutes who could be had for as little as two or three pence. The only requirement of the house was that they paid for the beds. Very few questions were ever asked and even fewer would have been answered.

Less than 200 yards south, on George Yard, lived Severin Klosowski. Investigating Klosowski for three unrelated murders during the 1902–3 police inquiry, Inspector Godley, who, as a young sergeant had worked on the Ripper case, was interviewed by the *Daily Chronicle*. On March 23, 1903, the paper reported that, "The police [Godley] have found that at the time of the first two [Ripper] murders Klosowski was undoubtedly occupying a lodging in George Yard, Whitechapel Road, where the first murder was committed. Moreover, he always carried a black bag and wore a 'P and O' cap. The man who was 'wanted' in connection with the Whitechapel murders always wore a P and O cap and carried a black bag, according to the tale of some of the women who escaped him. In pursuing their investigations into the movements of Klosowski, the London detectives have found that he *went to New Jersey City* [sic] *soon after the Whitechapel atrocities ceased*, and that he opened a barber's shop there."

Klosowski must have been well aware of the area's reputation before he moved there. An 1883 report had described Flower and Dean Street as, "Perhaps the foulest and most dangerous street in the whole metropolis." Locally the Spitalfields area of Thrawl Street, Flower and Dean Street, and George Street were known as the "evil quarter mile." On the edge of that "evil" stood yet another, even greater evil, preparing for his next killing. Charles Booth's, *Descriptive Map of London Poverty 1889, Volume 1*, shows that Klosowski had moved from the "middle class–well to do" area of West India Dock Road, to the "lowest class–vicious, Semi-Criminal" area of George Yard. He had found his lair and his killing ground. It was the evening of August 30, 1888, as London's night sky glowed red due to two raging dock fires, that he began his main work. With rains falling through a smoke filled backdrop, the Ripper once again came out to hunt. And the hunting was good.

If we are to believe Abraham Radin — that his assistant, Klosowski, only worked for him for "around five months" — then by late summer 1888, Klosowski was no longer working in Radin's hairdresser's shop at 70 West India Dock Road in Poplar. Radin never reported that he had fired Klosowski, so it is very possible that he left of his own accord to pursue other activities for which he wanted no witnesses. Or did he simply leave because he had been spotted by the salesman Levisohn? Whatever the reason for his departure, it is clear that with Radin's shop a full two miles away from the killing grounds, it would have been too far to travel to kill in the Whitechapel area. There would have been too many risks in walking, or riding, that far — cleaning himself up afterward being just one of them. He needed to be closer in order to be off the streets as soon as possible after the kill. From George Yard, Severin Klosowski would have been free to roam the dark alleys of Whitechapel for as long as he wanted, with no one to ask where he had been. But no one was watching Klosowski. And the police had no clear suspects for the series of crimes which were just beginning.

August 30–31, 1888

As that cold and wet August 30 came to an end, Polly Nichols could be seen walking along Whitechapel Road. It was 11 p.m., with a light rain washing the gray soot from the dark skies, as she continued her quest for yet another customer. It would not be for the money needed to pay for her room, but for one last drink that she would sell herself. By 12:30 a.m. she was recognized as she left the Frying Pan public house, which sat on the corner of Thrawl Street and Brick Lane. With no money, and feeling the effects of the night's activities, she walked the half block to the familiar and relatively safe doss house at 18 Thrawl Street. There was yet to be any great panic in the minds of the women of Whitechapel; that deep set fear would come later. For the time being it was just one more dangerous night in the East End for Polly, and if she was lucky she would not be bothered by any of the local gangs.

By 1:40 a.m., she found herself being ordered by the deputy of the lodging house to leave the kitchen because she did not have the required four pence for a bed. As she left, she asked him to save her a bed and said, "Never mind, I'll soon get my doss money. See what a jolly bonnet I've got now." Polly was drunk, tired and hungry. And she had less than two hours to live.

Where she went after leaving the doss house is not known, but she must have found another customer because by the time her friend Emily Holland met her at 2:30 a.m. (the time was known by the striking of the Whitechapel Church clock), Polly was very drunk and weaving. It is understandable that her customer never came forward. Emily had spent the evening and early morning watching the fires at the Shadwell Dry-dock near the river. Returning to her lodgings, she met Polly on the corner of Whitechapel Road and Osborn Street outside the small grocer's shop. Emily would later describe her as, "very drunk and [she] staggered against the wall." Klosowski's lodgings were less than 75 yards to the west, and Polly Nichols was the easiest of targets. Was he watching this last meeting from the darkness nearby or would he find his quarry later?

Polly told her friend that she had earned her doss money three times that day but had spent it on drinks. After one more attempt to find another customer, on that rainy early morning, she planned to return to Flower and Dean Street and sleep with one of the men who had paid for a bed there. Any one of them would do. After talking for seven or eight minutes Polly said, "It won't be long before I'm back," and started walking east along Whitechapel Road towards Buck's Row and Whitechapel Station, some half a mile and ten to 15 minutes away. Emily asked Polly to return with her to her lodging house, but Polly would hear nothing of it as she wove towards her fate. Emily was the last person, except the killer, to remember seeing Polly Nichols alive.

At 3:15 that morning, while on regular beat duty, Police Constable John Thain, 96J, walked down Buck's Row and saw nothing out of the ordinary. Sgt. Kerby had also passed through this area on patrol at about the same time and he too found nothing unusual. Although not very well lit, it would have been impossible for either man to have missed a body lying on the wet cobblestone street which was only 20 or so feet wide. These men were, after all, trained observers. For the most part, old two story rowhouses could be found on one side, with warehouses on the other. Buck's Row was described by police as "a narrow quiet thoroughfare frequented by prostitutes for immoral purposes at night." It was well known and well patrolled, but evidently not enough to catch the killer. On part of one side of this street, just where the body was located, there were some new cheap cottages for workers. But not a lot of money had been spent on lighting. At the end of the street was a single gas lamp.

Around 3:40 or 3:45 a.m., Polly Nichols' body was discovered by a carman, or carter, named Charles Cross, as he was going to work at Pickfords, in the City Road. She was murdered only 700 yards from Klosowski's doorstep in George Yard.

Cross saw that she was lying on her back against a gate which led into a stable yard. Was the Ripper in that yard waiting to flee? As he was looking at the body, a second carman named Robert Paul, who was also going to work, came down the road. Charles Cross's first thought was that she had been raped and was only unconscious. He called to Robert Paul and said, "Come and look over here, there's a woman." Polly's hands and face were already cold but her legs and arms were still warm. Her eyes were slightly open. Moreover, Paul thought that he could feel a faint heartbeat and told Cross, "I think she's breathing but it is little if she is." These men must have been very close to the killer as he murdered Polly and fled into the night. He may not have been able to finish his work, but he did have time to first strangle her then use his knife. By now the killer would most likely have been heading southwest along Whitechapel Road as he made his escape back to his lodgings. It was the only clear path out of Buck's Row. This route may simply have been a lucky one, or perhaps he chose it from a clear understanding of the area and police patrols.

Living in a room less than ten yards away from where Polly's body was found lodged Mrs. Purkiss, an elderly woman, who had been awake all night. She and her daughter would later report hearing and seeing nothing, even though their window overlooked the murder site. One of Mrs. Purkiss's sons would later wash off the small amount of blood, after the body

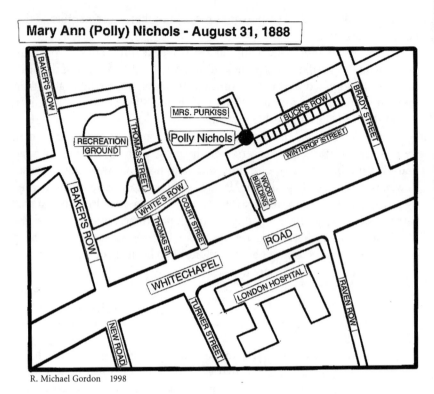

Mary Ann (Polly) Nichols - August 31, 1888

R. Michael Gordon   1998

Polly Nichols was the first Ripper victim to be purposely mutilated. She was discovered by a carman named Charles Cross around 3:40 a.m. August 31, 1888.

had been taken away. Because she had been murdered near a kosher slaughterhouse there were official concerns that the locals would blame one of the many Jewish immigrants who had crowded the East End. Also living nearby was Emma Green who would later recall, "I was awake at the time. I couldn't sleep. If the woman had screamed, I must have heard her."

Because of the darkness neither man noticed the blood on the street, nor any of the wounds, and simply went on to report the incident to the first policeman they could find. When they arrived at the corner of Hanbury Street and Old Montague Street, about 200 yards west of the scene of the crime, they found Constable Jonas Mizen, 55H, and told him what they had discovered. At about the same time Constable John Neil, 94J, on beat duty, came across Polly Nichols' body and began to investigate. The core Ripper murders had begun, and the hunt was now on to catch the multiple killer. Constable Neil had noticed nothing unusual before the discovery of the body and his beat never took him far from the murder site. "The farthest I had been that night was just through the Whitechapel Road and up Baker's Row."

From 3 to 4 a.m. Patrick Mulshaw, who had been dozing before, was awake and overseeing a sewage works on Winthrop Street. He was a night porter for the Whitechapel Board of Works and would testify that during the early morning he had seen no one. At around 4 a.m., he stated, "Another man then passed by and said, 'Watchman, old man, I believe somebody is murdered down the street.'" Mulshaw then walked southeast towards the murder site, as the mysterious other man disappeared into the darkness of Whitechapel. There is no surviving description of the man who spoke to Mr. Mulshaw.

The *Illustrated Police News*— September 8, 1888
The Murder in Whitechapel
Buck's Row, like many other miser thoroughfares in this and similar neighbourhoods, is not overburdened with gas lamps, and in the dim light the constable at first thought that the woman had fallen down in a drunken stupor and was sleeping off the effects of a night's debauch. With the aid of the light from his bulls-eye lantern [P.C.] Neil at once perceived that the woman had been the victim of some horrible outrage. Her livid face was stained with blood and her throat cut from ear to ear.

When he turned his lamp on P.C. Neil discovered that her throat had been deeply cut, almost severing the head. His first thought was that she had committed suicide but he could find no weapon close by so concluded it had to be murder. (Was this a failed attempt to take the head?) At that point Constable John Thain was called and was soon dispatched to Dr. Llewellyn's home located nearby at 152 Whitechapel Road. By 3:50 a.m. the doctor had arrived and under the lamps of several constables, he "pronounced life extinct and ordered the removal of the body to the mortuary." In fact Whitechapel had no public mortuary, just a workhouse mortuary where inmates cleaned the bodies for disposal. There was not much more added to the investigation at the murder site. As usual it was preliminary at best. In fact, Dr. Llewellyn had left the area even before the police removed the body.

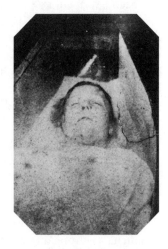

Mary Ann (Polly) Nichols — August 31, 1888. Throat cut down to the vertebrae; cut abdomen several times. She was the first Ripper victim to be intentionally mutilated. (Public Record Office.)

On arrival at the mortuary, Inspector John Spratling investigated under Polly's clothes for any wounds and found that the victim had been mutilated about the abdomen which had been deeply cut at several places "exposing the intestines." She had been literally gutted. Later that day, Spratling filed a report on what Dr. Llewellyn had so far discovered. "...[Her] throat had been cut from left to right, two distinct cuts being on left side, the windpipe, gullet and spinal cord being cut through; a bruise apparently of a thumb being on right lower jaw, also one on left cheek; the abdomen had been cut open from center of bottom of ribs along right side, under pelvis to left of the stomach, there the wound was jagged; the omentum, or coating of the stomach, was also cut in several places, and two small stabs on private parts; [all] apparently done with a strong bladed knife; supposed to have been done by some left handed person; death being almost instantaneous."

According to a Scotland Yard report, issued by Inspector Fred Abberline, "Dr. Llewellyn ... afterwards made a more minute examination and found that the wounds in the abdomen were in themselves sufficient to cause instant death...." Again from the *Illustrated Police News* of September 8: "...[The] lower part of the abdomen had been ripped up, and the bowels were protruding. The abdominal wall, the whole length of the body, had been cut open, and on either side were two incised wounds almost as severe as the centre one. This reached from the lower part of the abdomen to the breast-bone. The instrument with which the wounds were inflicted must have been not only of the sharpness of a razor, but used with considerable ferocity." Llewellyn felt that the murderer had anatomical knowledge and that the wounds could have been committed in four or five minutes. There was certainly tremendous anger indicated by these wounds. Most of the blood from the victim's injuries had been soaked up by the layers of her clothes, and only a little had flowed onto the street.

The Ripper had taken his victim to a street where prostitutes very often went to service their clients, but the lighting was very bad. It would have been easy to cut her throat and abdomen, but without any light to work from in the cloudy, red stained darkness of the night, it would have been next to impossible to accurately remove any targeted internal organs. The insufficient lighting may have been noticed by the Ripper only after his victim was nearly decapitated. If the purpose of the killing was to obtain an organ, for whatever reason, then once again the Ripper would have failed in his mission. It should also be noted that the victim was not left with her wounds exposed. For some reason the Ripper placed her clothes back over her, covering the ripped abdomen. It was a strange "kindness" which helped showcase the madness of the killer. It was a "kindness" he would display

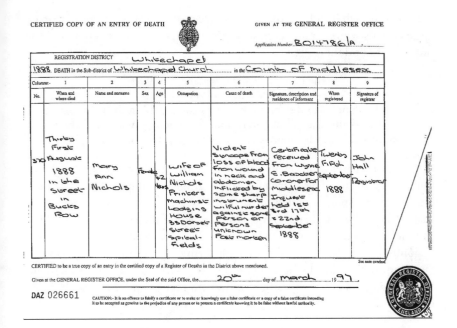

Copy of death certificate for Mary Ann Nichols.

again and again. The police could not find a motive for the murder. At first it was suspected to be the work of one of the gangs in the area, but that theory soon fell by the wayside.

A photo of Polly was taken and shown in the local workhouses in the hope of acquiring an identification of the murder victim. It was a mark, however, on petticoat bands, "Lambeth Workhouse — P.R.," which led police to Polly's eventual identification. As efforts got under way to locate the killer, Inspector Abberline, who had been sent to coordinate the work of local detectives, reported on September 19, that, "Inquires were made in every conceivable quarter with a view to trace the murderer, but not the slightest clue can at present be obtained." Abberline was considered one of the best investigators with a detailed and intimate knowledge of the East End. He had been on the force since January 5, 1863, when he joined as a 20-year-old constable. And he would need all the skills he could muster.

When her husband viewed her body at the mortuary he was overheard to say, "I forgive you for everything now that I see you like this." Polly Nichols was buried at the City of London Cemetery, Manor Park on September 6, 1888, in grave number 49500, square number 318. Her polished elm coffin bore a new brass plate with the words: "Mary Ann Nichols, aged 42; died August 31, 1888." There would not be any huge crowds for this victim, although hundreds did line the streets to view the hearse. The truly large crowds would come later, as more victims were discovered, and the outrage of Londoners grew.

> The London *Times*— September 1, 1888
> Another Murder in Whitechapel
> Another murder of the foulest kind was committed in the neighborhood of Whitechapel in the early hours of yesterday morning, but by whom and with what motive is at present a complete mystery.

That morning, L.P. Walter and Son wrote the Home Office and recommended a reward be offered for information about the killer. It was only one of many responses which showed this to be a strange new type of criminal being dealt with. Leigh Pemberton replied for the Home Office that the practice had been discontinued. Later that day, Robert Anderson was appointed Assistant Commissioner for Crime. He would choose Donald Swanson to head up the investigation of the Nichols murder, as Scotland Yard began to see that this situation was no regular murder case, but one of a very different nature.

> The *New York Times*— September 1, 1888
> A Terribly Brutal Murder in Whitechapel
> London, Aug. 31— A strangely horrible murder took place at Whitechapel this morning. The victim was a woman who at 3 o'clock, was knocked down by some man unknown and attacked with a knife. Her head was nearly severed from her body, which was literally cut to pieces, one gash reaching from the pelvis to the breastbone. The strangest part of the affair is that this is the third murder of the kind which has been done lately. In the last one, two weeks ago the victim was stabbed 39 times. The police have concluded that the same man did all three murders and that the most dangerous kind of a lunatic is at large.

The *New York Times* had included in its count the murder of Emma Smith, who was most certainly not a Ripper victim. But the details were coming in fast and it would be a while before fact could be separated from fiction.

Mr. Baxter's Inquest

The inquest into Polly Nichols' death began on Saturday, September 1, 1888, at the Working Lads' Institute and Mission, on Whitechapel Road, in an upstairs room lit by gas lamps. It was located across the street from London Hospital. Heading up the inquiries, and fresh from his holiday, was

Mr. Wynne E. Baxter, the well known Freemason and Coroner for South East Middlesex. He was noted for his flamboyant dress and his telegraphic address, "Inquest London." For this inquest the East London *Observer* reported that he wore "...white and checked trousers, a dazzling white waistcoat, a crimson scarf and a dark coat." However, he took his job very seriously and was not a man to be taken lightly.

> Oyez, Oyez, You good men of this district summoned to appear hear this day to inquire for our sovereign Lady the Queen when, how, and by what means Mary Ann Nichols came to her death, answer to your names.

The first to be called was Polly's father, Mr. Edward Walker, who lived at 15 Maldwell Street, Albany Road, Camberwell. It had been some time since he had last seen his daughter and his identification of her was understandably not an easy one.

> EDWARD WALKER: I have seen the body in the mortuary, and to the best of my belief it is my daughter, but I have not seen her for three years. I recognize her by her general appearance and by a little mark she had on her forehead a child. She also has either one or two teeth out, the same as the woman I have just seen. My daughter's name was Mary Ann Nichols, and she has been married twenty-two years. She was forty-two years.
> CORONER: Was she a sober woman?
> WALKER: Well at time[s] she drank, and that was why we did not agree.
> CORONER: Was she fast? [Was she a prostitute?]
> WALKER: No; I never heard anything of that sort. She used to go with some young women and men that she knew, but I never heard of anything improper.
> CORONER: Have you any idea of what she has been doing lately?
> WALKER: I have not the slightest idea.
> CORONER: She must have drank heavily for you to turn her out of doors?
> WALKER: I never turned her out. She had no need to be like this while I had a home for her.
> CORONER: Have you any reasonable doubt that this is your daughter?
> WALKER: No, I have not. I know nothing about her acquaintances, or what she had been doing for a living. I had no idea that she was over here in this part of the town.
> CORONER: Is there anything you know of likely to throw any light upon this affair?
> WALKER: No; I don't think she had any enemies, she was too good for that.

The next witness to be called was Police Constable John Neil, 97J, a 13 year veteran of the force from J Division, who gave a good account of his actions that early morning.

P.C. JOHN NEIL: On Friday morning I was proceeding down Buck's Row, Whitechapel, going towards Brady Street. There was not a soul about. I had been round there half an hour previously, and I saw no one then. [This effectively cuts off any direct route for the killer to leave the area going northeast.] I was on the right hand side of the street when I noticed a figure lying in the street. It was dark at the time, though there was a street lamp shining at the end of the row. I went across and found deceased lying outside a gateway, her head towards the east; gateway was closed. It was about nine or ten feet high, and led to some stables. There were houses from the gateway eastward. Deceased was lying lengthways along the street, her left-hand touching the gate. I examined the body by the aid of my lantern, and noticed blood oozing from a wound in the throat. She was lying on her back, with her clothes disarranged. I felt her arm, which was quite warm, from the joints upwards. Her eyes were wide open. Her bonnet was off and lying at her side, close to the left hand. I heard a constable passing Brady Street, so I called him. I did not whistle. I said to him, "Run at once for Dr. Llewellyn," and seeing another constable in Baker's Row, I sent him for the ambulance.

CORONER: Did you notice any blood where she was found?

P.C. JOHN NEIL: There was a pool of blood just where her neck was lying. The blood was running from … around … her neck.

CORONER: Did you hear any noise that night?

P.C. JOHN NEIL: No; I heard nothing. The farthest I had been that night was just through the Whitechapel Road and up Baker's Row. I was never far away from the spot.

CORONER: Whitechapel Road is busy in the early morning, I believe. Could anybody have escaped that way?

P.C. JOHN NEIL: Oh, yes sir. I saw a number of women in the main road going home. At the time anyone could have got away.

A JURYMAN: Knowing that the body was warm, did it not strike you that it might just have been laid there, and that the woman was killed elsewhere?

P.C. JOHN NEIL: I examined the road, but did not see the mark of wheels. The first to arrive on the scene after I discovered the body were two men who worked at a slaughter house opposite. They said they knew nothing of the affair and that they had not heard any screams. I had previously seen the men at work. That would be about a quarter past three, or half an hour before I found the body.

One activity which is common to many serial killers is putting their victims on display so that their work may be viewed and spoken of. It is a form of recognition which is greatly needed by many of these killers. The Ripper was no different, as he continued to display his work.

After Sergeant Kerby had come to Constable Neil's aid, Kerby began to check the houses in the area. He went to Mrs. Green's house which was just east of where the body had been found but she had heard nothing and could not give any evidence to aid the police.

Dr. Rees Ralph Llewellyn was then called to testify. He had been summoned at 4:00 a.m. the morning of Polly's death from his surgery at 152 Whitechapel Road. He was the first doctor to view the remains.

DR. LLEWELLYN: On Friday morning I was called to Buck's Row at about four o'clock. The constable told me what I was wanted for. On reaching Buck's Row I found the deceased woman lying flat on her back in the pathway, her legs extended. I found she was dead, and that she had severe injuries to her throat. Her hands and wrists were cold, but the body and lower extremities were warm. I examined her chest and felt the heart. It was dark at the time. I believe she had not been dead more than half an hour. I am quite certain that the injuries to her neck were not self-inflicted. There was very little blood round the neck. There were no marks of any struggle or of blood, as if the body had been dragged. I told the police to take her to the mortuary, and I would make another examination. I have this morning made a postmortem examination of the body. I found it to be that of a female about forty or forty five years. Five of the teeth are missing, and there is a slight laceration of the tongue. On the right side of the face there is a bruise running along the lower part of the jaw. It might have been caused by a blow with the fist or pressure by the thumb. On the left side of the face there was a circular bruise, which also might have been done by the pressure of the fingers. On the left side of the neck, about an inch below the jaw, there was an incision about four inches long and running from a point immediately below the ear. An inch below on the same side and commencing about an inch in front of it was a circular incision terminating at a point three inches below the right jaw. This incision completely severs all the tissues down to the vertebrae. The large vessels of the neck on both sides were severed. The incision is about eight inches long. These cuts must have been caused with a long bladed knife, moderately sharp, and used with great violence. No blood at all was found on the breast, either of the body or clothes. There were no injuries about the body till just about the lower part of the abdomen. Two or three inches from the left side was a wound running in a jagged manner. It was a very deep wound, and the tissues were cut through. There were several incisions running across the abdomen. On the right side there were also three or four similar cuts running downward. All these had been caused by a knife, which had been used violently and been used downward. The injuries were from left to right, and might have been done by a left-handed person. All the injuries had been done by the same instrument.

When the Ripper had finished his work he simply wiped off the blade on her skirt, covered over her wounds, and silently walked away. At this point in the series there were no descriptions for the police to work from so he did not need to be concerned about being stopped after he had left the immediate area. He had not yet been linked to the attacks on Annie Millwood and Ada Wilson.

The London *Times*— September 3, 1888
The Whitechapel Murder

Up to a late hour last evening the Police had obtained no clue to the perpetrator of the latest of the three murders which have so recently taken place in Whitechapel, and there is, it must be acknowledged, after their exhaustive investigation of the facts, no ground for blaming the officers in charge should they fail in unravelling the mystery surrounding the crime. The murder, in the early hours of Friday morning last, of the woman now known as Mary Ann Nichols, has so many points of similarity with the murder of two other women in the same neighbourhood — one Martha Tabram, as recently as August 7, and the other less than 12 months previously — that the police admit their belief that the three crimes are the work of one individual. All three women were of the class called "unfortunates" each so very poor, that robbery could have formed no motive for the crime, and each was murdered in such a similar fashion, that doubt as to the crime being the work of one and the same villain almost vanishes, particularly when it is remembered that all three murders were committed within a distance of 300 yards from each other. Detective-Inspector Abberline, of the Criminal Investigation Department, and Detective-Inspector Helson, J Division, are both of opinion that only one person, and that of a man, had a hand in the latest murder. It is understood that the investigation into the George Yard mystery is proceeding hand-in-hand with that of Buck's Row.

After Dr. Llewellyn's testimony, the inquest was adjourned for the day and began again two days later on Monday, September 3. On that day, Inspector John Spratling, J Division, testified that he had first heard of the murder around 4:30 a.m., while he was on Hackney Road, and he immediately proceeded to Buck's Row. He had little more to add to the case and his testimony basically backed up what had been stated by P.C. Neil. Next up was Henry Tompkins who worked as a horse slaughterer on Winthrop Street, one short half block south of Buck's Row. He testified that he normally went straight home after work but on that night he decided to go for a walk. As he was starting his walk a police constable came past the slaughterhouse at 4:15 a.m. and told the workers of a body being found nearby. The spot was very near the slaughterhouse but none of the men had heard any sounds which would have indicated a crime was being committed very nearby. It is not altogether clear that they would have even considered going to help if they had heard a cry — it was after all the East End.

> CORONER: Was all quiet, say after two o'clock on Friday morning?
> HENRY TOMPKINS: Yes, quite quiet. The gates were open, and we heard no cry.
> CORONER: Had anybody called for assistance from the spot where the deceased was found would you have heard it in the slaughterhouse?
> TOMPKINS: [No], it was too far away.
> JURYMAN: Did you hear any vehicle pass the slaughterhouse?
> TOMPKINS: No, Sir. If one had passed I should have heard it.

It would have been very easy for anyone up at that time to have heard the echoed sounds of wheels of any vehicle moving along cobblestone streets. It was therefore clearly established that the Ripper was on foot and had to have been working from the local area.

Detective Inspector Joseph Helson was then called before the inquest. He had inspected the body the morning of the murder, between 8 and 9 o'clock, when it still had the clothes on at the mortuary. According to a report in the *Illustrated Police News*, September 8, 1888, "There was blood in the hair and about the collars of the dress and ulster, but he saw none at the back of the skirts. He found no marks on the arms such as would indicate a struggle and no cuts in the clothing. All the wounds could, in my opinion, have been inflicted without the removal of the clothing. The only suspicious mark about the place where the body was found was one spot in Brady Street. It might have been blood."

> JURYMAN: Did the body look as if it had been brought dead to Buck's Row?
> INSPECTOR HELSON: No, I should say that the offense was committed on the spot.

Police Constable Jones Mizen, 55H, testified that at around 3:45 a.m., while he was at the corner of Hanbury Street and Baker's Row, he was approached by a passing carman, along with a second man, who told him, "You are wanted in Buck's Row by a policeman. A woman is lying there." When he arrived at the murder scene Constable Neil sent him to get the ambulance. His presence at the corner of Hanbury Street and Baker's Row effectively blocked any escape to the northwest by the killer, once again pointing to the Whitechapel area as the home of the Ripper.

Charles A. Cross was then interviewed by the coroner, as he was one of the first at the scene of the murder. He was passing through Buck's Row on his way to Messrs. Pickford & Company, where he worked as a carman. It was 3:30 a.m. when he saw what he at first thought was a tarpaulin sheet lying against a gate. Upon closer inspection, in the darkness, he saw that it was the body of a woman. "At this time I heard a man, about 40 yards off, approaching from the direction I myself had come. I waited for the man, who started on one side, as if he were afraid that I meant to knock him down. I said, 'Come and look over here. There's a woman.' We then went over to the body. I took hold of her hands, and the other man stooped over her head to look at her. Her hands were cold and I said, 'I believe she's dead.' I then touched her face, which felt warm. The other man put his head on her heart saying, 'I think she's breathing, but it is very little if she is.' The other man suggested that we should shift her but I said, 'I am not going to touch her.' I did not notice that her throat was cut." (This is an indication of just how dark it was on Buck's Row, which would have made it very difficult to successfully remove any organs from the body.)

The two men left the victim on the street and walked towards Baker's Row, soon meeting Constable Mizen. Cross informed him that, "She looks to me to be either dead or drunk." The second man said, "I think she's dead." Cross saw no one except Constable Mizen and the other carman. At the time there was no great excitement in the discovery of a body. This was not a unique event in the East End.

One of the last witnesses was Emily Holland who stated that she lived on Thrawl Street, Spitalfields, in a common lodging house. As reported by the *Illustrated Police News*, Holland testified that the "deceased had lived there about six weeks, but was not there during the last ten days. At about half past two o'clock on Friday morning witness [Holland] saw the deceased going down Osborn Street into Whitechapel Road. She was staggering along drunk and was alone. Witness tried to persuade her to go home with her. The deceased refused. She was a quiet woman, and kept herself to herself. Witness did not know whether she had any male acquaintance or not. She had never seen the deceased quarrel with anybody."

The coroner then informed the jury that the police had no further evidence at the time and requested the proceedings to be held for "sufficiently long" to give them an opportunity of obtaining further evidence. A two week delay was then ordered. The inquest was then continued on September 17 and finished on September 22. But not before one juryman would ask "Why don't the police offer a reward? If Mrs. Nichols had been a rich woman living in the West End of London they would have offered £1000." It was then up to the jury to come to a conclusion, which they did in 20 minutes. The conclusion was as expected: "wilful murder by some person or persons, unknown."

The London *Times*—September 4, 1888
The Whitechapel Murder
Yesterday morning Mr. Wynne E. Baxter, the Coroner for the South-
Eastern Division of Middlesex, resumed his inquiry at the Working
Lads' Institute, High Street, Whitechapel, respecting the death of Mary
Ann Nichols, whose dead body was found on the pavement in Buck's
Row, Whitechapel, on Friday morning. Inspector Spratling, continu-
ing [his testimony], said he and Sergeant Godley examined the East
London and District Railway embankments and lines, and also the
Great Eastern Railway yard, but they were unable to find anything
likely to throw any light on the affair. One of Mr. Brown's men wiped
up the blood. A constable was on duty at the gate of the Great Eastern
Railway yard, which was about 50 yards from the spot where the body
was found. He [Spratling] had questioned this constable, but he had
not heard anything.

As with the other murders, the police were on patrol or point duty
throughout the area, but to no avail. Although in the end, the coroner would
once again come to the conclusion that Polly Nichols had been murdered
by some person or persons unknown, the police were now convinced that
these were not the average everyday crimes they had grown familiar with
in the terror filled slums of the East End. These were something decidedly
different. They were the work of a madman, who in all probability, would
strike again and again. The authorities were convinced that it would only
be a matter of time. Serial killers are, after all, by definition successful at
what they do. As an interesting historic footnote to the Buck's Row murder, the officials in power would later change the name of the thoroughfare
to Durward Street. The Ripper, it seems, was bad on even a slum's image.

The London *Times* in its September 4, 1888, editorial remarked, "The
most salient point is the maniacal frenzy with which the victims were
slaughtered, and unless we accept, as possible alternative, the theory that
the assassin was actuated by revenge for some real or supposed injury
suffered by him at the hands of unfortunate women, we are thrown back
upon the belief that these murders were really committed by a madman...."

The *East London Observer* made its prejudicial opinions known about
the background of the killer when it stated "that no Englishman could have
perpetrated such a horrible crime, and it must have been done by a Jew...."

In a memo Sir Robert Anderson wrote, "I am convinced that the
Whitechapel murder case is one which can be successfully grappled with if
it is systematically taken in hand. I go so far as to say that I could myself
in a few days unravel the mystery provided I could spare the time to give
individual attention to it." He then went on vacation to mainland Europe.

Chapter Four

A Murder on
Hanbury Street

*"I pray God for sinners who are suffering unjustly in this country.
Believe me i an werry grievously sorry but it could not help now..."*

Severin Klosowski

As the police began to slowly gather their strength to confront the Whitechapel Killer, the Ripper himself was moving with great speed. For some as yet undiscovered reason he had a schedule, or at least a self-imposed time period, in which to do most of his work. It would be only one week before he would search again for a target. Seven days of rest before returning to the hunt on the killing fields of Whitechapel. As it was with the Ripper, it is the act of the hunt which draws many serial killers to their helpless victims. The killing itself is often just business as usual.

Her name was Annie Chapman. At her inquest, the doctor would state that "the deceased was far advanced in disease of the lungs and membranes of the brain, but they had nothing to do with the cause of death." Fate had decreed that Annie Chapman, or "Dark Annie," as some had known her, would not have much longer to walk the grim streets of Whitechapel and Spitalfields, but that time would be cut even shorter by Jack the Ripper. She would be described by her friend, Amelia Palmer, who lived at the lodging house at 30 Dorset Street, as a "sober, steady going woman, who seldom took any drink." But that must have been less than true. Rum was a favorite drink of Annie's and she had a drinking problem. It had not been an easy life for Dark Annie, and neither would be her death.

And what of Severin Klosowski? No evidence points to his moving away from his lodgings at George Yard Buildings just yet. There is also no clear evidence that he actually had a job at this time either, but the dates of the killings would suggest some type of employment was on hand for him during the daylight hours of the usual work week. He would need the weekends and holidays for his "real work," however; those periods would have to be free. And when his work was done he would be able to rest, before once again appearing in the daylight. It is even possible that Klosowski met and selected his victims from some of the customers who came into the hairdresser's shop where he had worked. They would have gone with someone they knew and trusted. They would have gone with someone familiar to most in the neighborhood; someone who blended into the confused and crowded matrix which was Whitechapel. The friendly hairdresser, quick with a joke and some pleasant conversation with the ladies, would have seemed perfectly safe.

It is also very possible that this future proprietor of barbershops could have worked in the barbershop located at the Brick Road end of Flower and Dean Street. Surely he was aware of it. This would have been a nearby and perfect place to return to in order to get off the streets and clean up after the murders. It was only three short blocks from his lodgings on George Yard and located across the street from where three of the Ripper's victims were living at the time of their deaths. Did Klosowski leave his job with Abraham Radin in order to find another, much closer position to his victims, and then use it as cover for watching his targets? It is a very good possibility, because his previous job was more than two miles away.

This is all speculation, though. But much is known. In 1932, former Detective Arthur Neil, who had worked on the investigation into the background of Severin Klosowski for his *1903 trial for three serial murders*, wrote in his memoirs, "Klosowski ... got a job at a barber's shop in High Street, Whitechapel. He was right on the scene of these atrocities [the Ripper series] during the whole period." He may not have been the owner or the operator of the barbershop under the White Hart public house on High Street at the time, but he was most certainly employed in one of the local barbershops during the Ripper murders. What is also known is that Annie Chapman's lodgings on Dorset Street were only 500 yards or so away from Klosowski's lodgings at George Yard, and only two short blocks from the barbershop on Flower and Dean Street. It would have required a five minute walk, at most, to find this victim. Detective Neil's investigation conclusively proves that Klosowski had easy daily access to *each and every victim* in the Ripper series.

She was born Eliza Anne Smith in September 1841. At her death she would be described as 45 years old, 5 feet tall, strongly built with pallid complexion, thick nose, dark brown wavy hair, blue eyes and possessing excellent teeth, of which possibly two were missing. She was also dying of tuberculosis and very possibly syphilis as well. Annie's parents, Ruth Chapman and George Smith, were married six months after her birth, on February 22, 1842, in Paddington. At the time, her father was a private in the 2nd Battalion of Lifeguards. She was the first of possibly five children; there may have been two brothers and two sisters. It has been reported that the siblings did not get along with their older sister, but no reason is given, only the suggestion of a long term drinking problem.

When Annie was 27 she married a relative of her mother by the name of John Chapman, on May 1, 1869. He was working "in the service of a gentleman" at the time, in Clewer near Windsor. (However, it was reported, by Amelia Palmer, who called him Frederick, that he was a veterinary surgeon.) During that early period they lived with her mother at 29 Montpelier Place, Brompton. The next year they moved to 1 Brook Mews, Bayswater, and stayed there until 1873 when they again moved, this time to 17 South Bruton Mews, Berkeley Square. During this period they had three children: Emily Ruth in 1870, who would die of meningitis 12 years later; Annie Georgina in 1873; and John Jr. in 1881. Their only son was a cripple who was eventually sent to live in a home. In the same year John Jr. was born, the family moved back to Windsor, when her husband accepted a job as a domestic coachman to a farm bailiff by the name of Josiah Weeks at St. Leonard's Mill Farm Cottage.

After 15 or 16 years of marriage, around 1885, they separated by mutual consent, but there is little record of the reason. However, by that time Annie had been arrested in Windsor several times for drunkenness and her husband John was known as a heavy drinker. This may have had something to do with the separation. There was at least one Windsor police report which touched on the subject when it stated that their marital problems were due to her "drunken and immoral ways." John Chapman died the next year, on Christmas day, of cirrhosis of the liver and dropsy. But until that time he had continued to support his wife, on a semi-regular basis, by sending her 10 shillings a week by postal order. Amelia Palmer reported that "since the death of her husband she seemed to have given away all together."

At the time of her husband's death she was living with John Sivvey, who made his living as a wire sieve maker. They lived at the common lodging house at 30 Dorset Street, Spitalfields, where she had met her friend Amelia Palmer. But Sivvey would soon leave her when the money from her husband stopped after his death. It was only then that Annie needed to turn to prostitution to support herself. Before that she did crochet work or sold flowers to supplement her allowance. Her only close relative was a married sister who lived on Oxford Street, Whitechapel, just south of London Hospital.

By June 1888, Annie surfaced at Crossingham's lodging house at 35 Dorset Street, Spitalfields. It was a common lodging house in which perhaps 300 people lived and it was in the central area of Jack the Ripper's hunting ground. Because of the large number of common lodging houses, or doss houses, along its short length, the street became known as "Dosset Street." It was also known for its many public houses (bars). At the western end, on the Chrispin Street corner, was located The Horn of Plenty. In the middle was The Blue Coat Boy operated by William Turner, and at the eastern end, on the Commercial Road corner, was The Britannia, which was also known as the Ringer after the family who ran it. Many of these public houses stayed open all night and they never lacked business. It is interesting to note that directly across the street from Crossinghams was the brick arched entrance which led into Miller's Court, the home of Mary Kelly, and the future scene of her murder. Towards the end of her life, Annie Chapman met, and had a steady relationship with, a man named Edward Stanley. He lived at 1 Osborn Places, Osborn Street in Whitechapel and was nicknamed "The Pensioner." He was not really drawing a military pension as he represented, but was actually a bricklayer's laborer. The two would spend their weekends at Crossinghams and it is strange that they would not go to his home on Osborn Street, unless it was a lodging house which did not allow couples. Most weekends they would be together until as late as 3:00 Monday morning.

A Last Long Night

Early on the evening of Friday, September 7, Amelia Palmer met Annie on Dorset Street. It was 5 p.m. and Annie was not feeling very well that day and told her friend that she was too ill to do anything. Amelia said her farewells and went on her way, but returned a few minutes later to find Annie still standing in the same spot. She told Amelia that, "It's no use my giving way, I must pull myself together and go out and get some money or I shall have no lodgings." It was the last time Amelia saw Annie Chapman alive. Later, she would be called upon to identify her friend's body and testify at the inquest into her murder.

Annie must have been somewhat successful during the evening because she was able to find enough money to pay for her drinks but seemed not to have enough for her bed. She would later tell one of the lodgers that she had been given five pence by her family, most likely to help her pay for her bed, but it was spent during the evening. By 11:30 p.m., Annie had returned to her lodging house and asked if she could go into the kitchen, and by 12:10 a.m. she was seen having another beer with Frederick Stevens, who also lived at Crossinghams. He later stated that she was the worse for drink and that she did not leave the lodging house until 1:00 a.m.. At around 12:12 a.m. another lodger, by the name of William Stevens, came into the kitchen. He saw Annie take out a box of pills she had gotten earlier from the casual ward to treat her illness. But the small box broke so she took an envelope piece from the mantelpiece to hold her pills. Stevens saw Chapman leave the kitchen area and later reported that he felt she had gone to bed. But she had not.

Instead of going to sleep, Annie went out to again earn some money for her bed. At 1:35 a.m., she was once more at Crossinghams, this time eating a baked potato. Before long the elderly night watchman, John Evans, was sent to collect her doss money for her regular bed, number 29. Because she had no money she went upstairs to speak with the deputy, Timothy Donovan, in his office. "I haven't sufficient money for my bed, but don't let it. I shall not be long before I'm in." Donovan then observed that, "You can find money for your beer and you can't find money for your bed." Not put out at all, the good-natured Annie stepped out of the office and two or three minutes later popped her head back into the office to say, "Never mind, Tim. I'll soon be back." As Annie left Crossingham's lodging house for the final time she ran into John Evans again and told him, "I won't be long Brummy [his nickname]. See that Tim keeps the bed for me." As she left, Evans watched her enter Little Paternoster Row heading north towards Brushfield Street. Annie then faded from view as she turned towards Spitalfields Market. It would be nearly four hours before anyone reported seeing Annie Chapman again. Then it would be for the very last time.

During those final four hours, Annie could have been with someone indoors for at least some of the time as witnessed by the fact that she had a little money with her. She had eaten a bit of food and no one had seen her moving about Whitechapel near any of her usual places. She was also not seen by any of the local constables who knew her by sight. She had not been engaged in any more drinking, as indicated by the postmortem, and was perhaps simply sleeping off her drunkenness out in the open, or in a doorway, before awakening to confront her killer. However, there was one report which placed her at the Ten Bells public house at around 5 a.m. but the report was not confirmed.

Five short blocks northeast of Spitalfields Market, stood 29 Hanbury Street. It would become Annie Chapman's final destination on that last long

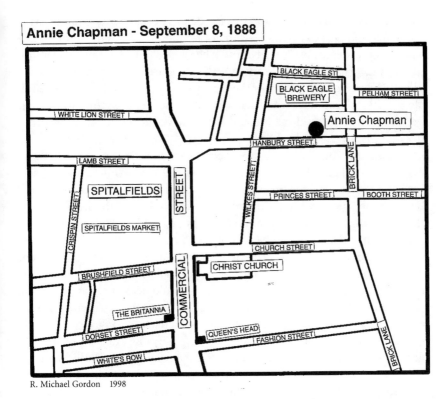

R. Michael Gordon   1998

Annie Chapman became the Ripper's third victim in a small backyard at 29 Hanbury Street. Her body was discovered by carman John Davis a little after 5:45 a.m. on September 8, 1888.

night. At 4:45 a.m., one of the residents of that crowded building, Mr. John Richardson, went into the small backyard before going to work. He sat on the step to remove a small piece of leather from one of his boots with his knife. It was very dark, but because he was sitting less than two feet away from where Chapman's head would have been lying, he could not have missed her, had she been there at the time. He would later report that he had seen and heard nothing out of the ordinary. "I could not have failed to notice the deceased had she been lying there then."

In 1888, 29 Hanbury Street was a yellow wood and brick, three story building, with attic and eight rooms. It was crowded inside with 17 people, and had two front doors. One door led into a small front shop, while the other, on the left, led through a passageway within the building directly into the backyard. On the ground floor lived Mrs. Annie Hardyman with her 16-year-old son. They used the front room as a small store, where they sold cat meat, as well as a bedroom after the day's sales. Richard G. Jones, writing in his *Unsolved Classic True Murder Cases*, 1987, reported, "Annie Chapman was murdered, in a yard behind a barber's shop." Certainly surviving photos of 29 Hanbury Street show a barber shop front, complete with a couple of Brylcreem signs, but was there a barbershop at that location in 1888, along with the cat meat store? If so, it would be one more link to the barber-surgeon Klosowski, who could hardly have missed its location in the heart of his own neighborhood.

John and Amelia Richardson occupied a first floor front room with her 14-year-old grandson, and rented the cellar for the manufacture of packing cases. She shared the first floor back room with Mr. Walker, who made tennis boots, along with his retarded 27-year-old son Alfred. The second floor was also crowded with a family of three, the Thompsons, using the front room and sharing the back room with two unmarried sisters named Copsey. The third floor was occupied by John Davis in the attic front, along with his wife and three sons. To the rear of the attic lived an elderly lady named Sarah Cox. None of the 17 residents would hear or see anything out of the ordinary, as the Ripper silently walked through their home into the early morning darkness and into the confined backyard.

As the clock on the Black Eagle Brewery, only one block away on Brick Lane, struck the half hour (5:30 a.m.) Elizabeth Long saw Annie Chapman standing in front of 29 Hanbury Street. Long lived with her husband, a parkkeeper, at 198 Church Row, Spitalfields and may therefore not have been a prostitute. Standing next to Annie was a man, "hard against the shutters." He certainly did not want to be seen. She noticed that they were speaking and Long heard the man say, "Will you?" and Annie reply, "Yes." Annie Chapman had just agreed to go into a secluded backyard, lit with the light of a sun just coming up, with Jack the Ripper. He would have, for the first time, the opportunity to work in the early light of day. It would be a great risk, but one he must have cherished. Elizabeth could see Annie's face clearly but the killer's back was towards her. Nevertheless, she was able to give a good general description of the man. At Annie's inquest, Elizabeth would describe him so: "...[Dark] complexion, and was wearing a brown deerstalker hat. I think he was wearing a dark overcoat but cannot be sure. Oh, he was a man over forty, as far as I can tell. He seemed a little taller than the deceased. He looked to me like a foreigner, as well as I could make out. He looked what I should call shabby genteel." Long did not stay and speak with either of them as she walked down the street. If she had stopped to speak with Annie and come face-to-face with the Ripper, would he have still gone into the dark yard with Annie? It would have been an added risk he may not have wanted to take. In fact, it could very well be that he had been seen face-to-face at other times, but in those cases decided not to take the chance to kill and of being later identified.

It would be only a few moments before the Ripper and Chapman would disappear into the hallway-passage of 29 Hanbury Street, walking a little over 23 feet, down the three steps and quietly into the backyard, closing the door behind them. As was the usual case, the door to the backyard was unlocked. At just that time, Albert Cadoch, a carpenter who lived next door at 27 Hanbury Street, walked into his backyard, reportedly to use the outhouse. As he passed the wooden five foot tall fence, separating the two yards, he heard a woman call out, "No, no!" He could not have been more than three feet from the fence when Chapman's throat was cut. He then heard "something fall against the fence." It was the body of Annie Chapman bouncing off the fence as it fell to the ground. This was the closest anyone would ever come to Jack the Ripper during one of his murders, and the witness would be completely unaware that anything out of the ordinary was happening, just an arm's length away. Cadoch never even looked over the fence. As he calmly used the backyard outhouse, over the fence an even calmer Ripper was beginning his work on Annie Chapman. Cadoch then went to work, passing Spitalfields Church at 5:32 a.m.

Upstairs on the third floor of 29 Hanbury Street, John Davis was having a restless night. He had been awake from about three that morning until about 5 a.m., finally finding a bit of rest for about half an hour. By 5:45 a.m. he had gotten up and prepared himself to go to work as a carman in Leadenhall Market. As he was getting ready for work and enjoying a cup of tea made by his wife, in the backyard below the Ripper continued working on Annie Chapman. Davis then went to the backyard, probably to use the outhouse, and there he found Annie Chapman's mutilated body. Seeing at once that she was dead he called two other men, James Green and James Kent, who rushed out to find a policeman. Davis himself went immediately to Commercial Street Police Station to report the murder. None of these men saw anyone in the backyard and no one saw the Ripper leave the building to mix with the early morning traffic going to work or to Spitalfields Market nearby. Davis directed the officers to this latest murder site but would go no further than the front door. "I can't face it again."

As with many modern day serial killers the Ripper seemed to have wanted his work displayed, even as he was doing everything he could to avoid capture. The arrangement of Annie Chapman's property is an excellent example of his madness and his directed actions. After the brutal murder and mutilation, he calmly laid out her property. He cut open her pocket and arranged her two combs and a piece of coarse muslin just beyond her feet. It was one more example of a type of deranged kindness which to this

Annie Chapman — September 9, 1888. Possibly strangled. Throat cut deeply; abdomen laid open; uterus, upper vagina and posterior two-thirds of bladder removed. (Public Record Office.)

day remains unexplained. The killer also required a souvenir from his latest kill, beyond the organs he had "needed." Chapman wore two or three inexpensive brass rings which were torn off by the Ripper. Because they were trophies of the hunt, they were, of course, never recovered. Theft was never the purpose of these killings, although the police did make the appropriate inquires, just in case. As the light of a new day began to illuminate the streets and backyards of the East End, the Ripper finished his work and blended into the swelling crowds. Many must have seen him, but none knew that this was the man they were all looking for. He did not waste very much time when he finished, indicated by the fact that he did not bother to wash his hands in a water filled basin under a tap in the yard.

It was at the tap where a leather apron would be found. It was at first speculated that it could have belonged to the killer but that was soon found to be a false lead. Mrs. Richardson explained, "Last Thursday I found the apron in the cellar, where it had mildewed. My son hadn't used it for a month, so I put it under the tap intending to wash it, and left it there. … On the Saturday morning, the police found it in exactly the same position as I had left it, and took it away with an empty nail box. On Friday night, there was a pan, full of water, by the tap, and that was also found in the same place on Saturday morning."

It was a remarkably risky murder. At any time he could have been spotted and easily trapped in that enclosed backyard. Even with a knife, he could not have gone far, as many in the area would have surrounded and captured him. He would have been lucky to have come out of it alive. It must have given him great pleasure to have successfully pulled off that kill.

It would later be reported that every doss house within half a mile of the murder site was checked out by the police, with the names of all those who had come in after 2 a.m. taken down. Surely Klosowski was on that list, as it was his habit to roam the streets at night. However, no list of these men has survived. If his name was on that list, it would have been the second time this cold blooded killer had come face-to-face with the men who were desperately seeking him.

GHASTLY
MURDER
IN THE EAST-END.
DREADFUL MUTILATION OF A WOMAN.

Capture : Leather Apron

Another murder of a character even more diabolical than that perpetrated in Buck's Row, on Friday week, was discovered in the same neighbourhood, on Saturday morning. At about six o'clock a woman was found lying in a back yard at the foot of a passage leading to a lodging-house in a Old Brown's Lane, Spitalfields. The house is occupied by a Mrs. Richardson, who lets it out to lodgers, and the door which admits to this passage, at the foot of which lies the yard where the body was found, is always open for the convenience of lodgers. A lodger named Davis was going down to work at the time mentioned and found the woman lying on her back close to the flight of steps leading into the yard. Her throat was out in a fearful manner. The woman's body had been completely ripped open, and the heart and other organs laying about the place, and portions of the entrails round the victim's neck. An excited crowd gathered in front of Mrs. Richardson's house and also round the mortuary in old Montague Street, whither the body was quickly conveyed. As the body lies in the rough coffin in which it has been placed in the mortuary —the same coffin in which the unfortunate Mrs. Nicholls was first placed—it presents a fearful sight. The body is that of a woman about 45 years of age. The height is exactly five feet. The complexion is fair, with wavy dark brown hair; the eyes are blue, and two lower teeth have been knocked out. The nose is rather large and prominent.

Poster announcing the murder of Annie Chapman and the capture of a Ripper suspect known as "Leather Apron."

At a little after 6 a.m., Inspector Joseph Chandler arrived to take charge of the body, as a crowd began to form in the yards adjacent to 29 Hanbury Street, as well as in the passageway within the building itself. No one went into the yard. Chandler had been on duty at Commercial Street, near the corner of Hanbury Street, when several excited men ran up to him. One of the men told him, "Another woman has been murdered." (The Ripper could have easily walked right past him, and with no description yet published, he would not have known it.) Although a crowd of people had already gathered at the murder site, none had entered the yard. Chandler later reported, for the record, what he saw. "I at once proceeded to number 29 Hanbury Street, and in the backyard found a woman lying on her back, dead, left arm resting on left breast, legs drawn up, abducted [spread], small intestines and flap of the abdomen lying on right side, above right shoulder, attached by a cord with the rest of the intestines inside the body; two flaps of skin from the lower part of the abdomen lying in a large quantity of blood above the left shoulder; throat cut deeply from left and back in a jagged manner right around throat." He covered the body and began his investigation of the yard. There was no sign of a struggle. By 6:30 that morning, Dr. George Bagster Phillips arrived to make the first medical examination of the body. Shortly afterwards he ordered it removed to the Whitechapel Workhouse Infirmary Mortuary on Eagle Street, which lay just off Old Montague Street. Doctor Phillips was described by Inspector Dew as "...a character. An elderly man, he was ultra-old-fashioned both in his personal appearance and his dress. He used to look for all the world as though he had stepped out of a century old painting."

Later, as even larger crowds began to gather at this latest murder site, five constables would stand guard at the outside of 29 and 27 Hanbury Street. They were there to ensure that no one, except residents, could gain entrance, and no one but the authorities were able to enter the yard. This was a problem for the residents who were, for a while, denied access to their outhouse. Twenty-nine Hanbury Street would stand until 1972 when it was torn down for a redevelopment project.

Many serial killers read and collect newspaper accounts of their crimes and follow police reports of their activities closely. In the late 1880s, the Whitechapel Killer would not have been disappointed in this regard, as all of London's newspapers began to give his crime spree almost daily coverage. It would have been very easy for him to gauge his effect on a now terrified public. The *East London Observer*, of September 8, 1888, noted some of the terror being produced, although it was discussing only the closely spaced murders of Tabram and Nichols. "The two murders which have so startled London within the last month are singular for the reason that the victims have been of the poorest of the poor, and no adequate motive in the shape of plunder can be traced. The excess of effort that has been apparent in each murder suggests the idea that both crimes are the work of a demented being, as the extraordinary violence used is the peculiar feature of each instance." The Ripper would also have been able to use these press reports to find ways around any known police investigations. In *The Star* of September 8, it was reported, "Whitechapel is garrisoned with police and stocked with plainclothes men. Nothing comes of it. The police have not even a clue. ... The horror and alarm this fourth crime — following so quickly on the others — has excited in the neighbourhood is inexpressible. ... The blood-crazy man or beast that haunts Whitechapel has done his latest work on the same line as its predecessors."

To the editor of the London *Times* a doctor wrote of his concerns:

> Sir, I would suggest that the police should at once find out the where-abouts of all cases of "homicidal mania" which may have been dis-charged as "cured" from metropolitan asylums during the last two years.
> Your Obedient Servant, September 9, A Country Doctor.

It would be a while before the police would take the "Country Doctor" up on his suggestion.

News of the Whitechapel murders was now reaching the rest of the civilized world, as major newspapers reported details of the continuing deaths. Some of the press coverage was none too kind to the police and their handling of the case. There was little coverage that did not have a sensational angle, as shown in the story about Annie Chapman's murder in the *New York Times*.

> The *New York Times*— September 9, 1888
> Whitechapel Startled by a Fourth Murder
> Its Curious and Shocking Detail by Commercial Cable
> London, Sept. 8.— Not even during the riots and fog of February, 1886, have I seen London so thoroughly excited as it is to-night. The Whitechapel fiend murdered his fourth victim this morning and still continues undetected, unseen, and unknown. There is a panic in Whitechapel which will instantly extend to other districts should he change his locality, as the four murders are in everybody's mouth. The papers are full of them, and nothing else is talked of. The latest murder is exactly like its predecessor. The victim was a woman street walker of the lowest class. She had no money, having been refused lodgings shortly before because she lacked 8d. Her throat was cut so completely that everything but the spine was severed, and the body was ripped up, all the viscera being scattered about. The murder in all its details was inhuman to the last degree, and, like the others, could have been the work only of a bloodthirsty beast in human shape. ... All day long Whitechapel has been wild with excitement. The four murders have been committed within a gunshot of each other, but the detectives have no clue. The London police and detective force is probably the stupidest

in the world. ... Both the character of the deed and the cool cunning
alike exhibit the qualities of a monomaniac. ... What adds to the weird
effect they [the murders] exert on the London mind is the fact that they
occur while everybody is talking about Mansfield's "Jekyll and Hyde"
at the Lyceum.

Richard Mansfield, 1854–1907, was a well known American actor who
was starring in the sensational play, based on the work by Robert Louis
Stevenson, at the time of the murders. However, the audiences were becoming smaller each time a murder was committed. His play was criticized for
showing the transformation of an educated Victorian gentleman into a
frightful fiend. Some individuals felt the play somehow encouraged the
killer to even greater atrocities. Before long (in October) the play was can-
celed, after only 10 weeks, but the Ripper had no such end to his run. His
would continue, and to even greater achievements and larger audiences.
Interestingly, Mansfield would find himself accused of being Jack the Ripper in one of the many thousands of letters written to the police. One man
wrote that after seeing the play he could not sleep for a day and claimed
that anyone who could change himself so convincingly on stage must surely
be the real Ripper.

The London *Times*— September 10, 1888
The series of shocking crimes perpetrated in Whitechapel, which on
Saturday culminated in the murder of the woman CHAPMAN, is something so distinctly outside the ordinary range of human experience that
it has created a kind of stupor extending far beyond the district where
the murders were committed. One may search the ghastliest efforts of
fiction and fail to find anything to surpass these crimes in diabolical
audacity. ... But, so far as we know, nothing in fact or fiction equals
these outrages ... in their horrible nature and in the effect which they
have produced upon the popular imagination. The circumstances that
the murders seem to be the work of one individual, that his blows fall
exclusively upon wretched wanderers of the night, and that each suc-
cessive crime has gained something in atrocity upon, and has followed
closer on the heels of, its predecessor — these things mark out the
Whitechapel murders, even before their true history is unraveled, as
unique in the annals of crime. All ordinary experiences of motive leave
us at a loss to comprehend the fury which has prompted the cruel
slaughter of at least three, and possibly four, women.... The details of
CHAPMAN'S murder need not be referred to here at length. It is
enough to say that she was found, early on Saturday morning, lying,
with her head nearly severed from her body, and mutilated in a most
revolting way, in the backyard of No. 29, Hanbury Street, Spitalfields.
... The fact that no cry from the poor woman reached any of the numerous inmates of the house shows that the assassin knew his business

well. ... But there is no room for doubt that the slayer of TABRAM, NICHOLS, and CHAPMAN meant murder, and nothing else but murder.

The always inflammatory *Star*, with a September 8 headline of "Horror Upon Horror," reported, "London lies today under the spell of a great terror. A nameless reprobate — half beast, half man — is at large, who is daily gratifying his murderous instincts on the most miserable and defenceless classes of the community."

After the Chapman murder, Chief Inspector, and Acting Superintendent, West, wrote to Scotland Yard. "I would respectfully suggest that Inspector Abberline, Central, who is well acquainted with H Division, be deputed to take up this enquiry as I believe he is already engaged in the case of the Buck's Row murder which would appear to have been committed by the same person as the one in Hanbury Street." Indeed, Inspector Abberline, one of the best known and respected officers in the area, had already been placed on the case the morning of Chapman's murder. From this request it could appear, however, that at the time Chief Inspector West had not yet assigned the Tabram murder to the same killer.

On September 10, Sir Charles Warren, a former major general of Royal Engineers, and Metropolitan Police Commissioner, forwarded a request by Member of Parliament for Whitechapel, Samuel Montagu, that a reward be given for information about the killer. Montagu was offering £100. But it was a request which would fall on governmental deaf ears. The government was not about to pay for information, even in this most unusual case. The question must be asked, though, whether this would have been so if the victims had come from a much more elevated stratum of Victorian society. Whatever the answer to that question, it was becoming clear that higher and higher levels of British government were becoming concerned about the series of deaths ongoing in the slums of the East End.

Once Again — A Ripper Inquest

Edwin W. Baxter began the next five-day Ripper inquest, on September 12, once again at the Working Lads' Institute in a hot and stuffy room on the second floor. He was accompanied by George Collier, the Deputy Coroner. Due to the overwhelming public interest and concern of Whitechapel residents, the inquest room was completely crowded, while many individuals waited outside for any news of the killer. The crowds were so large in fact that the building had to be guarded by several constables in case people tried to force their way in. It was difficult for the authorities to keep order as the citizens pressed for any information they could find.

The slum residents of Whitechapel and Spitalfields were beginning to demand straight answers to difficult questions, from the police and other officials. But these officials had no real idea what they were dealing with and would be slow to react. This was a new type of killer who invested no guilt or remorse in his deeds. These normal human emotions were not part of his composition. He was a cold blooded killer, and some unknown force was driving him hard. The police had no ready pool of suspects, as with most murders, from which to cull out the most likely. There was no easy to understand motive behind the murders such as greed, robbery, jealousy or revenge. This madman was a hunter, attacking generally random victims of opportunity, who, for the most part, were either unknown or little known to him and certainly not viewed with any normal human consideration. There was nothing obvious to link him to his victims. He was cold and relentless in the hunt and he did not panic. This was simply business as usual for him, and business was good. With very little to go on the Whitechapel Killer would be very hard to capture. This was a dark shadow moving through the even darker back streets of the East End. Only the victims he left and the circumstances of their deaths could bring any light to his identity. The bodies themselves would hold most of the clues, if only they could be properly understood and investigated.

After being impaneled, the jury went to the mortuary to view the remains of Annie Chapman, which had been laid out in a container. After the viewing, the jury returned to hear the testimony of Dr. George Phillips. Although his postmortem notes and the official records of his testimony have not survived, news reports did cover a great deal of the evidence and are thus the only records. He described the body as he viewed it in the backyard of 29 Hanbury Street. "I found the body of the deceased lying in the yard on her back, on the left hand of the steps that lead from the passage. The head was about 6 inches in front of the level of the bottom step, and the feet were towards a shed at the end of the yard. ... The left arm was placed across the left breast. The legs were drawn up, the feet resting on the ground, and the knees turned outward. The face was swollen and turned on the right side and the tongue protruded between the front teeth, but not beyond the lips. The tongue was evidently much swollen. [Evidence of strangulation.] The front teeth were perfect as far as the first molar, top and bottom and very fine teeth they were. The body was terribly mutilated... the stiffness of the limbs was not marked, but was evidently commencing."

Coroner Baxter reported on Dr. Phillips' further observations. "He noticed that the throat was dissevered deeply; that the incisions through the skin were jagged and reached right round the neck.... On the wooden paling between the yard in question and the next, smears of blood, corresponding to where the head of the deceased lay, were to be seen. These were about 14 inches from the ground, and immediately above the part where the blood from the neck lay. He should say that the instrument used at the throat and abdomen was the same. It must have been a very sharp knife with a thin narrow blade, and must have been at least 6 inches to 8 inches in length, probably longer. He should say that the injuries could not have been inflicted by a bayonet or a sword bayonet. They could have been done by such an instrument as a medical man used for postmortem purposes, but the ordinary surgical cases might not contain such an instrument. Those used by the slaughter men, well ground down, might have caused them. He thought the knives used by those in the leather trade would not be long enough in the blade. There were indications of anatomical knowledge... he should say that the deceased had been dead at least two hours, and probably more, when he first saw her [an error brought on by the coolness of the early morning and the massive loss of blood which helped drain the body of much of its stored heat]; but it was right to mention that it was a fairly cool morning, and that the body would be more apt to cool rapidly from its having lost a great quantity of blood. There was no evidence ... of a struggle having taken place. He was positive the deceased entered the yard alive.... A handkerchief was round the throat of the deceased when he saw it early in the morning. He should say it was not tied on after the throat was cut."

The coroner then reported to the jury the facts gained during the doctor's postmortem examination:

"He noticed the same protrusion of the tongue. There was a bruise over the right temple. On the upper eyelid there was a bruise, and there were two distinct bruises, each the size of a man's thumb, on the forepart of the top of the chest. The stiffness of the limbs was now well marked. There was a bruise over the middle part of the bone of the right hand. There was an old scar on the left of the frontal bone. The stiffness was more noticeable on the left side, especially in the fingers, which were partly closed. There was an abrasion over the ring finger, with distinct markings of a ring or rings. The throat had been severed as before described, the incisions into the skin indicated that they had been made from the left side of the neck. There were two distinct clean cuts on the left side of the spine. They were parallel with each other and separated by about half an inch. The muscular structures appeared as though an attempt had (been) made to separate the bones of the neck. There were various other mutilations to the body, but he was of the opinion that they occurred subsequent to the death of the woman, and to the large escape of blood from the division of the neck.

"The deceased was far advanced in disease of the lungs and membranes of the brain, but they had nothing to do with the cause of death. The stomach contained little food, but there was not any sign of fluid. There was no appearance of the deceased having taken alcohol, but there were signs of great deprivation and he should say she had been badly fed. He was convinced she had not taken any strong alcohol for some hours before her death. The injuries were certainly not self inflicted. The bruises on the face were evidently recent, especially about the chin and side of the jaw, but the bruises in front of the chest and temple were of longer standing — probably of days. He was of the opinion that the person who cut the deceased's throat took hold of her by the chin, and then commenced the incision from left to right. He thought it was highly probable that a person could call out, but with regard to an idea that she might have been gagged he could only point to the swollen face and the protruding tongue, both of which were signs of suffocation.

"The abdomen had been entirely laid open: the intestines, severed from their mesenteric attachments, had been lifted out of the body and placed on the shoulder of the corpse; whilst from the pelvis, the uterus and its appendages with the upper portion of the vagina and the posterior two thirds of the bladder, had been entirely removed. No trace of these parts could be found and the incisions were cleanly cut, avoiding the rectum, and dividing the vagina low enough to avoid injury to the cervix uteri. *Obviously the work was that of an expert — of one, at least, who had such knowledge of anatomical or pathological examinations* as to be enabled to secure the pelvic organs with one sweep of the knife, [in the dark or at least very low light] which must therefore have (been) at least 5 or 6 inches in length, probably more. The appearance of the cuts confirmed in him the opinion that the instrument, like the one which divided the neck, had been of a very sharp character. The mode in which the knife had been used seemed to indicate *great anatomical knowledge.*

"He thought he himself could not have performed all the injuries he described, even without a struggle, under a quarter of an hour. If he had done it in a deliberate way such as would fall to the duties of a surgeon it probably would have taken him the best part of an hour. ... The whole inference seems to me that the operation was performed to enable the perpetrator to obtain possession of these parts of the body."

The testimony was so detailed and disturbing that several spectators passed out on hearing the doctor's description.

As to what had been done to subdue his victim, Coroner Baxter pressed Dr. Phillips:

DR. PHILLIPS: I am of opinion that the person who cut the deceased's throat took hold of her by the chin, and then commenced the incision from left to right.
BAXTER: Could that be done so instantaneously that a person could not cry out?
PHILLIPS: By pressure on the throat no doubt it would be possible.
BAXTER: The thickening of the tongue would be one of the signs of suffocation?
PHILLIPS: Yes. My impression is that she was partially strangled.

The body of the victim had provided a vast amount of information about the killer, and to find this man the police would have to concentrate on understanding his victims and the mutilations. With this murder, the police could tell that the Ripper had great surgical skills and training. They were not looking for the average resident of Whitechapel. This was an educated man. Giving the police this knowledge was a grave error on the killer's part, and he would strive to rectify it in subsequent killings by covering up his skill. From a medical point of view, Annie Chapman's body was not mutilated. She was operated on and evidently with great facility. The Ripper would make sure the next time he killed he would do his best to hide that facility by genuinely mutilating the body, but then only after he had completed his "work."

...during the whole of that period he [Klosowski] performed his surgical functions with a full knowledge of the subject...

The London *Times*— September 11, 1888
The Whitechapel Murders
Two arrests were made yesterday, but it is very doubtful whether the murderer is in the hands of the police. The members of the Criminal Investigation Department are assisting the divisional police at the East-End in their endeavors to elucidate the mystery in which these crimes are involved. Yesterday morning Detective Sergeant Thicke, of the H Division, who has been indefatigable in his inquiries respecting the murder of Annie Chapman at 29 Hanbury Street, Spitalfields, on Saturday morning, succeeded in capturing a man whom he believed to be "Leather Apron." [Viewed as a possible suspect due to the water soaked leather apron found at the scene of Chapman's murder and yet it was quickly ascertained that the leather apron belonged to one of the men who lived in the building.] Sergeant Thicke, who has had much experience of the Thieves and their haunts in this portion of the metropolis, has, since he has been engaged in the present inquiry, been repeatedly assured by some of the most well-known characters of their abhorrence of the fiendishness of the crime, and they have further stated that if they could only lay hands on the murderer they would

hand him over to justice. These and other circumstances convinced the officer and those associated with him that the deed was in no way traceable to any of the regular thieves or desperadoes at the East-End.

While investigating the murders, police officers were informed by prostitutes that a local thug known as "Leather Apron" had been extorting them. He had threatened to beat them if he was not paid. The police were not sure if he was the Ripper but they definitely wanted to find him. There were, after all, other crimes being committed in the East End which were not linked to the Ripper murders.

Official Police Notice
Description of a man who entered a passage of the house at which the murder was committed of a prostitute at 2 a.m. on the 8th.—Age 37; height, 5 ft. 7 in; rather dark beard and moustache. Dress-shirt, dark vest and trousers, black scarf, and black felt hat. Spoke with a foreign accent.

As the police continued to search for the killer in the dark streets of the East End, the inquest continued into the death of Annie Chapman. John Davis, the carman who lived at 29 Hanbury Street with his family, and the discoverer of the body, testified that he had gotten up around 6 a.m. that morning. "I was certain of the time, because I heard the bell on Spitalfields Church strike." Because the front door to the backyard hall was never locked, and indeed at times left wide open, he did not find it unusual when he found the door unlatched. It was not a secret that the door was always unlocked. It could easily point to a local individual who targeted the secluded backyard as a good spot to "operate." Or possibly Annie herself chose the very location. A closed, small yard, however, would have also limited the escape routes the killer could use. The high risk nature of the selected spot is a very strong indication that the Ripper would have at least some familiarity with the location. For him, the risk would have greatly enhanced the thrill of the hunt as well as the kill. A trophy from this murder would have been of great importance.

When Davis went down the three short steps into the yard he saw the body of Annie Chapman. He saw that she was lying between the steps and the fence, with her head towards the house. He did not go into the yard itself but from his vantage point on the steps could see that her clothes had been "disarranged" and that she was lying on her back. He then called two local men who worked at a packing case plant nearby and showed them the body. He did not recall their names at the time, but testified that he then left the house and proceeded directly to the Commercial Street Police Station to report his find.

Amelia Palmer (Farmer), who lived at the common lodging house at 30 Dorset Street in Spitalfields, was then called. She testified that the body she had viewed in the mortuary was that of her friend, Annie Chapman. She stated that on Monday she had seen Annie, on Dorset Street, and that she had complained of feeling unwell. "At the time she had a bruise on one of her temples and I asked how she got it." Annie told her to look at her breast which also had a bruise. "You know the woman." Palmer could not remember the other woman's name. According to press reports, Palmer continued to explain some of the injuries found on Chapman. "Both the deceased and the woman referred to were acquainted with a man called 'Harry the Hawker.' In giving an account of the older bruises, the deceased told witness that on the 1st inst. she went into a public house with a young man named Ted Stanley in Commercial Street. 'Harry the Hawker' and the other woman were also there. The former, who was drunk, put down a florin, which was picked up by the latter, who replaced it with a penny. Some words passed between the deceased and the woman, and in the evening the latter struck her and inflicted the bruises. Witness again saw the deceased on Tuesday by the side of Spitalfields Church. The deceased again complained of feeling unwell, and said she thought she would go into the casual ward for day or two. She mentioned that she had had nothing to eat or drink that day, not even a cup of tea. Witness gave deceased two pence saying, 'Here is two pence to have a cup of tea, but don't have rum.' She knew that deceased was given to drinking that spirit. The deceased, who frequently got the worse for drink, used at times to earn money by doing crochet work, and at others by selling flowers. Witness believed she was not very particular what she did to earn a living and at times used to remain out very late at night."

Next to testify was Timothy Donovan who was the deputy of the common lodging house at 35 Dorset Street. He also identified the murder victim as Annie Chapman who he said had been living at the lodging house for the past four months, but not for the past week, except until Friday. Annie had told him that she had been "in the infirmary." On the morning of her death, shortly before 2 a.m., she told him "I have not any money now, but don't let the bed: I will be back soon." He testified that she had had "enough to drink" when he last saw her, but that she could still walk straight. The deceased generally got the worse for drink on Saturdays, but not on the other days of the week." He had never had any problems with her and stated that she was "always very friendly with the other lodgers."

The night watchman, John Evans, was the last to be called after identifying the body. He stated that he had seen Annie leave the lodging house at around 1:45 a.m., Saturday morning, and that she was "the worse for

drink. ... I had never heard any person threaten the deceased, and she never stated she was afraid of anyone."
The inquest was adjourned for the day.

> The London *Times* (Late Edition)— September 11, 1888
> Great excitement was caused in the neighbourhood of Commercial Street Police station during the afternoon on account of the arrival from Gravesend of a suspect whose appearance resembled in some respects that of "Leather Apron." This man whose name is William Henry Pigott, was taken into custody on Sunday night at the Pope's Head public house, Gravesend. Attention was first attracted to Pigott because he had some bloodstains on his clothes. ... The news of Pigott's arrival, which took place at 12:48, at once spread, and in a few seconds the police station was surrounded by an excited crowd anxious to get a glimpse of the supposed murderer. Finding that no opportunity was likely to occur of seeing the prisoner, the mob after a time melted away, but the police had trouble for some hours in keeping the thoroughfare free for traffic.

It was soon found that none of the witnesses could identify the arrested man as Leather Apron or as a Ripper suspect. But because of his dazed and bloodied condition it was decided to hold him for a while. After two hours or so of questioning, the suspect became "more strange and his speech more incoherent," so the divisional surgeon was called upon to certify that "the prisoner's mind was unhinged," and he was remanded for the time being into police custody.

The day before, a local man, John Pizer, had been arrested as a second possible Leather Apron. He was a well known thug who extorted money from the local prostitutes, and he carried a knife. Just after 8 a.m., Sergeant William Thick, known as "Johnny Upright," with two or three other officers, went to 22 Mulberry Street to find their man. As Pizer opened the door Sergeant Thick grabbed him and said, "You are just the man I want," and accused him of being involved with the death of Annie Chapman. He was taken, in considerable distress, to Leman Street Police station. Eventually, it would be shown that although he was of questionable character, he was not involved in the Chapman or other Ripper murders. He was released late the next day. Inspector Abberline stated that, "There was no evidence to connect him with the murder." Thick would later gain a level of fame on being described in Jack London's *The People of the Abyss.* London would meet Thick and his family during his journalistic visit to the East End.

The possibility of the killer wearing a leather apron came from the discovery of such a garment in a water filled basin in the yard where Annie

Chapman's body had been found. It was soon discovered that the apron belonged to one of the residents of the building and was completely unrelated to the murder. However, because many of the local Jewish men wore leather aprons in their work, some of them were grabbed and beaten on the streets by mobs of local men hell bent on finding the killer. It was also a way for the locals to vent their anger at the foreigners (mostly Jewish) who were crowding into the East End from all over Europe.

On September 14, Eliza Annie Chapman was buried at Manor Park, City of London Cemetery, number 78, square 148. Today, though, there is no above ground stone to mark its place. On her coffin was a simple plate which read: Annie Chapman — died Sept. 8, 1888, aged 48 years. Her family kept the arrangements secret from the public to avoid a problem with crowds and curiosity seekers. Her family members were with her as she was laid to rest, possibly including her 15-year-old daughter, Annie Georgina Chapman. Was the Ripper also at the funeral and therefore able to see the family of his latest victim? This would not be unusual behavior for a serial killer. If he did attend, he may have met Annie Georgina Chapman, who may then have gone to stay with her aunt still living in Whitechapel.

After the inquest had finished its work, the inevitable conclusion was reached that she had been murdered by some person or persons unknown. However, this time the Ripper had left clues to his skills and background. But would the clues be enough to eventually bring him to justice?

On the same day Chapman was buried, the *Weekly Herald* reported, "Another horrible murder in the East of London has been added to the swelling list of brutal outrages which have been perpetrated within the last few weeks, and all of which are buried in profound mystery. In each case the victim has been a woman of the class known as 'unfortunates' and the circumstances of each murder must have been of the most ferocious nature. ... There can be little doubt now that this latest murder is one of the series of fiendish atrocities on women which have been going on within the past few months, this making the fourth case in this short time in the same district.... [Only three can be placed in the Ripper's column.] Looking at the corpse, no one could think otherwise than that the murder had been committed by a maniac or wretch of the lowest type of humanity...."

The London *Times*— Editorial
Intelligent observers who have visited the locality express the utmost astonishment that the murderer could have reached a hiding place after committing such a crime. He must have left the yard in Hanbury Street reeking with blood, and yet, if the theory that the murder took place between 5 and 6 (a.m.) be accepted, he must have walked in almost broad daylight streets comparatively well frequented, even at that early

hour, without his startling appearance attracting the slightest attention. Consideration of this point has led many to the conclusion that the murderer came not from the wretched class from which the inmates of common lodging houses are drawn. More probably, it is argued, he is a man lodging in a comparatively decent house in the district, to which he would be able to retire quickly, and in which, once it was reached, he would be able at his leisure to remove from his person all traces of his hideous crime. It is at any rate practically certain that the murderer would not have ventured to return to a common lodging house smeared with blood as he must have been. The police are therefore exhorted not to confine their investigations, as they are accused of doing, to common lodging houses and other resorts of the criminal and outcast, but to extend their inquires to the class of householders, exceedingly numerous in the East End of London, who are in the habit of letting furnished lodgings without particular inquiry into the character or antecedents of those who apply for them.

(Perhaps the Ripper simply put on his black overcoat and walked the short blocks to his job at the nearby barber shop and cleaned up before going to work at his "other job.")

In the first 24 hours after Annie Chapman was murdered, the police investigated and interviewed the male occupants of over 200 common lodging houses. It was also after Annie Chapman's murder that James Monro's "Secret Department" went into action. Before the Ripper murders Monro had been the head of the CID as the Assistant Metropolitan Police Commissioner. The department was separate from the regular police and CID (Criminal Investigation Department), and was known as "Section D." This mysterious group established its own patrols in search of the Whitechapel Killer, with 27 men in plain clothes. Interestingly, they were not funded through normal Metropolitan Police funds but from "Imperial" funding.

As the search continued, there was something less than panic but more than apprehension moving among the people of London's East End. Businessmen, street thugs, constables and working men and women all had one thing on their minds. This madman must be caught and caught soon. He was completely alone and now most of the area's residents, on both sides of the law, wanted him off the streets. One thought was becoming clear to many in the police force and general public: that the killer could very well be a doctor, or at least a student with surgical skills. This would mean that the killer had a better than average education and would not be found among the lowest classes, at least, not as a general rule. The burning question was — who was he and would he strike again?

Henry Smith, the Assistant Police Commissioner, was not about to wait for the next body to drop. He had placed nearly one third of the force in plain clothes in order to spot the killer in the act before he could spot a policeman. He would later write that the instructions he had issued to them were, "...to do everything which, under ordinary circumstances, a constable should not do. It was subversive to discipline; but I had them well supervised by the senior officers. The weather was lovely, and I have little doubt that they thoroughly enjoyed themselves, sitting gossiping with all and sundry."

Chapter Five

"Perhaps Some of Us Will Be Killed Next!"

"Believe me, be careful in your life of dangers of other enimis whom are unnow to you."

Severin Klosowski

Without the words of the Ripper himself to explain his actions, no one will ever know for sure why there was a three week gap until his next successful kill in the East End, but a break indeed occurred. One explanation could be that the Ripper simply went on a weekend trip to Birtley, in the north of England. No one ever said that serial killers don't go on holidays!

On Saturday night–Sunday morning of September 22-23, 1888, a 28-year-old woman named Jane Beatmoor was murdered in Birtley in a manner quite similar to the ongoing Ripper series in London. At 7:30 p.m. Saturday evening, Jane left the home of a friend called Mr. Newell, and was reportedly on her way home. She had not arrived by 11 o'clock so her parents proceeded to search for her without success. It wasn't until early that morning, at around 7:30, that her body was found by a local miner named John Fish. Jane was in a ditch at the bottom of a railway embankment. She had been killed and then mutilated. It was not reported whether or not she was killed at that location, as in the Ripper series, or dumped at the spot, as in the Torso murders. It was clear, however, that vicious crimes were not confined to London alone.

As reported in the *Weekly Herald* of September 28, "A closer inspection revealed the fact that the lower part of the deceased's body had been cut open and the entrails torn out. She was also cut about the face. ... The unfortunate woman is stabbed in three places — once in the bowels and twice in the face. The wound in the body is very deep, the knife having knocked a piece off the vertebrae. [These were wounds which would match very closely those of one of the Ripper's next two victims.] The affair has caused quite a panic in the district; the resemblance to the Whitechapel tragedies encouraging the idea that the maniac who has been at work in London has travelled down to the North of England to pursue his fiendish vocation."

There is, after all, no reason to believe that the Ripper *had* to stay in London all of the time. He was not as poor as most of the inhabitants of the East End, and a weekend would be the best time to leave his regular job and visit new areas. Also, there were no Ripper murders in the East End that weekend, which means that he would have been available. Scotland Yard took no chances, sending Inspector North to investigate. This murder may not have been just a coincidence of timing, even though the authorities settled on the girl's boyfriend as the most likely suspect. Whatever the real story in Birtley, the Ripper would make up for lost time — with a "double event."

With the world now watching their every move, London authorities increased their efforts to find the killer. At the same time the residents of the East End braced themselves for the next atrocity they now felt sure had to be coming. But when would the monster strike? And who would his victim be? No matter what the answers to those questions, the East Enders were not about to just sit and wait. Two days after Annie Chapman's murder, 16 local men formed the Mile End Vigilance Committee to do all they could to aid the police in the capture of this mad slasher. The meetings were held at the Crown public house at 74 Mile End Road. This would not be a mob of men bent on trouble, but a group of businessmen serious about getting to the bottom of the murders. They would be only one of many formal and informal groups banding together to find the vicious killer among their own. And the police were happy to get all the help they could.

Elected to the presidency of the vigilance committee was builder, contractor, and Freemason, George Lusk, who lived at 1 Tollit Street, Alderney Road, Mile End, near where the now recovered Ada Wilson had been attacked. The committee's purpose was to "strengthen the hands of the police," and as stated by Joseph Aarons, the treasurer for the group and license holder of the Crown, "...the committee was in no way antagonistic to the police authorities, who were doing their best to bring the culprits to justice."

The first effort of the vigilance committee, on September 11, was to post handbills and posters on store windows throughout Mile End, Whitechapel and Houndsditch, which reported on a private reward for the capture of the killer. It is interesting to note that the exact amount alluded to in handbills was not mentioned, and despite the enthusiasm of the members and the community, the committee would find it difficult to raise the funds needed for the reward. There was not a lot of "extra" money lying around in the East End, even for the capture of a serial killer.

> IMPORTANT NOTICE
>
> To the tradesmen, Ratepayers, and Inhabitants Generally of White-chapel and District.— Finding that in spite of Murders being committed in our midst, and that the Murderer or Murderers are still at large, we the undersigned have formed ourselves into a Committee, and intend offering a substantial REWARD to anyone, Citizen, or otherwise, who shall give such information that will bring the Murderer or Murderers to Justice. A Committee of Gentlemen has already been formed to carry out the above object, and will meet every evening at nine o'clock, at Mr. J. Aaron's the "Crown," 74 Mile End Road, corner of Jubilee Street, and will be pleased to receive the assistance of the residents of the District...

The London *Times* of September 11, reported on the formation of the committee and stated that, "The movement has been warmly taken up by the inhabitants, and it is thought certain that a large sum will be subscribed within the next few days. The proposal to form district vigilance committees has also been met with great popular favor and is assuming practical form. Meetings were held at the various working men's clubs and other organizations, political and social, in the districts, at most of which the proposed scheme was heartily approved."

On September 16, Mr. B. Harris, the vigilance committee secretary, wrote to the Home Secretary, Henry Matthews, requesting the government augment private reward funds then being gathered. The request would be unsuccessful. The government's policy of never offering rewards, even in the face of such a disturbing run of murders, would not be compromised.

On September 15, the London *Times* reported on yet another arrest which would eventually prove to be one more false lead. "The police at the Commercial Street Station have made another arrest on suspicion in connection with the recent murders. It appears that among the numerous statements and descriptions of suspected persons are several tallying with that of the man in custody, but beyond this the police know nothing at present against him.... Last night he was handed over to a uniformed constable doing duty in the neighbourhood of Flower and Dean Street on suspicion in connection with the crime." The individual undoubtedly was found by one of the many civilian patrols scouring the area.

A New Name for a Serial Killer

Authentic words from the Whitechapel Killer were few and far between. In fact, most, if not all, of the hundreds of letters and postcards from "Jack" had nothing to do with the case. Indeed, this serial killer was doing everything he could think of to ensure that he would not be caught. Sending letters and giving himself a catchy name would certainly not have fit his profile or his needs. His purpose was to remain anonymous, in order to kill and to enjoy the process. The purpose of the press, though, was to sell newspapers, and sell them they did, by the millions.

On September 27, 1888, the *Central News Agency*, located at 5 New Bridge Street, London, received a letter under the signature of "Jack the Ripper." It was the first time the now legendary name had ever been used. The letter had most likely been written by a *Star* reporter named Best. He had been covering the murders since the discovery of Martha Tabram, as a freelance journalist, and would later admit to sending this and other such letters to "keep the business alive." It was also just as likely to have been the work of Tom Bulling who wrote for the *Central News Agency*. In fact, many officers involved in the Ripper case would later state their belief that the most widely publicized Ripper letters were hoaxes by "an identifiable journalist." The name of that journalist was never officially released, and no one was charged with the hoaxes. Indeed, if they were written by Bulling he would have actually been sending them to his own boss. However, these letters did give the Whitechapel Killer a name which would long be remembered.

The well known "Dear Boss" letter was written in red ink and postmarked September 25, 1888. It was mailed to "The Boss, Central News Office, London City," and was received on September 27. The letter was confirmed to have originated in the East End but the exact location was never pinpointed. It was the first use of the name Jack the Ripper, but it would not be the last, as other writers soon picked it up. Sending the letter to the news agency insured that it would be published, as would not have been the case if it had been sent to the police.

Dear Boss,   25. Sept. 1888
    I keep on hearing the police have caught me but they won't fix me just yet. I have laughed when they look so clever and talk about being on the right track. That joke about Leather Apron gave me real fits. I

am down on whores and I shan't quit ripping them till I do get buckled. Grand work the last job was. I gave the lady no time to squeal. How
can they catch me now. I love my work and want to start again. You
will soon hear of me with my funny little games. I saved some of the
proper red stuff in a ginger beer bottle over the last job to write down
with but it went thick like glue and I can't use it. Red ink is fit enough
I hope ha ha. The next job I do I shall clip the ladys ears off and send
them to the police officers just for jolly wouldn't you. Keep this letter
back till I do a bit more work, then give it out straight. My knife's so
nice and sharp I want to get to work right away if I get a chance. Good
luck.

Yours Truly
Jack the Ripper

Don't mind me giving the trade name

In the second postscript written on a 90 degree angle from the letter,
in red crayon, he wrote:

Wasn't good enough to post this before I got all the red ink off my
hands curse it. No luck yet. They say I'm a doctor now ha ha.

On October 1, a second communication, a postcard, again written in
red crayon, was received at the Central News Agency. It was written by the
same hand and it was postmarked "London, E., Oct. 1."
It read:

I was not codding dear old Boss when I gave you the tip. you'll hear
about Saucy Jackey's work tomorrow double event this time number
one squealed a bit couldn't finish straight off. had not time to get ears
for police. thanks for keeping last letter back till I got to work again.
Jack the Ripper

The letter and card were taken seriously by the police, who printed a
facsimile of them on posters and placed copies at every police station in the
area. The authorities requested the residents to view the handwriting and
report to them if it looked familiar. They were also sent to the news agen-
cies, and several papers published then on October 4. The die was now cast
as the Whitechapel Killer assumed a new and certainly more terrifying
name.

Long Liz

It was one thing for Elizabeth Long to have given a very good description of Annie Chapman's probable killer; it would be another thing entirely

to have her point out that suspect in a court of law. Is it possible that the Ripper knew Elizabeth Stride, known as "Long Liz," the next to be killed in the series. At her inquest hearing, Thomas Bates would inform the coroner that the woman he knew as "Long Liz" had made a living "charring" and was indeed Elizabeth Stride, also known as Annie Fitzgerald. It is possible that the killer mistook her for Elizabeth Long, whose name was becoming known throughout London, along with the fact that she had provided a detailed description of the suspect. Stride did live in one of the lodging houses on Flower and Dean Street, across from a barbershop where Severin Klosowski may have worked, and only three blocks from where he is known to have lived. It is a possibility that cannot be easily dismissed. It is also possible that she was the only one in the series to be killed, not for the need which devoured the Ripper, or the body parts he collected, but for the simple requirement of protecting his identity from the authorities who were desperately searching for him. He was by no means trying to be caught, and an excellent eyewitness was not a good thing to leave around.

With all of his victims living so close to each other, and three of them living on the same street, can it truly be said that any of them were actually randomly selected among the hundreds of prostitutes in the area? And how many of his victims knew each other? Surely the killer knew they were all prostitutes, so he surely had, at least, a superficial knowledge of their background. He must have known that none of his victims were ordinary working women or married housekeepers. He made no mistakes. He hunted and killed only known prostitutes, during the Ripper series in any case.

She was born Elizabeth Gustafsdotter on November 27, 1843, in the parish of Torslanda, Sweden, north of Gothenburg. Her father was Gustaf Ericsson who worked a farm with his wife Beata Carlsdotter. When she was nearly 17 she left home to become a domestic servant in the home of Lars Fredrik Olofsson. She moved again in 1862 when she was still reported to be working as a domestic servant. But by March of 1865 she had been registered by the Gothenburg police as a prostitute. In October of that year she was living in Philgaten, Ostra Haga, which is a suburb of Gothenburg. While there she was reported to have been treated for venereal disease twice. There can be no doubt about her occupation.

After giving birth to a stillborn girl ten months earlier, she moved to London in February 1866. She registered as an unmarried woman at the Swedish Church in Princes Square, St. George-in-the-East, on July 10, 1866. It was very near Whitechapel. On March 7, 1869, Elizabeth married a carpenter named John Thomas Stride in the parish church of St. Giles-in-the-Fields. At the time it was reported that he lived in Sheerness. (John Stride's nephew, Walter Frederick Stride, was a member of the Metropolitan Police and later identified Elizabeth's body from mortuary photographs. He retired from the force in 1902, the year of Klosowski's last murder.)

Very little is really known of this union owing to the fact that Elizabeth told many stories, including the tale that she had borne nine children. Very few verifiable facts remain. It is known that they lived for a while on East India Dock Road, Poplar, soon after their wedding. This was the same street Severin Klosowski would call his temporary home some 18 years later. In 1870, the couple were running a coffee room in Poplar on Upper North Street, and in 1872 the business was moved to 178 Poplar High Street.

By 1877, the marriage must have gone bad as Elizabeth became an inmate of the Poplar Workhouse, on March 21. From December 28, 1881, to January 4, 1882, she was in the Whitechapel Infirmary for treatment of bronchitis before being discharged, once again, into the workhouse. From 1882 until her death, she lodged on and off at the common lodging house at 32 Flower and Dean Street, when she was able to earn the night's rent. She was well known and liked at the house, and was referred to as Long Liz. However, she did live for three years with a laborer named Michael Kidney on Devonshire Street, Commercial Road. It is also known that Stride spoke fluent Yiddish, as did Klosowski.

The last week of Elizabeth Stride's life was confusing, as she was spotted here and there, in and around the killing fields of Whitechapel. By September 26, she was confirmed to have once again returned to 32 Flower and Dean Street for the first time in three months. She was seen in the kitchen by Dr. Thomas Barnardo, who preached on the streets, and would later open a home for boys. He was visiting the lodging house when he came across a group of women who were actively discussing the Whitechapel murders. He would later report that they were "thoroughly frightened." As one woman stated, "We're all up to no good, no one cares what becomes of us! Perhaps some of us will be killed next. If anybody had helped the likes of us long ago we would never have come to this!" Later, Dr. Barnardo would identify the body of Liz Stride and state that she was one of the women he saw in the kitchen discussing the murders.

One witness, Catherine Lane, stated that she had seen Stride at the doss house at 32 Flower and Dean Street on Thursday, September 27. Stride had told her that she had had "words" with the man she was living with, Michael Kidney. He would later deny this argument occurred, but considering the murders, including Stride's, his denial is understandable. There was, after all, a history of the two quarreling. An April 1887 charge by Stride of assault on her by Kidney was dropped when she failed to appear at Thames Magistrate's Court to prosecute. This violence was not an uncommon event in their lives, or the lives of many who lived in the area.

One report was presented by a local barber named Charles Preston, who knew Stride because he had also lived for 18 months at 32 Flower and Dean Street. He indicated that she had been arrested, of late, one Saturday night on a charge of being drunk and disorderly at a public house, the Queen's Head. It was by no means the first time that she had been charged. Indeed, Stride had been arrested no fewer than eight times in the preceding 20 months. The Queen's Head was located on Commercial Street, not far from where her body would be found. Is it possible that the local barber's assistant, Severin Klosowski, knew fellow barber Charles Preston and through him Liz Stride? Although there is no documented proof, in such a close living and working situation, it is a distinct possibility which cannot be ignored.

Again the Rains Bring Death

Cold winds moved across London on the evening of September 29, 1888, and along with them the rains which had become so much a part of that dark summer and fall in the killing ground. It was not a good night to be out looking for a customer. Long Liz spent the last afternoon of life earning her six pence by cleaning two of the rooms at her lodging house. She was paid by the doss house deputy, Elizabeth Tanner, who would see her later that evening at around 6 p.m. at the Queen's Head public house. They would later walk back to the lodging house together.

Sometime between 7 and 8 p.m. she was seen leaving 32 Flower and Dean Street by several people. She spoke to Charles Preston, the barber, as well as her friend Catherine Lane. As she left she passed the watchman Thomas Bates who reported that she looked "quite cheerful." Of Long Liz he would later say, "Lor' bless you, when she could get no work she had to do the best she could for her living, but a neater, cleaner woman never lived."

She eventually made her way to the Bricklayer's Arms public house on Settles Street, near Berner Street. Leaving the establishment at 11 p.m., she passed two men who were just going in. They were J. Best and John Gardner, hard working laborers, who later reported that Stride had been accompanied by a short man with a dark mustache and sandy eyelashes. He was said to be wearing a morning suit and coat with a billycock hat. Mr. Best recalled that "they had been served in the public house and went out when me and my friends came in. It was raining very fast and they did not appear willing to go out. He was hugging and kissing her, and as he seemed a respectably dressed man, we were rather astonished at the way he was going on at the woman."

As the rain continued to fall the couple were invited to come back inside for a drink but Stride's companion refused. It was at this point one of the men called out to her in a reference to the Whitechapel Killer, "that's Leather Apron getting round you." According to Best, "He and the woman went off like a shot soon after eleven." Stride and the man were soon out of sight as they walked, in the rain, towards Commercial Road and Berner Street. Berner Street had been known as "Tiger's Bay" when it was the home of many local criminals. By 1888 it had improved somewhat in reputation.

Forty-five minutes later another local laborer, by the name of William Marshall, saw Stride with what appeared to be a different man in front of 63 Berner Street. He saw them while he was standing in front of 64 Berner Street. As Marshall stood in the doorway, the man, described as wearing a sailor's hat and a short black cutaway coat told Stride, "You would say anything but your prayers." He would later report that they were "kissing and carrying on." He further reported that the man appeared "clerkly" and was 5'6" tall, and stout.

At 12:30 a.m., Charles Letchford, who lived at 39 Berner Street, decided to take a walk. He would later report that all was calm and that "everything seemed to be going on as usual."

At 12:35 a.m., as Police Constable William Smith, 452H, walked his beat, he spotted Elizabeth Stride with yet another man on the opposite side of the street from the International Workingmen's Educational Club on Berner Street. The man was described as wearing a dark coat with a hard deerstalker hat, and looking to be around 28 years of age, with a small dark moustache, and dark complexion. He was also said to be carrying a package measuring six inches wide and 18 inches long and wrapped in newspaper. (Long enough to house a knife with an eight-to-nine-inch blade, with plenty of space for any freshly removed organs.) And yet, only five minutes later Stride was seen with possibly a different man again.

The International Workingmen's Educational Club, at 40 Berner Street, was a well known local socialist club open to all who would enter, but it was mostly filled with Polish and Russian Jews (or those who posed as Jews, as did Severin Klosowski). It was also known for the loud goings on at all hours. It was only 500 yards from Klosowski's room and just north of where he would soon make his home. In the rear of the club was a print facility where the *Worker's Friend* was published. On the other side of the yard were row cottages, mostly full.

That evening, as with most Saturday nights, the club was crowded with upwards of 100 men in the first floor meeting room. The meeting ended between 11:30 p.m. and midnight, when all but a few dozen members went home. It was still a very busy building, with a high possibility of someone going into the yard next door at any moment. The lamps on Berner Street were not lit.

At 12:10 a.m., William West, a member of the club, decided to go out into the yard for a breath of fresh air, using the side door, going to the back office to pick up some papers. He later reported he saw and heard nothing at the time, but did notice that the yard gates were open. Five minutes later, West went home, leaving by the club's front door on Berner Street, along with his brother and a third man by the name of Louis Stanley. There was no one about as the three walked south towards Fairclough Street.

At 12:40 a.m., Morris Eagle, the chairman of the Workingmen's Club, returned to the club after escorting his lady home. By that time the front door was closed and locked which forced him to walk to the side of the building, through Dutfield's Yard, and through the side door. He was on the very ground which would soon hold the body of Elizabeth Stride, and he was able to report that he saw no one there. He would have stepped right on top of the body if it had been there. "I naturally walked on the right side (of the path), that being the side on which the club door was." The windows of the club were open and the side door was ajar. At the same time, or just after, at around 12:41 a.m., an American named Joseph Lave, who was temporarily living at the club, also decided to step out into the yard for some fresh air. He noticed that the yard was so dark that he had to feel his way along the wall. He was also sure that there was no one in the yard at the time. "I came out first at half past twelve to get a breath of fresh air. I passed out into the street, but did not see anything unusual. The district appeared to me to be quiet. I remained out until twenty minutes to one, and during that time no one came into the yard. I should have seen anybody moving about there."

Also, at approximately 12:40 a.m., a man, described by Israel Schwartz as 5'5" tall, about 30 years old, with dark hair, a small brown mustache, and a fresh complexion, was seen with Stride in front of the yard she would soon be found dead in. The man was dressed in an overcoat and wearing an old black felt hat with a wide brim. To further confuse the situation there was a second man in the area. Was he a lookout or simply in the wrong place at the wrong time? The encounter was described in the official Home Office files: "Israel Schwartz of 22 Helen Street, Backchurch Lane, stated that at this hour (12:40 a.m.), turning into Berner Street from Commercial Road, and having gotten as far as the gateway where the murder was committed, he saw a man stop and speak to a woman (he would later identify that woman as Elizabeth Stride after viewing her body), who was standing in the gateway. *He tried to pull the woman into the street* (was he trying to get her away from the club?), but he turned her around and threw her down on the footway as the woman screamed three times, but not very loudly.

"On crossing to the opposite side of the street, illuminated only by the light coming from the club, he saw a second man lighting his pipe. The man who threw the woman down called out, apparently to the man on the far side of the road, 'Lipski'. [A reference to a Jewish murderer named Israel Lipski who had poisoned a local girl one block east on Batty Street the year before. This is an indication that the individual who yelled out that anti–Semitic remark was not Jewish.] Schwartz then walked away, but finding that he was followed by the second man, he ran as far as the railway arch, but the man did not follow so far. Schwartz cannot say whether the two men were together or known to each other."

But the man did follow him for a while, leaving the area of Dutfield's Yard. This left only Stride and her assailant there. The yard was used by Arthur Dutfield, a builder of vans and carts.

Another witness, James Brown, stated at the inquest that as he was walking along Fairclough Street at 12:45 a.m. on his way home, he saw a woman, later identified as Elizabeth Stride. He testified that she was standing in front of the board school with her back to the wall talking to a stout man he thought to be 5'7" tall. The man was wearing a long coat and had placed his hand on the wall in a manner which indicated an attempt to stop her from leaving. Brown could hear Stride say, "No, not tonight. Maybe some other night." He was unable to see the man's face in the darkness.

The exchange is interesting in that it shows that Stride was perhaps looking, not for any client, but for a particular man. Also, if Brown's timing is correct, it probably puts the incident described by Israel Schwartz later, after the one described by Brown, not before it. It would make more sense if Stride's assault across the street in front of Dutfield's Yard was the latter of the two incidents.

That the area was well traveled by many club members would indicate that Stride or her attacker could not have expected to have engaged in sex in the dark walkway along the club wall. It seems to be an indication that this meeting had other purposes which were known to both the Ripper and his victim.

By 1 a.m., the deed was done. In this dark, small and confined Dutfield's Yard lay the still very warm body of Elizabeth Stride. At that point, a seller of inexpensive jewelry and the club steward, Louis Diemschutz, attempted to enter the yard with his pony and small cart. But the animal stopped at the entrance and would go no further, merely moving to the left and looking to the right. Because the yard was pitch black, Diemschutz was unable to see what had caused the pony to stop until he prodded in front with his whip and located Stride's body. His first thought was not of murder — he expected that the individual was asleep or drunk. He may even have thought it was his wife. Every Saturday night, after dropping off his unsold goods, Mr. Diemschutz would walk the pony to his stable located on George Yard, only a few feet from Klosowski's room at the lodging house. Coincidence? It is not unreasonable to believe that Klosowski had, during one of his late night walks throughout the area, seen Diemschutz stable his pony there. Perhaps he had when he walked back from Buck's Row after the murder of Polly Nichols early on the morning of Saturday, August 31. So, by extension, Klosowski could easily have known about the club as another stop on Mr. Diemschutz's regular itinerary.

Diemschutz then tried to light a match, but the winds, which had accompanied the rains all evening, soon made all but a brief glance impossible. But that was enough to show that the individual was a woman. He

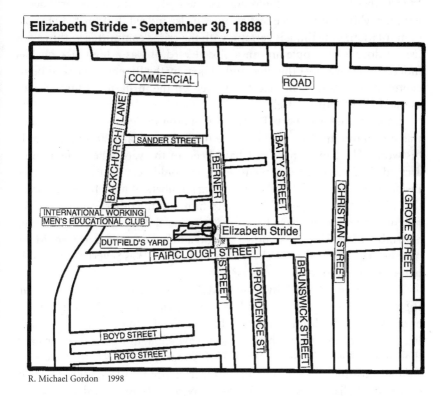

R. Michael Gordon   1998

Elizabeth Stride became the first to be killed during the night of the "double event." It has long been speculated that the Ripper was interrupted when Stride's body was discovered by Louis Diemschutz at 1 a.m. on September 30, 1888.

went from the yard into the Workingmen's Club to look for his wife and get help. "All I did was to run indoors and ask where my missus was because she is of weak constitution, and I did not want to frighten her." He informed the club members still in the dining room on the ground floor of the club, "There's a woman lying in the yard but I cannot say whether she's drunk or dead." It was at this point the murderer probably made his escape, if he was still in the yard.

Because of the odd, continued resistance of his pony, Diemschutz, even though he saw no one, felt that the Ripper must have still been in the yard when he attempted to enter, but the animal may only have been reacting to the dead body. Is it possible that the Ripper simply went *back* into the club to melt into a crowded room? Many researchers feel that with the arrival of Diemschutz the Ripper was interrupted in his mutilations. However, it must be remembered that the small yard was *totally black*. So dark in fact, that Diemschutz could not see the body, even after he prodded it with his whip two to three feet away. Murder indeed, but for the purpose of mutilation? One thing is certain, with the crime committed within a few feet of dozens of people and in a closed yard, it was a high-risk murder indeed. But it was just the type undertaken by the Ripper. He risked being captured again and again. He always needed the thrill of the hunt as well as the thrill of murder itself.

A man had been spotted in the area at around 12:40 a.m., but the body was not found until 1 a.m. This gave the killer perhaps 20 minutes to do his work. The Ripper need not have been in the yard when Diemschutz arrived. In fact, as already mentioned, he could very easily have stepped inside the club to mix with the remaining members. It must be remembered that Elizabeth Stride probably came to him, not the other way round. The risk of capture would have been greatly reduced if the murderer had been a member of the club, or a known visitor, and not a stranger. He would not have been questioned as to why he was in the yard. Was Severin Klosowski's name on the list of club members?

It has been reported, by Donald McCormick in *The Identity of Jack the Ripper*, that Joseph Lave would later inform the police that earlier in the evening a stranger had been in the club. He described the man as pretending to be a Polish barber (the American Lave thought he was Russian) and that he was *living in George Yard*. If this report is correct, then we have another possible close contact to a Ripper victim by Klosowski. After all, how many Polish-Russian barbers were living in George Yard at the time?

One witness, Mrs. Fanny Mortimer of 36 Berner Street, had been standing in her doorway between 12:30 and 1 a.m. "Nearly the whole time" she was overlooking Berner Street and the club, including the yard next to the club, and she saw no one exit the yard. "…[The] deed must have been done while I was standing at the door of my house." The Ripper *must* have gone back inside the club, and in the later confusion, left the area.

When Diemschutz moved back into the yard from the club, with fellow members Isaac Kozebrodsky and Morris Eagle, he discovered, with the help of a candle, that a murder had been committed and that the victim was indeed a woman. They tried to lift her up by her head and shoulders. It was easy then for the men to see that the Ripper had struck again, and this time on their very doorstep.

Standing at the side door, Mrs. Diemschutz had a view of the rain soaked yard. By the dim light of the men's candle she was also able to see the Ripper's work. "Just by the door I saw a pool of blood, and when my husband struck a light I noticed a dark heap lying under the wall. I at once recognized it as the body of a woman, while, to add to my horror, I saw a stream of blood trickling down [up] the yard and terminating in the pool I had first noticed. She was lying on her back with her head against the wall, and the face looked ghastly. I screamed out in fright, and the members of the club hearing my cries rushed downstairs in a body out into the yard." Diemschutz then lifted up Stride's chin and was able to see what had killed her. "I could see that her throat was fearfully cut. There was a great gash in it over two inches wide." Earlier, Mrs. Diemschutz had heard and seen nothing. "Just about 1:00 a.m. Sunday I was in the kitchen on the ground floor of the club and close to the side entrance. I am positive I did not hear screams or sounds of any kind."

Within a few short minutes Morris Eagle, and another man, had located Constable Henry Lamb, 252H, walking his beat on Commercial Road between Christian and Batty streets. As he moved towards them, the two excited men yelled out, "Come on, there has been another murder." As the group ran back to the yard another constable was picked up who had been on point duty on Commercial Road.

Arriving at the site, Lamb used his lantern to check for signs of life. The victim's face was still warm but her hands were cold. There was no pulse. He was not able to detect any signs of a

Elizabeth Stride — September 30, 1888. Throat cut deeply; not mutilated. (Public Record Office.)

struggle. "She looked as if she had been laid quietly down." Another sign of kindness after the murder had been committed. It was to be a continuing signature of this series of crimes. The yard was soon sealed off as the authorities began their work. Within short order the police were checking club members' hands and clothing for any signs of blood. Before they were allowed to leave members also had their names and addresses taken down.

By 1:16 a.m., Dr. Frederick William Blackwell arrived, having been aroused from his sleep. Under the light supplied by Constable Lamb he noted that, "The deceased had round her neck a check silk scarf, the bow of which was turned to the left and pulled very tight." This was of course an indication of strangulation. He further noted that her clothes were not rain soaked and thus she had not been lying in the yard for a long period of time. The doctor felt that Stride could not have been dead "more than twenty minutes, at the most half an hour." This places the murder somewhere from 12:46 a.m. to 12:56 a.m. If this estimate is accurate, the Ripper could have been gone at least four minutes before Diemschutz arrived with his cart. Before long Inspector Charles Pinhorn arrived to take charge of the case. By 5:30 that morning the investigation of the murder scene would be completed, as Reserve Police Constable Albert Collins, 12HR, under orders, washed away all traces of blood in Dutfield's Yard. At the time, this was standard operating procedure. After the investigation Stride's body was wheeled out of the small yard and taken to the mortuary on Cable Street, St. George-in-the East.

As the authorities and local residents attempted to understand the events which were unfolding on Berner Street, the Ripper was heading west towards the edge of the City of London proper, and Mitre Square. It was approximately three-quarters of a mile away and was very soon to become a part of his killing ground. This recent victim also lived on Flower and Dean Street, right across from the barbershop. She would become part of the "double event." With two women being murdered in one hour — women who had lived on the same street in Whitechapel — could those murders truly be random events? Or were these two women being silenced?

As for Diemschutz, the man who discovered Stride's body, he would be sentenced to hard labor in March 1889 for his participation in a brawl between members of the club and other local residents.

The Night of Terror Continues

She was 5 feet tall, with dark auburn hair, and hazel eyes, and was called Catherine Eddowes. (At times she was known as Kate Conway and

Kate Kelly.) She was born on April 14, 1842, in Graisley Green, Wolverhampton, in the English midlands. After her death she would have one of the most well attended funerals ever held in London's East End. Her mother was Catherine (Evans), and her father a tin plate worker named George Eddowes. She was one of five daughters of the couple. The others were Elizabeth, Eliza, Emma and Harriet.

Around 1848, when Catherine was only six years old, her father and Uncle William left their jobs during the tin men's strike in Wolverhampton. This caused both families to walk to London where the men eventually found work. Later, William would return to tin work in Wolverhampton.

Before her mother's death in 1855, Catherine and her sisters were educated at St. John's Charity School, Potter's Field. Upon her death they entered Bermondsey Workhouse and Industrial School. It was reported that her father George passed away a few months later, forcing Catherine, and probably her sisters as well, to move back to Wolverhampton to live with her aunt on Bison Street. While living there, Catherine attended Dowgate Charity School. She would later be described as a scholarly woman who was intelligent but one having a fierce temper.

She continued to live with her aunt until she was 21 at which point she became involved with a pensioner named Thomas Conway. He had been a member of the 18th Royal Irish Regiment and drew a pension under the name of Thomas Quinn. Catherine went off with him selling cheap books he had written. They also produced a series of gallows ballads and were even selling them in 1866 when her cousin, Christopher Robinson, was hanged at Stratford! Eventually, the couple returned to Wolverhampton, where in 1865 she gave birth to a girl named Annie. In 1868, she had a son named George and another son in 1875. There is no record of any marriage and in time Catherine would "run away from the pensioner," to return to her aunt. But her aunt refused to allow her to return, so she settled for a while in a lodging house on Bison Street near her aunt's home.

There is disagreement as to why the couple split up. Her sister Elizabeth stated, "My sister left because he treated her badly. He did not drink regularly, but when he drew his pension they went out together, and it generally ended with his beating her." Eddowes' daughter gave a story of her parents' separation some seven to eight years before her murder, as one caused by her mother's drinking. She said her father was a teetotaler but he was not on the best of terms with the Eddoweses. No matter what the reasons, the family broke up in 1880, with Conway taking the two boys and Annie going with her mother.

By 1881, Catherine had moved into Cooneys' lodging house at 55 Flower and Dean Street. By then her daughter Annie had married a lamp black packer named Louis Phillips. She had begun to move around so that she would be able "to avoid her mother's scrounging." It was at Cooneys that Catherine would meet John Kelly who she would stay with for the remainder of her life. She would also spend time with her sister who lived at 6 Thrawl Street, a nearby lodging.

The deputy of Cooneys was Frederick William Wilkinson who had known Catherine for years. He said she "was not often in drink and was a very jolly woman, often singing." He knew her to be in the lodging house usually no later than 10 p.m. and did not know her to be a prostitute. John Kelly would also state that he never knew her to "ever walk the streets," although he was well aware of her occasionally overdrinking. There is no evidence of prostitution, at least officially.

As was the couple's habit, each year they went hop picking but had little luck in September 1888. They could not earn enough money to keep themselves, so after less than a month they walked back to London from Hunton near Maidstone in Kent. They arrived in London on September 28, which was a Friday, and had to split up to find lodgings. John Kelly stayed at Cooneys and Catherine went to secure a bed at the Shoe Lane casual ward.

Catherine was well known at the casual ward but the superintendent had not seen her for a while. When she arrived she told him that she had been hop picking but, "I have come back to earn the reward offered for the apprehension of the Whitechapel murderer. I think I know him." After he warned her to be careful not to be murdered herself, she said, "Oh, no fear of that." She had less than 24 hours to live. She had recently told her friends, "He's got other girls to bother about instead of me. 'Sides, the minute I see any man carrying a shiny black bag, I'll throw my head back and scream it off!"

She spent the night at the casual ward but by 8 a.m. the next day she was once again at Cooneys in search of John Kelly. There had been some unspecified trouble at the casual ward and Catherine had been put out. It was at this point that Kelly, reunited with Eddowes, decided to pawn a pair of his boots at a shop on Church Street. Catherine took them inside and received two shillings and six pence for them under the name of Jane Kelly. They used the money to purchase some food and were seen between 10 and 11 a.m. sharing breakfast in the kitchen at Cooneys.

By that afternoon they were once again without funds, so Catherine told Kelly that she would go to see her daughter in Bermondsey to see if she could get some money. As she left him for the last time, at around 2 p.m. in Houndsditch, she promised to return "no later than 4 p.m." It was not possible for her to visit her daughter Annie, however, as she had once again moved to where her mother could not find her. In fact, they had not seen each other at all for the previous two years. There is no evidence to suggest who she actually went to meet. At the inquest John Kelly would lament, "I never knew if she went to her daughter at all. I only wish she had, for we had lived together for some time and never had a quarrel."

At around 8 p.m. that evening a very drunk Catherine Eddowes was seen entertaining a crowd who had gathered to watch her doing imitations of a fire engine along Aldgate High Street. She then lay down on the street outside 29 Aldgate High Street and went to sleep. It was not long before Constable Louis Robinson, 931 City, came along to make inquires of the crowd as to the woman's identity, but no one knew her. When he pulled her up on her feet to arrest her it was obvious that she was unable to stand by herself. As he leaned her up against the building she slipped sideways. But with help from Constable George Simmons, she was taken to Bishopsgate Police Station to sleep off the effects of her drinking.

When they arrived at the station Catherine gave her name as, "Nothing." She was then placed in a cell where, at 8:50 p.m., she was checked by Constable Robinson who found her fast asleep. At 9:45 p.m. Constable George Hutt, 968 City, assumed responsibility for the prisoners, which required him to check the cells every half hour. It was 12:15 a.m., when Catherine was again awake. She could be heard softly singing to herself. Fifteen minutes later she called to Constable Hutt and asked when she could be released. He replied, "When you are capable of taking care of yourself." To that she informed him that, "I can do that now."

By 12:55 a.m., it was becoming time once more to check the cells to see if any of the prisoners were sober enough to be released. Sergeant Byfield sent Constable Hutt to check and he found that Eddowes was indeed well enough to be set free. When asked again for her name she told the officers that it was *Mary Ann Kelly* and that she lived at 6 Fashion Street. Both pieces of information were incorrect and it is interesting to note that the name she gave was very close to that of another future Ripper victim — Mary Jane Kelly! Indeed, the real Kelly did, at times, use that exact name, Mary Ann Kelly. Some investigators have written that none of the victims knew each other, but the closeness of the names does beg the question. These women lived only two blocks away from each other. Or was it that the Ripper knew both of them? That would have been enough.

As Constable Hutt pushed open the station's swinging door for Eddowes at 1:00 a.m. she asked, "What time is it?" Hutt replied, "Too late for you to get anything to drink." "I shall get a damn fine hiding when I get home then," she said. Hutt replied, "And serve you right. You had no right to get drunk. This way missus, please pull it to." As she left and pulled open the door she said, "All right, good night old cock." Elizabeth Stride's body had just been discovered in a small enclosed yard some 1200 yards away.

Leaving the station she turned left back towards Aldgate High Street, and south on Houndsditch where she was earlier found drunk. In order to go back home to Flower and Dean Street she should have turned right. It was a fatal decision. It would take only ten minutes for her to walk to Mitre Square. There was plenty of time to meet the Ripper. It has been suggested that she did indeed plan to meet someone, witnessed by her insistence to be let out and the direction she went after her release. "*I think I know him!*"

Police Constable Edward Watkins, 881 City, on regular beat duty, entered Mitre Square at around 1:30 a.m., and found it quiet and deserted. The square was patrolled every 15 minutes and had an echo, so sound travelled very well. At about the same time (1:30) a night watchman named James Blenkinsop was looking after some roadwork in St. James Place, when a "respectably dressed man" came up to him and asked, "Have you seen a man and a woman go through here?" He informed the stranger that he had, but had taken no notice of them. With police at the other two entrances to Mitre Square there is a very good chance that James was speaking to the Ripper, yet there is no description of this individual and Blenkinsop was not called as a witness at the inquest. Also, at St. James Place (Orange Market) was a fire station, open all night. It was manned by two firemen who informed the police that no one came out of Mitre Square in that direction, which effectively cuts off that possible escape route.

Catherine was next seen by three men who were leaving the Imperial Club at 16-17 Duke Street. They had stayed late due to the rain that evening. The club was a local Jewish businessmen's club, which is significant because the next murder would be committed near another Jewish establishment, as was the last killing. It is entirely possible that the killer was trying to lead the police to believe he was Jewish and thus pull any suspicions away from himself, a Roman Catholic. As Joseph Lawende, a cigarette salesman, and Henry Harris and Joseph Levy left the club they saw Catherine talking with a man on the corner of Duke Street and Church Passage, which leads directly into Mitre Square from the north. They were no more than 15 or 16 feet away from the couple. They reported that she was facing the man with her hand on his chest in a friendly manner. He was described by Lawende as wearing a salt and pepper colored jacket with a gray cloth peaked cap and having a reddish handkerchief knotted around his neck. He further described him as 5'7" tall, 30 years old with fair complexion, medium build and a mustache. Eddowes' clothes would later be identified by Lawende as matching those worn by the woman he had seen. His description of the

Catherine Eddowes - September 30, 1888

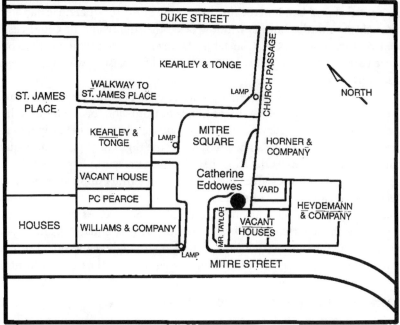

R. Michael Gordon   1998

Less than one hour after Stride's murder the Ripper struck a second time, murdering Catherine Eddowes in a dark corner of Mitre Square. Her body was discovered by Constable Edward Watkins at 1:45 a.m.

man would be published in the October 19, 1888, edition of the *Police Gazette*. It was 1:34 a.m., and Eddowes had less than ten minutes to live.

Just after that sighting Eddowes and a man described as "about thirty with a fair moustache," were apparently seen by two individuals talking at the St. James Place covered entrance into Mitre Square. This was reported in the *Daily Telegraph* of November 12, but these two individuals were never located by the police for follow-up interrogation. These witnesses must have been viewing the couple a few minutes or even seconds before Eddowes was murdered; Yet her killer felt comfortable enough to continue with his plan, even after having been seen by no fewer than five people.

Around 1:40 to 1:42 a.m., Police Constable James Harvey, 964 City, a 12 year veteran on beat duty, walked down Duke's Street and into Church Passage. He reported that he saw no one and could hear nothing when he looked into, but did not enter, Mitre Square. It could very well have been that the lamp at the Mitre Square end of Church Passage prevented him from seeing the body at the far end of the square by partially blinding his night vision. Interestingly, a city policeman, Constable Richard Pearse, 922 City, lived at number 3 on the northwest side of Mitre Square. He had slept through the murder but his window faced the square and he could easily see the murder site. As for Constable Harvey he would spend less than one more year on the force before being dismissed for reasons which have been lost to history.

George Clapp and his wife lived as caretakers at the Heydemann and Company warehouses. From their second- or third-floor back windows they had a clear view over the yard into Mitre Square where the next Ripper victim would soon be found. They retired for the night at 11 p.m. and would not hear any screams as the Ripper went about his work.

Forty-five minutes after the discovery of Elizabeth Stride's body off Berner Street, and only 12 minutes walking distance away, Constable Edward Watkins, 881 City Police, again entered Mitre Square. As detailed in the *Daily News*, he reported that, "I came round (to Mitre Square) again at 1:45, and entering the square from Mitre Street, on the right-hand side, I turned sharp round to the right, and flashing my light, I saw the body in front of

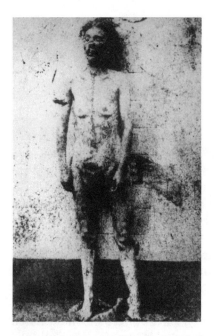 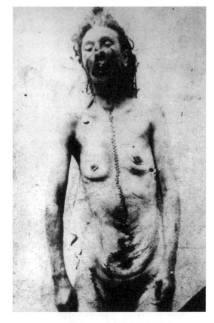

Left: Catherine Eddowes — September 30, 1888. Throat cut deeply; face mutilated; body opened from breast bone to pubes; liver stabbed; kidney and womb taken. *Right:* Catherine Eddowes. (Public Record Office.)

me. The clothes were pushed up to her breast, and the stomach was laid bare, with a dreadful gash from the pit of the stomach to the breast. On examining the body I found the entrails cut and laid round the throat, which had an awful gash in it, extending from ear to ear. In fact, the head was nearly severed from the body. Blood was everywhere to be seen. It was difficult to discern the injuries to the face for the quantity of blood which covered it... The murderer had inserted the knife just under the left eye, and, drawing it under the nose, cut the nose completely from the face, at the same time inflicting a dreadful gash down the right cheek to the angle of the jawbone. The nose was laid over on the cheek. A more dreadful sight I never saw; it quite knocked me over." When entering the square from the south, off Mitre Street, a blind corner on the right was formed by three unoccupied cottages. It was in front of these cottages that Eddowes' body was discovered.

Two constables effectively blocked two of three entrances into Mitre Square, making it almost certain that the Ripper used the dark covered passage from the Square towards St. James Place, to make his extremely close escape. Yet, even in that direction, the night watchman, Blenkinsop, was keeping his eyes open, albeit not for the Ripper. It is also possible that the Ripper was forced to stay in or near Mitre Square, trapped for a time, while the police began their searches. He may have been in the yard very near the body. It must have been an extremely close affair, and yet, once again, he slipped away into the darkness of that cloudy night. He must have heard the approach of the policemen's steps as he silently moved away from his latest killing grounds. He had killed two women within the space of a single hour, and he was still free.

After his pitiful discovery, Constable Watkins ran across Mitre Square to find a watchman at Kearley & Tonges Company. He pushed open the door, which had been left open towards the square, and found George Morris as he was sweeping the floor. Morris "had gone to the front door to look out into the square two moments before Watkins called," and had seen and heard nothing. Watkins yelled out, "For God's sake, mate, come to my assistance." Morris was a former police constable on pension who demanded, "What's the matter?" Watkins explained, "Oh dear, there's another woman cut to pieces!" Both men rushed back to the body and then, leaving Constable Watkins, Morris ran out of the square onto Mitre Street and then to Aldgate High Street. He was able to use his old police whistle to call Constable Harvey and James Holland. It is possible that when the constable ran into the warehouse to summon help he gave the Ripper just enough time to get away. Perhaps, if the constable had blown his whistle and stayed in the square with the victim, he may have caught the Ripper literally red-handed.

Morris would later say, "The strangest part of the whole thing is that I heard no sound. As a rule I can hear the footsteps of the policeman as he passes by every quarter of an hour, so the woman could not have uttered any cry without my detecting it. It was only last night I made the remark to some policemen that I wished the butcher would come round Mitre Square, and I would soon give him a doing, and here, to be sure, he has come, and I was perfectly ignorant of it."

As was becoming typical of the Ripper series, this was a very high risk killing. The square was virtually surrounded by beat officers or former officers and others, and there was little time to commit the crime. Even after he had been seen earlier by three witnesses, from a few feet away, the Ripper still committed the murder in an area, where, if he had been spotted, he would have surely been captured. This unnecessary high risk behavior is, however, a factor in many serial killings. It was the thrill of the hunt once again.

It was not long before Dr. George William Sequeria was called to the scene. The 29-year-old doctor lived at 34 Jewry Street, Aldgate, only 150 yards from Mitre Square, and he knew the area well. He was of course far too late to help this latest Ripper victim, as all he was able to do was pronounce death and have the body removed. He did not make an on the spot detailed examination of the body, but would later state that he felt it took no anatomical knowledge to inflict the fatal wounds.

The killer's ability to avoid apprehension is again evidenced by the searches conducted by three detectives who were also close by. Detectives Robert Outram, Edward Marriott and Daniel Halse were searching passages in the area, and were on the corner of Houndsditch and Aldgate High Street when they were informed of the Mitre Square killing at 1:58 a.m. After arriving at the murder site they split up going in three different directions looking for the killer. At the inquest Daniel Halse described their actions. "I gave instructions to have the neighbourhood searched and every man examined. I went by Middlesex Street into Wentworth Street, where I stopped two men who gave satisfactory accounts of themselves. I came through Goulston Street at 20 past 2 (a.m.) and then went back to Mitre Square. ... Inspector McWilliam, upon his arrival at the square also ordered immediate searches of neighbouring streets and lodging houses. Several men were stopped and searched but without any tangible result." Even though he was not found the Ripper may have still been in the general area, as he was about to leave a message for the police.

It is also possible that the Ripper himself was transparent to the police in that he may not have acted like a madman, which is the type of person the police were looking for. To those who must have seen him living in the area or near the crime scenes, the Ripper must not have seemed out of place. He somehow belonged there. How was he not a suspect? He indeed seemed to be able to blend into the background, and the police looked past him. And yet, living and working so close to the crime area, as he did, he must have been questioned several times during the height of the killings. This was a man who was completely calm before, during and after he killed. He did not panic, ever. Nothing he said or did gave him away. Nothing! Klosowski would, in his future manifestation of the American George Chapman, become friendly with police officers and their organizations. Perhaps he was also a helpful friend of the police during the Ripper period as well. It has also been suggested that the Ripper, upon completion of his work, donned the vestments of a priest as cover for his getaway.

To answer the question whether or not one man could have committed both crimes that evening, only two issues need be explored. The first is the time between the deaths. It easily allowed a man enough time to walk calmly from one site to the other. The second is the description given by individuals at both locations. Although he was described as respectably dressed by Schwartz, and rough and shabby by Lawende, by the time he reached Mitre Square, there are many similarities. Both witnesses described the probable killer as about 30 years old, with fair complexion, of medium height, and with a small mustache. They also both described him as wearing a jacket with a peaked cap. It is a good possibility that the Ripper simply went to his rooms on the way to Mitre Square and changed his clothes. At this point the police were very sure that he had some type of private quarters nearby. It must be remembered that he was trying not to be caught, and changing clothes would have been a very simple method to avoid identification as a suspect in that evening's first murder. By no means is it a difficult task to change coats.

There is one other description of the possible killer, given by Sergeant Steve White, which may shed some light on the situation. The story was reported in the September 26, 1919, issue of *People's Journal* so it must be viewed with a careful eye. However, it could be the only face-to-face contact with the Ripper by a police officer around the time of a murder. The sighting is said to have occurred on the night of the double event. "He was about five feet ten inches in height, and was dressed rather shabbily, though it was obvious that the material of his clothes was good. Evidently a man who had seen better days, I thought, but men who have seen better days are common enough down East, and that of itself was not sufficient to justify me in stopping him. His face was long and thin, nostrils rather delicate, and his hair was jet black. His complexion was inclined to be sallow, and altogether the man was foreign in appearance. The most striking thing about him, however, was the extraordinary brilliance of his eyes. They looked like two very luminous glowworms coming through the darkness. The man was slightly bent at the shoulders, though he was obviously quite young, about thirty-three at the most, and gave one the idea of having been a student or professional man. His hands were snow white, and the fingers long and tapering." Klosowski?

A Mysterious Message

For Police Constable Alfred Long, 254A, it was the first night of his new beat. As he walked along Goulston Street at 2:20 a.m., not yet aware of the two murders and two minutes before Detective Constable Daniel Halse made his way down the same street looking for the Ripper, he saw nothing to raise his suspicions. When he returned to Goulston Street, at approximately 2:55 a.m., he found a piece of a woman's apron, still wet with blood, at 108-119 Wentworth Model Dwellings. These were newly constructed lodgings serving mostly Jewish families. Once again the Ripper was attempting to point to the Jewish population and away from himself. It would be the fourth time that night that such an attempt would be made. The apron section was placed in the entryway to the staircase and just above it on the right hand side of that doorway was a message. It was written in white chalk on the black bricks and stated:

> The Juwes are
> The men That
> Will not
> be Blamed
> for nothing

This was the second anti–Semitic statement of the night; the first being the yelling of the slur "Lipski" at the Stride death site. No Jew would have written those words, which were very fresh. It should be noted that the Ripper's ego would not have allowed anyone else to claim credit for his work or his words. That is why he left the apron piece, as positive proof of the message's authenticity! He would soon leave another, even more dramatic, proof of his work.

It had been at least 35 minutes between the murder in Mitre Square and the 2:20 a.m. passage of Constable Long through this area. Long felt that the message would have been removed by the Jewish residents had it been seen so it had to have been written that night. Constable Long did not go inside the building to investigate but a close look at the staircases showed no footsteps or blood stains. It is also noted that the police forces were already on high alert due to the murder on Berner Street less than an hour before. The Ripper knew this would be the case. The graffiti was located five minutes from the murder site and yet, with police searching for him in all directions, he stayed in the area to drop off a piece of his latest victim's clothing and leave a message. Surely, if he was the author of the chalk message, he was playing the ultimate game of cat and mouse with the police.

As for Constable Long, he would remain on the force for one more year before being dismissed in 1889 for being drunk on duty.

The Ripper may have even found a dark spot to stand, possibly on the corner of New Goulston Street, so he could see the police officers walking past, before he left his message to prove he was there. This man was leaving his calling card. Or is it possible that he actually went home to his rooms, or workplace, and simply returned with a piece of chalk to the location to leave the message, after he cleaned himself up and changed his clothes? Did he need to remove his disguise? Certainly no one would have suspected a man calmly walking towards the murder site. Suspicion would have fallen on an individual moving away from Mitre Square. He would have been able to observe the activities, become involved, and yet remain above suspicion.

There is another aspect of the chalk message, involving high London police authorities. On site that early September 30 morning to view the message, were Sir Charles Warren, Commissioner of the Metropolitan Police, and Police Superintendent Thomas Arnold of H Division. Arnold had briefed Commissioner Warren on both murders as well as the message site. It was Arnold who first suggested that the message be removed as soon as possible. He felt that its Jewish aspect could possibly cause an anti–Semitic riot. The two men discussed covering part of it so that it could be later photographed, but in Warren's own words, "I considered it desirable to obliterate the writing at once, having taken a copy... I do not hesitate myself to say that if that writing had been left, there would have been an onslaught upon the Jews, property would have been wrecked, and lives would probably have been lost..." With that decision, a copy of what probably was the Ripper's own handwriting was forever lost. The message was wiped off at 5:30 in the morning. As reported by Major Smith, Warren himself removed it. However, with the Ripper living in one of the largest Jewish slums in Europe, killing non–Jews, and doing his best that night to place the blame on a Jew, it could just be that Warren and Arnold both made very good decisions that cold and wet early September morning in 1888. They were, after all, living through the "Autumn of Terror," and any increase in that terror was to be avoided at all costs. But why remove the entire message? That part of the effort was never fully answered by the police.

By now, having left unmistakable evidence of his passing, the Ripper was again on the move. He must have crossed Wentworth Street moving north on Bell Lane towards Dorset Street. It was here, in a darkened spot, he washed his hands "not more than six yards from the street." Major Smith, who claimed to have found the bloodstained water still moving in the sink, could have been very close to the Ripper, as he once again disappeared into the wet night streets of Whitechapel. The barbershop on Flower and Dean Street was only two blocks away and Klosowski's lodgings were five blocks away. This time the Ripper had defeated two police forces at the same time: the City and the Metropolitan. The terror in London, centered on Whitechapel, would now reach new heights. But his movements that night were pointing to his location which would soon be the site of a massive house to house search. He was leaving too many clues and the police were closing in.

A City Stunned

Early in the morning, crowds gathered at both the Berner Street and Mitre Square murder sites. In point of fact the crowds were more of a mob. They were loudly protesting the inability of London's finest to apprehend the Ripper. Their cries were being echoed even in the overseas press as witnessed by the headlines in the *New York Times*.

The *New York Times*— October 1, 1888
Dismay in Whitechapel
Two more murdered women found
One night's work of the mysterious assassin
who baffled the London police thus far
London, Sept. 30 — The Whitechapel fiend has again set that district and all London in a state of terror. He murdered not one woman but two last night, and seems bent on beating all previous records in his unheard-of crimes. His last night's victims were both murdered within an hour, and the second was disemboweled like her predecessors, a portion of her abdomen being missing as in the last case. He contented himself with cutting the throat of the other, doubtless because of interruption. Both women were street walkers of the lowest class, as before. These crimes are all of the most daring character. These made six murders to the fiend's credit, all within a half-mile radius. People are terrified and are loud in their complaints of the police, who have done absolutely nothing. They confess themselves without a clue, and they devote their entire energies to preventing the press from getting at the facts. ... The assassin is evidently mocking the police in his barbarous work. He waited until the two preceding inquests were quite finished,

and then murdered two more women. ... The vigilance committees which were formed after the first crimes were committed had relaxed their efforts to capture the murderer. At several meetings held in Whitechapel tonight it was resolved to resume the work of patrolling the streets in the district in which the murders have occurred.

On the morning of September 30, B. Harris, of the Mile End Vigilance Committee, again wrote to the Home Office requesting the Home Secretary, Henry Matthews, put forward a reward for information about the killer. His reply came three days later: "The Secretary of State saw no reason to alter his previous decision." That decision was of course to offer no reward. Indeed no official governmental reward would ever be offered by Her Majesty's Government.

On October 1, the editor of the *Financial News*, Harry Marks, sent a £300 cheque to the Home Office as a reward for the capture of the Ripper, but the cheque was returned. That afternoon, Queen Victoria herself voiced her concerns in a 3:30 p.m. phone call to the Home Office. She stated how shocked she was and requested information about the ongoing investigations.

In addition to requests for rewards and more police, the Mile End Vigilance Committee began sending out its own patrols. From the ranks of the many unemployed, men were hired to patrol the East End from before midnight to four or five in the morning. Each morning, by 12:30 a.m., these paid patrols were supplemented by the committee members themselves. The committee also hired a private detective agency, Grand & Batchelor, to supervise the patrols and advise the committee. The first patrols were in operation by midnight, October 3.

The *Los Angeles Times*— October 1, 1888
London Alarmed
The Whitechapel Fiend Again at Work
Two More Unfortunate Women Butchered in One Night
London, Sept. 30 — (By Cable and Associated Press) This morning the whole city was again startled by news that two murders had been added to the list of mysterious crimes that have been committed in Whitechapel. ... The police, who have been severely criticized in connection with the Whitechapel murders are paralyzed by these latest crimes. As soon as the news was received at police headquarters a messenger was dispatched for Sir Charles Warren, Chief Commissioner of Police. He was called out of bed, and at once visited the scene of the murders. ... The inhabitants of Whitechapel are dismayed.

The news of two women in one night being hunted down and murdered by the Whitechapel Killer, at once electrified and terrified the whole of London. That morning the *Central News Agency* interviewed Dr. L. Forbes Winslow about the individual being sought. He gave his opinion that the killer was a "homicidal monomaniac of infinite cunning." Many other local doctors were expressing the opinion that the killer must be a lunatic. By early morning the streets of the East End were crowded with residents pressing to hear the latest news. Thousands of people, at times leaving nowhere to move, crowded the two murder sites. Even though both sites had been cordoned off, the police could not stop the population from trying to get a look. Those lucky enough to have a view from one of the many buildings surrounding the sites sold window seats, and there was no lack of customers. The streets leading to the murder sites were literally choked with thousands of people.

The crowds were so large that many other individuals were taking advantage of the situation doing a brisk trade selling fruits, nuts and other snacks to the assembled onlookers. The news vendors also did a vast business as each special edition was quickly bought up. Those who could not read eagerly stood by as those who could read the latest reports. Crowds were also gathering in front of the local police stations with the inhabitants demanding some sort of action by the police. These crowds were to last for days.

Beyond what the police had already done was added some 80,000 handbills which requested information on the killer's identity. There were enough to deliver one to every household in the area. Redoubling their efforts, the police questioned over 2000 tenants of common lodging houses in the general areas of the murder sites in a house by house investigation. They even assigned plainclothes and undercover officers to lodging houses, and others to mingle with the customers at the local pubs. Every available man was put on the case. This was an all out effort to catch the killer. In the hope of finding someone to come forward and identify a suspect living in one of the local houses, the police issued the following notice.

POLICE NOTICE.
TO THE OCCUPIER
On the mornings of Friday, 31st August, Saturday 8th, and Sunday, 30th September, 1888 Women were murdered in or near Whitechapel, supposedly by some one residing in the immediate neighbourhood. Should you know of any person to whom suspicion is attached, you are earnestly requested to communicate at once with the nearest Police Station.
Metropolitan Police Office, 30th September, 1888

In addition to the official police patrols, there were many vigilance committee members who patrolled almost every street and alley within the

Ripper's killing ground. More and more vigilance groups were formed until the area was almost saturated with hundreds of eyes looking for one man. Many men would be stopped and questioned, with some even being escorted to local police stations, but none would turn out to be the Ripper. Even the local criminal gangs were on the lookout for the madman. After all, not only was he bad for their particular brand of business, but many of the women they were familiar with were targets of his demented attacks.

Monro's Secret "Section D" also responded to the double event by increasing its plainclothes patrols from the 27 established after the Chapman murder to 89. For the most part, there was at least one individual for each and every street in the Ripper's area, official or otherwise. The streets were being slowly taken back from the Whitechapel Killer.

One piece of evidence may have been placed into the hands of the police. At 12:30 a.m. on October 1, Thomas Coram, an 18-year-old laborer, was returning home from Bath Gardens. As he went past Mr. Christmas's laundry, at 252 Whitechapel Road on the north side, he noticed a dagger lying on the doorstep. The weapon's handle was wrapped in a bloodstained handkerchief and it had a nine- or ten-inch blade. Coram then called Constable Joseph Drage, 282H, who was on fixed point duty at Whitechapel Road and Great Garden Street. Constable Drage then took the weapon to the Leman Street Station. Dr. Bagster Phillips would later dismiss this as the weapon that killed Elizabeth Stride. But could it have been the dagger that killed Martha Tabram? The question was never asked.

At night, because of the murders, only the most populous and well lit areas held any foot traffic, as most of the other streets and alleys became deserted. Many who had no place to go and no money for a bed simply huddled together in dark corners or doorways in small groups for safety. Even as the temperatures began to push towards freezing many women were still being put out of lodging houses and on to the streets certain that they next would feel the Ripper's knife at their throats. For many the only protection they had were the knives they too were now carrying, as many were prepared to put up a fight to the end. Newspapers were carrying stories of well armed women which must have been read by the Ripper. They would not go down easily, and the killer would need to choose his targets with even greater care.

The terror was so real that at least one woman killed herself, rather than face the Ripper on the street. Mrs. Sodeaux of 65 Hanbury Street, not far from the Chapman murder site, hanged herself on October 10 from her stair banister. She had been reported to have been depressed and "greatly agitated" after the last two murders. Death by suicide was always an option in the slums of London's East End.

Undoubtedly, the Ripper himself read the reports of patrols and inquires and knew that it would not be an easy task to kill again. But he needed to kill. If he was keeping track of the news his eye would have caught one particular notice with considerable interest. On October 2 the *Evening News* reported that a particular area of Whitechapel had been pinpointed as the likely residence of the Ripper. It reported, "A belief is gaining ground that the murderer is not a frequenter of common lodging houses, but that he occupies a single room or perhaps finds refuge in an empty warehouse. He is supposed to make his home somewhere between Middlesex Street and Brick Lane." Severin Klosowski both lived and worked between these two streets, and he occupied a single rented room. This report was way too close for comfort. He would have to move, and move fast, if he wished to avoid the hangman. Because unknown to him and the general public, and perhaps most of the press, a major search was then being planned.

The *New York Times*— October 2, 1888
LONDON'S AWFUL MYSTERY
Indignation Against the Home Secretary and Police
London, Oct. 1.— Excitement over the Whitechapel murders has steadily increased during the day, the evening papers devoting all available space to the gory details. As in the preceding cases, however, the murderer continues unknown and unsuspected. ... As before, in all these horrible crimes, the duty of investigation seems to devolve on the Coroner, and the detectives sit at the inquest listening to the sworn testimony to find out who did it. The whole police management of the cases, as indeed the system under which they work, is idiotic in the extreme. Indignation meetings were held in several places in Whitechapel today to denounce Sir Charles Warren and Home Secretary Matthews. The "*Daily Telegraph*" this morning called loudly for Matthew's dismissal, since he had not sense enough to resign. A petition to the Queen is in preparation, asking her to offer a reward, Matthews having stupidly refused. The Lord Mayor promptly offered £500 reward this morning, the second murder having been committed within the precincts of the city. This, with other private rewards, makes a total of £1,200. (The Lord mayor of London had approved a recommendation for a reward from Colonel Sir James Fraser, Commissioner of Police.)

Whereas at 1:45 a.m. on Sunday, 30 September a woman, name unknown, was found brutally murdered in Mitre Square, Aldgate, in the City.
　　A reward of £500 will be paid by the Commissioner of Police of the City of London to any person (other than a person belonging to the Police Forces of the United Kingdom) who shall give such information

as shall lead to the discovery and conviction of the murderer or murderers.

Information to be given to the Inspector of the Detective Department, 26, Old Jewry, or any police station.

James Fraser, Colonel, Commissioner,
City of London Police Office, 1 Oct 1888

On October 2, George Lusk of the Mile End Vigilance Committee requested, once again, a reward be offered for the capture of the killer, and once again it was refused by the Home Office. The private rewards would be equivalent to nearly $100,000 in today's funds. The Ripper's identity was becoming a very valuable piece of information.

Twin Deaths Trigger Twin Inquests

On October 1, the inquest began into the death of Elizabeth Stride. There was little doubt, in the minds of the police, that she had met Jack the Ripper, and the evidence was widely publicized in the press. Edwin Wynne Baxter held the inquest in the Vestry Hall on Cable Street.

Dr. George Bagster Phillips, the divisional police surgeon, along with Dr. William Blackwell, had performed the autopsy at St. George's mortuary. Phillips and Blackwell had been the two medical men called to the murder scene. Earlier, Phillips had handled the Chapman inquiry and was familiar with the Ripper's work. He reported on October 3 that "The body was lying on its left side, face toward the wall, head toward the yard, feet toward the street, left arm extended from elbow, which had a packet of cashews in her hand. Similar ones were in the gutter. I took them from her hand, and handed them to Dr. Blackwell. The right arm was lying over the body, and the back of the hand and wrist had on them clotted blood. The legs were drawn up, the feet close to the wall, the body still warm, the face warm, the hands cold, the legs quite warm, a silk handkerchief round the throat, slightly torn. This corresponded to the right angle of the jaw. The throat was deeply gashed, and an abrasion of the skin about an inch and a quarter diameter, apparently slightly stained with blood, was under the right clavicle."

Dr. William Blackwell, who had arrived at the scene at 1:16 a.m., 20 to 30 minutes before Dr. Phillips, was called, and he added to the details of the crime scene. "The appearance of the face was quite placid. The mouth was slightly open. The deceased had round her neck a check silk scarf, the bow of which was turned to the left and pulled very tight. In the neck there was a long incision which exactly corresponded with the lower border of the scarf. The border was slightly frayed as if by a sharp knife. The incision in the neck commenced on the left side, 2½ inches below the angle of the jaw, and almost in a direct line with it, nearly severing the vessels on that side, cutting the windpipe completely in two, and terminating on the opposite side 1½ inches below the angle of the right jaw, but without severing the vessels on that side. I could not ascertain whether the bloody hand had been moved. The blood was running down the gutter into the drain in the opposite direction from the feet. There was about one pound of clotted blood close by the body, and a stream all the way from there to the back door of the club."

There was no attempt to mutilate the body or remove any organs. In fact, Stride's clothing had not been disturbed at all. Not even a button was out of place, and no blood was found on her clothing. It was also evident that she had not been dead for long before she was discovered, because when found her clothes were not wet from the rains, which had continued off and on for most of the night.

Doctor Blackwell concluded that she had been dead "more than twenty minutes, at the most half an hour." This testimony placed the murder between 12:46 and 12:56 a.m. He also felt that she had been dragged back by her handkerchief and pulled to the ground. She was laid down and not dropped. Once again a strange example of kindness by the killer. Then her throat was cut.

Neither of the doctors found any other knife marks or other abrasions. There was also no sign of strangulation or gagging. She did, however, have "pressure marks" on both shoulders which was evidence of two hands pushing hard on her shoulders. She also had a one-and-a-half-inch round mark on the right side of the jaw. It was an indication of a thumb which might have held her head as the killer's hand covered her mouth. This was identical to the bruise found on Polly Nichols' jaw. As for the weapon used, Doctor Phillips felt that it could have been a well ground down short knife, and very sharp. Could this have been the same clasp-knife used on Annie Millwood seven months earlier? Or perhaps it was the pen-knife used 38 times on Martha Tabram's body, on that dark morning in August? There is no reason to believe, or evidence to show, that the Ripper carried only one knife. It is interesting to note that when interviewed at the inquest Stride's sister reported that, "About twenty minutes past one on Sunday morning I felt a pressure on my breast and heard three distinct kisses." Was this a visit from her recently dead sister or just a bad dream?

After the doctor's report, witnesses were called forward who may have seen the killer. Among them was Police Constable William Smith who had seen Stride with a man shortly before her death.

CORONER BAXTER: Was the latter anything like the deceased?
CONSTABLE SMITH: Yes, I saw her face. I have seen the deceased in the mortuary and I feel certain it is the same person.
CORONER BAXTER: Did you see the man who was talking to her?
CONSTABLE SMITH: Yes, I noticed he had a newspaper parcel in his hand. It was about eighteen inches in length and six or eight inches in width. He was about five feet seven inches as near as I could say. He had on a hard felt deerstalker hat of dark color and dark clothes.
CORONER BAXTER: What kind of a coat was it?
CONSTABLE SMITH: An overcoat. He wore dark trousers.
CORONER BAXTER: Can you give any idea as to his age?
CONSTABLE SMITH: About twenty-eight years.
CORONER BAXTER: Can you give any idea as to what he was?
CONSTABLE SMITH: No sir, I cannot. He was of respectable appearance. I noticed the woman had a flower in her jacket.

The inquest would end on October 12 with the only conclusion possible. The jury decided that it was "Wilful murder by some person unknown."

The Whitehall Torso Mystery

Frederick Wildborn did not really trust some of the men who were working with him building the new Metropolitan Police Headquarters at New Scotland Yard. Wildborn had developed the habit of hiding his carpenter tools in dark places, out of sight, and out of other workers' minds. It was 2:20 p.m. on October 2, and Wildborn was working his way deeper and deeper into the dark and gloomy recesses of this latest construction project of Messrs. J. Grove & Sons, Ltd. As he went further in, the constant din of his fellow workers could barely be heard. From one sublevel to the next he walked down steps and through archways losing most, if not all, of the light from above, which was bright sunshine. Finally, he was only able to find his way by feeling along the wall. Finally, he came to his "nook" covered only by a board of wood. His tools were hidden inside.

It was a good hiding place in the basement archway, as it was slightly illuminated by a single stray beam of filtered sunlight. As Wildborn bent down to recover his tools he noticed again a large bundle lying near his nook — he had seen it the day before, too. He had had no time the previous day for an examination, but this time he did. Perhaps it belonged to another workman who had also found his spot? The package was large enough for him to require help in removing it, so he informed an assistant manager, Mr. Brown, of his discovery. It was two and a half feet long and two feet wide, tied with twine and wrapped in paper. They were soon carrying the heavy load into an area with better lighting, to get a better look.

On opening the bundle they discovered, to their great shock, the remains of a woman. This victim had literally been dumped in the heart of the new police headquarters. Neither man could speak for several seconds as they first stared at the remains and then at each other. Soon they recovered enough to move, as fast as they could, to the surface of the construction site in search of a constable. As reported in the *Police Chronicle* of October 6, 1888, "The prevailing opinion is that to place the body where it was found the person conveying it must have scaled the eight foot boarding which enclosed the works, and, carefully avoiding the watchman who does duty by night, must have dropped it where it was found."

Soon the site was covered with police and detectives. The authorities could quickly see that the murderer had to have made a very difficult climb in order to get over the wooden palings which encircled the construction site, then haul the torso to the depths of the building. It was by no means and easy task. Before long, the remains were removed to the mortuary on Millbank Street. Due to the advanced stage of decomposition the torso and arm were kept in alcohol until they were to be disposed of. It was at this time a photo was taken to aid in the possible identification of this latest East End victim. There the parts were examined by Dr. Thomas Bond, of A Division, and Dr. Charles Hibberd of Westminster Hospital. The remains were wrapped in a black silk woman's dress section of about two-and-a-half feet long. There was also a section of newspaper which appeared to be from the *Echo*, which was bloodstained. Dr. Bond looked at the headless and limbless torso and said, "I have an arm that will fit it !" The arm had earlier been found by some boys in the Thames River off Pimlico. It was soon discovered, by the medical men, that they indeed had a perfect match. The arm, with the hand still attached, was part of the latest victim. "Not only was the hand remarkably well shaped, but the fingers were long and taper, the fully shaped nails being carefully trimmed and kept. ...[It was] that of a person in all likelihood moving in a good position in life."

The *New York Times*—October 3, 1888
LONDON'S RECORD OF CRIME
Another Mysterious Murder Brought to Light
A Perfect Carnival of Blood in the World's Metropolis —
The Police Apparently Paralyzed
London, Oct. 2.— The carnival of blood continues. It is an extremely strange state of affairs altogether, because before the Whitechapel murders began several papers called attention to the fact that there have been more sanguinary crimes committed in London and its vicinity

this Summer than ever before known in this city in the same space of time. The Whitechapel assassin has now murdered six victims and crimes occur daily, but pass unnoticed in view of the master murderer's work in East End. A few days ago the right arm of a woman was found by some boys in the Thames near Waterloo Bridge. It belonged to a young woman, was plump, shapely and graceful, and had been rudely hacked from the shoulder. It was believed at first to be evidence of another murder, but as no young woman had been murdered, so far as known, the theory that it was a specimen from a dissecting room was generally adopted. Last week, however, another arm, corresponding to it, was found in a yard behind the asylum in Southwark, half a mile from Waterloo Bridge. The police took immediate possession of it, and refused absolutely either to give any information concerning its appearance, or to say whether it pointed to a fresh crime. ... This afternoon, however, a discovery was made in Pimlico, a mile up the river from where the arm was found, which throws some light on the mystery. ...[Some] workmen are engaged in tearing these [old buildings] down to prepare a site for the new police station. As they destroyed an old vault today they came upon a shapeless mass which, upon closer inspection, proved to be the trunk of the body of a young woman, perhaps 30 years old. The horribly mutilated head, arms, and legs had been cut off and carried away, only the trunk being left. The body was not ripped, however, as in the Whitechapel cases. It was very much decomposed, and in fact must have been there many weeks. ... Should the arms belong to the body they may serve as a clue. They seem in a much better state of preservation than the body. ... There is no clue to the identity of the murdered woman; in fact so many people disappear daily in this great city that the record of disappearances will not be of much assistance. ... No one suspected is at present in custody, though all Scotland Yard is at work on the case.

The doctors came to the conclusion that the victim had been a "very fine woman" between 25 and 30 years old who had been well nourished and stood 5'8" to 5'9". She had dark hair and fair skin, and suffered from pleurisy. (Pleurisy is an inflammation of the membrane that envelopes the lungs. It was not an uncommon problem visited on the people who lived in "the Abyss.") They also concluded that she had been murdered on or about August 20.

After the initial find the police, with the help of the workmen at the building site, continued to search the area for any more body parts. They were most interested in locating the head as the best way to aid in the identification of the victim, but it was reported that "No trace, however, of any kind was found within the area of the works, or, indeed, anywhere else in the vicinity."

On October 17, a *Central News* reporter, named Mr. Waring, received approval from the construction company, as well as the police, to bring his Spitzbergen dog to the torso dump site. Soon after they had made their way to the spot the dog began to scratch at the ground. It was soon discovered that the animal had found a leg with a "well formed foot attached." It was clearly part of the torso found earlier. What would never be found was the head.

During the inquest Dr. Neville was called, as he was the first to examine the arm which had been found in the river a few weeks earlier off Ebury Bridge. He testified that the limb he had examined had been "literally wrenched from its socket." He felt that the dissection of the arm showed "no understanding of anatomy." Finally, Dr. Bond and Dr. Troutbeck, who had both examined the remains, informed the inquest that the victim had "met with a violent death." Despite these seemingly definitive words of murder, the jury would only return a verdict of, "Found dead!"

It is easy to understand the problems in solving such cases given the conditions under which doctors had to conduct autopsies in the East End. Millbank Street mortuary was described as being "...in the yard attached to a dwelling house and shop, and it is almost devoid of the proper modern appliances. A few wooden partitions have been run up, but there is neither [sufficient] room to conduct post-mortem examinations, nor means for ensuring the most ordinary sanitation and assisting in the ready and safe identification of the dead."

It is not known if this was a Ripper related murder, but the question must be asked, just how many sexual serial killers were working the East End of London in 1888–89? It is also interesting to note that the police were very quick to discard the evidence of a murder placed right in front of them, and attempted to assign this death to some type of dissecting room specimen. This was slipshod work at best and speaks of a cover-up or at the very least a failure to do their jobs. After all, how many medical schools throw their specimens away in the River Thames? Adding to the many problems faced by those who worked these cases were the other bodies piling up in the same mortuary building. At the time the Whitehall torso was being examined there were also the bodies of a woman who had been murdered by her husband, a woman who had been killed in a boiler explosion, and a man who had hanged himself.

It is possible that this latest victim was also a prostitute, as no one came forward to attempt an identification. She must, however, have been poor, as no one seemed to care much about who she was or who killed her. Besides, the Ripper was commanding most of the attention during the Autumn of Death and no single extra body was going to change that fact, at least not for a while. Part of the coverage of this latest murder was a report which conveyed the problem the police were having with centralizing their efforts to combat crime in general. The *Police Chronicle* for October 6, 1888, reported on the building site where the torso was found. "The building which is in course of erection is the new police depot for London: the present scattered headquarters of the Metropolitan police force, and the Criminal Investigation Department in Great Scotland Yard and Whitehall Place, having been found too small for the requirements of the police system."

Another Inquest

On October 4, a second inquest began, this time into the death of Catherine Eddowes. It was conducted by Samuel Frederick Langham at the Golden Lane Mortuary. Once again, it was clear that the Ripper had struck down another woman. Doctor Frederick Brown once again testified as to the injuries. His report was very detailed and it was easy to see from his testimony the great deal of damage inflicted on Eddowes' body.

"The throat was cut across to the extent of about 6 or 7 inches. A superficial cut commenced about an inch and ½ below the lobe and about 2½ inches below behind the left ear and extended across the throat to about three inches below the lobe of the right ear. The big muscle across the throat was divided through on the left side. The large vessels on the left side of the neck were severed. The larynx was severed below the vocal cord. All the deep structure were severed to the bone, the knife marking intervertebral cartilage. The sheath of the vessels on the right side was just opened. The carotid artery had a fine hole opening. The internal jugular vein was opened an inch and a half, not divided. The blood vessels contained clot. All these injuries were performed by a sharp instrument like a knife and pointed.

"We examined the abdomen. The front walls were laid open from the breast bone to the pubes. The cut commenced opposite the ensiform cartilage. The incision went upwards, not penetrating the skin that was over the sternum. It then divided the ensiform cartilage. The knife must have cut obliquely at the expense of the front surface of that cartilage. Behind this the liver was stabbed as if by the point of a sharp instrument. Below this was another incision into the liver of about 2½ inches, and below this the left lobe of the liver was slit through by a vertical cut. Two cuts were shown by a jagging of the skin on the left side.

"The abdominal walls were divided in the middle line to within ¼ of an inch of the navel. The cut then took a horizontal course for two inches and a half towards right side. It then divided round the navel on the left

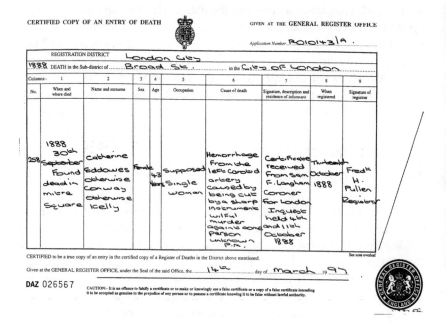

Copy of death certificate for Catherine Eddowes.

side and made a parallel incision to the former horizontal incision, leaving the navel on a tongue of skin. Attached to the navel was 2½ inches of the lower part of the rectus muscle on the left side of the abdomen. The incision then took an oblique direction to the right and was shelving. The incision went down the right side of the vagina and rectum for half an inch behind the rectum.

"There was a stab of about an inch on the left groin. This was done by a pointed instrument. Below this was a cut of three inches going through all tissues making a wound of the perineum about the same extent.

"An inch below the crease of the thigh was a cut extending from the anterior spine of the ilium obliquely down the inner side of the left thigh and separating the left labium, forming a flap of skin up to the groin. The left rectus muscle was not detached.

"There was a flap of skin formed from the right thigh attaching the right labium and extending up to the spine of the ilium. The muscles on the right side inserted into the Poupart's ligament were cut through.

"The skin was retracted through the whole of the cut in the abdomen, but the vessels were not clotted. Nor had there been any appreciable bleeding from the vessel. I draw the conclusion that the cut was made after death, and there would not be much blood on the murderer. The cut was made by someone on right side of body, kneeling below the middle of the body....

"The intestines had been detached to a large extent from the mesentery. About two feet of the colon was cut away. The sigmoid flexure was invaginated into the rectum very tightly.

"Right kidney pale, bloodless, with slight congestion of the base of the pyramids.

"There was a cut from the upper part of the slit on the under surface of the liver to the left side, and another cut at right angles to this, which were about an inch and a half deep and 2½ inches long. Liver itself was healthy.

"The gall bladder contained bile. The pancreas was cut but not through

on the side of the spinal column. 3½ inches of the lower border of the spleen by ½ an inch was attached only to the peritoneum.

"The peritoneal lining was cut through on the left side and the left kidney carefully taken out and removed. The left renal artery was cut through. I should say that someone who knew the position of the kidney must have done it. The lining membrane over the uterus was cut through. The womb was cut through horizontally, leaving a stump of ¾ of an inch. The rest of the womb had been taken away with some of the ligaments. The vagina and cervix of the womb was [*sic*] uninjured.

"The bladder was healthy and uninjured, and contained 3 or 4 ounces of water. There was a tongue-like cut through the anterior wall of the abdominal aorta. The other organs were healthy. There were no indications of connection.

"The face was very much mutilated. There was a cut about ¼ of an inch through the lower left eyelid dividing the structures completely through. The upper eyelid on that side, there was a scratch through the skin on the left upper eyelid near to the angle of the nose. The right eyelid was cut through to about ½ an inch. There was a deep cut over the bridge of the nose extending from the left border of the nasal bone

Top and bottom: Catherine Eddowes. (Public Record Office.)

down near to the angle of the jaw on the right side across the cheek. This cut went into the bone and divided all the structures of the cheek except the mucous membrane of the mouth. The tip of the nose was quite detached from the nose by an oblique cut from the bottom of the nasal bone to where the wings of the nose join on to the face. A cut from this divided the upper lip and extended through the substance of the gum over the right upper lateral incisor tooth. About ½ an inch from the top of the nose was another oblique cut. There was a cut on the right angle of the mouth, as if by the cut of a point of a knife. The cut extended an inch and a half parallel with lower lip. There was on each side of cheek a cut which peeled up the skin forming a triangular flaps about an inch and a half. On the left cheek there were two abrasions of the epithelium. There was a little mud on left cheek. Two slight abrasions of the epithelium under the left ear."

This was the first time the face had been a target of the Ripper. It could show that his anger was growing as he combined his attacks.

Despite the many wounds and mutilations inflicted, Doctor Brown felt that only one man was involved and that he had worked on her corpse where she was found. More importantly, to understand the background of the killer, Dr. Brown added, "I should say that someone who knew the position of the kidney must have done it.... I believe the perpetrator of the act must have had considerable knowledge of the position of the organs in the abdominal cavity and the way of removing them.... It required a great deal of knowledge to have removed the kidney and to know where it was placed." Dr. Brown, a respected surgeon and a powerful Freemason, who had been Grand Officer of England's Grand Lodge, did not want to report that only medical men would have this knowledge, so he made it known that slaughtermen or others could have the required skill to do the job. But was this what he truly believed or was he making a knee jerk reaction to the very real possibility that a fellow doctor or surgeon was responsible for these deaths? This question will be debated for a very long time. The bottom line from the examination was his report that, "It required a great deal of knowledge," both in surgical as well as anatomical areas. Only one realistic suspect fills those requirements and he is Severin Klosowski who had the documented skills.

"He performed his surgical functions with full knowledge of the subject."

D. Moshkovski

The *New York Times*— October 5, 1888
The Whitechapel Murders
London, Oct. 4 — The British Medical Journal, referring to the White-chapel murders says: The Coroner's theory that the assassin's work was carried out under the impulse of a pseudo scientific mania has been exploded by the first attempt at serious investigation. It is true that a foreign physician inquired a year ago as to the possibility of securing certain parts of the body for the purpose of scientific investigation, but no large sum was offered, and the physician in question is of the high-est respectability and came exceedingly well accredited.

This was the second or third murder in the series, depending on which observer was referenced, which required the killer to have anatomical knowledge and surgical skills. And yet the police, as well as some medical men at the time, refused to believe that they were dealing with a trained surgeon, despite the fact that the organs were removed with skill and great speed and in very low light. Chief Inspector Donald Swanson reported to the inquest that, "The surgeon, Dr. Brown, called by the City Police, and Dr. Phillips, who had been called by the Metropolitan Police in the cases of Hanbury Street and Berner Street, having made a postmortem examina-tion of the body, reported that there were missing the left kidney and the uterus, and that the mutilation so far gave no evidence of anatomical knowl-edge in the sense that it evidenced the hand of a qualified surgeon.... On the other hand, as in the Metropolitan Police cases, the medical evidence showed that the murder could have been committed by a person who had been a hunter, a butcher, a slaughterman, as well as a student in surgery or a properly qualified surgeon."

The mutilations were very possibly committed to cover up any skills possessed by the killer, which is exactly what he seems to have been able to accomplish. However, his pride would not allow him to do an unskilled job as witnessed by the skills required to remove the left kidney, cleanly and in conditions of extremely low light. It must also be remembered that there was the added stress of potentially being discovered at any moment. The mutilations came only after he had completed his work.

It was obvious, in both inquests, that these were murders, and the authorities had no solid clues pointing to any one suspect. However, it is interesting to note that during the Eddowes inquest, City of London solic-itor, Henry H. Crawford, acting on behalf of the police, requested that Joseph Lawende's detailed description of a man seen with Catherine Eddowes near Mitre Square be withheld. The only explanation the well known Freemason would offer was, "I have special reason for not giving details as to the appearance of this man." Was he providing the world a clue that the man seen, possibly the Ripper, was a Freemason and well known? Whatever the reason, it was clear that once again the Ripper had outfoxed the authorities. But it was becoming more and more difficult to do so. "Committed by person or persons unknown."

> The *Weekly Herald*—October 5, 1888
> The fiendish work of the man to whose account must be credited the six or seven recent brutal murders and mutilations that have put London, and Whitechapel especially, into a white terror, still goes on, and at the moment of writing the hand of justice seems as far as ever from paralyzing the onward course of the record of atrocious brutality. ... These murders have drawn men's minds with peculiar intensity to a consideration of the conditions under which so many people exist not only in the East End of the huge metropolis, but in all the large towns of the country. The horrible dens of vice and crime that blot the fair face of our most thriving communities, are whatever else may be said of them, crying impeachments of the indifference and carelessness with which those in responsible positions, both governmental and social, look upon their less fortunate fellow men. ... The wretched and abandoned frequenters of the streets fled in terror to their miserable shelters, and by half-past two not a woman was to be seen throughout the densely populated district.

As the search went on it was reported that members of the police forces on patrol duty were starting to place rubber on the taps of their boots to cut down on the noise they made as they walked their beats. It had been noted that the Ripper was able to walk very softly as well. More and more officers were being transferred to the killing fields, as the authorities saturated the East End. Most believed that they would be hearing from the Ripper again, and very soon.

These men hunting the killer knew by now that they were looking for a loner. He was a man who was extremely bold in his actions and skilled at avoiding detection. He had never given the authorities a solid clue to his identity, but his actions were coming into clear focus. These were not random murders on strangers; these were directed killings, only visited on prostitutes, and only those living in a tiny area some 200 by 400 yards. And he was terribly close. It was easily possible that the Ripper was interviewed on several occasions, and he must have enjoyed each and every one. But with all of the manpower being deployed in search of one man, could he once again test the limits? Could he risk another kill?

> *East End News*—October 5, 1888
> The marvellous inefficiency of the police in the detection was forcibly shown in the fact that in the very same block as that containing Mitre

Square, in the great leading thoroughfare, and at a moment when the whole area was full of police just after the murder, the Aldgate Post Office was entered and ransacked, and property to the value of hundreds of pounds taken clean away under the very noses of the "guardians of peace and order!"

Writing in *I Caught Crippen* some 50 years after the Ripper murders began, Inspector Dew lamented, "I have always thought that the higher police authorities in ignoring the power of the press deliberately flouted a great potential ally, and indeed might have turned that ally into an enemy."

Chapter Six

A Letter from Hell, as the Ripper Lies Low

"I regretted that day ever since I have stopped in this country."

Severin Klosowski

On that cold Saturday morning of October 6, 1888, Elizabeth Stride was buried in a pauper's grave in the East London Cemetery, Plaistow, London. Very few people attended her service as she was laid to rest in grave number 15509, square 37. That would not be the case on October 8, when Catherine Eddowes went to her grave. Eddowes was one of their own. The cortege left the mortuary in Golden Lane at 1:30 p.m., surrounded by a very large crowd. In the area of the mortuary, the streets, windows, and rooftops, were packed with onlookers as the elm coffin was taken to the cemetery. As John Kelly and Catherine Eddowes' four sisters, Emma, Eliza, Harriet and Elizabeth followed the carriage, crowds followed behind them.

The London *Observer* reported that "the footway was lined on either side of the road with persons who were packed in rows five deep, the front row extending into the roadway. Manifestation(s) of sympathy were everywhere visible, many among the crowd uncovering their heads as the hearse passed." By 3:30 p.m., the group had made its way to City of London Cemetery at Manor Park where hundreds gathered for the service, which was performed by Reverend T. Dunscombe, chaplain of the cemetery. The people of Whitechapel, from all walks of life, were coming together. Many witnessed her interment in grave number 49336, square 318. Eddowes' grave was just a few steps from where Polly Nichols had been buried a few short weeks earlier.

With the many reports and rumors coming in, it was not always easy to separate fact from fiction as reported in the newspapers of the day. One such example is a report from the *New York Times*.

> The *New York Times*—October 12, 1888
> THE WHITECHAPEL MURDER MYSTERIES
> London, Oct. 12 — The Pall Mall Gazette charges that the words "I have murdered four and I will murder 16 before I surrender myself to the police," written by the supposed Whitechapel murderer upon a shutter of a house adjoining the one in the yard of which the body of one of his victims was found, were erased by order of Sir Charles Warren, chief of the London police force, before the authorities had an opportunity of photographing them.

Of course the report of Sir Charles erasing a message was correct, but it was the imagination of the *Pall Mall Gazette* reporters which created this mysterious and fully imaginary message, as well as its location. With most of the East End looking for the Ripper it made logical sense for him to stay out of sight. Many serial killers continue their activities only as long as they feel comfortable and secure doing so. The thrill of the chase is one thing but being caught is another thing entirely. They will slow down or change their methods or timing if they truly feel that capture is a real possibility. However, logic was not the order of the day. This man thrilled to the excitement of the chase almost to the exclusion of every other consideration. Although he had no intention of being caught, he was not concerned with raising the stakes and increasing the risk which he was feeding off of.

He wanted to prove that he could not only beat the police but could outsmart the many vigilance committees as well. Additionally, the Ripper was not about to allow anyone else the opportunity to claim credit for his work. The Whitechapel Killer was about to send a major clue to the very men who were nightly trying to catch him. It would be sent to George Lusk, Chairman of the Mile End Vigilance Committee. Lusk had lately become concerned with his own safety. Just before he received his "package," he requested police protection. He had reported that he was being watched by a bearded man he described as "sinister!" Could this have been Jack in disguise? Perhaps he wanted some type of contact, face-to-face, with Lusk, before he trusted him with one of his prize possessions?

On October 7, Lusk had requested that a pardon be granted to anyone with knowledge of the murders, other than the killer himself of course. Police Commissioner Warren liked the idea and passed it along to the Home

Secretary, Henry Matthews, but Matthews rejected the plan. Once again, but perhaps not too surprisingly, the public were well ahead of the government when it came to inventive ideas.

The small, brown paper–wrapped package arrived on the evening of October 16, at 1 Alderney Road, Mile End, even though there was no street number written on the package. It had been mailed locally from the East End or nearby. Inside was half a human kidney and a blood stained letter from the man who had sent it. The quickly written letter read:

> From hell
>
> Mr Lusk
>   Sor
>   I send you half the
> Kidne I took from one woman
> prasarved it for you t other piece I
> fried and ate it was very nise I
> may send you the bloody knif that
> took it out if you only wate a whil
> longer
>   Signed Catch me when
>   you can
>   Mishter Lusk

As he thought that it may have been some kind of a bad joke, "Mishter Lusk" did not bring his new acquisition directly to the police. Instead, he waited and took both items the next evening to the regular meeting of the vigilance committee, held at the Crown public house on Mile End Road. Earlier, Lusk had received other letters from "the Ripper," which he had ignored, but this was something different. Showing the item to the committee treasurer, Joseph Aarons, he said, "I suppose you will laugh at what I am going to tell you but you must know that I had a little parcel come to me on Tuesday evening, and to my surprise it contains half a kidney and a letter from Jack the Ripper." At first Aarons laughed thinking that Lusk was trying to play some kind of a joke to get a reaction. He soon saw that Lusk was not joking and suggested that the matter be looked at by more of the committee members the next day. Neither man, however, thought to bring the box, and its contents, to the police at the time. Considering the seriousness of the matter one would have expected speed in bringing the police into the act. Their delay in contacting the authorities has never been explained.

The morning of October 18 found Joseph Aarons and three other committee members visiting George Lusk's home. When they arrived he went to his desk and removed the small, bloodied, three-and-a-half-inch square box, and gave it to them. He had gotten very tired of having it around and he told the other members to "Throw it away, I hate the sight of it!"

The men decided that a medical opinion was called for, so the package was taken to 56 Mile End Road; the surgery of Doctor Frederick Wiles. The doctor was not in his surgery when the men arrived but they were able to show the kidney to his assistant, Mr. Reed. Reed informed the group that the kidney was indeed human and further, that it had been preserved in wine. That would not have been expected if this were a medical sample that someone had used as a bad joke. He felt, though, that a second opinion was warranted, so he went over to London Hospital, a short distance away, and showed the kidney to the Curator of the Pathological Museum, Doctor Thomas Horrocks Openshaw. Dr. Openshaw was a well known and respected member of the hospital staff and his opinion carried a great deal of weight. Dr. Openshaw examined the organ closely under a microscope and, according to Joseph Aarons, reported that it "belonged to a female, that it was part of the left kidney, and that the woman had been in the habit of drinking. He should think that the person had died about the same time the Mitre Square murder was committed."

The *Star* reported a slightly different story on October 19 when it printed an interview with Dr. Openshaw. "Dr. Openshaw told a *Star* reporter today that after having examined the piece of kidney under a microscope he was of opinion that it was half of a left human kidney. He couldn't say, however, whether it was that of a woman, nor how long ago it had been removed from the body, as it had been preserved in spirits." At that point it was clear the time had come to bring the police into the case. The kidney and letter were taken to the Leman Street Police Station and delivered to none other than Inspector Frederick Abberline. From there, the kidney was sent by Abberline to Dr. Gordon Brown, the city police surgeon, who had already become familiar with the Ripper murders. For many years, Dr. Brown's report was lost and what remained was the Home Office report of Inspector McWilliam as given by Chief Inspector Swanson.

Swanson reported that "the result of the combined medical opinion they [the city police] have taken upon it, is, that it is the kidney of a human adult, not charged with a fluid, as it would have been in the case of a body handed over for purposes of dissection to an hospital, but rather as it would be in a case where it was taken from the body not so destined." When Dr. Brown's report was recovered, many years later, it stated that the liver remaining in the victim's [Eddowes] body was "pale bloodless, with a slight congestion at the base of the pyramid," these conditions all pointing to Bright's Disease.

It should be noted that Doctor Sedgwick Saunders, then working as the city pathologist, felt that upon first view, the kidney was not from Catherine Eddowes. He felt that it was probably a hospital specimen, but he was unable to explain the source of this "hospital specimen," and no one else was ever able to do so either.

Adding to the evidence, albeit 20 years later, as written in his book, *From Constable to Commissioner*, was Major Henry Smith, then acting Commissioner of City Police at the time of the murders. He wrote that the consulting surgeons reported, "The renal artery is about three inches long. Two inches remained in the corpse [Catherine Eddowes], one inch was attached to the kidney. The kidney left in the corpse was in an advanced stage of Bright's Disease; the kidney sent to me was in an exactly similar state." (In fact, Eddowes would probably have died within a year because of her condition if her life had not been cut even shorter by the Ripper.) "[Senior Surgeon Dr. Henry Sutton] said he would pledge his reputation that the kidney submitted to them had been put in spirits within a few hours of its removal from the body — this effectually disposing of all hoaxes in connection with it. The body of anyone done to death by violence is not taken direct to the dissecting room, but must await an inquest, never held before the following day at the soonest."

The overall meaning was clear. The kidney sent to George Lusk *was* taken from a woman who had recently been murdered. It was then placed in a container of wine or similar alcoholic substance. It could not have come from *any* other source. The question must be asked: How many women in the London area had been murdered in the previous two weeks and had their left kidneys removed after death, with one inch of renal artery still attached? The answer was one. The inch of renal artery left attached to the Lusk kidney corresponded with what remained in the body of Catherine Eddowes. And this information about the artery was *not*, at the time, printed in any published reports.

Finally, the fact that the Lusk kidney had Bright's Disease — as did the right kidney remaining in the murdered woman's body — leaves only one logical conclusion. There was no local source of a kidney which matched the one sent to George Lusk, other than the body of Catherine Eddowes. The kidney was sent by Jack the Ripper to show that his note to Lusk was real because no one else had taken any body parts from Eddowes or could deliver same. No other individual could have sent the note. The Ripper was trying to preclude some other letter writer taking the credit for his work. And this was the only way he could prove it was him writing, without walking right up to the authorities and handing them a sample of his work. The police now had a copy of his handwriting.

The Lusk letter, since lost by Scotland Yard, was examined by C.M.

MacLeod, a Canadian graphologist. As reported in *The Jack the Ripper, A to Z*, he "indicated the writer was aged 20 to 45." MacLeod further stated: "rudimentary education; possibly a heavy drinker; cockily self-confident ... showed a mind with vicious drive, great cunning, the capability of conceiving and carrying out any atrocity, and enough brains to hold down a steady job and mask his personality." In other words, the letter was not a hoax, and these were some of the many traits which can be found in the mind of a serial killer surely including Jack the Ripper. The term "catch me when you can" instead of "if" also displays a lack of understanding of English, possibly by someone who is relatively new to the language. It should also be noted that the writer of the letter did not use the name Jack the Ripper, as most of the phony letters had.

The Ripper murders also presented a forum for reformers to be heard loudly, whereas before their voices were barely a whisper in the ears of most. One of the better known East End religious reformers was Reverend Samuel Augustus Barnett, Rector of St. Judes, Whitechapel. He and his wife had been in the center of Whitechapel since 1873. He wrote often to the press during the Ripper series to suggest that the rich should pay for better street lighting in the East End, and purchase some of the slum property and build cheap but clean housing for the poor of Whitechapel and Spitalfields. Interestingly, his cries were not for the police to put an end to the killings by capturing the Ripper; rather, he felt the police would best spend their time working on vice in the "Wicked quarter-mile" that consisted of Flower and Dean, Thrawl, and Dorset streets. It would seem that saving souls was of greater importance to the good reverend than the saving of lives. He even felt that charity caused poverty, "because of the alms they [the poor] receive." In the end, his letters and words did nothing to bring about the capture of this killer, or for that matter better conditions in the East End. However, The 4 Percent Dwelling Company did purchase some of the more dilapidated sections of Flower and Dean Street on the northeast side, and by 1892 had built Nathaniel Dwellings. These consisted of 170 apartments which could house 800 people. Of course, they made only a slight dent in the dire need for housing in the area.

While the police were conducting their Ripper related searches, mainly between Middlesex Street and Brick Lane, Commissioner Warren was attempting to explain why he had the Goulston Street graffiti erased. The many radical papers of the day were quick to seize upon the series of murders to discredit the Home Secretary and attack the police forces for their activities against Irish Nationalists fighting for their rights. They were also against the firm measures taken by the police during demonstrations by the unemployed and socialist agitators. The radical press, led by the *Star* and

Pall Mall Gazette, were well into their campaigns against the government and Metropolitan Police when the Ripper appeared on the scene. These papers were using the murders to stir up the population. It was a tool their editors could not resist.

In a confidential letter to the Under Secretary of State for the Home Office Warren wrote:

4 Whitehall Place, S.W.

Confidential   6th November 1888

The Under Secretary of State
The Home Office
Sir,

In reply to your letter of the 5th instant, I enclose a report of the circumstances of the Mitre Square Murder so far as they have come under the notice of the Metropolitan Police, and I now give an account regarding the erasing the writing on the wall in Goulston Street which I have already partially explained to Mr. Matthews verbally.

On the 30th September on hearing of the Berner Street murder, after visiting Commercial Street Station I arrived at Leman Street Station shortly before 5 am and ascertained from the Superintendent Arnold all that was known there relative to the two murders.

The most pressing question at that moment was some writing on the wall in Goulston Street evidently written with the intention of inflaming the public mind against the Jews, and which Mr. Arnold with a view to prevent serious disorder proposed to obliterate, and had sent down an Inspector with a sponge for that purpose, telling him to await his arrival.

I considered it desirable that I should decide the matter myself, as it was one involving so great a responsibility whether any action was taken or not.

I accordingly went down to Goulston Street at once before going to the scene of the murder: it was just getting light, the public would be in the streets in a few minutes, in a neighbourhood very much crowded on Sunday mornings by Jewish vendors and Christian purchasers from all parts of London.

There were several Police around the spot when I arrived, both Metropolitan and City.

The writing was on the jamb of the open arch way or doorway visible in the street and could not be covered up without danger of the covering being torn off at once.

A discussion took place whether the writing could be left covered up or otherwise or whether any portion of it could be left for an hour until it could be photographed; but after taking into consideration the excited state of the population in London generally at the time, the strong feeling which had been excited against the Jews, and the fact that in a short time there would be a large concourse of the people in the streets, and having before me the Report that if it was left there the house was likely to be wrecked (in which from my own observation I entirely concurred) I considered it desirable to obliterate the writing at once, having taken a copy of which I enclose a duplicate.

After having been to the scene of the murder, I went on to the City Police Office and informed the Chief Superintendent of the reason why the writing had been obliterated.

I may mention that so great was the feeling with regard to the Jews that on the 13th ultimo, the Acting Chief Rabbi wrote to me on the subject of the spelling of the word "Jewes" on account of a newspaper asserting that this was Jewish spelling in the Yiddish dialect. He added "in the present state of excitement it is dangerous to the safety of the poor Jews in the East (End) to allow such an assertion to remain uncontradicted. My community keenly appreciates your humane and vigilant action during this critical time."

It may be realized therefore if the safety of the Jews in Whitechapel could be considered to be jeopardized 13 days after the murder by the question of the spelling of the word Jews, what might have happened to the Jews in that quarter had that writing been left intact.

I do not hesitate myself to say that if that writing had been left there would have been an onslaught upon the Jews, property would have been wrecked, and lives would probably have been lost; and I was much gratified with the promptitude with which Superintendent Arnold was prepared to act in the matter if I had not been there.

I have no doubt myself whatever that one of the principal objects of the Reward offered by Mr. Montagu was to show to the world that the Jews were desirous of having the Hanbury Street Murder cleared up, and thus to divert from them the very strong feeling which was then growing up.

I am, Sir,

Your most obedient Servant
[signed] C. Warren

Three weeks after the message was erased, and after a great deal of pressure, mostly unrelated to the Ripper case, Sir Charles Warren resigned.

There was a very real possibility that the inability of the Government to bring an end to the Ripper murders would do more than cost the jobs of a few ministers. When the members of Parliament again came back into session a vote of no confidence could bring about the resignation of the prime minister himself. As reported in the *New York Times* of October 7, 1888: "If it should happen when Parliament meets that the strange assassin is still undiscovered, or if more of these horrible crimes be committed and the perpetrator is tracked by outsiders, there would be a storm of indignation let loose in St. Stephen's under which certainly Mr. Matthews and very possibly his associates would go down. It seems odd enough to an American mind to wreck an imperial Government because an abnormal sort of criminal killed some women in the slums and escaped detection, but this is one of the risks of a system which gives executive powers to certain members of the majority party in Parliament and places their tenure of office at the mercy of a yea or nay vote. The House of Commons does not like or respect its police, and the Home Secretary is responsible for the police. ... [B]ut unless the Whitechapel scandal is cleared up before November and the Government unloads Mr. Matthews he is likely to be condemned by a majority so heavy as to discredit and destroy the whole Ministry."

Ladies' groups were also beginning to be heard. Mrs. Henrietta Barnett, representing a group called The Women of East London, sent a petition to Queen Victoria with over 4000 signatures. This social reformer, and wife of Reverend Samuel Barnett, was requesting that the Queen intervene in the East End herself by asking the police to close all of the brothels.

> To our Most Gracious Sovereign Lady Queen Victoria
> Madam — We, the women of East London, feel horror at the dreadful sins that have been lately committed in our midst and grief because of the shame that has fallen on our neighbourhood.
> By the facts which have come out in the inquests, we have learnt much of the lives of those of our sisters who have lost a firm hold on goodness and who are living sad and degraded lives.
> While each woman of us will do all she can to make men feel with horror the sins of impurity which cause such wicked lives to be led, we would also beg that your Majesty will call on your servants in authority and bid them put the law which already exists in motion to close bad houses within whose walls such wickedness is done and men and women ruined in body and soul.
> We are, Madam, your loyal and humble servants.

It would be the good reverend himself who would comment about what "good" could come from these murders when he said, "The Whitechapel horrors will not be in vain if at last the public conscience awakes to consider the life which these horrors reveal."

By October 9, another citizen's group called the Workingmen's Vigilance Committee, which had held its meetings at the Three Tuns public house in Aldgate, had developed 57 separate patrols in an attempt to locate the killer. Jack the Ripper may not have been on the run but the pressure of the increased patrols seemed to have kept him off the streets, as his next murder would not occur until nearly six weeks had passed, and that would be inside.

In mid–October, as a dense, coal-smoke–filled fog moved through parts of London, including the East End, it was becoming apparent that the terror on the night streets had also affected business in the area. Trade in the East End had dropped 50 percent and jobs would be lost, unless something was done, and done soon. To that end, 200 businessmen in Whitechapel, led by Samuel Montagu, wrote to the Home Secretary asking him to increase the number of police assigned to the area. He wrote, "The universal feeling prevalent in our midst is that the government no longer ensures the security of life and property in East London and that, in consequence, respectable people fear to go out shopping, thus depriving us of our means of livelihood." One look at London's East End in the 1880s would have easily confirmed that fact, with or without the Ripper.

Montagu's words would soon find their way to the authorities. He was, after all, the MP (Member of Parliament) for Whitechapel and was well respected. He would later become Lord Swaythling. The government was now slowly coming to the combined conclusion that something dramatic needed to be done.

It was during this period, just after the "double event," that a radical plan was developed. It was decided that a section of the East End would be searched completely. But the cooperation of each resident would be required if it was to be successful, since such a wholesale search would be illegal without warrants issued by the courts. It was unlikely that a blanket warrant would be issued, and martial law would have seemed excessive. Earlier, on October 4, the former Lord Mayor of London, Sir John Ellis, wrote to the Home Office to suggest a section of the East End be "cordoned off" for a massive search by whatever means necessary. He wanted no one in, and no one out, until the search was completed. Commissioner Warren was ready to conduct such an operation and wrote, "I am quite prepared to take the responsibility of adopting the most drastic or arbitrary measures that the Secretary of State can name which would further the securing of the murderer, however illegal they may be, provided H M Govt. will support me." Warren had informed the highest levels of government that it was time for them to put themselves on the record in support of this most remarkable effort.

By October 13, the unprecedented search operation had begun. The search area was bounded by the Central City of London on the west; Albert Street, Dunk Street, Chicksand Street and Great Garden Street on the east; by Whitechapel Road on the south; by Lamb Street, Commercial Street, The Great Eastern Railway and Buxton Street on the north. Much to the delight and surprise of the authorities almost everyone in the affected area cooperated. Excluding of course the Ripper, who was indeed living within the search area.

On October 18, Charles Warren reported, "With few exceptions the inhabitants of all classes and creeds have freely fallen in with the proposal, and have materially assisted the officers engaged in carrying it out." In a mostly immigrant population, and one suspicious of police, the cooperation was remarkable. The *Star*, the radical newspaper which rarely published articles in favor of police actions, was quick to note: "The failure of the police to discover the Whitechapel murderer is certainly not due to inactivity. No one who has had occasion to visit the police officers whence the investigations are being conducted can escape the impression that everybody is on the move, and it is probably a fact that very few of the chief officials and detectives have had their regular rest since last Sunday morning. One hears no complaint against the demand for extra duty, except in instances where the pressure is unevenly applied, for the police are individually more interested in the capture of the murderer than anyone else."

The operation was finished by October 18. It did not uncover any evidence of the killer, but it did prove to have a quieting effect on the general East End population, which may have been the primary reason for the search in the first place. Here, in the population's point of view, was a police action they could understand and support. It was visible evidence that at least some type of grand effort was being made on their behalf. But was the Ripper still living or working in the area?

Sir Robert Anderson reflected on the search effort in his 1910 memoirs, *The Lighter Side of My Official Life*. "One did not need to be a Sherlock Holmes to discover that the criminal was a sexual maniac of a virulent type; that he was living in the immediate vicinity of the scenes of the murders; and that, if he was not living absolutely alone, his people knew of his guilt, and refused to give him up to justice. During my absence abroad the police had made a house-to-house search for him, investigating the case of every man in the district whose circumstances were such that he could go and come and get rid of his blood-stains in secret. And the conclusion we came to was that he and his people were low-class Jews. ... In saying that he was a Polish Jew I am merely stating a definitely ascertained fact. And my words are meant to specify race, not religion. For it would outrage all religious sentiment to talk of the religion of a loathsome creature whose utterly unmentionable vices reduced him to a lower level than that of the brute."

Be that as it may, it really does not make any sense for any group, no matter what their beliefs, to allow an individual to continue murdering people in such a small area in which they lived. If he was known to "his people" it makes logical sense that they would find some way to prevent him from continuing to kill women under their very noses. After all, they would have known him, by then, to be an insane serial killer. At any time he could begin killing them as well.

The Police Gazette— October 19, 1888
At 12:35 a.m., 30th September, with Elizabeth Stride, found murdered
at 1 a.m., same date, in Berner — street — A MAN, age 28, height 5 ft
8 in., complexion dark, small dark moustache; dress, black diagonal
coat, hard felt hat, collar and tie; respectable appearance. Carried a
parcel wrapped up in newspaper.
    At 12:45 a.m., 30th, with same woman, in Berner — street — A MAN,
age about 30, height 5 ft 5 in., complexion fair, hair dark, small brown
moustache, full face, broad shoulders; dress, dark jacket and trousers,
black cap with peak.
    At 1:35 a.m., 30th September, with Catherine Eddowes, in Church —
passage, leading to Mitre — square, where she was found murdered at
1:45 a.m., same date — A MAN, age 30, height 5 ft 7 or 8 in., complexion fair, moustache fair, medium build; dress, pepper-and-salt
colour loose jacket, grey cloth cap with peak of same material, reddish
neckerchief tied in knot; appearance of a sailor.
Information to be forwarded to the Metropolitan
Police Office, Great Scotland — yard, London, S.W.

A Time to Move?

Public outcry, massive house-to-house searches, added police, vigilance committees, rewards, and hundreds of patrols, were perhaps starting
to show results. Whatever the reason, the Ripper knew that he would have
to lie low for at least a few weeks. Also, with all the search activities going
on, the Ripper had another problem to be concerned with — body parts.
The Ripper, as with many serial killers, was a collector. Many collect some
piece of clothing, or other article, so the experiences of the kills can be
relived at a later date. If the Ripper was going to keep his trophies now
would be the time to move them to a safer location, before one of the constables stumbled upon them.
    The 1889 *Post Office Directory of London (Kelly's Office Directory of Lon-
don)* lists an address for Severin Klosowski as 126 Cable Street, St. George-
in-the-East. The reference can be dated to early 1889, but that is only a
starting point. It was an address in an area of the East End of London not
known for being particularly safe. It ran parallel to Pinchin Street and just
south. Pinchin Street was known as "dark lane," and was, at the time, uninhabited, but it would soon be the scene of *yet another murder only yards
from Klosowski's new front door.* As he moved, it seems, so did the murders.
There are *no* documents which are known to have survived to indicate
exactly when he moved from his lodgings at George Yard Buildings to the
barber-hairdresser's shop on Cable Street. However, with such a long break

in the murder series, and massive searches in his general area, the logical time to move would have been in early October 1888. It was an interesting place to relocate to, as a section of Cable Street had recently been declared "unfit for human habitation" by the Metropolitan Board. It was described as dilapidated, dirty, and overflowing with filth.

The argument can be made, but not conclusively, that the 1889 directory was compiled and possibly even printed in 1888. Yet, what month would the directory have been finalized? Surely not in the early or even mid-point of the year. The most logical conclusion would place its completion at the very end of the year so as to make it as up-to-date as possible for 1889 usage. And that fits in very nicely with a move by Klosowski during the latter part of 1888. It should also be remembered that there is no listing for Klosowski in the 1888 directory which would probably have been compiled in late 1887.

It would have taken Klosowski time to find a new home, to hide his "work samples," and to plan new escape routes for his next killing. The Lusk letter shows signs of a man on the run, or at least one who was busy moving his base of operations: "if you only wate a whil longer Signed Catch me when you can." Was he telling the head of this vigilance committee that he would need time before once again communicating, because he needed to move? The letter was *written and mailed* during the search operations, so it is a good possibility.

In a series of narratives titled *Chronicles of Crime* (apparently lost), written by Dr. Thomas Dutton, who lived in the Whitechapel area, it was reportedly written that the then 32-year-old Dr. Dutton knew Inspector Abberline at the time of the Ripper murders. The work is reported to have stated that the good inspector would, at times, go to Dutton's home for advice on the case, of both a medical and personal nature. Tom Cullen in his work *When London Walked in Terror* has written that Dutton "...was a close crony of Inspector Abberline." It is further reported that Abberline suspected Severin Klosowski of being the Ripper as early as 1888, but could bring no proof forward to convict him in a court of law. However, without any other references, or the rediscovery of the work itself, it must be left as an interesting side story, as yet unproven.

By this time a great deal of information was coming in from the public. They were much more willing to cooperate with the police than usually was the case. With rewards being offered, many people came forward with statements, all of which had to be checked out, but for the most part they were of no value. Men were, however, being picked up on suspicion, which was having a marked effect on regular criminal activity. On October 19, Chief Inspector Swanson reported that 80 people had been detained at

Metropolitan Police Stations and some 300 others had been investigated. He further stated that "The absence of motives which lead to violence and of any scrap of evidence either direct or circumstantial, left the police without the slightest shadow of a trace."

Officers were being sent to all of London's lunatic asylums. These men were checking on any individuals who had recently been released or admitted. Commissioner Warren, himself a powerful and well known Freemason, who had founded the Quatuor Coronate Lodge Number 2076 in 1884, was even looking into the possibility that the deaths were part of some ritual, played out by a secret society. On October 12, Warren wrote a memo to the Home Office in which he stated, "As Mr. Matthews is aware I have for some time past been inclined to the idea that the [murders] having been done by a secret society is the only logical solution to the question, but I could not understand them being done because the last murders were done by someone desiring to bring discredit on the Jews and Socialists or the Jewish Socialists." And of course, all butchers and slaughtermen were being carefully investigated. It was becoming a huge task to keep track of all of the inquires. The Ripper, it would seem, would be lost in the details.

Many medical professionals thought the killer had medical knowledge or training, so officials began to look closely at the medical schools and hospitals. The nearby London Hospital, on Whitechapel Road, came under close investigation because it was the closest hospital to the Ripper area. Several students were actually detained for questioning. In 1959 94-year-old Dr. D.G. Halsted published his book *Doctor in the Nineties*. He commented on the Ripper investigation when he wrote, "Naturally those of us at the London Hospital were in the limelight. ... On more than one occasion I became aware that I was being shadowed by the plain-clothes men.... I must be the only man living to have been suspected of being Jack the Ripper." He had been at the hospital since 1884 as an intern. He was only 23 years old when the Ripper was most active which would suggest, despite descriptions to the contrary, the police were looking for a younger man. Perhaps it was luck, or good prior planning, that kept the surgically trained Klosowski from working at a major hospital within walking distance of his lodgings. If this was the case he had played his cards correctly. The investigating officers would not find 22-year-old Junior Surgeon Klosowski at Whitechapel Hospital.

It was also considered a possibility by some that if the Ripper's targets were no longer accessible perhaps this would end his killing spree. The authorities, after all they had done, still did not have a motive for the killings. So this was as good as any other idea. With that proposal in mind, the new head of CID, Dr. Robert Anderson, wrote in his memoirs, "I went on to say that the measures I found scandalous; for these wretched women were plying their trade under definite police protection. Let the police of that district, I urged, receive orders to arrest every known street woman found on the prowl after midnight, or else let us warn them that the police will not protect them." Even with many additional uniformed and plain-clothes detectives patrolling Whitechapel, it could hardly have passed as protection for the "wretched women." Indeed, Anderson passed along the word that prostitutes could not expect to be protected by the police as long as they continued to conduct their street activities. He failed to grasp the concept that for many of these women it was not a choice but a matter of survival which kept them on the streets. He was later quoted as saying, "No amount of silly hysterics could alter the fact that these crimes were a cause of danger only to a particular section of a small and definite class of women, in a limited district of the East End; and that the inhabitants of the metrop-olis generally were just as secure during the weeks the fiend was on the prowl, as they were before the mania seized him...."

Even the military wanted to get into the search for the killer. Colonel Sir Alfred Kirby, commander of the Tower Hamlets Battalion, Royal Engi-neers, offered the services of 50 soldiers from his unit. The offer was not accepted. Involving the military would not have been politically advanta-geous, and would have been seen as repression by the residents of the East End. However, if these men were put on single point duty in civilian clothes perhaps they could have been of some help. For now, at least, it seemed the Ripper had gone to ground.

More Ripper Rewards

Finally, convinced that help from other sources was required, Com-missioner Warren, on October 6, wrote to Home Secretary Matthews urg-ing a free pardon and a reward of £5000. "[If] other murders of a similar nature take place shortly ... the omission of the offer of a reward on the part of the government may exercise a very serious effect upon the stabil-ity of the government itself." Warren was becoming frustrated at the lack of progress in the case, and the Home Office was being ridiculed in the press on a daily bases.

On October 7, George Lusk once again pressed the government for action on the series of murders plaguing the East End. The Mile End Vigi-lance Committee members were the most persistent of the many groups and individuals writing the government requesting that rewards be offered. In a new letter to the Home Office he once again asked that an official government reward be offered to anyone who could name the killer. He also asked that a pardon be given to anyone who had aided the killer, but was not directly responsible for these deaths. In his letter he stated "...that the present series of murders is absolutely unique in the annals of crime, that the cunning, astuteness and determination of the murderer has hitherto been, and may possibly still continue to be, more than a match for Scotland Yard and the Old Jewry combined, and that all ordinary means of detection have failed."

Demands were coming in from many individuals for a pardon, as well as cries from the local press for some kind of positive action. Editors were calling on the Government to change its position on offering no rewards. Sir Charles Warren and the Home Secretary were coming under greater and greater pressure. Two days earlier Matthews had written a letter to his secretary, Evelyn Ruggles-Brise, discussing the position he had backed himself into. "I have never myself shared to the full extent the HO prejudice against rewards; nor have I thought Harcourt's [Sir William Harcourt, a leading Liberal member of Parliament, and then Chancellor of the Exchequer] reasoning on the subject at all conclusive. I am disposed to regret now that in the first instance I did not sacrifice to popular feeling and offer a considerable reward. But in as much as I did yield to the official view and refuse to make an offer and subsequently repeated that refusal, I feel that my hands are tied.... I feel very strongly that to make such an offer now, after what has passed, so far from conciliating public opinion ... would cover me with ridicule and contempt — as having given way to popular pressure — with nothing to justify or call for a change which would of itself be the strongest condemnation of my previous action." It was one more example of a politician more interested in personal power and saving face than actually doing something that might help the people he represented. Personal pride and ego were now part of the situation, as the authorities attempted to protect their own interests possibly at the cost of more lives lost to the Whitechapel Killer.

Commissioner Warren responded to the latest vigilance committee letter on October 9, with his report to the Home Office. He had changed his mind about the usefulness of pardons. "[D]uring the last three or four days I have been coming to the conclusion that useful results would be produced by the offer of a pardon to accomplices.... Relatives or neighbors may have gradually unwittingly slid into the position of accomplices and may be hopeless of escape without a free pardon." Home Secretary, Henry Matthews, declined the suggestion. Matthews and the Metropolitan Police were roundly criticized by the press for not offering a reward or a pardon. The Government, in the guise of Home Secretary Matthews, officially did not want a reward offered because it was feared that such an offer would bring information on individuals not involved in the crime series, and could cause an innocent person to be charged and possibly hung. At least this was the published reason. It was not a view shared by the public, as private citizens continued to bring monies forward for more rewards. No matter what superficial differences separated the many groups in the East End, there was no doubt that all were united in the desire to remove this killer from their midst as soon as possible, and by any means available. It would, however, take one more brutal death at the hands of the Ripper before the Government would move on the pardon issue. It seems, by the record, that five murders were not sufficient for action; it would take a sixth.

On October 9, Scotland Yard received an anonymous letter from an individual who claimed to be the Ripper's accomplice. Within the letter was a request for a Queen's pardon. Commissioner Warren reported its contents to the Home Office and attempted to make contact with the writer through a journal advertisement. It would seem that a general press announcement would have made more sense but possibly too many people would have responded. Perhaps the journal was chosen by the writer of the letter. A week later, Warren again wrote to the Home Office and reported, "The alleged accomplice did not turn up and it looks like a hoax: but a communication has come in from another source which looks more genuine. We have not tested it yet." Whether or not these were real communications cannot be investigated, as they have not been passed down, and there are no further references to them in the official surviving files.

On October 23, Sir Robert Anderson issued a confidential memo to the Home Office. In it, he reported that after five murders and thousands of hours of police investigation, the CID did not have "the slightest clue of any kind." He felt that it was "extraordinary" that no real clues to the murderer's identity had been found after so much work had been done. The day before, Superintendent Arnold, noting the general situation in the Whitechapel area, reported that "...with the exception of the recent murders crime of a serious nature is not unusually heavy in the district." Perhaps, but the Ripper was enough to bring terror to a whole city, and any other crimes were beginning to seem somewhat unimportant.

By the end of October, the East End was starting to get back to what, on those filthy, crime ridden streets, passed for normal. The women were once again walking the dark night streets in search of customers, as the days turned into weeks after the Ripper had last struck. Surely he would not dare strike again, at least not with all of the patrols and rewards for his capture.

On October 24, Charles Warren wrote a reply to Secretary Matthews' request to bring him up to date. Warren wrote: "Very numerous and searching enquires have been made in all directions and with regard to all kinds of suggestions which have been made: they have had no tangible result...."

Three days earlier, 21-year-old Maria Coroner of Bradford was charged with a breach of the peace for sending several letters signed "Jack the Ripper" to a local paper and to police. She would become the only individual ever identified and prosecuted for sending fraudulent Ripper letters. By this time the police were receiving upwards of 1000 letters a week from citizens who felt that advice to the authorities was needed, just as many or more were being sent to the newspapers in and around London. One letter informed the police that some native tribes, specifically in East India, carried small weapons shaped as needles which had been dipped in poison. It was said that one prick by such a weapon could kill or paralyze instantaneously. The question must be asked whether or not Klosowski, with his medical training and book of poisons, was aware of such methods. Is this why the Ripper victims were never heard to cry out?

On patrol duty and assigned to CID was Inspector Walter Dew, who knew the Whitechapel area very well. He was from H Division of the Metropolitan Police, and he knew many of the "ladies of the night" by sight. One of the women he was familiar with was Mary Jane Kelly. He would later report that, "Often I had seen her parading along Commercial Street, between Flower and Dean Street and Aldgate, or along Whitechapel Road."

Mary Jane would not be on parade for very much longer.

"I may send you the bloody knif that took it out..."
Catch me when you can

Chapter Seven

Death Moves
Off the Streets

"Oh, I could give her that and she wouldn't be no more..."

Severin Klosowski

As the Ripper's respite went on and the people of London's East End began to return to their daily activities, the newspapers continued to report on arrests and on Ripper scares outside of London. The fear was starting to spread even beyond national borders as London nervously waited for the next attack they seemed to know had to come. On November 7, the *New York Herald* would report, "A woman found stabbed on the Boulevard de la Chapelle [in Paris] last night stated that a man attacked her and stabbed her with a knife, saying he was 'Jack the Ripper' and had already killed 10 women in London and two in Paris. He is believed to be mad and is still at large."

The *Weekly Herald*— October 26, 1888
The "Ripper" Scare in Aberdeen
The credulity of the public, intensified for the time being by the sensational reports of Whitechapel horrors, is being played upon by a clumsy imitator who succeeded on Saturday in getting publication for a grossly ridiculous effusion signed "One of the Ripper Gang." The author of this very indifferent copy of the style of the original "Jack the Ripper" warns all decent girls not to venture out after ten p.m., and accompanies his threat, which is written on a scrap of paper sent to one of the local evening papers, by a rude drawing of a big knife.

Of her true history there is much mystery, the majority of it of her own making. That which is known, true or otherwise, comes mainly from the man who shared part of her life, just prior to her death, Joseph Barnett. And the story he told was given to him by the lady herself: Mary Jane Kelly. She is practically the only source of her own background and family. She was also known, in the East End, as Mary Ann Kelly, Fair Emma, and Ginger. (Mary Ann Kelly was one of the names used by Ripper victim Cathy Eddowes.)

She was born in Limerick, Ireland, around 1863, but while she was young the family moved to Wales. Her father was an Irish Catholic iron worker named John Kelly employed at a plant in Carnarvonshire or Carmarthenshire. Of her mother nothing is known. At various times she claimed to have six or seven brothers as well as one sister. The only verifiable sibling was a brother named John, said to be a member of the 2nd Battalion of Scots Guards stationed in Dublin, Ireland, in 1888. Barnett and Mrs. Carthy, a local friend, stated that Mary came from a family that was "fairly well off," and "well to do people." Mrs. Carthy further reported that Mary was "an excellent scholar and an artist of no mean degree." She spoke fluent Welsh and her friend, Maria Harvey, would say that Mary was "much superior to that of most persons in her position in life."

When Mary was 16 she married a coal miner named Davis, around 1879, but he was killed two or three years later, while on the job, in a pit explosion. So perhaps she should be called Mary Davis. The marriage may have produced a child but no information has been located to confirm this point. After her husband's death she moved to Cardiff to live with her cousin. It was at Cardiff that, according to sources, she began her life as a prostitute, but the Cardiff police have no records of her ever having been arrested for any related crimes. Mary also told her friends that during her stay in Cardiff she was ill and spent a great deal of time in an infirmary. By 1884, Mary Jane Kelly had made her way to London, but not yet into the darkness of the East End.

The story is then picked up by a reporter working for the *Press Association*. He had investigated Kelly's background in the Breezer's Hill District and reported, "It would appear that on her arrival in London she made the acquaintance of a French woman residing in the neighborhood of Knightsbridge, who, she informed her friends, led her to pursue the degraded life which had now culminated in her untimely end. She made no secret of the fact that while she was with this woman she would drive about in a carriage and made several journeys to the French capital, and, in fact, led a life which is described as that 'of a lady.' By some means, however, at present, not exactly clear, she suddenly drifted into the East End. Here fortune failed her and a career that stands out in bold and sad contrast to her earlier experience was commenced. Her experiences with the East End appear to have begun with a woman (according to press reports, a Mrs. Buki) who resided in one of the thoroughfares off Ratcliffe Highway, known as St. George's Street. This person appears to have received Kelly direct from the West End home, for she had not been there very long when, it is stated, both women went to the French lady's residence and demanded the box which contained numerous dresses of a costly description."

Mrs. Elizabeth Phoenix claimed that Mary had lived in her brother-in-law's house on Breezer's Hill. She said that Mary was "Welsh and that her parents, who had discarded her, still lived in Cardiff, from which place she came. But on occasions she declared that she was Irish. ... [She was] one of the most decent and nice girls you could meet when sober." Mary was described as having "considerable personal attractions," and as being 5'7" tall, stout, with blonde hair, blue eyes, and a fair complexion, and aged around 25 at the time of her death. No one from her family would attend her funeral, and they could not be found by any of the reporters working on the story.

It is possible that she spent some time living with the Catholic nuns at Providence Row Convent and Night Refuge on Crispin Street, Spitalfields. She is said to have scrubbed floors there and was subsequently placed into domestic service. The nuns who run the present day convent do have a tradition that a Ripper victim stayed for a while at the convent before going into the streets.

By 1886, after moving around a good deal, Mary could be found living in Colleys' lodging house on Thrawl Street. It was while living at Colleys that she met Joseph Barnett. Barnett was 39 years old at the time of the murders, in 1888. He worked as a fish market porter and riverside laborer, and was of Irish background, but had been born in London. While walking along Commercial Street they ran into each other and quickly decided to have a drink. They then arranged to meet the next day and subsequently decided to live together. It was Saturday, April 9, 1887, when the couple rented a lodging on George Street, Whitechapel. During that same time period a young man named Severin Klosowski was running away from his past, and traveling towards the East End of London from Warsaw, Poland.

They would not stay long on George Street, soon moving to Paternoster Court off Dorset Street. The stay at Paternoster Court would also be short as they were soon evicted for being drunk and behind on their rent. From there they moved to Brick Lane, and then again to George Yard Buildings—the same lodgings as Severin Klosowski. This move to the George Yard Buildings places a future Ripper victim closer to a Ripper suspect than does any other known event in the entire case. Klosowski and Kelly could not have missed seeing each other. This is no circumstantial event, *it is a matching of victim to killer,* and clearly places Klosowski at the top of any suspect list. It also removes, at least for one of his victims, the suggestion that all of his targets were random and unknown to their killer. Was Klosowski a customer of Mary's and was it some type of rejection by her which finally pushed him over the edge of insanity?

In March of 1888, Barnett and Kelly moved to her final home. It would be a single 12 foot square, barely furnished, dirty room, at 13 Miller's Court, just off Dorset Street. The dimly lit court itself was approximately 40 by 10 feet. Mary's room, at number 13, was actually the back parlor of 26 Dorset Street which had been partitioned off by what appeared to be a set of doors which had been nailed shut. Mary's bed had been positioned so that it sat up against that partition, which served as one of her four dirty walls. The small room had a fireplace opposite the door which, when opened from left to right, banged up against a small bedside table. A second smaller table and a chair sat opposite the bed facing her two windows to the left as one entered the room. Next to the fireplace was the understocked cupboard with some bread and drinks. For some reason Mary had lost her key to the door, but it did not matter. The window nearest the door had earlier been broken by her when she was drunk, which made it easy to reach inside and pop open the spring lock. On the wall there was an old print of the painting, *The Fisherman's Widow.*

Countdown to Another Murder

It was late August or early September, as the Ripper series was just picking up momentum, that Joseph Barnett lost his job, and Kelly decided to return to prostitution. This was also when Barnett decided to leave 13 Miller's Court, and Mary, to live elsewhere. He would later testify, at the inquest into her death, that he left because she had begun to share her room with other prostitutes. "She would never have gone wrong again and I shouldn't have left her if it had not been for the prostitutes stopping at the house. She only let them [stay] because she was good hearted and did not like to refuse them shelter on cold bitter nights. We lived comfortably until Marie allowed a prostitute named Julia to sleep in the same room; I objected: and as Mrs. Harvey afterwards came and stayed there, I left and took lodgings elsewhere." It was on October 30, sometime between 5 and 6 p.m., that Elizabeth Prater, who lived above their small room, heard the argument which led to his leaving. Mary stayed in Miller's Court and Barnett went to Buller's boarding house at 24-25 New Street, Bishopsgate. Mrs.

Maria Harvey was not to board with Mary for long. After staying overnight, on November 5 and 6, she moved to 3 New Court, off Dorset Street, just west of Miller's Court. Barnett continued: "I left her because she had a person who was a prostitute whom she took in and I objected to her doing so. That was the only reason; not because I was out of work. I left her on the 30th October between five and six p.m. I last saw her alive between half-past seven and a quarter to eight on the night of Thursday before she was found. I was with her about one hour. ... We were on friendly terms. I told her when I left I had no work and nothing to give her, of which I was very sorry."

On November 7, a Wednesday, Mary was seen at John McCarthy's shop buying a candle. Some time later, Thomas "Indian Harry" Bowyer saw her with a man in Miller's Court. Bowyer was a British Army pensioner, a veteran of India, who worked for McCarthy collecting the rents at Miller's Court. He described the man he had seen with Kelly as having "...very peculiar eyes," and as being 27 or 28 years old with a dark mustache. He was dressed "very smart and attention was drawn to him by his showing very white cuffs and a rather long white collar, the ends of which came down in front over his coat." It would be Bowyer who, only days later, would discover the mutilated corpse of Mary Kelly inside her tiny room. He would later report that he saw Kelly speaking with a man that night who very closely resembled Matthew Packer's description of a man said to have been seen with Elizabeth Stride shortly before her death. That man was also dressed in a long black coat, white cuffs and white collar.

If these reports are correct, and there is no reason to believe they are not, then they are evidence of not only a very local individual committing the murders, but of an individual who was targeting a specific woman he knew. Klosowski could have been known to Mary Kelly from George Yard, and after several meetings she certainly would have felt very safe going with him to her room. For Klosowski, it was an opportunity to commit an almost risk free murder of someone who would not only be inside, but would not suspect that he was the Ripper.

Thursday, November 8, found Barnett visiting Kelly as he had done most days since he had left. He arrived between 7:30 and 7:45 p.m. to visit, but another woman, possibly a prostitute who lived in Miller's Court, was already there. It was the last time he would see Mary alive. Later, he would be called to identify her body in the Shoreditch Mortuary, which he could only barely accomplish and then only by being able to recognize her eyes and hair. The other woman may have been Kelly's friend, 20-year-old Lizzie Albrook, who lived at 2 Miller's Court and worked at a lodging house on Dorset Street. Of her friend, Albrook would say, "About the last thing she said to me was, 'Whatever you do don't you do wrong and turn out as I have.' She had often spoken to me in this way and warned me against going on the streets as she had done. She told me, too, that she was heartily sick of the life she was leading and wished she had money enough to go back to Ireland where her people lived. I do not believe she would have gone out as she did if she had not been obliged to do so to keep herself from starvation." Mary had told Lizzie, "This will be the last Lord Mayor's Show I shall see. I can't stand it any longer. This Jack the Ripper business is getting on my nerves. I have made up my mind to go home to my mother. It is safer there." The parade was held the following day but Mary Jane Kelly would not see it after all.

Barnett left to go back to Buller's boarding house at 8 p.m. After he arrived he played a card game called whist, a forerunner of bridge, which is played with four people. After the game ended, at 12:30 a.m., he went to bed. He would have nothing to do with the death of Mary Kelly, even though for a while he was a logical suspect. He is still considered by some investigators to be a good possibility in the Kelly murder, but there has *never* been anything to show the slightest evidence that he was involved.

From 8 p.m. until around 11:00 p.m. that Thursday, very little is known about what Kelly was engaged in. The only contemporary report said that she had been seen drinking with another prostitute named Elizabeth Foster at the Britannia public house. The Britannia, which was demolished in 1928, was a favorite drinking spot of Mary's, located on the north corner of Dorset and Commercial Streets. It was 11 p.m. when she was spotted at the Britannia drinking with a dark mustached young man who was said to have been dressed respectably and well. This could have been a late night contact with Klosowski. Mary Kelly was very drunk but apparently not yet ready to go to her room.

At 11:45 p.m. she was again seen, but this time with a different man. She was still drunk and weaving back and fourth as she entered Miller's Court. The man with Kelly was described as 35 or 36 years old 5'5" tall, blotchy faced, with small side whiskers, and a carroty mustache. He is further described by Mary Ann Cox, who followed them into Miller's Court, as being in a long overcoat, shabbily dressed with a billycock hat and carrying a pail of beer. This man was not the Ripper. Passing them on her way to her room at 5 Miller's Court, Mrs. Cox said "Good night" to Mary who, barely able to speak coherently, replied, "Good night, I am going to sing." Within a few minutes Kelly could be heard singing, "It was only a violet I plucked from my dear mother's grave." When Mrs. Cox went out again at midnight, after warming up for a while in her room, she could hear Mary singing the same song.

By 1 a.m., as the cold of the night turned to a drizzle of rain, Mary Ann Cox once again came back to her room to warm herself. As she passed Kelly's room she saw that a light was on and heard Mary still singing. There was no indication anyone else was with her in the small room. At about the same time Elizabeth Prater, who lived in number 20, directly above Mary's room, came home and stood in the brick archway entrance from Dorset Street leading into Miller's Court. This effectively blocked the entrance, as she would have been aware of anyone coming from or going into the court — they would have had to have brushed past her. She was waiting for the man who lived with her but he was nowhere to be seen. After about a half hour, exposed to the cold rainy weather, she went into McCarthy's shop next door. After a few minutes of conversation in the shop she went back into Miller's Court and entered her room. She remembered hearing no singing at that point, as she placed two chairs in front of her door as her security against the Whitechapel Killer. She was very drunk and went to bed without undressing, which was not an uncommon occurrence.

Years later, a woman named Kitty Ronan would be murdered in the same room Elizabeth Prater lived in above Mary Kelly. Miller's Court would long live up to the reputation of the evil quarter-mile.

Just after 1:30 a.m. Mary must have left her room after having a meal of fish and potatoes. She was warmed up against the cold, and the effects of drink had begun to wear off. She was seen by George Hutchinson — who knew her very well and was reported to have been one of her customers — as she walked along Commercial Street at 2:00 a.m. Mr. Hutchinson, three days later, would recount what he had seen that early morning to officers at the Commercial Street police station. "About 2 a.m. 9th I was coming by Thrawl Street, Commercial Street, and just before I got to Flower and Dean Street, I met the murdered woman Kelly, and she said to me, 'Hutchinson will you lend me sixpence?' I said, 'I can't, I have spent all my money going to Romford.' She said, 'Good morning, I must go and find some money.' She went on her way towards Thrawl Street. A man coming in the opposite direction to Kelly, tapped her on the shoulder and said something to her. They both burst out laughing. I heard her say, 'all right' to him, and the man said, 'You will be all right, for what I have told you.' (A clear indication that she had met this man before and thus he was not a complete stranger.) He then placed his right hand around her shoulders. He also had a kind of small parcel in his left hand, with a kind of strap round it. I stood against the lamp of the Queen's Head public house, and watched him. (The Queen's Head is on the corner of Commercial Street and Fashion Street.) They both then came past me and the man hung down his head, with his hat over his eyes. I stooped down and looked him in the face. He looked at me stern. They both went into Dorset Street. I followed them. They both stood at the corner of the court [Miller's Court] for about three minutes. He said something to her. She said, 'all right my dear come along you will be comfortable.' He then placed his arm on her shoulder and [she] gave him a kiss. She said she had lost her handkerchief. He then pulled his handkerchief a red one, and gave it to her. They both then went up the court together. I then went to the court to see if I could see them but I could not. I stood there for about three quarters of an hour to see if they came out. They did not, so I went away." It was 3:00 a.m. as a clock in the distance struck the hour and Hutchinson walked away, unknowingly leaving Kelly to her fate at the hands of Jack the Ripper.

As published in the *Laborer's Press*, Hutchinson's description of the man last seen with Kelly was detailed: "The man was about 5'6" in height,

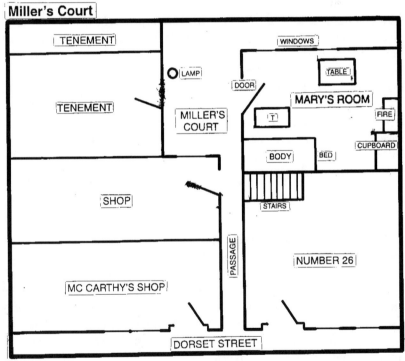

R. Michael Gordon   1998

Only one Ripper murder occurred inside a room: that of Mary Jane Kelly, killed in her small room at 13 Miller's Court, just off Dorset Street. Her greatly mutilated body (greatest of the series) was discovered at 10:45 a.m. by rent collector Thomas "Indian" Bowyer.

and 34 or 35 years of age, with dark complexion and dark moustache, turned up at the ends. He was wearing a long dark coat, trimmed with asrachan [sic], a white collar, with black necktie, in which was affixed a horseshoe pin. He wore a pair of dark 'spats' with light buttons over button boots, and displayed from his waistcoat a massive gold chain. His watch chain had a big seal, with a red stone, hanging from it. He had a heavy moustache curled up and dark eyes and bushy eyebrows. He had no side whiskers, and his chin was clean shaven. He looked like a foreigner.... [Other than the age this is a very good description of Klosowski who is reported to have looked older than he was.] The man I saw did not look as though he would attack another one [man]. [Another general trait of Klosowski's.] He carried a small parcel in his hand about 8" long, and it had a strap round it. He had it tightly grasped in his left hand. It looked as though it was covered with dark American cloth [oil cloth]. He carried in his right hand, which he laid upon the woman's shoulder, a pair of brown kid gloves. One thing I noticed, and that was that he walked very softly. *I believe that he lives in the neighbourhood*, and I fancied that I saw him in Petticoat Lane on Sunday morning, but I was not certain." (The actual name was Middlesex Street, but it was called Petticoat Lane due to its famous Sunday street markets. It was a major commercial center for the Jewish community throughout London.)

Inspector Abberline went over Hutchinson's statement again and again to test his validity. He wanted to be very sure of this description, as it would turn out to be one of the best yet to come into his hands.

> ABBERLINE: How could you see a red handkerchief so far away?
> HUTCHINSON: He flourished the handkerchief in front of her. It caught the lamplight. He waved it about like a bullfighter and made her laugh.

It will be remembered that the man seen just outside Mitre Square with Catherine Eddowes just before her murder also had a red handkerchief.

Inspector Abberline was so impressed with Hutchinson's testimony, and description, that he forwarded them to Scotland Yard with the note, "An important statement has been made by a man named George Hutchinson which I forward herewith. I have interrogated him this evening, and I am of opinion his statement is true."

Inside her room Mary had folded her clothes and placed them neatly on the only chair she had, at the foot of the bed. She placed her boots in front of the small fireplace and the light was turned off as she went to bed. Inspector Abberline would later find the remains of clothing which had been burned in the fireplace, and surmised that the fire which consumed them was used to illuminate the room. Dr. Roderick Macdonald, the district coroner, would also examine the ashes in the grate looking for human remains, but none were found. This was not some type of ritual human sacrifice or cult killing.

Around 3 a.m., but after Hutchinson left, Mrs. Cox again returned to her room at 5 Miller's Court as the cold rain came down hard on London. When she passed Mary's room she heard no sounds and her light was out. The Ripper may have already been working quietly in the room lit only by a fire, fed by clothes. For the rest of the night she stayed awake but did not go out again. She never heard anything from Kelly's room, but did report that she occasionally heard men going in and out of the court. There were people, once again, all around as the Ripper did his work. He had, by medical accounts, at least two hours to do anything he wanted to do before he simply disappeared.

Sarah Lewis, who had argued with her husband, came to stay with Mrs. Keyler at number 2 Miller's Court. She arrived at 2:30 in the morning, according to the clock on Christ Church, Spitalfields, then sat awake in a chair. "Just before four o'clock," she heard a "loud scream of 'murder.'" She said that it sounded close and that it was from a young woman. She did not even bother to get up and look out the window—it was not an uncommon event even in the time of the Ripper. Between 3:30 and 4 a.m. Mary Jane Kelly was murdered by Jack the Ripper.

At a little after 4 a.m., Elizabeth Prater was awakened by her kitten walking across her neck. She also heard the cry of "Oh, murder!" faintly, and ignored it. She felt that it was after 4 a.m. because the lodging house light was out. By this time, Mary Jane Kelly was little more than a mutilated corpse a few feet away, just below Mrs. Prater's room, and the Ripper was continuing his night's work on her body. Later examination of Kelly's hands and arms would indicate an attempt by her to fend off her killer's attack. But it would not have been a long struggle. Mrs. Prater slept until 5 a.m. when she got back up to get a drink of rum at the Five Bells public house. She would then be ready for her work on the streets of the East End. She saw and heard nothing.

By 6:15 a.m. Mrs. Cox was again awake and could hear someone walking down the narrow passage out of Miller's Court and onto Dorset Street. She could not tell who it was but she did notice that whoever it was did not close a door so that it could be heard.

Those who feel that the serial killer known as Jack the Ripper did not adjust his method to suit the situation, need only look at this murder, conducted off the streets over an extended period of time. It was a dramatic new twist in a series of vicious crimes. And although it has been discounted, intercourse may have been at least attempted with this victim, thus explaining the massive destruction of the genitalia of Mary's body. She was found lying on the near side of the bed, but she had been killed as she lay on the far side, leaving plenty of room for her killer to lie next to her.

A Most Bloody Discovery

The morning promised Londoners a good show as the new Lord Mayor of London, James Whitehead, paraded to the Royal Courts of Justice in the Strand to take his oath of office. The promise would soon dissolve in the realization that the Ripper had struck again, and this time in the insane mindless attack of a mad dog. The parade would be stopped cold, in front of St. Paul's Cathedral, as newsboys pushed through the crowds of onlookers with cries of — MURDER! The parade was over.

As John McCarthy checked his books he found that Mary was six weeks behind in her rent on the room she had shared with Joe Barnett. He had allowed her to be behind, but some type of payment would be nice if he could get it. It was 10:45 in the morning of November 9 when McCarthy told his assistant, Thomas Bowyer, to try to collect the rent. Bowyer went around the corner into Miller's Court from the store and twice knocked on her door at number 13. There was of course no answer, so he walked around the corner to the broken window. Pulling aside the curtain, his eyes became adjusted to the darkness of the room and the mutilated corpse of Mary Jane Kelly came into focus. Later McCarthy would say, "All those lumps of flesh lying on the table — it was more the work of a devil than of a man."

Shocked beyond words, Bowyer ran back to McCarthy's shop and stammered, "Governor, I knocked at the door and could not make anyone answer. I looked through the window and saw a lot of blood." McCarthy replied, "Good God, do you mean that, Harry?" Both men ran back to the room and McCarthy looked through the window. It was enough for him. When he turned away, all the blood had drained from his face. He told Bowyer to, "Go at once to the police station and fetch someone here."

Bowyer went to the Commercial Street station and, barely able to speak, told Inspector Walter Beck, "Another one, Jack the Ripper. Awful. Jack McCarthy sent me." Beck immediately rushed out with Detective Walter Dew hot on his heels. Dew's nickname was "Blue Serge" for the suit he always wore. Upon arriving a little after 11 a.m., Detective Dew later reported, "I tried the door. It would not yield. So I moved to the window, over which, on the inside, an old coat was hanging to act as a curtain and to block the draught from the hole in the glass. Inspector Beck pushed the coat to one side and peered though the aperture. A moment later he staggered back with his face as white as a sheet. 'For God's sake, Dew,' he cried, 'don't look.' I ignored the order, and took my place at the window. When my eyes had become accustomed to the dim light I saw a sight which I shall never forget to my dying day. ... It remains with me — and always will remain — as the most gruesome memory of the whole of my police career. ... All this was horrifying enough, but the mental picture of that sight which remains most vividly with me is the poor woman's eyes. They were wide open, and seemed to be staring straight at me with a look of horror." Dew soon telegraphed Divisional Police Superintendent Arnold of his investigation and stood by for reinforcements.

It did not take long for them to get there. The divisional police surgeon, Dr. George Bagster Phillips, arrived at 11:15 a.m., and Inspector Abberline was on hand by 11:30. Abberline's first order of business was to seal off the murder site. Movement into and out of Miller's Court was by his order alone. No one entered the murder room until photographs could be taken of the corpse through the window which had been removed to allow a clear shot. The door was finally broken in by McCarthy with a pickaxe at 1:30 p.m., as Superintendent Arnold arrived, and it would be Dr. Phillips who entered first. When "Blue Serge" Dew stepped in, he promptly slipped on the remains and fell to the floor. The air in the room was stifling.

> The *London Times*— November 10, 1888
> Another Whitechapel Murder
> During the early hours of yesterday morning another murder of a most revolting and fiendish character took place in Spitalfields. This is the seventh which has occurred in this immediate neighbourhood, and the character of the mutilations leaves very little doubt that the murderer in this instance is the same person who has committed the previous ones, with which the public are fully acquainted.
> The scene of this last crime is number 26 Dorset Street, Spitalfields, which is about 200 yards distance from 35 [should be 29] Hanbury Street, where the unfortunate woman, Mary Ann Nichols, was so foully murdered. Although the victim, whose name is Mary Ann (or Mary Jane) Kelly, resides at the above number, the entrance to the room she occupied is up a narrow court, in which are some half a dozen houses, and which is known as Miller's Court; it is entirely separated from the other portion of the house, and has an entrance leading into the court. The room is known by the title of number 13. The house is rented by John McCarthy, who keeps a small general shop at 27 Dorset Street, and the whole of the rooms are let out to tenants of a very poor class. As an instance of the poverty of the neighborhood, it may be mentioned that nearly the whole of the houses in this street are common lodging houses, and the one opposite where the murder was enacted

has accommodation for some 300 men, and is fully occupied every night....

Mr. Arnold (the police superintendent), having satisfied himself that the woman was dead, ordered one of the windows to be entirely removed. A horrible and sickening sight then presented itself. The poor woman lay on her back on the bed, entirely naked. [Incorrect, but considering the conditions the error is understandable.] Her throat was cut from ear to ear, right down to the spinal column. ... While this examination was being made a photographer, who, in the meantime, had been sent for, arrived and took photographs of the body, the organs, the room, and its contents. Superintendent Arnold then had the door of the room forced. ... There was no appearance of a struggle having taken place, and, although a careful search of the room was made, no knife or instrument of any kind was found... [However, reports have survived of a hatchet being discovered at the scene, which would have most certainly been a formidable weapon.] After the examination of the body it was placed in a shell, which was

"Is He the Murderer?" Man seen by Hutchison with Kelly; 1888 composite of murder suspect. (Published in the *Illustrated Police News* on Saturday, November 24, 1888, on the front page.)

put into a van and conveyed to the Shoreditch mortuary to await an inquest....

After the examinations the windows were boarded up, and the door padlocked by direction of the police, who have considerable difficulty in keeping the street clear of persons. ... The news that the body was about to be removed caused a great rush of people from the courts running out of Dorset Street, and there was a determined effort to break the police cordon at the Commercial Street end. The crowd, which pressed round the van, was of the humblest class, but the demeanor of the poor people was all that could be described. Ragged caps were doffed and slatternly looking women shed tears as the shell, covered with a ragged looking cloth, was placed in the van.

Once again shock waves of disbelief and frustration flowed across the wet, gray, dismal cobblestone streets of London's East End. The news brought despair and anger directed at the authorities, as the residents around Dorset Street heard the news of yet another vicious murder. There was a deep seated fear on the people's faces as they crowded every street near the murder site by the thousands. This was a body blow to the minds and souls of the desolate East Enders. No one knew what would happen next as the police moved as fast as they could to cordon off both ends of Dorset Street. The streets were so crowded at one point that no one could even move. No one could understand what was driving this killer and no one could be sure that he would not kill again.

Mary Jane Kelly — November 9, 1888. Photo taken in situ at murder site. Throat cut deeply; body and face greatly mutilated; body parts removed; heart taken. (Public Record Office.)

As reported by the London *Times*, "The excitement in the neighbourhood of Dorset Street is intense, and some of the low women with whom that street abounds appear more like fiends than human beings. The police have great trouble to preserve order, and one constable, who is alleged to have struck an onlooker, was so mobbed and hooted that he had to beat a retreat to Commercial Street Police Station, whither he was followed by a huge crowd, which was only kept at bay by the presence of about half a dozen constables, who stood at the door and prevented anyone from entering."

To inform the government, Sir Charles Warren sent a telegram to the Under Secretary of the Home Office, Godfrey Lushington, in which he wrote, "I have to acquaint you, for the information of the Secretary of State, that information has just been received that a mutilated dead body of a woman is reported to have been found this morning inside a room in a house in Dorset Street, Spitalfields." Commissioner Anderson would later telephone the Home Office. A surviving note of the call records:

Body is believed to be that of a prostitute much mutilated. Dr. Bond is at present engaged in making his examination but his report has not yet been received. Full report cannot be furnished until medical officers have completed enquiry.

After the body (and remaining parts) were removed at 3:45 p.m., the police allowed the public to reenter Dorset Street. The crowds of curiosity seekers would last for hours. No one was allowed into Miller's Court, other than those who lived there: it was now guarded by two constables stationed at the entrance to keep sightseers away. On a wall near the entrance a poster announced a £100 reward for Jack the Ripper offered by the *Illustrated Police News*. It must have given the Ripper a great deal of pleasure as he walked past it with his latest victim. Perhaps they looked at it together, and laughed.

Later that evening, John McCarthy, who had broken down the door to the murder site for the police and was one of the first to enter the room, reported, "The sight we saw, I cannot drive away from my mind. It looked more like the work of a devil then of a man. ... I had heard a great deal about the Whitechapel murders, but I declare to God, I had never expected to see such a sight as this." The *Pall Mall Gazette* reported that "the rest [of the face] was so scored and slashed that it was impossible to say where the flesh began and the cuts ended." Not unexpectedly, some reports in the local press exaggerated even this murder, like the one in the *Weekly Herald* of November 16: "The head rested upon the floor, away from the body; an arm lay apart from the trunk...." The fact remains that such reporting could very well have been true had this been one of the Torso murders occurring in and around the East End.

That evening as East Enders tried to control their terror, the Lord Mayor, Sir James Whitehead, hosted some 850 upper crust guests, including Prime Minister Lord Salisbury, at a banquet held in Guildhall. The Ripper was not about to be allowed to put a dent on the evening's entertainment.

Even Queen Victoria, who normally did not comment on the great and small events of the day, once again contacted her Government. She had phoned the Home Office after the double event and had been closely following news reports of the Ripper killings. A day after the murder of Mary Kelly she sent a telegram to the Prime Minister voicing her concerns.

> This new most ghastly murder shows the absolute necessity for some very decided action. All these courts must be lit, and our detectives improved. They are not what they should be. You promised, when the first murder took place, to consult with your colleagues about it.

With unrelenting pressure from all sides, and an argument with the Home Secretary over the policy regarding publishing articles about his department, Commissioner of Police Sir Charles Warren resigned his post on November 8. He would continue until November 27, but to all intents and purposes his police career was finished. Before he left office, however, he brought forth a controversial response to demands from the public for more action.

On Saturday, November 10, the cabinet met and decided that, although rewards would not be forthcoming, it was acceptable to offer a pardon to any accomplice of the murderer of Mary Kelly. It should be noted that only the Kelly murder was covered in the document — it could not have been expected to accomplish much if someone had been involved in all the Ripper murders. Perhaps it was designed only to placate the public and not really to be effective in the apprehension of the killer.

> MURDER — PARDON — Whereas on November 8 or 9, in Miller's Court, Dorset Street, Spitalfields, Mary Janet [sic] Kelly was murdered by some person or persons unknown: the Secretary of State will advise the grant of Her Majesty's gracious pardon to any accomplice, not being a person who contrived or actually committed the murder, who shall give such information and evidence as shall lead to the discovery and conviction of the person or persons who committed the murder.
> CHARLES WARREN, the Commissioner of
> Police of the Metropolis
> Metropolitan Police Office, 4 Whitehall Place,
> S. W., Nov. 10, 1888

There was not much chance that this pardon would bring forth any witnesses. The police may not have fully realized what type of individual they were dealing with but most felt that these crimes were being committed by a single madman who was not sharing his deeds with anyone. The very best they could hope for would be for someone to step forward who suspected another person or who may have been reluctant to turn in a friend or relation before. It could very well be that the pardon's major consequence was its ability to show the people of London that the authorities were going to extreme lengths to catch the killer, whether they were successful or not.

Once again the local, as well as foreign press, had a field day with this latest Ripper murder. The *Manchester Guardian* of November 10 reported, "Terrible mutilation of a Woman in Spitalfields — Escape of the Murderer … This forenoon the inhabitants of the East End of London were thrown into a state of consternation by the discovery in their midst of another revolting crime, far worse in its barbarity than any of the previous five murders which have shocked London during the past five months. The victim is again a woman of the impure class, and the murderer committed the crime under her own roof in broad daylight and easily escaped. Dorset Street, Spitalfields, is filled with lodging houses, tenanted chiefly by the

Home Office file holding murder pardon.

lowest classes, amongst them some of the most degraded thieves and immoral women.... [The] excitement in the neighborhood was spreading, and among the dwellers in the immediate locality amounted to a perfect frenzy. Women rushed about the streets telling their neighbours the news, and shouting in angry voices their rage and indignation."

The London *Times* of November 10 reported, "The murders, so cunningly continued, are carried out with a completeness which altogether baffles investigators. Not a trace is left of the murderer, and there is no purpose in the crime to afford the slightest clue, such as would be afforded in other crimes almost without exception. All that the police can hope is that some accidental circumstance will lead to a trace which may be followed to a successful conclusion."

Once again the streets were alive with people seeking the killer. Shouts of "Jack the Ripper!" and "Lynch him!" were directed at several men who had to run for their lives to the closest police station.

The *New York Times*— November 10, 1888
Exciting London Events
The discovery today of the seventh Whitechapel murder, this time believed to have been committed in broad daylight and involving the most terrible wholesale mutilation it is possible to imagine, overshadows all other topics in the London mind tonight. ... The conclusion is now universal that the assassin is a periodic lunatic, who unless detected at once, is likely to commit a fresh series of crimes within a few days before his frenzy passes away.

Murder

Pardon.

Whereas on November the 8th or 9th in Millers Court Dorset Street Spitalfields, Mary Janet Kelly was murdered by some person or persons unknown, the Secretary of State will advise the grant of Her Majesty's gracious pardon to any accomplice not being a person who contrived or actually committed the murder who shall give such information and evidence as shall lead to the discovery and conviction of the person or persons who committed the murder.

(Sd) Charles Warren
Commissioner of Police
of the Metropolis.

Metropolitan Police Office
4 Whitehall Place
sw
16 November 1888

Handwritten copy of murder pardon by Charles Warren for any accomplice to the Kelly murder.

The *Los Angeles Times*— November 10, 1888
The Whitechapel Fiend
Another Woman Butchered and
Horribly Mutilated in London
The murder fiend has added another to his list of victims. At 11 o'clock this morning the body of a woman cut into pieces was discovered in a house on Dorset Street, Spitalfields. The remains were mutilated in the same horrible manner as those of the women murdered in Whitechapel.

Mary's funeral took place on Monday afternoon, November 19. Just as the church bell began to toll its noon message thousands of residents gathered in front of St. Leonard's Church, Shoreditch. Soon, from the church, four men bore the casket through the gate to the open car, as the crowd massed forward to touch it. The emotion of the gathered crowd was unconstrained and spontaneous; many had tears on their faces. The polished oak and elm coffin had on it a plate reading: Marie Jeannette Kelly, died 9th Nov. 1888, aged 25 years.

The cortege moved with great difficulty as thousands of people blocked the streets for a view of the procession. It finally made its way to St. Patrick's Roman Catholic Cemetery at Leytonstone, London. (Klosowski would later find work as a hairdresser in Leytonstone.) The sky had been dark and cloudy all day, as it was when her remains were lowered into the ground at public grave 16, row 67. In attendance were those who had been acquainted with Mary, but few who knew her well. No members of her family were there to see her off, but Joseph Barnett was. And, if his tormented mind was typical of the serial killer, so was Jack the Ripper!

On November 10, in a letter now in the Public Record Office (MEPO 3/141), Dr. Thomas Bond reported to Robert Anderson, then head of the CID, his thoughts on the ongoing Whitechapel murders. Dr. Bond had just finished his post-mortem of Mary Jane Kelly.

> 7 The Sanctuary,
> Westminister Abbey
> November 10th '88

Dear Sir,
    Whitechapel Murders
    I beg to report that I have read the notes of the four Whitechapel Murders viz—:
        1. Buck's Row
        2. Hanbury Street
        3. Berners Street
        4. Mitre Square
I have also made a Post Mortem Examination of the mutilated remains of a woman found yesterday in a small room in Dorset Street—:

1. All five murders were no doubt committed by the same hand. In the first four the throats appear to have been cut from left to right, in the last case owing to the extensive mutilation it is impossible to say in what direction the fatal cut was made, but arterial blood was found on the wall in splashes close to where the woman's head must have been lying.

2. All the circumstances surrounding the murders lead me to form the opinion that the women must have been lying down when murdered and in every case the throat was first cut.

3. In the four murders of which I have seen the notes only, I cannot form a very definite opinion as to the time that had elapsed between the murder and the discovery of the body. In one case, that of Berners Street the discovery appears to have been immediately after the deed. In Buck's Row, Hanbury St., and Mitre Square three or four hours only could have elapsed. In the Dorset Street case the body was lying on the bed at the time of my visit at two o'clock quite naked and mutilated as in the annexed report. Rigor Mortis had set in but increased during the progress of the examination. From this it is difficult to say with any degree of certainty the exact time that had elapsed since death as the period varies from six to twelve hours before rigidity sets in. The body was comparatively cold at two o'clock and the remains of a recently taken meal were found in the stomach and scattered about over the intestines. It is therefore, pretty certain that the woman must have been dead about twelve hours and the partly digested food would indicate that death took place about three or four hours after food was taken, so one or two o'clock in the morning would be the probable time of the murder.

4. In all the cases there appears to be no evidence of struggling and the attacks were probably so sudden and made in such a position that the women could neither resist nor cry out. In the Dorset St. case the corner of the sheet to the right of the woman's head was much cut and saturated with blood, indicating that the face may have been covered with the sheet at the time of the attack.

5. In the first four cases the murderer must have attacked from the right side of the victim. In the Dorset Street case, he must have attacked from the left, as there would be no room for him between the wall and the part of the bed on which the woman was lying. Again the blood had flowed down on the right side of the woman and spurted on to the wall.

6. The murderer would not necessarily be splashed or deluged with blood, but his hands and arms must have been covered and parts of his clothing must certainly have been smeared with blood.

7. The mutilations in each case excepting the Berners Street one were all of the same character and showed clearly that in all the murders the object was mutilation.

8. In each case the mutilation was inflicted by a person who had no scientific nor anatomical knowledge. In my opinion he does not even

possess the technical knowledge of a butcher or horse slaughterer or any person accustomed to cut up dead animals.

9. The instrument must have had been a strong knife at least six inches long, very sharp, pointed at the top and about an inch in width. It may have been a clasp knife, a butchers knife or a surgeons knife, I think it was no doubt a straight knife.

10. The murderer must have been a man of physical strength and of great coolness and daring. There is no evidence that he had an accomplice. He must in my opinion be a man subject to periodical attacks of Homicidal and erotic mania. The character of the mutilations indicate that the man may be in a condition sexually, that may be called Satyriasis. It is of course possible that the Homicidal impulse may have developed from a revengeful or brooding condition of the mind, or that religious mania may have been the original disease but I do not think either hypothesis is likely. The murderer in external appearance is quite likely to be a quiet inoffensive looking man probably middle-aged and neatly and respectably dressed. I think he must be in the habit of wearing a cloak or overcoat or he could hardly have escaped notice in the streets if the blood on his hands or clothes were visible.

11. Assuming the murderer to be such a person as I have just described, he would be solitary and eccentric in his habits, also he is most likely to be a man without regular occupation, but with some small income or pension. He is possibly living among respectable persons who have some knowledge of his character and habits and who may have grounds for suspicion that he isn't quite right in his mind at times. Such persons would probably be unwilling to communicate suspicions to the Police for fear of trouble or notoriety, whereas if there were prospect of reward it might overcome their scruples.

Dr. Thomas Bond

An Inquest in Shoreditch

The coroner for the North Eastern District of Middlesex, Dr. Roderick MacDonald, began and ended his inquest into Kelly's death on Monday, November 12, at Shoreditch town hall, beginning at 11 a.m. It would be the only inquest of a Ripper murder to be completed in a single day. Because the murder was committed in Spitalfields and not Whitechapel, the body had been taken to Shoreditch Mortuary. The inquest room was filled beyond capacity and the doors had to be padlocked and guarded by constables to keep the crowds outside from forcing their way in.

Very little came out of the inquest, as Dr. MacDonald felt his job was to simply consider whether or not a crime had been committed. In that light, very little was released to the public through the inquest process. "There is other evidence which I do not propose to call, for if we at once

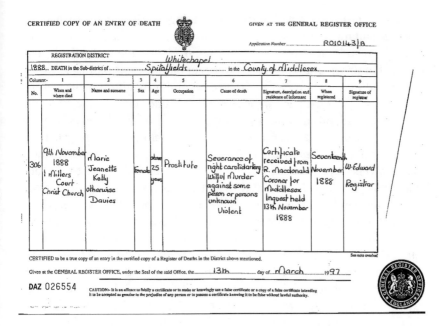

Copy of death certificate for Mary Jane Kelly.

make public every fact brought forward in connection with this terrible murder, the end of justice might be retarded." Dr. Phillips was called and briefly explained that the victim had died because of "the severance of the right carotid artery." There were no discussions about the mutilations. By the end of the day's testimony the jury was asked if they had come to any conclusions, and indeed they had.

Wilful murder against some person or persons unknown.

For more details of the event at Miller's Court we are left in the hands of Dr. Thomas Bond. (In 1901, after a long illness, Dr. Bond committed suicide by throwing himself out of his bedroom window.) He examined Kelly's remains and wrote down his notes the day after. The notes were delivered to Scotland Yard and later went missing for years before being returned, anonymously, in 1987. Dr. Bond wrote:

"The body was lying naked [this was incorrect] in the middle of the bed, the shoulders flat, but the axis of the body inclined to the left side of the bed. The head was turned on the left cheek. The left arm was close to the body with the forearm flexed at a right angle and lying across the abdomen, the right arm was slightly abducted from the body and rested on the mattress, the elbow bent and the forearm supine with the fingers clenched. The legs were wide apart, the left thigh at right angles to the trunk and the right forming an obtuse angle with the pubes. The whole of the surface of the abdomen and thighs was removed and the abdominal cavity emptied of its viscera. The breasts were cut off, the arms mutilated by several jagged wounds and the face hacked beyond recognition of the features, and the tissues of the neck were severed all round down to the bone. The viscera were found in various parts viz: the uterus and kidneys with one breast under the head, the other breast by the right foot, the liver between the feet, the intestines by the right side and the spleen by the left side of the body. The flaps removed from the abdomen and thighs were on a [bed-side] table. The bed clothing at the right corner was saturated with blood, and on the floor beneath was a pool of blood covering about two feet square. The wall by the right side of the bed and in a line with the neck was marked by blood which had struck it in a number of separate splashes.

"The face was gashed in all directions, the nose, cheeks, eyebrows and ears being partly removed. The lips were blanched and cut by several incisions running obliquely down to the chin. There were also numerous cuts extending irregularly across all the features. The neck was cut through the skin and other tissues right down to the vertebrae the 5th and 6th being deeply notched. The skin cuts in the front of the neck showed distinct ecchymosis. The air passage was cut at the lower part of the larynx through the cricoid cartilage. Both breasts were removed by more or less circular incisions, the muscles down to the ribs being attached to the breasts. The intercostals between the 4th, 5th and 6th ribs were cut and the contents of the thorax visible through the openings. The skin and tissues of the abdomen from the costal arch to the pubes were removed in three large flaps. The right thigh was denuded in front to the bone, the flap of skin, including the external organs of generation and part of the right buttock. The left thigh was stripped of skin, fascia and muscles as far as the knee. The left calf showed a long gash through skin and tissues to the deep muscles and reaching from the knee to 5 inches above the ankle. Both arms and forearms had extensive and jagged wounds. The right thumb showed a small superficial incision about one inch, with extravasation of blood in the skin and there were several abrasions on the back of the hand and forearm showing the same condition. [These wounds would appear to indicate that Mary had been able to put up some kind of a fight before she was overcome by her killer. Once again, however, no one heard any real screams so the killer must have also grabbed her by the throat or mouth to silence her. But due to the massive destruction of her throat, strangulation could not be proven by the medical examiners.] On opening the thorax it was found that the right lung was minimally adherent by old firm adhesions. The lower part of the lung was broken and torn away. The left was intact: it was adherent at the apex and there were a few adhesions over the side. In the substances of the lung were several nodules of consolidation. The pericardium was open below and the heart absent. In the abdominal cavity was some partially digested food of fish and potatoes and similar food was found in the remains of the stomach attached to the intestines."

Dr. Phillips, who was also able to examine the remains, gave testimony at the inquest:

"The mutilated remains of a female were lying two-thirds over towards the edge of the bedstead nearest the door. She had only her chemise on, or some under linen garment. I am sure that the body had been removed subsequent to the injury which caused her death from that side of the bedstead that was nearest the wooden partition, because of the large quantity of blood under the bedstead and the saturated condition of the sheet and the paillasse at the corner nearest the partition. The blood was produced by the severance of the carotid artery, which was the cause of death. The injury was inflicted while the deceased was lying at the right side of the bedstead."

All of this damage and yet the killer *never* attacked the eyes. He did, however, remove any humanity from the face. It is possible that he knew her and was trying to render her unrecognizable as he mutilated her.

Once again the vigilance committees stepped up their patrols of streets which had become all but deserted after midnight. The killing ground was now saturated with every type of officer, from beat constables and men undercover to inspectors, as well as with the private patrol forces. The secret Section D increased its patrols, this time to 143 men. However, for the most part they were looking in the wrong places.

Once again from Queen Victoria came a letter, in the third person, to the Home Secretary, Henry Matthews:

> The Queen fears that the detective department is not so efficient as it might be. No doubt the recent murders in Whitechapel were committed in circumstances which made detection very difficult; still, the Queen thinks that, in the small area where these horrible crimes have been perpetrated, a great number of detectives might be employed and that every possible suggestion might be carefully examined, and, if practicable, followed.
>
> Have the cattle boats and passenger boats been examined?
>
> *Has any investigation been made as to the number of single men occupying rooms to themselves?*
>
> The murderer's clothes must be saturated with blood and kept somewhere.
>
> Is there sufficient surveillance at night?

These are some of the questions that occur to the Queen on reading the accounts of these horrible crimes.

There were no direct clues to point to the killer and no real suspects to trace. He had left nothing at the crime scenes to show what drove him or where he had come from. He had once again committed a vicious, brutal murder, in one of the most densely populated areas of London and indeed the world, and simply walked away, once more blending in with the street traffic of the East End. No one could guess his next move, but few doubted that he would strike again. But how and where? And what *would* those in power do?

The rage continued.

Chapter Eight

The Madness Continues

"Bah, the doctors! I could give her that and none of them would ever know!"

Severin Klosowski

During the dark nights, the cold dilapidated streets of London's East End were no longer owned by the people who lived on them. They were owned by a terror so overwhelming it consumed daily life. The residents could not see the terror; they could only feel it all around them. They could not escape it. The terror was primal, pressing down hard on a captive population within the killing grounds. No one could know when, or if, the killing would ever end. The question being asked in the pubs and on the streets was: would these deaths satisfy the killer or would he need more? The Ripper would soon answer that question.

Everyone knew the killer only came out at night. He had killed from one to six in the morning. During those hours no woman would, if she could help it, walk alone in the East End. Those men who did were likely to be on some type of patrol, official or otherwise, or quickly moving towards their jobs. Indeed, at this point, anyone who walked through those dark streets at night could not go any great distance without being stopped and questioned. The *Times* reported, "It seems at times as if every person in the streets were suspicious of everyone else he met, and as if it were a race between them who could first inform against his neighbour."

Even though fear ruled the night, the days were a different matter. During the daylight hours, groups of men roamed the streets looking for anyone who could possibly match the Ripper's description, and perhaps those strangers who did not as well. Men who wore good clothes or looked respectable automatically came under suspicion. After all, what were they doing in the working man's area of the East End? Men were being grabbed by mobs and dragged to local police stations, many somewhat the worse for wear.

One, who was silly enough to declare in public that he was Jack the Ripper, was grabbed by two young men at the corner of Wentworth and Commercial Streets. The crowd, which quickly gathered, screamed "Lynch him!" As reported in the *Illustrated News*, "Sticks were raised, and the man was furiously attacked, and but for the timely arrival of the police he would have been seriously injured." There was a very *real* possibility that in a relatively small section of London, centered on Spitalfields and Whitechapel, that mob rule was going to take over the streets. For as much as there was real terror, there was an equal or greater amount of anger and rage, and those feelings would need to be directed at someone.

> The *Illustrated Police News*— November 17, 1888
> Intense Excitement in the East-End
> On Sunday the excitement created by the murder in Whitechapel had not abated to any appreciable extent, and the streets of the district were crowded, Dorset Square, the scene of the tragedy, being in the afternoon and evening in a practically congested condition. The crowds which extended even into Commercial Street rendered the locomotion all but impossible. Venders of pamphlets descriptive of the Whitechapel crimes advertised their wares in shrill tones which could be heard even above the cries of the proprietors of fruit barrows and confectionary boxes, who appeared to be doing a thriving trade. Two police constables guarded the entrance to Miller's Court, where of course the crowd was thickest, and the adjacent shop of the landlord of the house in which the body of the murdered woman had been found was besieged with people anxious to glean further particulars regarding the crime. A very short distance away an itinerant street preacher sought to improve the occasion. The assemblage within and about Dorset Street comprised men and woman of various classes, and now and then vehicles drove up containing persons impelled by curiosity to the scene of the tragedy.

The police themselves were bringing in a number of suspects who even remotely resembled the individual they were looking for, or simply acted in a strange manner. With all the extra work generated by the investigations and by the efforts of the many patrols, private and otherwise, the police forces were barely able to keep up. As an example of the level of inquiry into the Ripper case which was being demanded, the London *Times*— as published in Philip Sugden's definitive work, *The Complete*

History of Jack the Ripper— reported: "Since the murders in Berner Street, St. George's, and Mitre Square, Aldgate, on September 30, Detective-Inspectors Reid, Moore and Nairn, and Sergeants Thicke, Godley, McCarthy and Pearce have been constantly engaged, under the direction of Inspector Abberline (Scotland Yard), in prosecuting inquires, but, unfortunately, up to the present time without any practical result. As an instance of the magnitude of their labors, each officer has had, on an average, during the last six weeks to make some 30 separate inquires weekly, and these have had to be made in different portions of the metropolis and suburbs. Since the two above-mentioned murders no fewer than 1,400 letters relating to the tragedies have been received by the police, and although the greater portion of these gratuitous communications were found to be of a trivial and even ridiculous character, still each one was thoroughly investigated. On Saturday [November 10] many more letters were received, and these are now being inquired into. The detective officers, who are now subjected to a great amount of harassing work, complain that the authorities do not allow them sufficient means with which to carry on their investigation."

Despite all of the fear and terror brought on by the murders, prostitutes continued to walk the streets of Whitechapel and Spitalfields, with some even taking advantage of the situation. One such case was that of Annie Farmer. On November 20 she had picked up a customer at 7:30 in the morning. He was wearing a suit described as "shabby-genteel." They both walked over to the lodging house at 19 George Street (the same one last used by Martha Tabram), where her "gentleman friend" paid for a bed. By 9:30 a.m. the man could be seen running out of the doss house behind the screams of Annie Farmer, fully clothed. Passing two men on the street he stated, "What a ____ cow!" and was never seen again. Although Annie did have a shallow cut on her throat and claimed to have been attacked by the Ripper, the police believed that she had tried to rob the man and that the Ripper claim was used to cover up her own activities. The case was not heavily investigated by the police, but it remains an example of the lengths some individuals would go to in the slums of the East End.

By December 7, James Monro, Head of the Detective Service, had acquired new funding for even more manpower to be used in search of the killer. Monro's secret department was separate from the uniformed police department and the CID and he reported directly to the Home Secretary. His men were also expected to do their jobs with "extreme confidentiality" at all times. The new funding brought one inspector, nine sergeants, and 126 constables to the case. These men were transferred from uniform duty in different divisions and placed in patrol situations at night throughout the killing grounds of the East End. But would it be enough, and were they even looking in the right place? Even with all this activity the *Weekly Herald* of December 7, under a heading, "The Whitechapel Fiend," declared, "The new Chief Commissioner of Police has not done anything yet towards unravelling the Whitechapel mysteries." The press were still making good saleable copy out of the Ripper murders.

With all of the talk of the Ripper around London the possibility of copycat killings always existed. The *New York Times*, in its December 11 issue, reported under a headline, "Is this Jack the Ripper?: London, Dec. 10 — In a cheap restaurant in Bermondsey, a suburb of London, tonight a man, without provocation, cut the throat of the landlord's daughter. She is not expected to recover. There are rumors that the would-be murderer is 'Jack the Ripper.'" This was clearly not a Ripper case, being far too public an attack, but any such attack was bound to be reported as a Ripper possibility.

As for the Ripper himself, he was very lucky and did have evasive skills. But he was not brilliant. On the other hand, he was not stupid either. It would have taken a complete fool, or one who wanted to be captured, to continue his activities in the Whitechapel area. The Ripper had no intention of stopping and he also had no intention of allowing himself to be caught. He would return to a place he had earlier known very well. It was a place where the police protection had been reduced, as it had in many areas, because of the Ripper murders elsewhere. It would be another perfect killing ground.

When Severin Klosowski first came to London, in 1887 or early 1888, this surgical student found work, as earlier stated, in a hairdresser's shop owned by Abraham Radin at 70 West India Dock Road, Poplar, in the East End. He worked and possibly lived there for at least five months, a little more than five blocks from where the body of Rose Mylett would later be found in Poplar. She had lived in Limehouse Causeway, two blocks from Radin's shop, but was now living on George Street, Whitechapel, two blocks from where Severin Klosowski had lived very recently. It would have been impossible for them not to have walked past each other's Whitechapel lodgings many times, and they could even have known each other in Poplar. Once again, we are faced with the possibility that a Ripper victim was not a random choice. On December 14, 1888, living alone, Severin Klosowski celebrated his 23rd birthday. There is no record of what he did on that day or what present he may have given himself. Perhaps he was simply planning his next murder. Maybe he would wait until December 20 to give himself a proper gift.

A Wider Field of View

Not much is really known about Rose Mylett, and what is known can be confusing. According to her mother she was born in 1862. She had been married to an upholsterer named Davis, so perhaps she should be called Rose Davis. In fact, she was known by friends as "Drunken Lizzie Davis," because of her many drinking episodes throughout Spitalfields and Whitechapel, which considering the area must have been substantial. In 1881, she gave birth to a son who, at the time of his mother's murder, was at school in Sutton. During the years just prior to her death she lived in Limehouse in the Poplar area, and with her mother in Pelham Street, Baker's Row, Spitalfields, and at 18 George Street, Whitechapel. Most of the time she stayed at various lodging houses. There is no doubt, however, about her occupation. Rose was a known prostitute who had many aliases, including Catherine Millett or Mellett, but in Poplar her friends knew her as "Fair Alice Downey."

As with her life, little is known of her final movements leading up to her death. On the evening of December 19, 1888, Rose was seen by Charles Ptolomay at 7:55 p.m. Ptolomay worked as a night attendant in a local infirmary and saw her speaking with two sailors on Poplar High Street, near Clark's yard. This would not have been very unusual for the most part, as the London docks were nearby. But Ptolomay heard Rose say to one of the men, "No, no, no!" He would report that their conduct and suspicious manner drew his attention to them.

Hours later, on that cold morning of December 20, Rose was again seen, this time by Alice Graves, at 2:30 a.m., outside the George public house on Commercial Road. Graves related that Mylett was with two men and that she was drunk. It would be the last reported sighting of Rose Mylett alive. Where she went and what she did for the next hour and a half is unknown. At 4:15 that morning, Police Constable Robert Goulding was on his usual patrol duty on Poplar High Street. As he walked past Clark's yard (named after George Clark, the owner who stored building materials on the lot), located between 184 and 186 Poplar High Street, he noticed a woman lying in the disused lot. It was the still warm body of Rose Mylett resting on its left side. The manner in which the body was laid out, with the left leg drawn up and other leg straight out, reminded him of the bodies in recent Ripper cases.

This murder was, after all, only two miles from the Ripper's central killing ground: an easy walk from the major search area, yet far enough away from the patrols to make another attack feasible. The body, however, did not show any signs of knife wounds or any other mutilations, which had

Rose Mylett - December 20, 1888

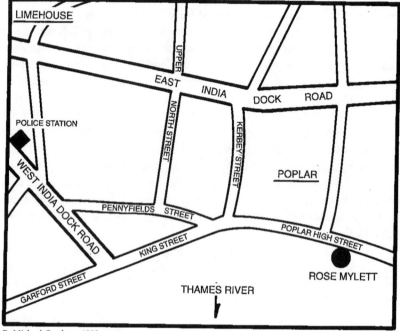

R. Michael Gordon   1998

The "Autumn of Terror" extended into December with the murder of Rose Mylett on December 20, 1888. It was a killing well outside the central killing zone but well known to Severin Klosowski. Her body was discovered at 4:15 a.m. by Constable Robert Goulding.

become the hallmark of the Ripper murders. In fact, the victim's clothes were not disheveled in any way, not unlike Stride's. Although Constable Goulding did not believe that this was a Ripper case, it is possible that the Ripper only had time to strangle this victim and not enough time to use his knife on her. He could have been very close by when the constable came across the body. And the Ripper *never* attacked a man. In fact, one witness of a suspect commented that he felt the fellow would not attack another man. There was also nothing to prevent the Ripper from killing without using his knife, as a change of pace, then as usual carefully laying his victim down in the yard. He may have even tried a murder by strangulation alone, just to see how well he could accomplish the task. Serial killers do at times try out different methods, and in order to fully understand this killer it is important that we not assume he always used his knife. We cannot become blinded by the Ripper name which the killer himself *never* used.

As with many of the Ripper cases, this possible Ripper murder is strewn with controversy. When Dr. Robert Anderson, Assistant Commissioner of the Metropolitan Police CID, investigated the murder site personally, he found evidence which pointed to no murder having been committed at all, at least in his view. He observed that there were no extra footprints "anywhere among the soft ground of the yard," and that the body "lay naturally." He also noticed that there was no struggle around the lot and no evidence of a struggle on the body. With these observations Anderson concluded that murder had not been done. And yet, with all the officers and medical men who must have been in the yard before he arrived, how could he have determined that there were no extra footprints?

It must be remembered that there were very few, if any, signs of struggle in any of the other Ripper cases, yet they were certainly murders. The Ripper did indeed use strangulation as the primary means of subduing his victims, as do many sadistic sexual serial murders of this day and age. It is also possible that the killer strangled his victim just outside the yard, then took her body into the yard. There is no evidence either way.

Later that day, Dr. Matthews Brownfield, Metropolitan Police Surgeon for K Division, became the first to examine Mylett's body. In his postmortem report he stated: "Blood was oozing from the nostrils, and there was a slight abrasion on the right side of the face…. On the neck there was a mark which had evidently been caused by a cord drawn tightly round the neck, from the spine to the left ear. Such a mark would be made by a four thread cord. There were also impressions of the thumbs and middle and index fingers of some person plainly visible on each side of the neck. There were no injuries to the arms or legs. The brain was gorged with an almost black fluid blood. The stomach was full of meat and potatoes, which had only recently been eaten.

"*Death was due to strangulation.* Deceased could not have done it herself. The marks on her neck were probably caused by her trying to pull the cord off. The murderer must have stood at the left rear of the woman, and, having the ends of the cord round his hands, thrown it round her throat, crossed his hands, and thus strangled her. If it had been done in this way, it would account for the mark not going completely round the neck." Or did the Ripper simply use his bare hands?

When Dr. Anderson read Brownfield's report he completely disagreed. It is not clear whether Anderson, and the police, truly felt that this was not a Ripper murder, or they simply did not want the general public to believe that the murderer had expanded his killing ground and be required to cover a much larger area. Police resources were, at the time, stretched to an all time limit and a much larger area could not have been covered in the way being done in Whitechapel and Spitalfields. Whatever the reason, Anderson demanded a second opinion. He called on Dr. Thomas Bond, the police surgeon from Division A, who had worked on the Mary Jane Kelly and Torso cases, to have a look at the victim. It would, however, be a few days before Bond could view the body. Because of Dr. Bond's unavailability the Senior Police Surgeon for Westminster Division A, Alexander McKellar, and Bond's personal assistant both went immediately to examine the body — the two men also came to the conclusion that it was a case of "willful murder by strangulation."

Only after five days was Dr. Bond himself able to view the remains. In two separate examinations, he could not see the marks on the neck which would have indicated strangulation, and he saw no secondary indications of this type of murder, such as a protruding tongue or clenched fists. He put forth the theory that Mylett had fallen down in a drunken stupor and was choked to death by her own stiff collar. This was his conclusion, though, only after being sent back for the second examination by Anderson. What pressure had Anderson placed on the doctor? After the first examination he, too, had concluded that the victim had been strangled. At that point four fully qualified medical men had declared the case a murder by strangulation. However, the medical examination found no alcohol in Rose Mylett's stomach, only a meal of "meat and potatoes, which had been recently eaten." She was simply *not drunk* and thus could not have fallen down in a "drunken stupor." Anderson, it would seem, was grasping at straws for any explanation which would rule out murder. Why?

The inquest was held on January 2, 1889, and reconvened on January 9. It was conducted by Wynne Baxter at Poplar Coroner's Court and would prove to be very controversial. Dr. Brownfield's report was not "acceptable" to the police or to Anderson. The police brought up the point that the marks on the neck — which they now accepted as being present, despite Dr. Bond's report — only encircled it one-quarter the way around. Further, the police were not able to find a string or ligature in the yard and therefore felt that it did not exist. Not a very good piece of deduction to say that a weapon does not exist simply because it was not found. Weak evidence to be sure since they never found the Ripper knife either, but it most certainly existed.

Robert Anderson and the police forces, for whatever reason, did not want this case to be placed in the murder files, and certainly nowhere near the Ripper case. Dr. George Phillips, who had worked on five of the Ripper cases, felt that Mylett's murderer "had studied the theory of strangulation, for he evidently knew where to place the cord so as to immediately bring his victim under control." This was now the fifth respected doctor to state that it was murder by strangulation. So there was evidence the killer had anatomical knowledge, and it must be stated that the Ripper was very adept at strangulation.

Coroner Baxter was not about to put up with any police reports which pointed to, as he put it, "this nonsense of death by natural causes." On January 9, he summed up for the jury and stated, "After Dr. Brownfield and his assistant, duly qualified men, came to the conclusion that this was a case of homicidal strangulation, someone had a suspicion that the evidence was not satisfactory. At all events, you've heard that doctor after doctor went down to view the body without my knowledge or sanction as coroner. I did not wish to make that a personal matter, but I had never received such treatment before." (What were these officials trying to cover up?)

"Of the five doctors who saw the body, Dr. Bond was the only one who considered the case was not one of murder. Dr. Bond did not see the body until five days after her death and he was, therefore, at a disadvantage. Dr. Bond stated that if this was a case of strangulation he should have expected to find the skin broken, but it was clearly shown, on reference being made to the records of the Indian doctors in the cases of Thug Murders, that there were no marks whatever left. Other eminent authorities agreed with that view."

It was not long before the jury came up with the now familiar verdict of "Willful murder by person or persons unknown." Despite the conclusion reached by the coroner and the jury, both Anderson and the CID refused to put any men on the case, stating that it would be a waste of time and manpower. Anderson was, however, required to file a report with the Home Office explaining his reasons for not investigating the death beyond the inquest.

In the Scotland Yard files on the Ripper case, a file may be found which lists victims, and possible victims, of the Whitechapel Killer. *Rose Mylett is on that list.* So no matter who her killer was, the police not only knew that Rose Mylett was indeed murdered, they were also quite aware the Ripper could have done it. The bottom line is: they covered up.

It was 22 years later when Sir Robert Anderson wrote of the Rose Mylett murder. In his book, *The Lighter Side of My Official Life*, published in 1910, he said, "Poplar [Mylett] case of December, 1888, was death from natural causes, and but for the 'Jack the Ripper' scare, no one would have thought of suggesting that it was a homicide." It would appear that a cover-up sometimes lasts a lifetime.

He was, perhaps, unfamiliar with a man named Klosowski. The facts, however, are crystal clear. This was another dead woman, located at night, in an area *very* familiar to Klosowski, where he had both lived and worked. The coincidences, if that is what they are, were starting to pile up high against him. Either Klosowski was the Ripper, or the Ripper was following him around and dropping off bodies to incriminate him.

The bloody year of 1888 was finally over and the police officials did not want, for obvious reasons, anyone thinking the Ripper was still active and expanding his hunting ground even though they knew better. The Ripper himself had no such idea and was not about to end his work, at least for now. The press were also fully aware that the chase was still on and not just in London. On the last day of 1888 the *Pall Mall Gazette* would report, "Inspector Andrews of Scotland Yard, has arrived in New York from Montreal. It is generally believed that he has received orders from England to commence his search in this city for the Whitechapel murderer." Scotland Yard *knew* the Ripper was still out there!

1889

Throughout that cold winter, both police and unofficial vigilance patrols continued to search for the Ripper without success. There were men who were stopped and taken to police stations, but none was the serial killer. By February, the Toynbee Hall students, who were working with the St. Jude's Vigilance Committee, ended their efforts, in part due to the lack of reported Ripper activity and because of the long hours required, at night, in the miserable weather.

On January 26, 1889, Assistant Metropolitan Police Commissioner James Monro informed the Home Office that he would be "gradually reducing the number of men employed on this duty as quickly as it is safe to do so." By mid–March, the special patrols by Monro's forces would end, as the Ripper seemed to have ended his carnage. In fact, it has been reported that in March 1889, William Bachert, of the Mile End Vigilance Committee, had been informed by the police that the Ripper had died by drowning, possibly at his own hand, at the end of 1888. However, there is nothing in the actions of the police or their files to indicate that *they* actually believed the Ripper was indeed dead. It is very possible the authorities simply wanted to rid themselves of an individual who had badgered them for months. Actually, the police were actively searching for the killer well into the new year, so it could not have been a story believed by the officers working on the case. But the information about this story is at best third hand as it is said to come from Dr. Thomas Dutton through Donald McCormick.

As stated earlier, overlaying the terror of the Ripper series was a second series of murders becoming known as the Thames Torso murders. They were so named because the torsos of four women, as well as several arms and legs, were recovered in or near the Thames River in 1887-89. None of the heads of these four murder victims were ever recovered. Could there have been a second sexual serial killer working the same small area of East London, at the same time as the Ripper, killing the same type of women? This serial killer, like the Ripper, was never caught and convicted of these crimes and the police authorities, who did not solve this case either, were quick to assign this series of deaths to a killer other than the Ripper. But were they correct in that assessment?

The Torso of Elizabeth Jackson

From the evening papers of June 4, 1889, London residents were once again to be shocked by another East End murder. What made this torso murder different from the others was the fact that the victim would eventually be identified. Her name was Elizabeth Jackson.

At the time of her death she was 24 years old. She was described by her mother, Catherine Jackson, as being plump, well formed, around 5 feet 5 inches tall, with a fair complexion and reddish gold hair. She also reported that Elizabeth had a "beautiful set of teeth and nicely shaped hands." She was the youngest of three daughters, with sisters named May and Annie. And not unlike the Ripper victims she was also a prostitute.

Elizabeth was 16 years old in 1881, when she began work as a domestic servant in Chelsea in London, where she came from. Considered of "excellent character," she continued in that line of work until suddenly leaving it, and her home, in November 1888. It was around this time that her sister Annie met her on Turk's Row, Chelsea. Elizabeth had been speaking to a man when Annie called to her. Hearing the call, Elizabeth went over to talk with her sister, who promptly accused her of picking up men for immoral purposes. The meeting ended in an argument with an angry Elizabeth walking away. It was the last time her sister Annie would see her younger sister.

Around the end of November, Elizabeth met a man named John Faircloth in a pub on the corner of Turk's Row. She told Faircloth that she had been living with a man named Charlie for a while, but that did not stop her from going off with Faircloth. The evidence indicates that she was "easy." They both went off to Ipswich where they remained for around four months. Faircloth was described as being a miller by trade and a native of Cambridgeshire who had served in the 3rd Battalion of the Grenadier Guards. He had a twisted nose, fair complexion, stood 5 feet 9 inches tall, and was 37 years of age when he met Elizabeth.

On March 30, 1889, the pair went to Colchester to find any kind of work they could, but it was a vain attempt. Neither finding employment soon forced them to walk all the way to London, ending up in Whitechapel. There they stayed at one of the common lodging houses. On April 18, the pair moved into a room at Mrs. Paine's house on Manila Street, Millwall. "The man called himself John Faircloth." Mrs. Paine described him as being older than Elizabeth and violent towards her.

The move to the East End did not go well for John and Elizabeth, as once again no work could be found. It was at that point that John asked her to go with him to Croydon but Elizabeth decided not to make the move. Instead, she told Faircloth that she would go and stay with her mother. She did not tell him that her mother was in the workhouse. It would be on April 28 that John went to Croydon, and he never saw Elizabeth again. The next day she left the room at Mrs. Paine's owing a week's rent.

Not long after she left her room she was spotted walking the streets of Chelsea by Mrs. Mary Minter of Cheyne Road who had known Elizabeth for years. She told Mrs. Minter that she had been living for a few months with a man who had not treated her well. He had left her penniless, and she had only been able to sleep "out in the raw" for the past few days on the Thames Embankment. She was dressed very shabbily and Mrs. Minter gave her threepence for food and told her that she should go to the workhouse. Crying, she told Mrs. Minter, "I don't like to do that because for one thing, my mother is there, and she would be angry with me, and, for another thing, I am expecting."

Mrs. Minter tried to give her some comfort and gave her an ulster; a very long loosely worn overcoat named after Ulster, Ireland. With the gift she said, "At any rate, it will keep you warm." The last time Mrs. Minter saw her, the next day, Elizabeth was still wearing the long coat. It would be the coat, and a small piece of linen with the name L.E. Fisher, which would lead to her identification after her murder. The linen clothing had been purchased, secondhand, at the Ipswich lodging house, by John Faircloth.

Elizabeth would later be seen by a woman named Annie Dwyer who lived on Turk's Row in Chelsea. It was the Monday before Whit Sunday, and she was still wearing the ulster. She described the man she saw walking with Elizabeth as looking like a sailor. He was wearing a dark cloth coat, rough cap and light moleskin trousers.

On May 31, Catherine Jackson saw her daughter for the last time, and quite by accident. While walking along Queens Road she spotted Elizabeth, who quickly began to walk away but turned around after her mother begged her to stop. She was still wearing the old coat and after much discussion Elizabeth agreed to spend the afternoon with her mother. She told her that she was expecting and that the father, John Faircloth, was not able to find any work and had left her in Poplar. She was also wearing a brass ring to indicate that she was married, which of course she was not. For both mother and daughter it was a long and well spent day.

It was 10:30 in the morning of June 4 when the first body parts were discovered. A dock worker named John Regan was standing along the bank of the Thames waiting for work to begin near St. George's Stair at Horselydown. He saw a couple of young boys throwing stones at an object floating off the river bank at about three yards distance. The boys pulled the bundle to the shore and at once were able to see that it contained a portion of a body wrapped in what looked like an apron. At that point a Thames River Police boat passed by and was hailed by the small unlucky group. The remains were then taken to Wapping police station for further investigation.

Later that day, a young man named Isaac Brett, who worked as a woodchopper in Chelsea, found a wrapped bundle under the Albert Bridge where he had gone to bathe. What he found was a woman's leg and thigh wrapped in a section of an ulster and tied with a bootlace. He immediately retied the parcel and brought it to the nearest police station. It was on closer inspection, at the station, that the piece of old linen was found with the name L.E. Fisher on it.

June 6 would bring to light still more remains. In the afternoon, Joseph Davis, who worked as a gardener in Battersea Park, found what he described as a "curious looking bundle" in a secluded section of the park among some shrubbery. He opened the linen-wrapped package to discover, to his great shock, a section of human remains. It took a while before he could recover his composure but when he had done so sufficiently he rushed off to deliver the package to the closest police station. It is quite possible that the killer had fully meant to dispose of all his parts in the Thames but was somehow prevented from doing so by some unforeseen event or passerby.

Two days later, a newspaper reporter named Claude Mellor was walking past Mr. Percy Shelley's home on the Chelsea Embankment on the Thames when he spotted something unusual. In the house's garden he could see what he thought was a small section of a human body which had seemingly washed up just inside the fence. Other body parts were washing up off of Copington Wharf, Southwark, Bankside and West India Dock. By June 25 the last of the body parts had been located along the Thames.

The remains were put together and examined by Dr. Bond, along with Doctors Hibberd and Kempster. They were able to find that the single victim had been a woman from 24 to 25 years of age and of fair complexion. They also found that she had, on her left hand, worn a ring which was missing. (Similar to Annie Chapman.) Perhaps it was kept by the killer as a trophy of the kill. They were also able to see that she was pregnant when murdered. But due to the condition of the much mutilated remains the exact cause of death could not be ascertained. Dr. Bond also stated that the cutting was more along the lines of the work of a butcher than someone familiar with anatomy. But he admitted that firm conclusions were difficult to draw due to the poor condition of the remains, some of which had spent weeks in the water. By scars on it, the body would be identified as that of prostitute Elizabeth Jackson by friends who knew her very well. She would become the only victim in the torso series to be positively identified. Once again, however, the head would never be recovered.

The inquest jury, after a very short session, came to the only reasonable conclusion it could find: "Wilful murder against some person or persons unknown." There was however, at least one classic error in the handling of the case: Jackson's death certificate records her death as June 4–10. This last date would be at least six days after her body parts were starting to wash up on shore.

Most who say this was not a Ripper case look at the method of disposal as the deciding factor. But serial killers do not stay with one method as a strict rule. They learn and change as needed. Perhaps the heads held too much evidence and had to be disposed of in a different manner. Or perhaps he was just a collector. One New York City serial killer, working in the late 1980s and early 1990s, stated that some of his killings were committed on the spur of the moment and he had a body to dispose of and no plan to do so. This killer turned to dismemberment as the way to handle the problem. But he did not always cut up his victims. For him it was trial and error, as it could have been for the Ripper. Without knowing for sure why the Ripper killed, we cannot state for a fact that at times he would not change his method of operation. We simply do not know, and without such knowledge, these Torso murders cannot be attributed to some other killer. Poison was of course another option not to be dismissed for the future.

In the House of Commons on July 29, Mr. Howard Vincent reported to the members on the increase of crime occurring in the City of London:

> Crime during the year has shown a decided tendency to increase. This fact may be accounted for to a certain extent by circumstances which affected the administration of the force in a peculiar manner at different periods of the year. The agitation which centered in Trafalgar Square, and the murders in Whitechapel, necessitated the concentration, in particular localities, of large bodies of police, and such an increase of force in one quarter of the Metropolis, it must be remembered, is only procurable by diminishing the number of men ordinarily employed in

other divisions. In the present state of the force, increase of protection in the East End means diminished numbers of police in other quarters, and so long as the available force is hardly sufficient, as it is just now, for the performance of the ordinary and every day duties of the police, any additional drain on its resources leads to diminished protection against, and consequent increase of, crime…. The fact [is] that the force is overworked, and, under such circumstances, crime cannot be met or coped with in a satisfactory and efficient manner.

On July 25, another contrived Ripper letter arrived at Scotland Yard, probably from the same journalist author of the first letters. It could be assumed that newspaper sales were going down. This new letter read:

Dear Boss
Have not caught me yet you see, with all your cunning, with all your "Lees" with all your blue bottles. I have made two narrow squeaks this week, but still though disturbed I got clear before I could get to work — I will give the foreigners a turn now I think — for a change — Germans especially if I can — I was conversing with two or three of your men last night — their eyes of course were shut and thus they did not see my bag. Ask any of your men who were on duty last night in Piccadilly (Circus End) if they saw a gentleman put 2 dragoon guard sergeants into a hansom. I was close by and heard him talk about shedding blood in Egypt I will soon shed more in England. I hope you read mark and learn all that you can if you do so you may and may not catch
Jack the Ripper

Marriage Is Such Good Cover

As published in many of the local papers, the police were looking for a single man who lived alone. With things getting hot there could be no better cover for the Ripper than to be married and looking respectable. In late June or early July of 1889, only days after the final parts of Elizabeth Jackson's remains were found, Severin Klosowski decided to visit the Polish Club in St. John's Square, Clerkenwell. There he met Stanislaus Baderski who worked as a tailor in Walthamstow. Baderski would later recall, "He was introduced to me as Severin Klosowski and said that he had a barber shop." Klosowski also met Stanislaus's sister Lucy at the same club. Within four or five weeks Klosowski and Lucy were living together at 126 Cable Street, St. George-in-the-East.

On October 29, 1889, Severin and Lucy were married in a German Roman Catholic ceremony, even though he may well still have been married to a first wife in Poland. From this point on he would have someone very close to him who would be able to report on what type of individual he was and what his habits were. When interviewed by Inspector Fred Abberline, years later, for another series of murders, Lucy would state, "He was often out until three or four in the morning." After extensive questioning, Abberline reported, she could "not throw any light on these absences." One thing is clear: his late night activities could not have been a new activity just when Lucy arrived; that would not make any logical sense. It is much more reasonable to assume that his nighttime "walks" were a general part of his lifestyle, begun when he first came to London and perhaps even before.

Before he began living with Lucy, however, and before another marriage was entered into, there was one more piece of business he had to attend to.

Her name was Alice "Clay Pipe" McKenzie.

She was born around 1849, and may have been raised in Peterborough. Sometime about 1874, at 25 or so years of age, she moved to London's East End. Of her early life there is not much more that can be known. It is possible that she had two sons who did not live in England. Time has erased the facts as it has with many who lived so long ago. Nine years after her arrival in the East End, around 1883, she began living off and on with an Irishman named John McCormack. He worked for some Jewish tailors on Hanbury Street as a porter. For six years they shared rooms in various doss houses more or less as man and wife. Yet McCormack would prove of little help to the police as he knew so little about Alice's background. It was reported that before her time with McCormack she lived with a blind man, but he was never identified. In April 1889, they moved to Mr. Tenpenny's lodging house at 52 or 54 Gun Street, Spitalfields. It was managed by Mrs. Elizabeth Ryder.

Those who knew Alice gave her the nickname "Clay Pipe" for her constant use of the pipe for smoking. The freckle-faced Alice worked doing housework and as a washerwoman. But to the police she was just another common prostitute, one of many hundreds still walking the dark streets of the East End, despite the atrocities of the Ripper. She was also one of the many who had syphilis.

On Tuesday, July 16, 1889, around 4 p.m., as soot-choked air mixed with moisture-laden clouds, John McCormack returned to the room he shared at Mr. Tenpenny's lodging house. He was a bit drunk. He met Alice, and he gave her 1s. 8d. The money was for the rent and other expenses. Alice accepted the money and left. But she failed to pay the rent, and slipped into the gray overcast afternoon of London's East End.

For three hours there was no word of her whereabouts. But at 7:10

p.m. she was seen with a blind boy named George Dixon. Dixon would later report that he had heard Alice speaking to a man he referred to as "strange." Alice had asked the man to buy her a drink later and the man had accepted. With the date arranged, she brought the young boy home to Gun Street. At 8:30 p.m. Mrs. Ryder again saw Alice at the doss house and would report that she was "more or less drunk." Alice was leaving the house after an argument with McCormack, which was not an uncommon event. It would not be until 11 p.m., when McCormack went downstairs, that he found out, from Mrs. Ryder, that Alice had not paid the rent.

At 11:40 p.m., Alice was spotted by three women on Flower and Dean Street. It was while they were seated on the steps of either a "*barber's shop*" on the Brick Lane end of the street or of a lodging house on the Commercial Street end, depending on the source of the story. Either way, her friend Margaret Franklin spotted Alice "walking hurriedly" towards Whitechapel. When she asked her how she was doing, Alice replied, "All right. I can't stop now." Was she late for a meeting with Jack the Ripper? As Alice continued on, the three women noticed that she was not wearing her bonnet but did have over her shoulders a "light coloured shawl." It was the last confirmed sighting of Alice McKenzie alive. She had less than an hour to live as she rushed on into the darkness of the London night.

Police Constable Joseph Allen, 423H, was taking a break under a street lamp two-thirds the way into Castle Alley at 12:15 a.m. He was just off Whitechapel High Street, having a bite to eat, during just one more long night on patrol duty. He saw no one. After five minutes he left when he saw a brother officer, Constable Walter Andrews, 272H, enter the 135-yard-long alley. Andrews stayed in the alley for three minutes and he also saw no one. He left at 12:23 a.m. The alley itself was entered from Whitechapel High Street through a very narrow covered brick entry, and as with most such paths in the area, except for the street lamp, it was very dark. The area was used mostly by those familiar with Whitechapel, as it appeared to be a dark dead end to any casual viewers walking past.

At around 12:25 a.m., Sarah Smith, the deputy of the Whitechapel baths and washhouses, which ran along Castle Alley, went to her room. She also saw no one. In her room, she started reading near a window which overlooked the entire alley. She would later report that she heard nothing and saw no one until she heard the police whistle.

At 12:45 a.m., rain once again came to Whitechapel, but this time it would bring a clue. Walking his regular beat, just after speaking with Sergeant Badham at the corner of Old Castle Street, Constable Andrews stepped into Castle Alley at 12:50 a.m. It was around 27 minutes since he had last walked through the area. This time, only feet away from the street

Alice McKenzie - July 17, 1889

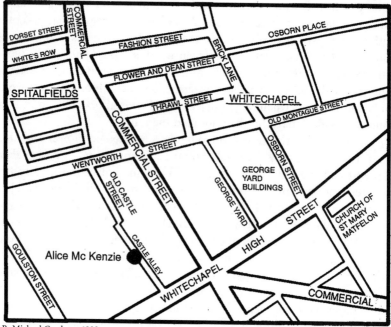

R. Michael Gordon   1998

Returning to the central killing fields the Ripper murdered Alice "Claypipe" McKenzie only two short blocks west of his first murder of Martha Tabram, 11 months earlier. McKenzie's body was discovered at 12:45 a.m. on July 17, 1889, by Constable Walter Andrews.

lamp PC Allen had used during his break, Andrews discovered the body of Alice McKenzie. She was lying on the pavement, feet towards the wall, just outside the back door to David King's Contractors. Blood was still flowing from the two four-inch jagged stabs on the left side of her neck. This was the same type of neck wound inflicted on Ada Wilson nearly 16 months earlier. Her skirt had been pulled up and her abdomen attacked with a knife. A closer view of the body showed that the ground under her was still dry which placed her death between 12:25 a.m., when Sarah Smith went to her room, and 12:45 a.m. when it began to rain. Later, one of her clay pipes and a farthing would be found under her body, possibly dropped by her as she struggled with her silent killer.

As Constable Andrews was inspecting the body, he heard Lewis Jacobs walking towards the alley on his way to purchase a meal. As Jacobs arrived Andrews ordered him to watch over the body as he went for help. He soon located Sergeant Edward Badham, 31H, whose job it was to inspect the beat constables. Badham had heard Andrews' whistle after only going 150 yards down the street, and hurried back to Castle Alley. At around 1:10 a.m. Inspector Reid arrived in the alley and recorded that blood was still flowing from her throat and into the gutter. Two minutes later, Dr. Bagster Phillips arrived and noticed that the blood was beginning to clot. He certified death and recorded that the cause was two stabs on the left side of her neck, which had severed the left carotid artery, and were "carried forward in the same skin wound." She also had bruises on her chest and five bruises on the left side of her abdomen. There was a wound seven inches long "but not unduly deep" from the bottom of the left breast to the navel, as well as seven or eight "scratches" from the navel towards the genitalia. Finally, it was found that she had a small cut on the mons veneris.

As police forces began to converge on the alley they were dispatched in all directions to search for the killer. They entered the nearby lodging houses and local coffee houses still open but they were unable to come up with any suspects.

By 3 a.m. James Monro was on the spot to see the murder site for himself. He was not about to pass up the chance to personally investigate. If this was another Ripper crime he wanted to be part of the investigation.

But Was It Jack?

Almost immediately there was disagreement, again, among officials as to whether or not this victim was one of the Ripper's. It is true that the victim died due to the severing of the left carotid artery, which is in line with the Ripper series, but there was no evidence this time of strangulation. Also, most of the Ripper victims had deeper and longer wounds to the throat right down to the spinal column. This victim also had no damage to her air passages as the others had. But the Ripper could have been adjusting his technique. Dr. Phillips did note that there was some level of anatomical knowledge required to commit the murder. He stated that the murderer "knew the position of the vessels, at any rate where to cut with reference to causing speedy death." It would be investigatively incorrect to expect a serial killer to murder time after time in only one way. It was clear, however, that this was not a robbery-murder — it was, once more, a killing for pleasure and, of course, the victim was a prostitute.

It could simply be that this victim was able to struggle, perhaps not yell out, but struggle. The bruises on her chest do point to her being held down on the ground while she was stabbed on the left side of her neck by a right handed attacker. Also, the five bruises on the left side of her abdomen could very well indicate the victim was punched by her assailant before being held down. Her killer was a powerful man. But there was no disagreement as to what killed her: both doctors on the case asserted that it was a "sharp pointed weapon."

After his post-mortem examination, Dr. Phillips gave his opinion as to the possible continuation of the Ripper's work when he wrote: "After careful and long deliberation, I cannot satisfy myself, on purely anatomical and professional grounds that the perpetrator of all the 'Wh Ch. murders' is our man. I am on the contrary impelled to a contrary conclusion in this noting the mode of procedure and the character of the mutilations and judging of motive in connection with the latter.

"I do not here enter into the comparison of the cases neither do I take into account what I admit may be almost conclusive evidence in favor of the one man theory if all the surrounding circumstances and other evidence are considered, holding it as my duty to report on the P. M. appearances and express an opinion only on Professional grounds, based upon my own observation."

Alice McKenzie — July 17, 1889. Neck cut with two four-inch jagged stabs on left side, severing the carotid artery; seven-inch wound on chest; bruises on chest and left side of abdomen. (Public Record Office.)

Dr. Thomas Bond, in his capacity as police surgeon for A Division, examined the body, as it began to decompose, the day after the post-mortem. He reported the results of his examination to Assistant Commissioner Anderson. "I see in this murder evidence of similar design to the former Whitechapel murders viz. sudden onslaught on the prostrate woman, the throat skillfully and resolutely cut with subsequent mutilation, each mutilation indicating sexual thoughts and a desire to mutilate the abdomen and sexual organs. I am of opinion that the murder was performed by the same person who committed the former series of Whitechapel murders." Only eight months after the Kelly murder it is significant that Doctor Bond used the words "former series."

Even though he was not in the city, but on leave at the time of the murder, Anderson gave an opinion which made it clear that he felt the Ripper was not responsible for the latest atrocity. "I am here *assuming* that the murder of Alice McKenzie on the 17th of July 1889, was by another hand. I was absent from London when it occurred, but the Chief Commissioner investigated the case on the spot and decided it was an ordinary murder, and not of a sexual maniac." Once again, Anderson would do his best to discount a murder as being that of the Ripper, even when he was out of the country and had no first hand knowledge of the events.

Many of the powers-that-be were trying hard to put the Ripper murders behind them. They had now been searching for him for the better part of a year, without success. The only way he was going to stop was if he was captured or became an inactive killer. The Government needed some type of closure as the costs continued to pile up. However, Home Secretary Matthews felt that "The circumstances of the present murder are so far as known, almost identical with those of last year...."

The head of the detective service, James Monro, stated, "I need not say that every effort will be made by the police to discover the murderer, who, I am inclined to believe, is identical with the notorious Jack the Ripper of last year." Monro had not let up his search for the killer, and his Secret Department still consisted of 39 constables and 3 sergeants working in the Whitechapel area. To this force he added an additional 22 men hoping to move with speed on a hot new trail. But where would he look?

Once again Coroner Wynne Baxter chaired an inquest. This time it was begun on the very day of the murder. Held on July 17 and 19, and then adjourned to August 14, it ultimately came to the inevitable conclusion, that McKenzie's death was an act of murder by "person or persons unknown."

The *New York Times*— July 18, 1889
The Whitechapel Crime
No Clue to the perpetrator of the latest murder
London, July 17.— The woman whose body was found in Castle Alley, in the Whitechapel district, last night was a middle aged female of the disreputable class. Her throat had been cut to the spine. When the body was found it was lying on its back. ... A policeman, who with the watchman of an adjacent warehouse must have been within a few yards of the spot when the crime was committed, heard no noise. Policemen have been placed at fixed points in Whitechapel since the murders of this character began there, and since the one preceding that of last night officers have been stationed at a point within a hundred yards of the scene of the last tragedy. ... Several arrests of suspected persons have been made, but they were discharged from custody, there being no proof on which to hold them.

The *New York Times* then reported, in its July 21 edition, the goings-on in Whitechapel because of the revival of the killing spree. "This sinister revival of the Whitechapel butcheries has not specially excited the well-to-do parts of London, where, in fact, it seems to be taken as an interesting variation upon the midsummer monotony of existence; but people who saw something of the slums in the east and south parts of the metropolis last night will never forget the unprecedented and terrible spectacle. Thousands of the lowest gutter type of street women were drunk in very bravado; all the refuse population of countless stews was swarming aimlessly from one gin shop to another, shouting, quarreling, and shrieking hideous jokes. Many hundreds of extra police, seemingly more stolid, heavy-footed, and thick-witted than ever, pushed their pompous way through the throngs, and nobody talked or thought for a moment about anything but Jack the Ripper. ... It takes an event like this to show the London press and London police at their very worst, and it would be hard to say in the present instance which is the least adorable. There seems to be no more prospect now than there was a year ago that the remarkable criminal who is committing these murders will be detected, unless it be by chance."

During August 1889, a few weeks after the death of Alice McKenzie, Severin Klosowski moved Lucy Baderski into his rooms above his hairdresser's shop at 126 Cable Street, St. George-in-the-East. (According to Lucy's brother, Stanislaus Baderski, Klosowski had told him that it was his barbershop.) It was not an area of great safety. Many of the buildings were run down and abandoned, and many unsavory individuals could be found in and around the area at all hours of the day and night. Indeed, according to the excellent research found in *The Jack the Ripper A to Z*, just off Cable Street to the west was "full of cheap taverns, brothels, opium dens (at the Limehouse end), slop shops (selling seamen second hand clothes) and exotic pet shops (where seaman could sell animals collected in foreign lands). Mugging, pocket-picking and shanghaiing (kidnapping to provide crews for shorthanded merchantmen) were rife." These were also excellent hunting grounds for a serial killer. Many passed that way but few would have been missed or even noticed.

The street itself ran along a railroad line which ended its run in the Railway Goods Depot. It was not a place where a great deal of hairdressing business could be expected to be conducted. It was outside the Ripper search area, though, and the River Thames was only a few blocks away to the south. It was as close as it could be to the river and yet still be within a short walking distance of central Whitechapel. Although it was no place to live or conduct business, it did afford an excellent hideout and base of operations beyond Whitechapel ... for a serial killer.

Another Torso —
The Pinchin Street Mystery

As Klosowski was roaming the dark streets of the East End during the early morning hours, the authorities continued their search for the elusive Jack the Ripper. It had been nearly two months since a murder had occurred in which the name of the Ripper had been spoken. The time would come again.

A news vendor out of Charing Cross, later identified as John Arnold, made a statement that as he was leaving the King Lud public house on the night of September 7 he ran into a soldier on Fleet Street. The soldier reported to him that he should, "Hurry up with your papers. Another horrible murder in Backchurch Lane." Arnold proceeded to the London offices of the *New York Herald* to tell his story. He described the soldier as "...between 35 and 36 years old standing five feet six inches, fair complexion and mustache." He also stated that the soldier carried a parcel. It was an interesting tale with only one problem — a body had yet to be discovered in that area because a murder had yet to be committed.

Around September 8, 1889, a well-known prostitute and East End character named Lydia Hart, came up missing. This in itself was not unusual in a city the size of London. And no one was keeping track of prostitutes, except Jack. It was, however, the one-year anniversary of Annie Chapman's death. It was also the estimated date of Hart's death, if indeed the torso was hers. The name of Lydia Hart was reported in the *World* newspaper, out of New York, on September 11, 1889, as the possible name of the victim, only because she was a missing East End prostitute who had not been seen by her friends for almost a week. There was never any positive evidence for the claim.

On regular beat duty on September 10, 1889, at 5:15 a.m., Police Constable William Pennett, 239H, discovered the mutilated corpse of a woman under a Great Eastern Railway arch in Pinchin Street. The stench of the decomposing body had first attracted his attention. The corpse had no head or legs, and the abdomen had been mutilated with a 15-inch gash (similar to the Ripper mutilations). Constable Pennett had patrolled the same area some 15 minutes earlier and had neither seen nor smelled anything out of the ordinary. The torso had the remains of a cheap chemise still on which was similar to the one found on Mary Kelly's body. It had been torn down the front and cut with a knife. Both women could very well have been sleeping at the time they were murdered. The dumping of the torso between police patrols echoed the Ripper technique of close contact with danger of discovery, and he was familiar with the area. The corpse was also just a few blocks away from where Elizabeth Stride had been murdered a little less than a year earlier.

Pennett could see no pool of blood on the ground nor were there any footprints to be found under the arch. He stood still so that he could take in the area around him. He had thought about using his whistle to call for assistance but feared that it may alarm the murderer who he felt would still be very near the area.

Constable Pennett, after his discovery and survey of the area, called for assistance and began to search the ground around where he had found the torso. A street cleaner came along at that point and Pennett told him to go and get the constable who was on patrol at the bottom of the street just to the east. "Tell him I've got a job on, and make haste." It was obvious that the woman had been killed elsewhere and dumped on the Pinchin Street site, but it was just as obvious that a man could not have been expected to walk very far carrying an object as large as a torso without being noticed. It was starting to get light, and there were simply too many police in the area. Not long after the discovery Inspector Charles Pinhorn arrived and took charge of the investigation. Later, Inspector Moore would be put in charge of the case. He had earlier been responsible for the investigation into Stride's murder on Berner Street.

A search of the area quickly uncovered two sailors, one named Richard Hawk, and a shoeblack, Michael Keating of 1 Osborn Street, who had been sleeping under an arch right next to the one where the body was found. They all reported that they had heard and seen nothing unusual, but that may have been due to their intoxicated condition. However, all three were taken into custody for further questioning, but were soon released when it was shown they had nothing to do with the crime. Some bloodstained clothes were found on Batty Street, by none other than Sgt. Godley, but they were not successfully linked to the victim.

It should be noted that the northern entrance of Pinchin Street was fenced off by wooden palings and thus difficult to access from that direction, especially by a person carrying a body. Behind the wooden palings was Pinchin and Johnson's paint and oil company. It seems reasonable then to assume that the killer came into deserted Pinchin Street from the south. Just to the south, and just across the tracks, lived *Severin Klosowski on Cable Street.* From his location he could have viewed the police patrols and easily dumped a body a mere 150 yards away. He would have been familiar with the street, called "dark lane," and would have known it to be uninhabited. To the south of his "shop" flowed the River Thames: it could well have carried away the legs and head of this latest murder victim. Klosowski was literally *in between the body and its parts*. It would have taken no more than five minutes to dump the torso in the early morning and return to his home to dump the rest in the river. Once again we are faced with a murder committed right in front of Klosowski's front door. This *cannot* be said of any other *alleged* suspect. And, there is no disagreement as to Klosowski's location at the time of this murder. Also, Klosowski would have had the opportunity to work in his own home without interruption. It is doubtful his "wife" would have gone into a particular room or a basement if Severin had told her not to. He was always in control of the situation. At least, he was for the time being.

In Home Office file HO 144/221/A49301 K dated September 11, 1889, it is reported that:

"The body then must have been concealed where the murder was committed during Sunday night, Monday, Tuesday.... This leads to the inference that it was concealed in some place to which the murderer had [access] over which he had control and from which he was averse to move the corpse. We may say then that the murder was committed probably in the house or lodging of the murderer, and that he conveyed the portion found to Pinchin Street to get rid of it from his lodging where the odour of decomposition would soon [bother] him."

And as for whether or not the authorities believed the Ripper was either dead or confined in a mental hospital at the time the report continues:

"If this is a fresh outrage by the Whitechapel murderer known by the horribly familiar nickname of Jack the Ripper the answer would not be difficult.... [This] murder, committed in the murderer's house [is] a new departure from the system hitherto pursued by this ruffian." This statement clearly shows that the authorities did not believe the Ripper was dead or confined in a mental hospital, whether this was a Ripper murder or not.

"There is no sign of frenzied mutilation of the body, but of deliberate or skillful dismemberment with a view to removal." The report stated that had the body been dropped off anywhere other than Whitechapel that the Ripper's name would not have come up. Perhaps, but as the report continued with its author's own underscores: "But the body has been found in Whitechapel and there is a gash on the front part extending downwards to the organs of generation — and we have to account for these facts...." Scotland Yard could not then or now rule out the Ripper in this case. "As to how the body got to Whitechapel ... [how could it have] unless it be supposed that the murderer — being other than the 'Ripper' — had good knowledge of the localities."

Certainly the police officers must have questioned all those in the area who may have had any knowledge concerning this latest murder. They must

have come face-to-face with Klosowski again, but his studied coolness under
questioning would not have revealed anything. Did Sgt. Godley interview
Klosowski? He did work on the case. Once more the police would have looked
right past this man, as he would have seemed, on the surface, to have been
a respectable shopkeeper who was married and settled down. But where was
his real "wife" who had just come to England from Poland? A clue to the
woman's identity may be found in police reports that she was possibly a factory worker and not a prostitute. Perhaps other reasons were on the mind
of the killer in this case. Perhaps there was a different need for this murder?

> The *New York Times*— September 11, 1889
> Another London Murder
> London, Sept. 10.— At 5:30 o'clock this morning a policeman found the
> body of a fallen woman lying at the corner of a railway arch on Cable
> Street, Whitechapel. The head and legs had been cut off and carried away
> and the body opened. Policemen pass the spot every fifteen minutes.
> Those on duty last night say they saw nothing suspicious. The manner
> in which the limbs had been severed from the body shows that the *mur-
> derer was possessed of some surgical skill.* The woman was about thirty
> years old. There was no blood on the ground where the body was found,
> neither was there any blood on the body. From this it is evident that the
> murder was committed in some other place. It is believed that the woman
> had been [dead] for two days. *The body has not been identified.*

A later examination of the remains by Doctors Phillips, Clark and
Sargeant showed that the woman was stoutish, around 5 feet 3 inches in
height. She was also thought to be about 33 years old, with dark brown hair,
dark complexion, fair skin and soft hands. The abdominal area of the torso
had been heavily mutilated with some reports indicating that the womb had
been removed. It was also discovered that she did not have clenched fists,
which indicated to the doctors that she had not died in great pain. The body
had also been recently washed. Perhaps she had been drugged before she
was killed?

Mr. Percy John Clark, assistant to Dr. Phillips, had been called to the
murder site to examine the remains. He reported at the inquest that "On
the back were four bruises, all caused before death. ... About the middle of
the back also, over the spine, was a bruise about the size of half a crown [a
little smaller than a 50 cent piece]. On a level with the top of the hip bone,
and three inches to the left of the spine, was a bruise two and a half inches
in diameter, such as might be caused by a fall or a kick. ... On the right
arm there were eight distinct bruises, and seven on the left, all caused before
death and of recent date. ... The bruises on the right arm were such as
would have been caused by the arm having been tightly grasped."

Doctor Phillips stated: "The cut surface at the neck ... impressed me greatly with the general even surface. ... The neck had been severed by a clean incision commencing a little to the right side of the middle line of the neck behind leaving a flap of skin at the end of the incision. It had severed the whole of the structures of the neck, dividing the cartilage of the neck in front, and separating the bone of the spine behind. ... I believe that death arose from loss of blood. ... [The] mutilations were effected by someone accustomed to cut up animals or to see them cut up; and that the incisions were effected by a strong knife, eight inches or more long. ... [To] my mind ... there had been a former incision of the neck... [the cause of death?]."

Dr. Phillips further stated: "...[The] division of the neck and attempt to disarticulate the bones of the spine were very similar [to the Kelly murder].... The *Evening Standard* reported on September 24, 1889, "He [Phillips] believed that in this case there had been greater knowledge shown in regard to the construction of the parts composing the spine, and on the whole there had been a greater knowledge shown of how to separate a joint."

The coroner's panel, once more headed by Wynne Baxter, came to the verdict of, "Wilful murder against some persons unknown."

In direct response to the latest murder the police increased plainclothes patrols in Whitechapel, and Monro requested 100 more men to again saturate the area. By now, however, the Ripper was becoming more than just lucky, he was outthinking the authorities. The woman he had killed did not live in the same small area of Whitechapel, as the others had, and she was killed in St. George-in-the-East, yet the police were increasing their patrols in the Whitechapel area. They must have realized that the killer had moved. At the same time the New York Police received a letter from an individual using the name Jack the Ripper. The letter was superscribed "Hell" and mailed from the City of London. Was the Ripper doing some prior planning or just playing with the New York Police Department?

On February 23, 1894, Sir Melville Macnaghten produced a memorandum in response to the *Sun* newspaper reports that a Thomas Cutbush was the Ripper. Macnaghten had worked on the Pinchin murder and, as part of his memorandum, wrote his views about the case:

"On 10th Sept. '89 the naked body, with arms, of a woman was found wrapped in some sacking under a railway arch in Pinchin St: the head and legs were never found nor was the woman ever identified. She had been killed at least 24 hours before the remains, (which had seemingly been brought from a distance) were discovered. The stomach was split up by a cut, and the head and legs had been severed in a manner identical with that of the woman whose remains were discovered in the Thames, in Battersea Park, and on the Chelsea Embankment on 4th June of the same year; and these murders had no connection whatever with the Whitechapel horrors. The Rainham mystery in 1887, and the Whitehall mystery (when portions of a woman's body were found under what is now New Scotland Yard) in 1888 were of a similar type to the Thames and Pinchin St. crimes."

It should be taken into consideration that Macnaghten once stated that he had "documentary proof" of the Ripper's identity, but he had destroyed the papers. With this type of declaration, can we place any credence in his suspect list or what crimes were actually committed by the Ripper?

Once more referring to HO 144/221/A49301 K, we find evidence of a connection to the other torso murders. The Home Office report concludes: "...[This] is the hand which was concerned in the murders which are known as the Rainham Mystery—The New Police building case—and the recent case in which portions of a female body (afterwards identified) were found in the Thames." And yet, if Scotland Yard officials truly believed that the torso murder on Pinchin Street was unrelated to the Ripper murders, why is the post-mortem report on Mary Kelly and the Ripper "Dear Boss" letter found in the same Metropolitan Police file (MEPO 3/3153) as a report on the Pinchin Street inquest signed by Inspector Moore and dated September 24, 1889, fully ten months after Kelly's murder? The answer is simple. Scotland Yard suspected that there was indeed a connection to the Ripper case.

As for the Ripper's chosen targets—the prostitutes—many of them had, by their long experiences in the slums of the East End, developed a fatalistic approach to the murders occurring in their midst. When Chief Inspector Henry Moore, working as the liaison officer between Scotland Yard and Inspector Abberline, was interviewed about the women in the area for the November 4, 1889, issue of the *Pall Mall Gazette*, he said, "I tell many of them to go home, but they say they have no home, and when I try to frighten them and speak of the danger they run they'll laugh and say, 'Oh, I know what you mean. I ain't afraid of him. It's the Ripper or the bridge with me. What's the odds?' And it's true, that's the worst of it." Indeed, suicide was not uncommon along the dark streets and in the chilling river waters of London's East End. In 1889, the Ripper was not the only terror to be confronted on a daily basis for those existing in the "Abyss."

As for the remains of the Pinchin Street torso, they were preserved in "spirits" and then placed in a sealed container. The container was buried on October 4, 1889. Perhaps they were preserved well enough to give a few answers about who killed her, even today.

"I'm the next for Jack"
East End prostitute, London 1888

Chapter Nine

One Last Time?

"You can see I am not believed. Therefore you see where there is Justice."

Severin Klosowski

Despite his October marriage, Klosowski continued to move through the night streets and back alleys of London's East End. The question is, what was he doing until the early morning hours? The simple answer would be that this misogynist and womanizer was looking for and using prostitutes. Unfortunately, we have no direct evidence of such activity during the major Ripper period. But there is testimony of it from some people, including his "wife" Lucy, in reference to the period of the end of the series and beyond.

The "real" wife coming onto the scene is an example of the type of individual Klosowski was, and of the type of women who were drawn to him and what they were willing to put up with. It is not recorded how the other woman located her "husband" in London, or for that matter how she found out he was once again "married," but locate him she did. Perhaps she ran into Levisohn. As recounted by Hargrave L. Adam in his *Notable British Trials, The Trial of George Chapman*, 1930: "It is indeed probable that he was already married before he came to this country. At any rate, a woman came to England from either Russia or Poland, and claimed him as her husband. Her arrival, however, was at a most inopportune time, for Klosowski, who had been without female companionship for as long as he could possibly endure, had already gone through a marriage ceremony with another woman. The two women met at his house. Both claimed the distinction of

being the real wife, and neither would give way to the other. For some time
the two women actually lived in the same building with this enterprising
barber. The records do not concern themselves with the kind of life led by
the man during the struggle between his devoted spouses, but probably it
was not without considerable excitement. At length, one of the women went
away—*disappeared*—leaving the other, mistress of the situation. The one
who remained was the more recently wedded one, a Polish woman, whose
maiden name was Lucy Baderski."

Disappeared!

There is no record of when this first wife arrived or when she finally
left the situation to Lucy. But it must have been sometime between August
1889, when Lucy and Severin moved in together on Cable Street, and September 1890, when they moved away. So, was the torso, which was discovered across the tracks from Klosowski's shop on September 10, 1889, that
of a prostitute, or Klosowski's disappeared first wife? She would have been
a great threat to him as she could have known much about his activities in
Poland from which he had suddenly run. She probably knew that he was
illegally married and might have been threatening to inform the English
authorities. She was a loose end that Klosowski could not afford to leave
dangling. It is a big unknown but a tantalizing one. There is certainly no
record of his Polish wife after the move into 126 Cable Street. She never
reported him to the police. And at no point did Klosowski file a missing
person's report on her.

By May 1890, Parliament was still debating the criminal activities in
and around Whitechapel centered on Flower and Dean Street. With or without an active Ripper in residence, the area was still the "evil quarter-mile."
Samuel Montagu, the MP for Whitechapel, pressed the Home Secretary for
answers to the continuing criminal activities in the area.

> MR. MONTAGU: I beg to ask the Secretary of State for the Home Depart-
> ment whether any report or complaint has been received at the
> Home Office or by the Police Authorities respecting an area in
> Whitechapel intersected by Flower and Dean Street; whether the
> police have reported as to the existence of crime and vice in that
> locality; and if he will allow that report to be made public; and
> whether any effort has been made by the owner or by the police to
> remedy the evils complained of?
> MR. MATTHEWS: Yes, Sir; in December last the vicar of St. Jude's brought
> under my notice the evil state of the district referred to. The Com-
> missioner of Police, whom I consulted on the subject, reported in
> substance that vice of the lowest type finds a refuge in parts of

Whitechapel. The police do all in their power to keep violence and
vice within bounds, but their duties are confined to the streets; in
fact, extra constables are continuously on duty there on special
beats. It is only by bringing influence to bear on the landlords that
a better class of dwellings can be provided, and so, gradually, a better class of tenants secured. I regret to say that I am informed by
the Commissioner that no substantial efforts have been made by the
owners of the property in this neighbourhood to effect improvements, the neighbourhood being in much the same condition as it
has been for years. The lease of some of the property is running out,
and it is to be hoped that at the expiration changes will be effected
and improvements made.

It would take the bombs of World War II to finally affect substantial
change to the buildings and lodging houses of Whitechapel, as well as to a
large portion of the East End. In 1890, that was a generation or two in the
future.

By the time Mr. and Mrs. Klosowski moved back to Whitechapel in
September 1890, most of the Ripper excitement had died down, and Lucy
had given birth to a son named Wohystaw Klosowski, born in either April
or September (depending on the source). Immediately before, they had been
moving around quite a bit, during 1889–90: to Greenfield Street, Commercial Street and possibly others. This could be expected of a man trying
to hide from the authorities. But by September 1890, the family could be
found at 89 Whitechapel High Street. Klosowski was working as an assistant in the dilapidated basement barbershop located below the White Hart
public house. He would later become the proprietor, but the circumstances
of his "promotion" are now lost.

It is a possibility that his family was actually living on Greenfield Street
at that point, which would have given Severin time alone and away from
his wife. Mrs. Rauch, Lucy's sister, met Klosowski only after he married
her and was running the barbershop on Whitechapel High Street. "When
I came to London my sister was living with him in Greenfield Street, and
I used to go and see them there." It was at the Whitechapel High Street location that Wolff Levisohn, the travelling hairdresser salesman, once again ran
into Klosowski, or "Ludwig" as he knew him. The men spoke to each other
for the most part in Yiddish, so Levisohn would later be unable to testify
as to Severin's ability to speak English. At Klosowski's trial a witness by the
name of George Schumann would state that he was familiar with
Klosowski's barbershop, "Underneath the public house in High Street,
Whitechapel in 1891."

The Ripper Returns

There were no Ripper murders in 1890 and Whitechapel had, for the most part, gotten back to business as usual, such as it was in the destitute East End. Even Inspector Abberline had moved on to other cases and had been promoted to Chief Detective Inspector on December 22, 1890. Very few individuals who lived in the area were still actively looking for the elusive killer who seemed to have simply vanished. Then again, Severin Klosowski was running a full-time business, as well as adjusting to life as a married man with a newborn son at home. He was a very busy man. But not so busy he could not stay out late at night for a little hunting. He simply could not hunt as often as he had when he was single.

Frances "Carrotty Nell" Coles was born in 1865 to James William Coles, probably in London. Of her mother there is no record. Her father had worked as a boot maker and was considered respectable. At the time of her murder, he was very advanced in age, and was an inmate at the Bermondsey Workhouse, on Tanner Street. She had one sister, Mary Ann Coles, a respectable spinster living at 32 Ware Street, Kindsland Road.

Five feet tall, Frances had brown hair and eyes, and has been called one of the most beautiful of the Ripper victims. She worked for a while "stopping" bottles at a wholesale chemist's shop in the Minories. At the drug store she could earn around seven shillings a week, but the work hardened the skin on her knuckles which caused her pain. In fact, it was so bad that she often complained about her job to her sister. She left the job sometime around 1883–84, but told none of her family.

After her death, one of her "clients," James Murray, informed the police that she became a prostitute around 1883, when she was 18 years old. She had met Murray while she was staying at Wilmot's lodging house at 18 Thrawl Street — then, she had been working the streets of Shoreditch, Bow and Whitechapel for eight years. It was a secret she kept from her family, including her father, who learned about her "situation" only after her death. (As an interesting aside, Klosowski would later move to Rushton Street, Shoreditch.)

Despite her situation, Frances kept in contact with her family and could be found attending church services with her father on most Sundays. He last saw her on February 6, 1891, a week before she was killed. It has been suggested that on that final visit she informed him that she had left the chemist's but did not reveal that she no longer lived with an older woman in Richard Street, Commercial Road. Her sister may have been a little more aware of the situation. Frances visited Mary Ann for tea on Boxing Day (December 26) 1890, and though she claimed to still be living on Richard

Street and working at the chemist's, her sister was skeptical. Mary Ann noticed a faint odor of alcohol on Frances' breath, and the fact that she "was very poor, and looked very dirty."

On February 11, 1891, a fifty-three-year-old merchant seaman named Thomas Sadler was discharged from the S.S. *Fey* at the London docks. Sadler had known Coles for some time and had been a "customer" of hers. Leaving the ship, he proceeded to the Princess Alice public house on Commercial Street. After having a few drinks he came upon Frances and they decided to spend the night together. After more drinks they made their way over to a common lodging house a few blocks away, at 8 White's Row, Spitalfields. They were probably unaware that this was where Annie Millwood had lived on February 25, 1888, when she was attacked by "a stranger" and stabbed. It was nearly three years to the day since that first attack and the series was about to come full circle.

Tuesday, February 12, found Frances and Sadler barhopping throughout the area, and it was not long before both were the worse for drink. Around 7:30 that evening, Frances went into a hat shop at 25 Nottingham Street, Bethnal Green, north of Whitechapel. She purchased a new black crepe hat with money that had been given to her by Sadler earlier in the day. The salesman, Peter Hawkes, would later inform the police that she was "three sheets in the wind." This was just the way the Ripper liked his targets.

Later that night, between 9 and 11 p.m., Frances and Sadler had an argument which resulted in their going their separate ways. The breakup was not the best thing for either of them. Frances made her way back to 8 White's Row and plopped herself down in the kitchen. All she was able to do was drink herself into a stupor, and was soon fast asleep on a bench at the table. Sadler then came in showing the signs of a beating. He had been attacked on Thrawl Street when a woman in a red shawl had come at him from behind and knocked him to the ground, aided by two male accomplices. He had been kicked, beaten and robbed of his money and watch, and had nothing but a bloodied and bruised face to show for it. It has even been suggested that Frances had arranged the attack because of her anger at Sadler. He would later state that, "I was then penniless and I had a row with Frances for I thought she might have helped me when I was down." He informed the lodging house night watchman, Charles Guiver, "I have been robbed and if I knew who had done it I would do for them." Guiver helped Sadler get cleaned up, but because he had no money Guiver had to ask him to leave.

Sometime after 12:30 a.m., Frances woke up and left the lodging house. A lodger named Samuel Harris placed the time at 12:30 a.m., but watchman

Charles Guiver placed the time at 1:30 or 1:45 a.m. It may be possible that Frances came and went twice, hence the difference in the two statements.

By 1:30 a.m. Frances had made her way to Shuttleworth's eating house, located on Wentworth Street. She ordered three half pence of mutton and bread from Joseph Hassell the attendant. It took her 15 minutes to eat her meal. During that period the demanding Mr. Hassell asked her to leave no fewer than three times. Frances returned the rudeness by shouting back, "Mind your own business!" Nevertheless she did leave, and by around 1:45 a.m. she was seen walking past Commercial Street towards Brick Lane. At Commercial Street at 1:45 a.m., Frances met fellow prostitute Ellen Callagher as she was passing "a violent man in a cheese cutter hat." According to Callagher, she had known the man before as a client and he had given her a black eye. She told Frances not to approach the "violent man" but to no avail. Frances solicited him and both headed off towards the Minories. There is no surviving description of the man Frances walked away with less than 30 minutes before her death.

The bruised Thomas Sadler was not having much of a night. By 1:50 a.m., he had gotten into his third fight. He tried to force his way back on board the S.S. *Fez*, but some of the dock workers at St. Katharine Dock had other ideas, and Sadler got the worst of it. He had called them "dock rats," and for that was left with a large wound on his scalp. Then he attempted to enter a lodging in East Smithfield, but was unsuccessful. And by 2:00 a.m. he was drunk and bloodied and sitting on the pavement outside the Mint. At this point, Sergeant Edwards came across the much the worse for wear seaman, who was "decidedly drunk." It was evident that Sadler could barely stand let alone walk. He could not have attacked anyone, and within 15 minutes Frances Coles would be murdered.

At the same time, 2 to 2:12 a.m., the two Knapton brothers, along with Carman "Jumbo" Friday, were walking through a Great Eastern Railway arch at Swallow Gardens. They saw a man and woman at the Rosemary Lane corner of Swallow Gardens. Although they later turned out to be Kate McCarthy and Thomas Fowles, friends of Jumbo Friday, Friday did not recognize them. He and the Knapton brothers described the man as looking like a ship's fireman, which proved to be a problem for Sadler when it was found that he had spent the better part of the previous two days with Coles. Within minutes of the Swallow Gardens sighting, Frances Coles would be dead.

Twenty-five-year-old Constable Ernest Thompson, 240H, had been on the force for less than two months, and that early morning of February 13 was his first night of beat duty on his own. It was a night he would remember for the rest of his life, and he would always question his actions,

Frances Coles - February 13, 1891

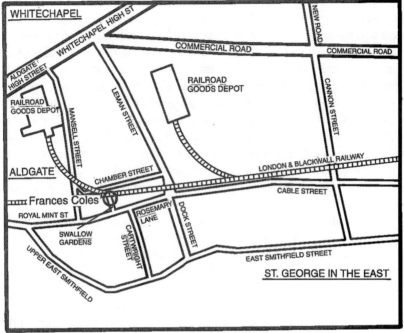

R. Michael Gordon   1998

It had been many months since the Ripper had taken a life and no one has ever fully explained the long break. The series in London would end with the death of Frances Coles on February 13, 1891. When she was found by Constable Ernest Thompson at 2:15 a.m. she was still alive but died soon after he arrived.

wishing he had gone after the attacker. At 2:15 a.m., Thompson was walking in a westerly direction along Chamber Street. Ahead of him, not hurried, he could hear the footsteps of a man. He could not see the individual, who was too far away in the darkness, but he could tell he was moving towards Mansell Street. (From the north end of Mansell Street it would have been less than 300 yards to the White Hart and Klosowski's basement barbershop.)

As Thompson continued on his beat he came to the short passage called Swallow Gardens, and turned left. Walking towards Rosemary Lane he came across the mortally wounded Frances Coles lying under the railway arch, as the footsteps of the man he had heard faded away. She had been thrown violently to the ground, perhaps because her killer did not have the time he needed to do his work.

Shining his lamp on her he was able to see that her throat had been deeply cut, and to his heightened horror, he saw the woman open and close one eye. She was still alive. Thompson's first thought was to blow his whistle for assistance. He wanted desperately to run after the man he had heard walk away, for surely this man must have been the killer. But the woman was still alive and he had no choice but to follow police procedure, which stipulated that he stay with the victim. That was his first duty. But had he gone after her killer he may very well have captured Jack the Ripper. He would forever believe that he was right behind the Ripper, and that he should have gone after him. Of course, he did the right thing by staying where he was, with Frances. In the darkest part of the street, which at times was used as a public toilet by locals, Frances died, as Constable Thompson continued to summon help. Thompson himself would later die from a knife wound, in 1900, while attempting to arrest a man named Barnett Abrahams who was causing a disturbance at a coffee stand.

The first officer to come to Thompson's aid was Constable Hart, 161H, at 2:25 a.m. Following closely behind was Constable Detective George Elliot, a plainclothes man working the same general area. Hart then went off to find a doctor. He located a local physician named F.J. Oxley who rushed to the scene, but it was too late.

Frances Coles had been murdered 250 yards away from where the torso had been dumped on Pinchin Street, under the same type of railway arch and a little more than 300 yards from the barbershop Klosowski had vacated merely months before. It was an area he knew very well.

With news of another possible Ripper murder the police were quick to call in their top men. First to arrive, around five in the morning, were Chief Inspectors Moore and Swanson. Assistant Police Commissioner Robert Anderson made his way to the site in the morning as did Assistant Chief Constable CID of Scotland Yard, Melville Macnaghten.

> The *New York Times*— February 13, 1891
> Jack the Ripper Again
> Another Woman Murdered and Her Body Mangled
> London, Feb. 13.— A renewal of the "Jack the Ripper" scare terrorizes that quarter of the city where the performances of the mysterious murderer have heretofore been the cause of so much alarm. At an early hour this morning the body of a young woman was discovered in a secluded locality in Chambers Street. She had been horribly gashed with a sharp instrument. Nothing is yet known as to who she is or who her murderer was. The woman's head had been severed almost entirely from the body, and it was a ghastly spectacle that met those who viewed the remains. Detectives quickly began a search for the murderer.

For his part, Sadler was still having a bad night, but he was alive. At 3 a.m. he made his way back to the lodging house at 8 White's Row. He was still very bloody and barely able to walk and talk. The house deputy, Sarah Fleming, noting that he was drunk and unable to pay for his bed, turned him away. As he left, Sadler told her, "You are a very hard-hearted woman. I have been robbed of my money, of my tackle and half a chain." By 5 a.m. he checked himself into London Hospital to have his injuries treated. On the way he had been stopped by a constable who was suspicious of Sadler's condition and searched him. The constable then helped him to the hospital. After his head was bandaged he was allowed to sleep on the couch in the Accident Ward. He did not stay long and by 10:15 a.m. that same morning, according to a seaman Duncan Campbell, Sadler was selling him his knife for a piece of tobacco and a single shilling. The blunt knife was later purchased by a marine stores dealer named Thomas Robinson. It was a dull knife indeed, and could not have been used on Frances. A sailor with a blunt-ended knife was not so unusual at the time. Sailors of that day often did not sharpen their knives in order to avoid personal injury while at sea.

It was Sadler who came under immediate suspicion because of the time he had spent with Coles during the days and hours before her death, and because of his condition. He would also be suspected as a result of the erroneous testimony of the witnesses who saw a woman with a man they described as a seaman just before the killing. Sadler was charged with Coles' murder on February 16 and held while the coroner conducted an inquest.

The *New York Times*— February 14, 1891
The Whitechapel Mystery
London, Feb. 14 — The latest Whitechapel victim has been identified as a woman named Frances, who was last seen with a suspicious looking sailor. The police have searched the wharves and shipping, but without success. One man, a stranger, has been arrested on suspicion. Whitechapel is thronged with people who have come from all parts of London to visit the scene of the latest murder mystery.

The Final Ripper Inquest

Once again, Coroner Edwin W. Baxter was called upon to impanel a jury into a Ripper murder. For this one, however, he would, for a time at least, have a possible suspect. The inquest was held at the Working Lads' Institute, and began on February 15.

The police, as would be expected, were delighted to finally have a suspect. But if they had looked closely at the Ripper's descriptions, then at Sadler, the joy would have soon evaporated. He simply did not fit the descriptions, or the pattern. He was not even close. The police investigation soon found that Sadler was at sea during the murders of Nichols, Chapman, Stride and Eddowes. He was on board the *Winestead* from August 17, 1888, to October 1, 1888, for a voyage to the Mediterranean. He was *not* the Ripper, and his condition at the time of the Coles murder also excluded him.

Sadler was well represented at the inquest. The Seamen's Union had hired solicitors Wilson and Wallace for his defense. They had seven witnesses who would testify to his movements and physical condition during the evening before and the early morning of the day of the murder. It all proved unnecessary when Kate McCarthy and Thomas Fowles came forward and testified that they were the couple seen by the Knapton brothers and Jumbo Friday near Swallow Gardens. Also, Sergeant Edwards and Sarah Fleming both testified as to Sadler's drunken condition at 2 and 3 a.m. Finally, Doctor Oxley, the first doctor on the scene of the murder, testified that "If a man were incapably drunk and the knife blunt, I don't think he could have produced the wound.... If a man were swaying about I don't think he could control the muscles of his hand and arm sufficiently to cause the wound."

Doctor George Bagster Phillips performed the post-mortem examination and came to the conclusion the Coles had been thrown to the ground violently, evidenced by the wounds on the back of her head. This could have excluded the need for strangulation in subduing her. The killer then knelt by her, tilted her body away from himself, held her head by the chin, and cut her throat three times. This was the Ripper's style. The manner in which he cut her throat would have allowed him to inflict the wounds without becoming covered in blood. Dr. Phillips also reported that no anatomical knowledge was needed to kill Frances, but it certainly required skill. The body was not mutilated, as

Frances Coles — February 13, 1891. Throat cut deeply three times. Only Ripper victim to be found alive. Died shortly after being found. (Public Record Office.)

many of the others were, but with a constable moving in his direction, the Ripper may not have had time.

Inspector Edmund Reid, head of CID for Whitechapel, had worked on the Alice McKenzie case and testified at the inquest into her death. He had also worked on the Coles murder. Although he did not believe the Ripper had any surgical skills, he did believe there had been nine murders in the Ripper series, and that Frances Coles' was the last.

On February 27, the jury brought in a verdict of "willful murder against some person or persons unknown." Four days later, all charges against Thomas Sadler were dropped by the Thames Magistrate's Court. Sadler was released to the cheers of a crowd, and he slowly faded into the confused history of the Ripper murders. The police were apparently back to square one without a suspect. Or were they? Sadler's movements were still coming under police investigation even after he was discharged. The authorities did not want to let go of the only suspect they had ever brought before a coroner's inquest into a Ripper murder, despite the overwhelming evidence that he could not possibly have been their man.

A Suspect at the Seaside Home

Although Thomas Sadler was clearly not the Ripper, there may have been a substantive suspect, according to statements made by officials very close to the case. Although charges were never brought against the man, it is possible he was identified as the Ripper and actually captured. In volume IV of the *Police Encyclopedia*, Hargrave L. Adam reported on a letter he received from Sir Robert Anderson who, as Assistant Commissioner of Metropolitan Police–CID, was the officer in charge of the overall Ripper investigation from October 6, 1888, to the time when the last report was filed in 1892. Adam wrote: "A great deal of mystery still hangs about these horrible Ripper outrages, although in a letter which I have just received from Sir Robert Anderson, he intimates that the police knew well enough at the time who the miscreant was, although unfortunately, they had not sufficient legal evidence to warrant them laying hands upon him...." This letter from the officer in charge of the case is critical, as it not only states that the Ripper was known but that he *could not be held in any way.*

In 1910, Anderson published his memoirs, *The Lighter Side of My Official Life*, in which he further discussed the identity of the Ripper: "For I may say at once that 'undiscovered murders' are rare in London, and the 'Jack-the-Ripper' crimes are not in that category. And if the police here had powers such as the French police possess, the murderer would have been brought to justice. ... I will merely add that the only person who had ever had a good view of the murderer unhesitatingly identified the suspect the instant he was confronted with him, but he refused to give evidence against him." He did not identify the witness or the suspect.

In an earlier serialized version of his book, published in *Blackwood's Magazine*, he had written that the suspect was then "caged in an asylum." It can be assumed that the first reference about the asylum was incorrect and for that reason removed from his memoirs. But once again, Anderson is saying that the Ripper was known but not held.

Anderson never named the suspect, which does not make any real sense. However, he does state that the man identified was a poor Polish Jew who lived in the immediate area of the murders. This is a pretty good description of Severin Klosowski who spoke fluent Yiddish, was posing as a Jew, and he was Polish.

There is one man who could very well be the unidentified witness. That man is Wolff Levisohn, who seemed to be just about everywhere Klosowski went. He knew Klosowski in Poland, as well as in Whitechapel, both before and after he went to the United States. He also knew that Klosowski had tried to acquire poison, was using different names, and was living with two "wives" at the same time. And yet, he said nothing to the police even during the Ripper series. Surely this man knew more about Severin Klosowski than he was willing to share with the police, or swear to.

The final word on the Anderson suspect can be found in the introduction of the *Police Encyclopedia*. Written in 1920, two years after Anderson's death, it states: "So again with the 'Whitechapel Murders' of 1888. [Clearly he felt they ended with Mary Jane Kelly.] Despite the lucubrations of many an amateur 'Sherlock Holmes,' there was no doubt whatever as to the identity of the criminal, and if our London 'detectives' possessed the powers, and might have recourse to methods of foreign police forces, he would have been brought to justice. But the guilty sometimes escape." The Ripper, according to Sir Robert Anderson, did not pay for his crimes, period. And not paying must include not being held in an insane asylum.

From September 1 to October 6, 1888, the Whitechapel murder investigation was under the control of Chief Inspector Donald Swanson. After October 6, Swanson became the desk officer when Anderson took charge. Swanson then was responsible for reading and reviewing all materials gathered in the case. He acquired a personal copy of Anderson's *The Lighter Side of My Official Life*, and wrote in the margins and end papers his own personal comments about the Ripper case. These notes are referred to as "Swanson Marginalia," and they expand on the previous information greatly. But it must be remembered that they were made 20 years after the crimes were committed, by the 72-year-old Swanson, without any reference material. Still they are important to understanding the overall police activities in the case.

At the place in Anderson's book where he wrote that a witness identified a suspect as the Ripper but "refused to give evidence against him," Swanson added: "[B]ecause the suspect was also a Jew and also because his evidence would convict the suspect, and witness would be the means of murderer being hanged, which he did not wish to be left on his mind. D.S.S." He continued in the margin: "And after this identification, which suspect knew, no other murder of this kind took place in London."

Finally, Swanson wrote on the end papers: "[The] suspect had been identified at the Seaside Home [a reference to the Convalescent Police Seaside Home, opened in March 1890 at 51 Clarendon Villas, West Brighton] where he had been sent by us with difficulty in order to subject him to identification and he knew he was identified." Up to this point Swanson and Anderson are in agreement as to the identification of "a" suspect, but Swanson then diverges stating: "On suspect's return to his brother's house in Whitechapel he was watched by police by day and night. In a very short time the suspect with his hands tied behind his back he was sent to Stepney Workhouse and then to Colney Hatch and died shortly afterwards — Kosminski was the suspect — D.S.S."

The question must now be asked, did Swanson truly write down the Ripper's name in the margins, or did he pick the name of a lunatic arrested at the same general period and simply write it in? There are many problems with Kosminski as a suspect. Firstly, after the lunatic Aaron Kosminski was taken into custody he was sent to Mile End Infirmary, hardly the place one would expect the police to bring Jack the Ripper. Secondly, although Kosminski was transferred to Colney Hatch Asylum, he did not die there "shortly afterwards," but lived until 1919, some nine years after Swanson wrote his notes in Anderson's book. So Swanson's identification of Kosminski must be viewed with the utmost skepticism. Simply stated, Swanson was wrong when he wrote his notes in the copy of Anderson's book.

It must also be remembered that Sir Melville Macnaghten wrote his memorandum on the three main (according to Macnaghten) suspects in the Ripper murders in 1894. In those notes, he records that the three were; "No 1. Mr. M. J. Druitt a doctor of about 41 years of age and of fairly good family, who disappeared at the time of the Miller's Court murder [Mary Kelly], and whose body was found floating in the Thames on 31st Dec...[;] No 2. Kosminski, a Polish Jew, who lived in (the very) heart of the district where the murders were committed. ... He was (I believe still is) detained in a lunatic asylum about March 1889[;] No 3. Michael Ostrog, a mad Russian doctor and a convict and unquestionably a homicidal maniac."

Macnaghten agreed that Kosminski was in a lunatic asylum but wrote, "Personally, after much careful and deliberate consideration, I am inclined to exonerate the last 2, but I have always held strong opinions regarding No. 1...." So in Macnaghten's opinion Kosminski was not Jack the Ripper. A witness to the certification that Kosminski was a lunatic was Jacob Cohen. He is reported to have testified that Kosminski ate bread from the filthy gutters and would drink water from standpipes. He was also said not to have washed or worked for years. He did not report that Kosminski was dangerous. And could an unwashed, dirty, smelly individual pick up women in the dead of night? The Ripper, it must be remembered, was a good dresser; Kosminski was not.

And what of Suspect No. 1, Montague John Druitt? Inspector Frederick George Abberline, in an interview with the *Pall Mall Gazette* in 1903, stated, "I know all about that story. But what does it amount to? Simply this. Soon after the last murder in Whitechapel the body of a young doctor was found in the Thames, but there is *absolutely nothing* beyond the fact that he was found at the time to incriminate him. A report was made to the Home Office about the matter, but that it was 'considered final and conclusive' is going altogether beyond the truth.... [The] fact that several months after December 1888, when the student's body [was] found, the detectives were told to hold themselves in readiness for further investigations seems to point to the conclusion that Scotland Yard did not in any way consider the evidence as final."

Abberline, in the same interview, spoke of Kosminski when he said, "I know that it has been stated in certain quarters that 'Jack the Ripper' was a man who died in a lunatic asylum a few years ago, but there is nothing at all of a tangible nature to support such a theory." Therefore, the detective on the ground, responsible for the investigation, eliminated in his own mind, both Druitt and Kosminski as suspects.

Macnaghten would later make a strange statement to the press: "Of course he was a maniac, but I have a very clear idea who he was and how he committed suicide, but that, with other secrets, will never be revealed by me. I have destroyed all my documents and there is now no record of the secret information which came into my possession at one time or another." With his obviously self-serving comments can we now trust *any* *reports*, or statements, made by Macnaghten about the Ripper case? Yet, it has also been reported that his files were not destroyed but simply vanished just after his death. One thing becomes clear. Someone, for whatever reason, wanted information about the Ripper investigation kept out of the public record for a very long time. Hargrave L. Adam writing in the introduction to his 1930 work, *The Trial of George Chapman*, made it known that he had been told by Henry Smith, Robert Anderson and Macnaghten that the Ripper's identity was indeed known to the police.

With all three official suspects no longer viable, what does that leave? It leaves a suspect who was identified, warned that he was known, but released due to a lack of solid evidence linking him to the crimes, and a comment that there were never any more Ripper-style murders in London after he had been confronted. It is very possible that after his identification, and very lucky release, the Ripper decided he had to leave London. The final Ripper murder occurred on February 13, 1891, with Frances Coles the victim. Within six weeks of her murder, Severin Klosowski and his wife left London on a ship bound for New York City, and new hunting grounds. During the time Klosowski was away, there were no new Ripper or torso murders committed in London. Those would come much later.

Severin Klosowski was ultimately proven to be a serial murderer of women. Is it possible that in the prime of his life during the Ripper series, he could have lived through the entire period right there in the East End and not killed any women? Possible yes, but most unlikely. Severin *enjoyed killing women* far too much to wait until he was in his thirties to start doing it. At the very least he could have taken advantage of the situation in Whitechapel to drop off a body or two. Klosowski was a sexual killing machine, and nothing, save death, was going to stop him. *Nothing.*

"And after this identification which suspect knew, no other murder of this kind took place in London."

Macnaghten's Memorandum
Confidential

The case referred to in the sensational story told in "The Sun" in its issue of 13th, & following dates, is that of Thomas Cutbush who was arraigned at the London County Sessions in April 1891, on a charge of maliciously wounding Florence Grace Johnson, and attempting to wound Isabella Fraser Anderson in Kennington. He was found to be insane, and sentenced to be detained during Her Majesty's Pleasure.

This Cutbush, who lived with his mother and aunt at 14 Albert Street, Kennington, escaped from the Lambeth Infirmary, (after he had been detained only a few hours, as a lunatic) at noon on 5th March 1891— He was rearrested on 9th idem. A few weeks before this, several cases of stabbing, or jabbing, girls behind had occurred in the vicinity, and a man named Colicott was arrested, but subsequently discharged owing to faulty identification. The cuts in the girl's dresses made by Colicott were quite different to the cut(s) made by Cutbush (when he wounded

Miss Johnson) who was no doubt influenced by a wild desire of morbid imitation. Cutbush's antecedents were enquired into by Ch. Inspr.
(now Supt.) Chris ( ), by Inspr. Race, and by P.S. McCarthy C.I.D.—
(the last named officer had been specially employed in Whitechapel at
the time of the murders there,)—and it was ascertained that he was
born, and had lived, in Kennington all his life. His father died when
he was quite young, and he was always a "spoilt" child. He had been
employed as a clerk and traveller in the Tea trade at the Minories, &
subsequently canvassed for a Directory in the East End, during which
time he bore a good character. He apparently contracted syphilis about
1888, and, — since that time, — led an idle and useless life. His brain
seems to have become affected, and he believed that people were trying to poison him. He wrote to Lord Grimthorpe, and others, — & also
to the Treasury, — complaining of Dr. Brooks, of Westminster Bridge
Road, whom he threatened to shoot for having supplied him with bad
medicines. He is said to have studied medical books by day, & to have
rambled about at night, returning frequently with his clothes covered
with mud; but little reliance could be placed on the statements made
by his mother or his aunt, who both appear to have been of a very
excitable disposition. It was found impossible to ascertain his movements on the nights of the Whitechapel murders. The knife found on
him was bought in Houndsditch about a week before he was detained
in the Infirmary. Cutbush was the nephew of the late Supt. Executive.
	Now the Whitechapel murderer had 5 victims —& 5 victims only, —
his murders were
	(i) 31st Aug. '88. Mary Ann Nichols — Buck's Row — who was found
with her throat cut —& with (slight) stomach mutilation.
	(ii) 8th Sept. '88. Annie Chapman — Hanbury Street: — throat cut —
stomach & private parts badly mutilated & some of the entrails placed
round the neck.
	(iii) 30th Sept. '88. Elizabeth Stride — Berner's Street — throat cut,
but nothing in shape of mutilation attempted, & on same date
	(iiii) Catherine Eddowes, Mitre Square, throat cut, & very bad muti-
lation, both of face and stomach.
	(iiiii) 9th November. Mary Jane Kelly — Miller's Court, throat cut,
and the whole of the body mutilated in the most ghastly manner.
	The last murder is the only one that took place in a room, and the
murderer must have been at least 2 hours engaged. A photo was taken
of the woman, as she was found lying on the bed, without seeing which
it is impossible to imagine the awful mutilation.
	With regard to the double murder which took place on 30th Sep-
tember, there is no doubt but that the man was disturbed by some Jews
who drove up to a Club, (close to which the body of Elizabeth Stride
was found) and that he then, "mordum satiatus," went in search of a
further victim who he found at Mitre Square.
	It will be noted that the fury of the mutilations increased in each case,
and, seemingly, the appetite only became sharpened by indulgence. It

seems, then highly improbable that the murderer would have suddenly stopped in November '88, and been content to recommence operations by merely prodding a girl behind some 2 years and 4 months afterwards. A much more rational theory is that the murderer's brain gave way altogether after his awful glut in Miller's Court, and that he immediately committed suicide, or, as a possible alternative, was found to be so hopelessly mad by his relations, that he was by them confined in some asylum.

No one ever saw the Whitechapel murderer; many homicidal maniacs were suspected, but no shadow of proof could be thrown on anyone. I may mention the cases of 3 men, any one of whom would have been more likely than Cutbush to have committed this series of murders:

(1) A Mr. M. J. Druitt, said to be a doctor & of good family—who disappeared at the time of the Miller's Court murder, & whose body (which was said to have been upwards of a month in the water) was found in the Thames on 31st Dec.—or about 7 weeks after that murder. He was sexually insane and from private information I have little doubt but that his own family believed him to have been the murderer.

(2) (Kosminski)—a Polish Jew, & resident in Whitechapel. This man became insane owing to many years indulgence in solitary vices. He had a great hatred of women, specially of the prostitute class, & had strong homicidal tendencies; he was removed to a lunatic asylum about March 1889. There were many circumstances connected with this man which made him a strong "suspect."

(3) Michael Ostrog, a Russian doctor, and a convict, who was subsequently detained in a lunatic asylum as a homicidal maniac. This man's antecedents were of the worst possible type, and his whereabouts at the time of the murders could never be ascertained.

And now with regard to a few of the other inaccuracies and misleading statements made by the "Sun." In its issue of 14th February, it is stated that the writer has in his possession a facsimile of the knife with which the murders were committed. This knife (which for some unexplained reason has, for the last 3 years, been kept by Inspector Race, instead of being sent to Prisoner's Property Store) was traced, and it was found to have been purchased in Houndsditch in February '91 or 2 years & 3 months after the Whitechapel murders ceased!

The statement, too, that Cutbush "spent a portion of the day in making rough drawings of the bodies of women, & of their mutilations" is based solely on the fact that 2 scribble drawings of women in indecent postures were found torn up in Cutbush's room. The head & body of one of these had been cut from some fashion plate, and legs were added to show a woman's naked thighs & pink stockings.

In the issue of 15th inst. it is said that a light overcoat was among the things found in Cutbush's house, and that a man in a light overcoat was seen talking to a woman at Backchurch Lane whose body with arms attached was found in Pinchin Street. This is hopelessly incorrect! On 10th Sept. '89 the naked body, with arms, of a woman was found wrapped in some sacking under a Railway arch in Pinchin Street: the head & legs were never found nor was the woman ever identified. She had been killed at least 24 hours before the remains, (which had seemingly been brought from a distance), were discovered. The stomach was split up by a cut, and the head and legs had been severed in a manner identical with that of the woman whose remains were discovered in the Thames, in Battersea Park, & on the Chelsea Embankment on the 4th June of the same year; and these murders had no connection whatever with the Whitechapel horrors. The Rainham mystery in 1887, & the Whitehall mystery (when portions of a woman's body were found under what is now New Scotland Yard) in 1888, were of a similar type to the Thames & Pinchin Street crimes.

It is perfectly untrue to say that Cutbush stabbed 6 girls behind — this is confounding his case with that of Colicott. The theory that the Whitechapel murderer was left-handed, or, at any rate, "ambidexter," had its origin in the remark by a doctor who examined the corpse of one of the earliest victims; other doctors did not agree with him.

With regard to the 4 additional murders ascribed by the writer in the "Sun" to the Whitechapel fiend:

(1) The body of Martha Tabram, a prostitute, was found on a common staircase in George Yard buildings on 7th August 1888; the body had been repeatedly pierced, probably with a bayonet. This woman had, with a fellow prostitute, been in company of 2 soldiers in the early part of the evening. These men were arrested, but the second prostitute failed, or refused, to identify, and the soldiers were accordingly discharged.

(2) Alice McKenzie was found with her throat cut (or rather stabbed) in Castle Alley on 17th July 1889; no evidence was forthcoming, and no arrests were made in connection with this case. The stab in the throat was of the same nature as in the case of the murder of

(3) Frances Coles, in Swallow Gardens, on 13th February 1891 — for which Thomas Sadler, a fireman, was arrested, & after several remands, discharged. It was ascertained at the time that Sadler had sailed for the Baltic on 19th July '89 & was in Whitechapel on the night of 17th idem. He was a man of ungovernable temper & entirely addicted to drink, & the company of the lowest prostitutes.

(4) The case of the unidentified woman whose trunk was found in Pinchin Street: on 10th September 1889 — which has already been dealt with.

M.S. Macnaghten
23rd February 1894

A Last Word on Jack

There is an aspect to the Ripper murders which becomes lost in the minutiae of victims and evidence. This is more than simply a case of a sexual serial killer at work. The Ripper began as a spree killer, then when things got hot he continued on as a serial killer, and later in life moved on to simple murder with poison as his weapon of choice. Certainly he was learning as he went along, and was most likely following the newspaper reports closely as he hunted his victims. He changed his tactics when it was reported that surgical skills were evident in the taking of body parts even as the testifying surgeons attempted to downplay some aspects of his expertise. He attempted to mask his skills with the trademark mutilations of his victims.

He was also trying very hard not to be caught, even as he took great risks in killing and mutilating his victims. This is clear from the close proximity of witnesses and the closed-in locations of the Hanbury Street and Berner Street murder sites, as well as the nearly surrounded Mitre Square. He seemed to be able to track, by news reports, who was being arrested on suspicion and from this know exactly how far off the police were from discovering his identity.

Towards the end of the spree series, the Ripper struck inside where he had cover from witnesses and plenty of time to do his work, but that was only after weeks had gone by without an atrocity. It is fully possible that the killer felt he could no longer risk living or working in the central killing area and thus needed to move out of the general area. This move would have made killing on the streets a much more risky venture as he would have been required to travel a greater distance before finding refuge, hence the need to kill indoors. Yet he killed again out of doors, and safely.

We are asked to believe, in conventional theories about the Ripper, that this individual was an insane sexual serial killer who only killed for a few weeks, and then for some unknown reason stopped. And yet, this type of individual does not simply stop killing without a very good reason, such as death or capture. And the Ripper did not die in the 1880s, and he was never caught. These types of killers may move around and perhaps graduate to a different type of victim or method, but if he was a true serial killer, he was by definition, a success, and would likely not have stopped on his own. A true insane killer would not understand his own insanity and would continue to kill even as the authorities closed in. But the police never closed in; indeed, the killer may not have even been interviewed. Certainly Klosowski's name has not been found on any surviving police documentation ascribed to the case. And because the Ripper was never brought to trial, Klosowski's name not being on a suspect list is a major plus in favor of his being the killer. The important consideration is, he had no reason to stop killing as long as he was successful. Nonetheless, in order to continue he would need to change his style.

It is possible that after the Ripper series the killer felt he had, for some reason, enough body parts and that aspect of his insane desires was somehow fulfilled. (We do know that at least one body part was briefly preserved in alcohol and then a section of it was sent to George Lusk.) Despite probably having as many "samples" or "mementos" as he needed, he was still a serial killer, though, and more deaths would have to come to fulfill that basic requirement of his deranged mind. To continue he would need to find a new killing ground. From Detective Walter Dew, "I was on the spot, actively engaged throughout the whole series of crimes. I ought to know something about it. Yet, I have to confess I am as mystified now as I was then by the man's amazing elusiveness."

Much has been made of murder by knife and murder by poison seeming to constitute different MOs. They might if this was a case of everyday run-of-the-mill murder. It was not. This was a serial killer at work, and these types of killers do indeed modify their killing styles when needed. The FBI's Serial Killer Task Force has investigated many cases in which the killer used seemingly different styles or MOs to put the authorities off the track, or simply because the previous method of murder no longer appealed to them. Peter Kurten, a serial killer from Germany, born in 1883, murdered for at least 20 years, and changed his MO because, as he later stated, "I hoped by changing the method to bring about the theory that there were several murderers at work." He was thinking all of the time — so was Jack. He also confessed that he had experimented with his murder style to see which would give him the greatest sexual satisfaction. Stabbing, strangulation and poisoning were all used by Kurten. He used arson too.

There is no reason to believe that Jack the Ripper was any less creative than Kurten. In fact, because the Ripper was never convicted of his murders, perhaps he was just a bit better at killing than Kurten and most of the others.

As for the Ripper case files, the last report was filed in 1891, and no further follow-up investigation was conducted by the Metropolitan Police. And 1891 was the year Klosowski left England for the United States. The police had no *official* strong suspect, no physical evidence to speak of, no official knowledge that the killer was dead or even inactive, but they closed the case. Why?

As was standard practice with such a serious set of crimes, the files were closed from public view for 75 to 100 years. It seems that those who reached high office must treat the people they represented as somehow less able to understand the realities of life than they. Closing the files was one of officialdom's methods of keeping the masses subdued, ignorant, and subservient to those few who had decided, "We know better." It is no different today, as President Kennedy's files are only ever so slowly opened. Of great interest is the fact that the Ripper suspect's file (MEPO 3/141 32-135) went missing before it could be copied. It was reported to have contained investigations of at least 100 men who were taken to local police stations on suspicion. Most of the men were released after they were able to prove who they were, but the names of those men could have been most instructive if not critical to understanding the Ripper case. If it has not been destroyed and was simply "taken," then perhaps it could still have the name Klosowski in it.

In the 1950s, the records were transferred to the Public Record Office and have been open to researchers since 1976. The Home Office files concerning the case were opened in 1986. With these files now part of the public domain it is likely that interest in the case will continue for many years to come.

The Ripper "Victims Folder" has individual case files marked:

EMMA ELIZABETH SMITH, aged 45, murdered on 3rd April 1888.
MARTHA TABRAM alias TURNER, aged 35 to 40, murdered on 7th August 1888.
MARY ANN NICHOLLS, murdered on 31st August 1888.
ANNIE SIFFEY alias CHAPMAN, murdered on 8th September 1888.
ELIZABETH STRIDE, murdered on 29th September 1888.
CATHERINE EDDOWES, murdered on 29th September 1888.
MARIE JEANETTE KELLY, murdered on 9th November 1888.
ROSE MYLETT alias LIZZIE DAVIS, murdered on 20th December 1888.
ALICE McKENZIE, murdered on 17th July 1889.
TRUNK OF A FEMALE, found on 10th September 1889.
FRANCES COLES, murdered on 13th February 1891.

From Chief Inspector Frederick George Abberline, "It is a remarkable thing that after the Whitechapel horrors America should have been the place where a similar kind of murder began...." The case now shifts across the Atlantic Ocean, as Klosowski begins a bloody new life.

"That Chapman's [Klosowski's] career coincides *exactly* with the movements and operations of Jack the Ripper must appeal strongly to all who endeavor to throw light upon the shadows of the latter's obscurity."
From *The Trial of George Chapman*, edited by Hargrave L. Adam

Chapter Ten

A Time to Run,
and a Time to Kill

"One thing whod I wish is this to be remembered as I am an American orphend of good family and I left my foster father, against his wish, and I took to erning my own living at age of ten."

Severin Klosowski

When Klosowski was arrested, in late 1902, for the murder of his latest "wife," he had in his wallet a piece of paper which he had drafted himself. It read: "Came from America in 1893, independent. Deposits £100, when from America I had £1000."

This was a complete fabrication. Yet, why would an individual bother to construct a piece of "evidence" which appears to indicate that he had never been in England before 1893? The only logical answer has to be that he was trying to hide his criminal past during that year and create a completely new identity, as that of an American. He was also trying to remove any link to himself and Jack the Ripper.

But before he could accomplish any of that, he would need to leave London for New York City. America was about to come face to face with Jack the Ripper.

On March 3, 1891, Klosowski's son, Wohystaw, died of pneumonia asthenia. It has not been recorded how Klosowski reacted to this event but considering his past and future behavior his reaction could not have been very deep. It has been called by some researchers, however, the pivotal event which caused him to leave London, along with his wife, and begin a new

225

life in the United States. This may have been a normal reaction, but Klosowski was not a normal human being. In future years he would not acknowledge his son or either of his other two children, and made it very clear that he wanted nothing to do with them. So the death of his first son could not have meant much to him. Indeed, considering his distaste for human life, there is a good possibility that the child died at the very practiced hands of Severin himself.

March 3, 1891, is important because it is the last confirmed date that Klosowski was in London before moving to New York. A second major date is April 5, 1891, which was the day of the National Census. In that census, Klosowski and his wife Lucy were *reported* to have been living at 2 Tewkesbury Buildings, Whitechapel. But is this oft-quoted information correct? The census taken on that date does place them living at that London address at that time, but there is no way of knowing how accurate the census takers were in recording the information. Did they actually speak with Klosowski and his wife at their home, or did they simply report on what others told them about who lived there? In other words, Klosowski and his wife could have moved before the census was taken. There is no other documentation to either confirm or deny this census report.

The reason the accuracy of it is important, but not critical, is because a Ripper type murder was committed in New York City on the night of April 23-24. If Klosowski left London before the census he could have easily traveled to New York in time to have committed the murder. If he moved on or just after the day of the census he would still have had time, but it would have been a much closer affair. Still, he would have had a full 18 days to reach the United States, and that would have easily been sufficient time to arrive on the docks of New York City, near where the murder occurred. And, going to new areas was no problem for Klosowski. He liked to keep on the move, and he moved a lot. It should also be remembered that there were no Ripper style murders *before* Klosowski came to New York.

Earlier, during the Ripper murders of 1888, Chief Inspector Thomas Byrnes, the highest ranking New York City police official at the time, had stated that if those murders had occurred in New York the killer would be "in the jug" within 36 hours. That boast was about to be put to the test.

"Old Shakespeare"

Her name was Carrie Brown, but her friends called her "Old Shakespeare," because of her habit of quoting passages from the works of the Bard, usually as she stood in a prison cell intoxicated. She was born around

1830, which would have placed her in her early sixties when she was murdered. Carrie was reported to have been a "highly educated woman and something of a writer." In her earlier days she had also been an actress, even well known. She had told of her birth at sea and informed her acquaintances that "all of her relatives were seafaring people." Her husband, who had died years earlier somewhere along the Pacific coast, was named Charles S. Brown (or Beane), and was said to have been well off. Carrie also spoke of two daughters who were still alive, one of whom she said was 36 years old. Carrie herself was described in the *New York Times* as "an old, gray-haired, and wrinkled woman who had for years past haunted the neighborhood." The police had been aware of her presence in the general area for at least ten years before her death.

Three weeks before Carrie was murdered, she had been released from Blackwell's Island. She had been held for a "short sojourn for some unspecified infraction," but it was likely to have been in connection with her work as a streetwalker.

With no money to speak of, she could be seen walking the afternoon streets of the waterfront on April 23, 1891. The area was little more than a filthy slum, not unlike the East End of London. As she walked she met Alice Sullivan. Carrie told Alice that she had not eaten for three days so Alice took her to a saloon on Water Street and bought her a cheese sandwich. Later, Carrie would find her way to the free-lunch counter nearby, for some corn beef and cabbage. These were to be her last meals. It was 8:30 in the evening when Alice Sullivan spotted Carrie again, this time with a man called "Frenchy," and she would testify to that fact at the upcoming trial.

Later, during that evening of April 23, Carrie Brown could be seen in the company of a younger woman named Mary Healey. The assistant housekeeper of the East River Hotel, Mary Miniter, who was on duty at 9 p.m., reported that the two women came into the saloon at about that time. The East River Hotel was a very run down lodging house, referred to as a "bawdy resort," located near the docks on the southeast corner of Catharine Slip and Water Street, fronting on the latter. The four story, dirty, brick building was owned by James Jennings and was reported to have been a "lodging house of unsavory reputation, and is chiefly resorted to by the women who prowl about the neighborhood after nightfall." The bar was on the first floor, with an office on the second floor and small squalid rooms occupying the rest of the building. It had also been rumored that the hotel had a subterranean tunnel built for the dumping of underworld bodies into the East River.

Mary Healey and Carrie Brown stayed in the bar drinking beer for more than half an hour before Mary went off with another woman named

Lizzie. Overseeing the saloon's operation that night was bartender Samuel Shine who was also playing the role of night clerk. It was at this point that the intoxicated Brown began to tell housekeeper Mary Miniter, who had never seen her before, about her life and family. From there, "Old Shakespeare" walked over to Mrs. Harrington's Lodging House on 49 Oliver Street at around 9:45 p.m.

On that evening of April 23, Isaac Perriger had taken a 35 cent a night room at the lodging house operated by the Seventh Presbyterian Church on Ridge Street. He had told the desk clerk that he wanted to be awakened at 9:30 so that he could meet a woman, and he left at around 10 p.m. He went to Mrs. Mary Harrington's Lodging House, located near the docks. At Mrs. Harrington's he asked about a woman named Mary Ann Lopez. (Lopez was acquainted with Brown and also knew the local man named "Frenchy.") However, it would seem that he was unable to find the woman as he was soon seen leaving the location with Carrie Brown. They proceeded to the Water Street Hotel, located near James Street and not far from the East River Hotel. From the Water Street Hotel, Brown and Perriger went to a saloon owned by John Speckman on Oliver Street. They were seen going out of that saloon together. But she would soon leave Perriger, and meet Jack the Ripper.

Between 10:45 and 11 p.m., a still intoxicated Carrie Brown returned to the East River Hotel with a younger man. He tried his best to keep in the background, apparently not wishing to be remembered. It was a hotel Carrie knew well. Mary Miniter, the assistant housekeeper, who had been temporarily placed in charge, would later describe the man as "apparently about 32 years old, five feet eight inches in height; of slim build, with a long, sharp nose and a heavy mustache of light color. He wore an old black derby hat, the crown of which was much dented." (From a recent voyage perhaps.) She further described him as a foreigner and said she had the impression that he was German. It was a detailed word picture of Severin Klosowski. Mrs. Miniter asked the man for his name so that she could place it in the register, and he replied that it was C. Nicolo. It was the name that Mrs. Miniter heard, but could he have said "Nichols"? Was this just one more game being played by the Ripper? Perhaps he was recalling the East End slum around the Brick Lane barbershop and Old Nichol Street known locally as "The Nichol." Or maybe he was using the last name of one of his London victims, Polly Nichols. (Other writers have given the name as C. Knick, so there is some doubt as to which false name he used.)

Miniter went over to Edward Fitzgerald, the room clerk, and he wrote in his grease stained register, "C. Nicolo and wife," and assigned the pair to room 31. It is also possible that Brown requested that room since she was familiar with it. The odd couple retired with a "tin pail of beer." Theirs was the corner room on the top floor of the hotel, which had six rooms on it in total. Of the six, four apparently had guests that night. But no one would ever report hearing any cries for help from their neighbor in room 31. It would be a great risk to murder in this seedy hotel-saloon, but the Ripper had taken risks before and this would not be the last time. Besides, Carrie Brown was intoxicated—just the way Jack the Ripper liked his targets— and he was far away from London and the many eyes still looking for the Whitechapel Killer. With the murder of Carrie Brown, the Ripper moved into the realm of the "international sexual serial killer." He was indeed a rare bird.

The *New York Times*—April 25, 1891
Choked, Then Mutilated
A murder like one of "Jack the Ripper's" deeds
Whitechapel's Horrors Repeated
in an East Side Lodging House—
An Aged Woman the Victim—
Several Arrests on Suspicion

A murder which in many of its details recalls the crimes with which "Jack the Ripper" horrified London was committed late Thursday night or early yesterday morning in a small room in the squalid lodging house known as the East River Hotel, on the southeast corner of Catherine and Water Streets.

The discovery of the murder was made by (Edward) Fitzgerald [some reports identify the man who made the discovery as a clerk named Eddie Harrington] about 9:30 o'clock yesterday morning. He was on his rounds waking up the late sleepers, and when he reached Room 31 he knocked, but got no answer. The door was unlocked, and he entered. [In point of fact the door was locked and needed to be opened with a pass key.] Such a sight met his gaze that he rushed from the room like one demented and raised the house with his cries for help. The old woman was lying dead on the bed. She was naked from her armpits down and was disemboweled. Her head and face were tightly enveloped in portions of her clothing. There were marks about her throat to indicate that the woman had been choked or strangled before the mutilation was performed.

The woman was lying on her right side with her face to the wall, and her arm was twisted under her back. There was a gash extending from the base of the spine around the abdomen to the front of the body. The incision was begun near the base of the spine and carried from below upward in an oblique direction to a point halfway up on the right side. On the back was a mark like an "X" made by drawing the knife lightly across the skin; this was evidently the murderer's sign manual.

This was indeed a sign which was meant to be read. It was not a deep mutilation as some reports said. It was even reported to have been *the* mark of Jack the Ripper, but there is nothing to indicate that the Ripper ever left such a mark on any of his other victims. But what did the X signify? According to the dictionary, it could simply be something to be emphasized, or it could be the killer's cryptic signature. For an individual trained in the medical arts, and thus familiar with Latin, the X is always shown as "KS." When reversed, as the body is turned over, the KS becomes "SK": Severin Klosowski! It could also be that she was his tenth (X) murder victim and he wanted all the world to know it.

After this murder and mutilation, at around 2 a.m., the killer dropped the four-inch-bladed knife on the floor next to the bed. It was an ordinary table or cooking knife with a black handle and its normally rounded end had been broken off and ground down to a sharp point. It was exactly like the type of knife used by the Ripper in London only a bit smaller. When it was found it was still quite wet with Carrie Brown's blood. Her killer could have walked down the stairs and left the hotel by the private drinking room door without being seen, but it must have seemed to have been too great a risk to do so. Instead, the Ripper walked along the short hall on the sixth floor to an iron ladder which directed him to a "scuttle" opening leading to the roof. This route was discovered by bloodstains later found in the general roof area. From there he climbed to the next roof and made his escape into the darkness of that New York City night.

From the cheap hotel on the Manhattan waterfront, which in modern times has become a parking lot, the Ripper moved through the darkness to another rundown lodging house in Chatham Square, not more than five minutes walking distance. At the Glenmore Hotel the night clerk, named Kelly, came face to face with Jack the Ripper. He saw that his hands and clothing were smeared with blood and described him as "about five feet nine inches in height, light complexion, long nose and light mustache." The man had what Kelly said was a "pronounced German accent," and that he wore a "shabby cutaway coat and a shabby old derby hat." There is little doubt that this was the same man who had just murdered Carrie Brown.

As reported in the *New York Times* of April 26, "Night Clerk Kelly ... says that the man was very nervous and agitated. 'His hat was pulled down over his eyes,' Kelly explained, 'and he acted queer. He asked me in broken English if I could give him a room for the night. At the time his right hand rested on my desk and I noticed it was all bloody. I noticed it looked as though he had tried to wipe the blood off, but it was smeared all over. There were also two blotches of blood on his right cheek, as through he had put the bloody hand to his face. There was also blood on his right coat sleeve and it was spattered on his collar. Altogether the fellow looked very bad. I asked him what priced room he wanted. He answered nervously that he wanted me to give him a room as he did not have a cent. I told him that I could not give him a room as the house was full. He turned to go away, but instead of going down the stairs to the street he started for the washroom. I came out from behind my desk and told him we only allowed the guests of the house the use of that room. He turned then without a word and went down into the street. As he did so I turned to Tiernman, our night watchman, who was in the office at the time, and said: That man looks as though he had murdered somebody.'"

Once again, the Ripper, this time bloodied and seemingly confused, melted into the dark of the night. It was later reported that the key to room 31 was missing. It was the key to Carrie Brown's room. He had once again taken a memento of his kill. Perhaps he was confused by the fact that he had not been long in the area or perhaps the risks were beginning to play on his mind.

After the body was discovered, "a messenger" was sent to the Oak Street police station. Before long Captain O'Connor, and several other detectives, were at the site. Hot on their trail — in fact, accompanying the detectives — were several newspaper reporters. It was this large crowd of police and reporters that trampled the evidence in the case — an act which would eventually lead to the wrong man being accused and convicted. Blood evidence was soon "accidentally" placed in locations other than the crime scene. Actually, when the body was first discovered by the clerk he noticed no bloodstains on the door or in the hallway. Only later would the police "discover" blood in these and other incriminating areas.

The assembled group quickly examined the blood-soaked mattress, blood-spattered surfaces all around the room, and the victim's clothes which had been scattered about. To prop open a window the killer had used one of Carrie's shoes which was still in place. Along with the knife, found on the floor, the detectives found two pairs of Carrie's old spectacles, and a cotton cloth shopping bag. They also recorded that there was no blood on the knob or the lock of the door to room 31.

A preliminary examination, by Coroner Schultze, indicated that she had been strangled while she was asleep, and then mutilated. According to preliminary reports, the throat was not cut, and no body parts were removed this time. But it had been a vicious multiple stabbing attack. Perhaps the Ripper had not enough time, up to that point, to locate a proper hiding place for new samples. He was, after all, new to the country. It was an attack which seemed, somehow, even to have disturbed the killer himself.

The police began a house-to-house search of the general area and along the waterfront. All downtown lodging houses were searched for anyone answering the description given by Mary Miniter. Dozens of detectives from police headquarters supplemented the precinct detectives, some in civilian clothes, as they looked for "dissolute companions" of the victim. Police Headquarters sent Captain McLaughlin, who was in charge of the detective bureau, along with detectives Grady, Crowley and McClusky. This was going to be an all out effort, as the name Jack the Ripper was already being spoken in the press.

Since Mary Miniter was the only person at the East River Hotel to get a close look at the killer she was taken into custody. Mary Healey, who had been drinking with Carrie earlier in the evening, was located in room number 12 at the East River Hotel. She was so drunk, however, that she was unable to even give a statement to the police at the time. She was also taken to the police station and held. It was an easy task for the police to find people who knew Old Shakespeare, but attempting to retrace her movements would prove to be a difficult task, as, for the most part, she moved on the edge of life and not in the mainstream.

The body was removed to the morgue at 6 p.m., but a post-mortem was not immediately performed because the coroner's office had been closed for the day. There was no doubt that this had been a brutal murder, but it is surprising that the authorities would wait until the next day to perform an autopsy. As for Carrie's body, it would not be buried until August 30, 1891, a full four months after her murder. In death, as in life, it seemed that no one wanted to claim Carrie Brown. No one that is, except the Ripper.

The *New York Times*— April 26, 1891
Byrnes Says He Has a Clue
He Thinks He Has Solved the East River Hotel Murder
There are two "Frenchys"
he has one and wants the other —
The victim of the crime
identified as Mrs. James Brown

The murder of the old woman in the East River Hotel Thursday night is still as deep a mystery as ever. The best detectives of the city force, headed by Inspector Byrnes, are working like beavers to clear it up. Information as to what they are doing and what they have done and hope to accomplish they refuse to give. They hope to catch the murderer, and this hope is warranted by the fact that there is reason to believe that he is absolutely without means.

The most important clue that came to the police yesterday was from the Glenmore Hotel, a Chatham Square cheap lodging house. The morning of the murder. About three hours after the murderer and his victim went to their room in the East River Hotel, a man went [to] the

Glenmore and asked for a room. Kelly, the night clerk of the house, noticed that the man's hands, face, and clothing were smeared with blood.
Inspector Byrnes refuses to say whether in his opinion the old woman was killed by the genuine "Jack the Ripper" or not.

After the arrest of "Frenchy," the police took into custody several other individuals either as suspects or witnesses. Annie Lynch, Lizzie Mestrom and Annie Corcoran, most likely prostitutes, were taken in because they were known to have been around the East River Hotel quite often. It was also reported that three Italians were arrested for a short time but were released after questioning by police.

Mary Miniter, who was still being held, was taken before Frenchy to see if he was the man who she had seen with Carrie Brown at the Hotel, but she was unable to identify him. But the police put out an arrest order for a suspect based on her description:

General Alarm!— Arrest a man 5 feet 9 inches high, about thirty-one years old, light hair and mustache; speaks broken English. Wanted for murder. THOMAS BYRNES, Acting Superintendent.

It should be noted that she never said the suspect had light hair, only a light mustache.

As the medical examiner began his work, the Brooklyn police force joined "New York's Finest" in the hunt for the killer. Inspector Byrnes, the officer in charge of the case, consulted with Brooklyn Commissioner Haryden and Superintendent Campbell. The result was the issuance of a general arrest order to all precincts. The order quickly resulted in the arrest of a Frederick Strube, of 68 Fulton Street. He was brought before Mary Miniter. She could not identify him, and so he was discharged. The "dragnet" was in full effect.

With the case now catching the attention of the public, the *New York Times* of April 26 reported on the results of the autopsy. "The autopsy held on the old woman's body yesterday by Deputy Coroner Jenkins was a four hours' task. He concluded that the woman was between sixty and sixty-five years old. The condition of the lower part of the trunk of the body cannot be described. There were cuts and stab wounds all over it. Dr. Jenkins' opinion was that the murderer had tried entirely to cut out his victim's abdomen, but that his fury and her struggles prevented him. There were two cuts that penetrated for several inches into the abdominal cavity which would have caused death.

"There were *evidence of strangulation about the throat,* and blood from the left ear indicating that she had been struck on the head. Col. Vollum, President of the United States Board of Army Medical Examiners, was at the autopsy. He said that, in his opinion, the murderer had clutched the woman by the throat and when she was half dead had begun to slash her with the knife. He thought that there was a struggle while the butchery was in progress. When Dr. Jenkins had finished his work he said that he thought death was caused by a combination of *asphyxia and weakness resulting from hemorrhage.*" The coroner would later state that he felt the wounds were inflicted by a right handed individual. Carrie Brown's death certificate, numbered 15143, states that the cause of death was due to, "strangulation by a portion of clothing tied around the throat," as well as "incisions to the lower abdomen, intestines, and vagina." With such a well-known and respected doctor as Colonel Vollum at the autopsy, the question must be asked: just how important was this murder of an old prostitute? Did they believe that this was indeed a Ripper case?

The New York papers continued to report, "The Murderer Still At Large," and, "No Light as Yet on the East River Hotel Mystery." The Brooklyn police arrested every man they could find who was known as "Frenchy." A man, named Nils Hansen, who happened to be Swedish, was taken in for a lineup but was soon dismissed; as was another man named John Williams. The press and public were being reminded that Inspector Byrnes had bragged that he would capture the killer before he could kill again.

Williams was a much better suspect. The 45-year-old laborer not only lived in a local lodging house, but two years earlier had occupied nearby 114 Roosevelt at the same time a woman was murdered there. This Frenchy had known Old Shakespeare, and was himself well known in the area. But he was dark and short, and so did not fit the description of the suspect. The police even arrested a local fruit stand owner who was also known as Frenchy. His real name was Christian Rey. Rey had been away from his stand for a few days due to illness, so he too became a suspect for a short period of time, until his story could be verified.

On April 29, Jersey City Police Detective Kilcauley filed a report from a train conductor who was then employed on the New Jersey Central Line. The conductor had informed the detective that a man, fitting the suspect's description, had boarded the train in New York for a ride to Easton, New Jersey, just after the murder of Old Shakespeare. It would be in New Jersey that Klosowski and his wife would live and work during his "Americanization."

As reported in the *New York Times* of April 29, the Frenchy theory was starting to wear thin. "The 'Frenchy theory,' which was advanced by Inspector Byrnes late on Friday night, now seems to be completely exploded. He then stated that the murderer was a ruffian known as 'Frenchy,' a cousin of another ruffian known as 'Frenchy,' whom the police had in custody. Yesterday, the Inspector said that he did not think that Frenchy No. 2 was the murderer. 'Then,' he was asked, 'why don't you discharge Frenchy No. 1, whom you are holding?' 'How do you know I have not?' he answered. 'But have you?' he was asked. 'I refuse to answer,' he responded. 'Well, what do you think of the murder now?' he was asked. 'I have no theory for publication,' he answered. 'I don't know anything more about the murder than you do....'"

"Washington April 28. Inspector Byrnes of the New-York police force has communicated with Major Moore, Superintendent of the Washington Police concerning the murderer who is supposed to be 'Jack the Ripper,' and the result of the correspondence was the sending out of an order requesting the officers to look out for and arrest the supposed murderer."

There would be no request sent to London for information on the Ripper. Perhaps Byrnes felt that it would not be good for his career to ask for any help from across the ocean.

The Wrong Suspect Goes on Trial

It would not be long before the New York Police were able to make good on their promises. If they could not find the real murderer then a scapegoat would do just as well. They would soon arrest a suspect, albeit the wrong one, and bring him to the bar of justice. He was arraigned on April 30, before Judge Martine, and held for murder. It was simply not a good move for the French Algerian, Ameer Ben Ali, alias Frenchy, to have taken room number 33, across the hall from Carrie Brown and her evening's "guest," that fateful night. He was described as being "[A] typical Algerian Arab, with a dark, sallow skin, coal-black hair and eyes, and a thin, aquiline nose."

He had come to New York via South America when some people, possibly steamship agents, had convinced him that he could do well in America. He had first gone to Brazil but could not find work, so he travelled north. It was not much better in the United States as all he could find were odd jobs he came across as he walked the streets of New York. Ameer had already decided to return home to Algiers when Carrie Brown was found murdered.

On May 1, Ben Ali was taken to the jail at the "Tombs," where he would await his murder trial. The police argued that Ali, a veteran of the Franco-Prussian War, had gone into Brown's room after her "guest" had left, and murdered her for her money. There was one glaring problem in that reasoning: Carrie Brown had no money and was well known in the area to be poverty stricken. And what of the bloodied man seen at the other hotel?

On June 27, the *New York Times* reported that "Ameer was brought up a soldier in the French Army in Algiers ... serving in one of the Turco regiments that was taken to France on the outbreak of the war with Prussia. He fought in several engagements with the Germans, and in one of them was shot in the leg. After the war he returned with his regiment to Algiers, and several years later was discharged, and got married and settled among his own people."

Before long it was discovered that the poor Algerian had been earlier picked up for vagrancy and had spent the past March and April in the Queens County Jail. Further, the authorities reported that fellow inmates, Edward Smith and David Galloway, had made statements to the effect that Ben Ali had owned a knife similar to the one used in Brown's murder. It was not reported how these two men in jail could have possibly seen such a knife, but the information was nevertheless used to further the case against Frenchy. One possibility the police were able to point to was that Ben Ali had known Brown and may have been with her in the murder room a week before — a point possibly obtained by other prostitutes in the area who knew Brown. In fact, Ali was a regular at the hotel and would have known that Brown had little or no money. It is interesting to note that in some coverage by the *New York Times* he was referred to as "George Frank ... or Aamer Ben Ali as he calls himself in Arabic...."

The short trial began on June 24, 1891, in the Court of General Sessions before Recorder Smyth, as the French Algerian fought for his life, seated on a bench in the prisoner's cage. It would take three days to seat the jury and five days for evidence to be presented. On June 27 the jury was taken to the "scene of the murder" and soon returned to the courtroom to begin the trial. The prosecution was handled by Assistant District Attorneys Simms and Wellman. However, on July 1, District Attorney Nicoll himself took the floor of the court to present blood evidence based on Dr. Formand's investigations. It would be the climax of the prosecution's case, and the most damaging evidence to the defense.

For the most part, the case against Ameer Ben Ali was based on the blood evidence found on his clothes and in his room, number 33; evidence which would later be shown to have been either planted by the police or allowed to be "accidentally" placed in his room by sloppy procedures. The medical experts' testimony was reported in the *New York Times* on July 2. "Their evidence was to the effect that the intestinal matter mingled with blood of Carrie Brown was identical with that found upon 'Frenchy,' upon his clothing and in the room where he slept. Prof. Henry N. Formand of Philadelphia ... testified that he, Dr. Austin Flint, and Dr. Cyrus Edson of the Board of Health, together made microscopic, stereoscopic, and chemical examinations of the blood spots upon the mattress upon which the murdered woman lay, the spots upon the bed tick in the room in which 'Frenchy' slept, and the spots upon his clothing. He found traces of intestinal matter in all but six of the pieces of material upon which there was blood. In the scrapings of 'Frenchy's' fingernails traces of the same matter were discovered. ... They believed that the intestinal matter found in the various places were identical...."

Blood stains were also found on the walls of the hallway as well as on both sides of Frenchy's room. It did not help matters when Ameer stated that he had fought with a different woman that night and that "some blood was spilled." He could only add that if this other woman could be located she would support his statement. The woman was never located and never came forward.

The blood evidence would, on the surface, seem to have pretty much wrapped up the case. But on cross examination, all three medical doctors admitted that they could "not swear that the blood was even human, but would swear that it was mammalian." On the other hand, something was allegedly found under Ameer's fingernails. It may have been possible that Ameer was actually in Brown's room after all. However, several reporters stated that when they had visited the room Ameer had for the night, there was no blood anywhere to be seen. In fact, the police did not find any blood in room number 33 until the second day of the investigation, and then, only after many reporters and police had moved all over it. It was simply no longer a protected crime scene. Yet, none of these reporters came forward during the trial.

This closed the case for the prosecution. Court-appointed attorney Levy, backed by attorneys House and Friend, took up the case for the defense on July 2. In his first statement Levy informed the jury that "with no testimony as to the whereabouts of the man who accompanied Carrie Brown to the East River Hotel on the night of her death," Mr. Ameer Ben Ali could in no way be found guilty. He also stated that the police had not done enough to track down this most likely suspect, who was, at the very least, the most important witness in the case. The New York police, and prosecutors, had *a* man and they were not about to let any real evidence get in the way of a conviction.

First to be called by the defense was officer James R. Hiland, who testified that when Ben Ali was arrested in Queens, he had no weapon on him. He also did not have the key to room 31, which had been taken by the murderer after he closed and locked the door. There was also no link between Ben Ali and the murder knife. The defendant himself then took the stand.

> QUESTION: Did you know Carrie Brown or Old Shakespeare?
> BEN ALI: I don't know her.
> QUESTION: Upon the night you slept in a hotel did you kill a woman?
> BEN ALI: I don't kill her. I don't know her.
> QUESTION: Have you ever owned or seen the knife found in the dead woman's room?
> BEN ALI: I never saw the knife till I saw it here.

In Arabic, which was even difficult for the translator to understand, he screamed, "I am innocent. I am innocent. Allah il Allah [God is God]. I am innocent. Allah Akbar [God is great]. I am innocent. Oh Allah, help me. Allah save me. I implore Allah to help me." After which the Arab slumped in his chair, for a while unable to continue.

When he had recovered, Ben Ali further testified that he had gone to Castle Garden Park during the evening of Carrie's murder. He had then proceeded to the East River Hotel at around 11 p.m. He stated that he slept the rest of the night and got up at 5 a.m. to take a walk along the waterfront. While he was walking he was looking for work and not hiding. When confronted with the testimony of Detective Aloncle, who had told the court that Frenchy had informed him that the blood on him had come to be on him during a trip to Jamaica, Ben Ali jumped up and shouted, "He don't tell the truth, by Allah!" Finally, as he ended his testimony Ben Ali cried out, "If they want to kill me they can. ... They say that the man who was with the woman had large and lovely mustaches. Just look at my mustaches. They are neither long or thick." Ameer's mustache was described as "very medium size."

When interviewed by a *New York Times* reporter, Ameer "began to speak of old Carrie Brown and he again denied that he had killed her. 'Why should I strangle her and cut her up?' he cried, and, becoming excited, he went through a very dramatic pantomime of strangling a person by catching himself by the throat and then stabbing and slashing at an imaginary person as he spoke. 'Why should I kill her?' he repeated. 'She did not have any money.'" The police were also never able to find the key to Carrie Brown's room, number 31, and Ameer certainly did not have it.

To finish up the defense testimony, four experts — two doctors, a professor and a Mr. Justin Herald — were called to contradict the State's expert medical witnesses. By July 3, the case had gone to the jury. It was a jury who wanted to be finished in time for the holiday — being on a murder case was not where most of them would have preferred to be. It was reported that juror number three asked the judge how long they should deliberate. The court stated, "That depends on you." The juror then reminded the judge, "You know tomorrow's the Fourth of July!" At which point he, and the other jurors were reminded that the holiday should have no bearing on the deliberations. The jury would soon be free to enjoy their holiday nonetheless.

That evening Ali was interviewed about his future. "God knows what they will do with me. Perhaps they will hang me, but I swear that I never killed any woman." When asked what he would do if he were found innocent he replied: "In that case I shall go home to my wife and children in Algiers as soon as possible. I'd go and ask the French Consul to send me home, as I have served in the French Army. ... I swear that I did not kill that woman or any other woman. I did not know her; never had anything to do with her. Why should I kill her? She never did me any harm. Women like her never have any money about them. She might have 50 cents or $1, or perhaps $2 at the most, and who is going to kill a person for a couple of dollars?"

The *New York Times*—July 4, 1891
Frenchy Found Guilty
Convicted of murder in the second degree
Three Ballots settled the fate of the Algerian—
He will be imprisoned for life—
More Protestations of Innocence

Imprisonment for life was the message the jury had for Ameer Ben Ali, or "Frenchy," in the court of General Sessions last night after two hours deliberation. The courtroom was packed to the doors when the jury came in. A low murmur of surprise ran over the crowd when the foreman announced, "Guilty—guilty of murder in the second degree."

On the first ballot the jury stood 8 to 4 for murder in the first degree, on the second 11 to 1 for that degree of crime, and after some argument a compromise verdict of murder in the second degree was agreed upon.

Mr. House [a defense attorney] discussed the evidence at length. It was circumstantial he said, and of the most unsatisfactory kind and bearing the least weight. "Where is the man who went upstairs in the Fourth Ward hotel with Old Shakespeare the last time she was seen alive?" he cried. "When he went upstairs he passed out of sight. No one knows where he went or where he is."

Inspector Byrnes returned to Police Headquarters after the verdict was rendered. He was very much pleased with the result.... Asked if he thought the man had committed the London murders, he replied that he would not like to express an opinion on that subject, but he had in his possession a statement tending to show that the man had been in London at the time that some of the murders were committed.

Of course no such "statement" was ever given, and Inspector Byrnes was allowed to place one final lie on the record. Despite published reports of Byrnes being pleased with the results of the verdict, he was anything but pleased. He wanted a verdict of guilty of murder in the first degree, and when that verdict was not forthcoming he was shocked. He wanted Frenchy executed.

The man who went to Carrie Brown's room that night was never found, and thus he lived to kill another day. In point of fact, very little, if any, work was done by the police to locate this critical witness. As for Ameer Ben Ali, he continued to deny any knowledge of the murder. On July 10, 1891, he was sentenced to life in prison and spent 11 years of his life behind bars at Sing Sing and Mattewan State Hospital for Insane Criminals, before being pardoned by then Governor Benjamin Odell on April 17, 1902. It would take the work of a few journalists, notably Charles Russell and Jacob Riis, who had worked on the case from it inception, and others, to unearth facts which would cast doubts on the Algerian's conviction.

The governor when granting the pardon was acting on requests from the French Ambassador, Jules Cambon, and others: "persons of credit, some of whom had had experience in the investigation of crime." To them, there was a very real possibility that Ben Ali had been "railroaded" for the murder. New evidence showed that police incompetence (or planting) in the handling of blood evidence could have placed the blood stains in Ben Ali's room and on his clothes. Because the blood evidence was the primary cause of his conviction, the Governor stated that he had "grave doubts of the prisoner's guilt. ... To refuse under such circumstances would be plainly a denial of justice, and after a very careful consideration of all the facts, I have reached the conclusion that it is clearly my duty to order the prisoner's release." Upon his pardon the Governor declared Ameer Ben Ali innocent of Carrie Brown's murder. It would be left up to the government of France to arrange the transportation of Ameer Ben Ali back to his home in an Algerian village. After his pardon, the police, still believing they had had the right man, never brought anyone else to trial for Brown's murder.

In newspaper stories in April 1902, it was reported that the Carrie Brown murder had occurred only a "few days after the [final] Whitechapel murder in London." It would seem that they were referring to the Coles murder in the East End. As far as the New York Times was concerned, the Brown murder was still very much linked to the Ripper series in London, and not to a poor Algerian who had had the misfortune to be in the wrong room at the wrong time. And the New York police files on the Brown murder? They were destroyed, after 75 years, sometime in the 1960s.

The New Jersey Barber

After "passing through" New York City, Severin Klosowski and his wife, Lucy, made their way across the Hudson River to Jersey City, New Jersey, where before long, he found work as a barber. However, it would not be long before he once again turned to his misogynistic ways. Had he also been to Easton by train?

The couple were never happy in New Jersey, most likely due to Klosowski's continuous roving eye and late night outings. At one point he even attacked his wife while he was working in the barbershop. The incident was reported on March 23, 1903, in the *London Daily Chronicle*, after his trial. "Klosowski's real wife, Lucy Klosowski, who was present in the Central Criminal Court last week, has made a startling statement as to what occurred in the New Jersey shop. She states that on one occasion, when she had a quarrel with her husband, he held her down on the bed, and pressed his face against her mouth to keep her from screaming. At that moment a customer entered the shop immediately in front of the room, and Klosowski got up to attend him. The woman chanced to see a handle protruding from underneath the pillow. She found, to her horror, that it was a sharp and formidable knife, which she promptly hid. Later, Klosowski deliberately told her that he meant to have cut her head off, and pointed to a place in the room where he meant to have buried her. She said, 'But the neighbours would have asked where I had gone to.' 'Oh,' retorted Klosowski, calmly, 'I should simply have told them that you had gone back to New York.'"*

The burning questions are: Would Lucy have been the victim of a Ripper type murder or a Torso murder? And, are there any heads still buried on the grounds of 126 Cable Street, St. George-in-the-East, London?

The incident was more than Mrs. Klosowski could put up with. So, after less than a year in the United States, the six months' pregnant Lucy returned to the East End of London, in February of 1892. She stayed with her sister at her home at 26 Scarborough Street, Whitechapel. It was while living there that she gave birth to her second child, Cecilia, on May 15, 1892. Since she arrived in London in February it is very probable that she left New Jersey at the end of January.

Klosowski was now alone with no one to watch his movements, from January or February to June 1892, when he returned to London and the East End, with very little money to his name. With such a small amount of cash on hand it does not make any real sense for him to have left his new

---

*The "gone back to New York" portion of the statement would seem to indicate that the couple stayed in New York somewhat longer than simply passing through!

home, and his job in the New Jersey barbershop, for what must have been a chancy reunion with Lucy in London. He certainly had no feelings for her. Unless, of course, he was once again running away from more crimes committed in and around the New Jersey area.

The *New York Times*— February 1, 1892
A Brutal New Jersey Murder
An Old Woman Killed and
Her House Ransacked for Plunder
NEWARK, N.J. Jan. 31.— When Joseph Senior, a watchman at Fouratt's hat shop in Milburn, entered his house this morning, he was surprised at not finding his wife in the room. Going to the stove he found in front of it the body of his wife, who had been brutally murdered during the night. The body lay at full length on the floor. The throat was cut, there were eleven stab wounds in the breast, and both arms were frightfully gashed.

It may have been a close affair for Klosowski to have arrived in New York City in time to have murdered Carrie Brown, but there is absolutely no doubt that he was living and working in New Jersey when 73-year-old Elizabeth Senior was murdered. He had just recently attacked his wife with a knife, and was still in the habit of roaming the streets at night, and Milburn was not far away from Jersey City. And, as with many of the murders in the East End of London, it was a weekend the killer stalked the streets to do his bloody work. Klosowski still had his barbershop to be concerned with during the week.

That day, 70-year-old Joseph Senior had worked, as usual, as a watch repairman and taxidermist. At night he supplemented his income by working as the night watchman in Fouratt's hat shop in the quiet village of Milburn. The couple had lived for 40 years in their small two story house located on Springfield Avenue. It was just across the street from the Milburn schoolhouse. The town, it would seem, had grown up around them. As reported, "The news of the murder created intense excitement in the village." The peaceful core of the city had been literally ripped away.

The authorities established that around 10 p.m., before Elizabeth had gone to bed, her assailant had entered the house and attacked the old woman. However, Mrs. Senior was not about to give up without a struggle, easily witnessed by the spattered blood all around the murder scene, as well as the many deep gashes on her hands and arms. And yet, no one in that quiet town would ever report hearing any screams from this latest victim. Despite the struggle, her killer was finally able to find his mark and cut her throat. Then, perhaps as an indication of his frustration, he stabbed her breast 11 more times. After he had finished his work, her killer calmly washed off the blood from his hands and carefully ransacked the house. According to reports, he was only able to acquire around $45 for his trouble. Murder for pure delight was not the only reason for this attack—his funds were low.

After the murder had been discovered a shocked Joseph Senior ran out of his house and began to alert the neighbors, and soon the local constable was on the case. It would not be long before a suspect came to the attention of the police. August Lyntz, who was described as a "dissolute character," had worked as an engineer in Fouratt's hat shop before being fired for drinking on the job. He had been seen in the area of the Senior home late that night and would not be able to show where he had been during the time of the murder. Although two other men had also been seen in the area, and would be searched for, no one knew their names and they would never be located. The only name known to the police was August Lyntz. The telegraph wires sprang into life.

> Arrest for murder August Lyntz, German, Thirty-three, 5 feet 7 inches, dark hair and mustache, dark complexion, small brown eyes, dark suit, brown overcoat, old-style derby hat, with a wide brim and high crown; clothes must have some blood on them; working shoes, with strap and buckle. Information to the District Attorney of Newark.

It would not be long before the police had their hands on the man. He was arrested on February 3 by Constable Manderville and subsequently turned over to Police Superintendent Brown who, with the help of Detective Cosgrove, took over the case. After his arrest Lyntz was taken before a night clerk, who had been working at a lodging house at 5 New Chambers Street, in New York City. The clerk identified Lyntz from a police lineup as the man who had come to the lodging house between 4 and 6 a.m. that Sunday. "That is the man. I could pick him out of a hundred men. ... He had on a brown overcoat." The clerk reported that Lyntz had "...taken off a bloody shirt and put on a clean one." But it was not reported exactly how this clerk had acquired that particular piece of information. It would certainly not have been volunteered by Lyntz if he had just killed someone. It is also interesting to note that there was no mention of blood on Lyntz's overcoat which had, by then, been removed by the authorities, and was in the custody of the County Physician, Doctor Wrightson. Moreover, the so called "bloody shirt" was never reported found, nor was any knife found on Lyntz when he was arrested. He did, however, tell Constable Manderville, when he was approached, "All right; I supposed you were after me."

On February 6, the press were reporting that the case was, for the most part, cleared up. A conductor named Bell had reported that a man, whom he identified as August Lyntz (occasionally spelled Lentz in the *New York Times*), had been his only passenger on a run from Short Hills station, near Milburn, all the way to Hoboken. The conductor further stated that Lyntz had "disappeared at once into the toilet room" until the train arrived at South Orange. After which his passenger took a seat and slept the rest of the way. What the conductor did not report were any signs of blood on Lyntz's clothing. Nor did he report that his passenger felt concerned about being seen — indeed, he seemed to make no attempt to hide his identity. He appeared unconcerned and simply went to sleep. Upon arriving at Hoboken station Lyntz was observed leaving the train and appeared to be making his way towards the New York City ferryboat.

It was on February 17, as the morning papers were warning their readers about the new "Electric Cars" racing through town at breakneck speeds of 20 miles per hour, that the inquest was held into the death of Mrs. Elizabeth Senior. It was conducted at Bonnell's Hall in Milburn and was very well attended, although it would be short — less than a full afternoon. Over 12 witnesses were called to testify, but not much information could be gathered into the facts of the case. There was simply no great body of evidence, other than circumstantial, in which to point to any one suspect, including August Lyntz. Although the police felt sure that they had their man, the jury soon came to a verdict of "death at the hands of persons unknown." Once again the killer had escaped. But would he be heard from again?

A Close Call?

Around 3 a.m. on the morning of April 25, an Elizabeth, New Jersey, policeman named William Martin was found walking his usual beat and enjoying the coolness of the air. Suddenly, and without warning, a man came out of the night and ran directly into him while fleeing from another officer named Martz. As reported in the *New York Times*, "Martin demanded what he was doing. The man quickly drew a knife and slashed Martin from the mouth to the neck within half an inch of the jugular vein." The surprise attack put the officer temporarily off balance and prevented his attacker's capture, but Martin would not be put off for long. Despite being seriously wounded, he almost immediately took up the chase. During this wild run through the darkened streets of Elizabeth the two men exchanged several shots. Martin was able to fire all four rounds from his service revolver as he ran, with the suspect firing twice at the very determined officer. Although Martin did not hit the suspect, his fleeing attacker was able to graze the officer's head with one of his two shots. Even with these severe wounds the officer continued to press the chase after the desperate fugitive.

It would not be long before a loss of blood would compel officer Martin to give up. However, by that time three other officers had joined the pursuit alerted by the sounds of the running gun battle. One of the officers stayed with the badly wounded Martin, escorting him to a local doctor, as the other two men continued the chase. Despite the added manpower the attacker was able to make his escape into the darkness of the early morning. The only evidence to his identity would be his method of attack and a general description supplied by the policemen who had pursued him.

> He is about five feet eight inches in height, of rather sturdy build, and had a good suit of dark clothing and a derby hat.

One month later, it was reported by the press that a 27-year-old local criminal named Michael Sullivan, who lived on Pearl Street in New York City, was charged with the attack in Elizabeth, New Jersey. He had also been accused of burglary but was only convicted of the assault of the police officer, which he never admitted committing. On June 4 in Union County Court in Elizabeth, he was sentenced to ten years in State prison. Considering the lack of credibility of some of the convictions in the New York and New Jersey courts, it must be asked whether or not the police actually got the right man this time. Did the Ripper get away yet again, with some other individual paying the price for his crime? Perhaps.

With one murder to mark his arrival in the United States and a second to mark his departure, Klosowski left to find new and safer hunting grounds. London was once more calling this serial killer, as New Jersey became far too risky a place to pursue his work.

For a while, after talking his way into his sister-in-law's home, he stayed with his wife and new child in the East End. But he was not about to change his misogynist ways. Before long, he was staying out late and seeing other women, and not long after that his wife left him for the final time, taking their daughter with her. Klosowski never attempted to see either of them again.

The next and last time Lucy saw Klosowski would be after he had been arrested for a second series of murders, and at that time he would not even admit to knowing her. He may not have enjoyed being reminded of the one who got away. But, at the time they separated, there would be years of killing yet to come, and London was preying on his mind.

As Klosowski was making his way back to London the *New York Times* in its June 9, 1892, issue once again reported on the brutality of daily life in the East End. "Last evening the body of a boy of four years who had been murdered was found tied to the railings in front of a house in Goulston Street…. The boy's throat was cut and there were numerous gashes on the body."

Chapter Eleven

Mr. Chapman
Comes to Town

"I don't know anything about that fellow."

George Chapman

Klosowski must have felt assured of his success in the Ripper series when he returned to Whitechapel in mid–1892. For the most part the investigation had stalled, due to an appalling lack of tangible evidence, and there were no lines of inquiry to be followed at the time. Inspector Abberline had retired and the investigation was, to all intents and purposes, finished and closed — without the capture and conviction of the man who had led London police forces on such a grand and bloody chase. Klosowski could breathe easy as he retraced his steps along Buck's Row and Flower and Dean Street, reliving recent events. He also had the time to recover and move the body parts he had worked so hard to acquire.

After Klosowski and his "wife" separated for the final time, within weeks of his return to London, there began a period in the life of Severin Klosowski which is unrecorded. His travels and occupation are unknown, but a clue may be gleaned from the handwritten document found in his wallet when he was arrested in 1902. He had written on a small piece of paper, "Came from America in 1893..." Certainly this was false. He had returned to London in 1892, still "married" and with little or no money. Clearly he was trying to mislead anyone who might pick him up and search his possessions. But why did he not want anyone to know that he had been in England during 1892? Perhaps there was a different series of crimes

247

committed during that year which he did not want to be associated with. Indeed, from mid-1892 until late 1893 there are no surviving records of Klosowski's whereabouts. Certainly Klosowski himself held no documents from this time period, nor did he hold any from the Ripper period either. In the later period of time, there could have been many crimes as yet unsolved — crimes he was responsible for as he walked the dark streets of England. If, indeed, he was on the streets at all. Perhaps, just perhaps, Klosowski was being held in an asylum somewhere in England. If this is so and he was not held under his own name, it would be nearly impossible to prove. All that can be said is, the 1892–3 period is unexplained.

A Link to the Past

Towards the end of 1893, Klosowski could be found working in Mr. Haddin's hairdresser's shop, located at 5 West Green Road, South Tottenham. He was now away from the East End killing area and was possibly using the name Schloski (by some witness accounts). From Alfred Wicken, who worked at Mr. Haddin's along with Klosowski, comes this report on his use of the name Schloski: "Never heard him called by any other name other than Schloski." It could also be that some of the people in the area could not, or chose not, to pronounce his name properly. Klosowski also claimed to be an American, but clearly this was a tall tale. Few, including those women who lived with this serial killer, believed he was an American. He simply did not look or really act the part. German perhaps, but American? And was the name "Schloski" the one he used during his missing time during 1892–3?

It would be at Haddin's that Severin would meet a young woman named Chapman. It is entirely possible that this woman was the daughter of Ripper victim Annie Chapman — Annie Georgina Chapman. If true, Klosowski may have been playing a dangerous egotistical game with this direct link to his Ripper past. And, it would be well beyond simple coincidence with the Ripper murders. It is an open risk the Ripper would have delighted in.

The couple lived together as Mr. and Mrs. Klosowski from November 1893 to December 1894, possibly in some of the rooms at Haddin's. However, it would not be long before Severin's wandering eye focused on a new woman. Earlier, he had talked his "wife," Lucy, into allowing his "real" Polish "wife" to live with them for a while on Cable Street, before she "disappeared." But this time, when he brought a second woman to live with Annie in a threesome, his charms seemed to have failed him. Even though she was pregnant, in the fall of 1894, Annie Chapman removed herself from Klosowski's household. She could only take so much. The new woman's name, however, has been lost. Perhaps it could be found on a long forgotten list of missing persons. Whatever her fate, she did not go with Klosowski on his next move. It must be noted, though, that serial killers do not always kill, as Annie Chapman was able to walk away with her life and leave Klosowski behind, as did Lucy. It is a very important point.

Once again, testimony from Wolff Levisohn, who seemed to be in many of the right places at the right times, gives us a brief look at Klosowski's multiple lives. During Klosowski's trial, Levisohn spotted him and blurted out, "There he sits! That is his description. He has not altered from the day he came to England; he has not even a grey hair. Always the same — same la-di-da, 'igh 'at and umbrella. Two wives he had while at Tottenham — one English, one foreign." This is an indication that Klosowski may have looked older than he was 14 years earlier, more in line with the age of the suspects in the Ripper murders.

It was during this general period that Klosowski purchased a house, under his real name, on High Road, Tottenham. Perhaps he felt more room was needed if two women were going to be living with him. The extra room, however, would not be needed. In February 1895, Annie Chapman visited Klosowski, in South Tottenham, to inform him that she was "with child." She wanted his acknowledgment for official records but Klosowski would have none of that. But that was all — she would not be moving in with him and the other woman. Later, at his trial, she would recount his actions at the time for the court: "When I told him I was going to have a baby he did not take much notice." She confirmed that Klosowski was the father of the child and also stated her belief that he had then gone to Whitechapel after their final encounter. Is that where he left the other woman? Annie would not see him again until the second day of his trial, on March 17, 1903. As for the child, she would never meet her father at all.

It is interesting to note that if this was Annie Georgina Chapman, then her child would not only be the grandchild of a Ripper victim, but the child of the Ripper himself. Perhaps, through this child, there is a direct descendant of Jack the Ripper today.

After Annie had gone for good, an interesting transformation occurred. Klosowski changed his name to George Chapman. Again, if Annie was Annie Georgina Chapman, then he would have simply taken her name and cut out the female parts of it. It was not greatly creative, but it would have given him a permanent and very personal link to his past series of murders as Jack the Ripper. It would also provide a small look into the mind of this serial killer: while trying his best to distance himself from past crimes, he appears to have been doing much to keep their memory alive deep within himself. His taking the names of a Ripper victim and her daughter offers a glimpse, too, perhaps, of his hatred of women and his own self-hatred. As for the rest of the world, he would never again admit to being Severin Antonovich Klosowski, Polish surgical student from Warsaw. He was now the American barber, George Chapman from Jersey City. And he was looking for a wife.

The Quiet Time

For "George Chapman" the period from early 1895 to early April 1897 was a time for him to grow into his new identity. He was now a single man-about-town who was free to seek employment and a place to stay. His travels would lead him to a home and work in Leytonstone. As with some serial killers, he took a break from killing before once again inevitably hunting prey.

In early 1895, Chapman took up residence in a home owned by the Rentons in Leytonstone. It was there that he would meet the former Mary Isabella Renton, then Mrs. Mary Spink, who was married to a Great Eastern Railway Company porter named Shadrach Spink. However, Mrs. Spink would say her husband was a doctor. She had been living at the family home since her husband had left her because of her drunkenness. He had gone off with their first son, leaving Mary pregnant and about to give birth to a second son, who would be named William. Mrs. Spink was the ideal victim for Chapman. She was a woman who would be more than happy to subject herself to his every whim. She was described as being short and plump with short blonde hair, and not overly intelligent.

By mid–1895, Chapman could be found working as an assistant barber in William Wenzel's shop at 7 Church Lane, Leytonstone. Wenzel had advertised for an assistant and Chapman had answered the ad. "I knew him as George Chapman and he told me he had come from Tottenham." It would be a position that Chapman would hold for six or seven months. He was never one to stay in any place too long.

Chapman was soon changing his lodgings once again. He moved out of the Renton home around October of 1895, and moved to new lodgings with Mr. John Ward of Forest Road. "He said he was a Polish Jew." Chapman and Mrs. Spink could be seen together a great deal. An affair had begun, which had caught the eye of the very proper Mr. Ward, who commented to Chapman about it. "My wife has seen you kissing Mrs. Spink. We cannot allow that sort of thing to go on in the house." Not taken aback, and without missing a beat, Chapman replied, "It's all right, Mr. Ward, we are going to get married about Sunday week."

On October 27, George and Mrs. Spink made a show of going out as if they were to be married. Chapman told Mr. Ward and his wife that they would be going to Whitechapel. However, since both were already married, any "real" marriage between them would have been bigamy, and it certainly would have caught the eye of the authorities. As they returned to John Ward's that evening they declared themselves to be Mr. and Mrs. Chapman. Chapman stated, "Allow me to present you my wife." With the help of Mrs. Spink, Chapman was able, once more, to fool those around him with his lies. But not before Mrs. Ward asked to see the marriage certificate. Chapman simply dismissed the request by replying, "Oh, our laws are different to your laws."

It was a good enough cover to even fool Mrs. Spink's relations. A cousin of hers, Joseph Smith Renton, commented years later, "I noticed my cousin was keeping company with the accused, whom I knew as Chapman, and who was employed at Wenzel's. About March 1896, my cousin left Leytonstone. I was given to understand she was married to Chapman, as she passed as Mrs. Chapman." But the immediate family, at the very least, must have known that it was not a real marriage, and yet no one seemed prepared to inform the authorities. It would be a fatal omission for the wife of Shadrach Spink.

With the entry into his life of his newest "wife," George Chapman came into a fresh source of funding. Mrs. Spink's grandfather had passed away and left her around £600 which had been placed in a trust fund. Soon after the "marriage" the fund trustees sent £250 to the couple. Two years later, the final payment of £300 would find its way into the account of Mr. and Mrs. Chapman. It was a princely sum.

The new cash flow allowed Chapman to quit his job at Wenzel's and start a shop of his own. Early in 1896, he leased a small storefront in Hastings in southeast England. However, he chose a bad section of town where business was poor. After a short time, around March 1896, he moved the hairdressing business to George Street, in Old Hastings. It proved to be a much better location, behind the Albion public house, and in a more affluent section of town.

Mr. and Mrs. Chapman were now able to live "off site," and moved to rooms at 10 Hill Street, Hastings, near his new business. Also living in the lodgings on Hill Street was Mrs. Anna Helsdown. Mrs. Helsdown would later report that the Chapmans lived there with a young boy named Willie. "After they had been there some time the accused [Chapman] opened a barber shop in George Street. That was in 1896. I left them there in 1897." It would be to Anna Helsdown that the former, and in reality still, Mrs. Spink, showed marks around her throat from Chapman's not infrequent attacks. For some unknown reason, though, she stayed with this vicious thug. More than once Mrs. Helsdown also saw bruises on Mrs. Spink's face, and later stated that she heard her cries in the night from Chapman's abuses. It is not recorded why Mrs. Spink stayed with her abusive partner, despite the fact that legally he had no hold on her whatsoever. Moreover, Chapman showed his contempt for her son by having him sleep in a cellar below his barbershop, in the company of rats and filth. The alcoholic Mrs. Spink was not a very protective mother.

Despite the less than ideal living arrangements, the Chapmans did indeed stay together, with Mrs. Chapman working in her "husband's" shop. She would lather up many of the customers before the "Mister" would use his well practiced blade to give the men their close shaves. How would they have felt if they had known they were being shaved by Jack the Ripper! On occasion Mrs. Chapman would try her hand at shaving, but she was not always "in full control of her faculties," due to her frequent drinking, and perhaps other reasons. It was not the best way to be shaved, and the number of customers began to slow down. After all, the neck is a very sensitive area. And it was also quite rare at the time to find a female barber.

It would not be long before a new method of customer relations was tried. Chapman rented a piano and placed it in the front of his barbershop. After she lathered the customers, Mrs. Chapman would sit at the piano and play. These "musical shaves" rapidly became very popular with the locals and prosperity seemed assured for the Chapmans. With this new security Chapman was able to purchase a small sailing boat he christened the *Mosquito*. (Interestingly, the dictionary defines the word mosquito as an insect, the female of which has a long proboscis capable of puncturing the skin of man and animals for extracting blood!)

It was on the *Mosquito* that an interesting event would occur, which, in light of Mr. Chapman's past and future activities, needs to be recounted. Chapman, being a boastful but not a particularly skilled sailor, set out dressed in nautical garb, with Mrs. Chapman, on a day cruise along the coast. During the sailing the reckless Chapman capsized the boat throwing both him and his drunk wife overboard. It was reported that both nearly drowned but for the quick rescue of a fisherman who saw the event. It is not recorded whether or not he could swim. But in view of his many killings, it is a good bet that Mrs. Chapman could not. (Serial killers change their MO.)

After the "accident" Chapman would once again be on the move. Keeping on the move and covering his tracks was a way of life for him, with or without a woman at his side. In February 1897, Mr. and Mrs. Chapman moved to 1 Coburg Place in Hastings. It would be at the Coburg Place lodgings that they would meet Mrs. Harriet Greenway. Mrs. Greenway, at

Chapman's later trial, would relate what she knew of the small family who moved in just as she was about to leave. It would seem that Mr. Chapman had forgotten that he was posing as an American at the time, and let slip one or two secrets. "A family named Chapman came to live (in) the same house about a month before I left. There was a man, a woman and a child. He went to a hairdresser's shop in George Street. He said he was a Russian Pole, and that he had been in America."

It would be to Mrs. Greenway that Mary Spink would confide a dark secret about her "husband." "Once Mrs. Chapman showed me a black bag, secretly. Prisoner George Chapman used to keep the bag." Was this the bag he carried as Jack the Ripper? Inspector Godley did report that Chapman, at the time of the murders, carried such a black bag and that some reports suggested the Ripper did as well. And, if it was the same bag, did Mary Spink know that Chapman had such a dark past? It is of course speculation as to how much she may have guessed at the time, but this much is sure: Mary Spink knew that bag held some dark secrets which she understood Chapman did not want anyone to find out about. History does not record what was in the black bag, but soon after its "showing" to Mrs. Greenway, George Chapman began heading towards his poisoning career. Mrs. Spink would be his first victim.

The Little White Powder

It was not long before Chapman began to tire of his newest wife. And his eye focused on a domestic servant by the name of Alice Penfold. During one of her Sunday evening walks Alice was intercepted by Chapman, who introduced himself as a single man working as the manager of a piano shop in Hastings. They would meet again several times, but with this young woman his charms would not succeed. Perhaps it was because he had other things on his mind. The powerful control he had over most women seemed to fail him with Miss Penfold. She would live to tell the tale of her encounters with the "Borough Poisoner."

On April 3, 1897, George Chapman walked into Chemist William Henry Davidson's shop at 66 High Street in Hastings, and purchased one ounce of tartar emetic, a poison which contained antimony and a small amount of arsenic. The Ripper had put down his knife to begin a career as the Borough Poisoner. He was intelligent enough to realize that the violent methods of the Ripper would only bring attention to him if the victims were too closely linked to him. He needed a new method and he had the skills for it. The poison he had tried to get in 1888 would no longer elude him.

Mr. Davidson had been an occasional customer of Chapman's at his barbershop, and during his shaves the two of them discussed many things. One of the subjects was medicine. Through these discussions Davidson was able to gather that his barber had a great deal of medical knowledge. Chapman must surely have told the chemist that he was a surgeon and perhaps shown Mr. Davidson his medical papers. All of this was to impress the chemist so that he would sell him the tartar emetic, which Davidson readily agreed to do. Chapman acquired the poison in white powder form in a small bottle. The red label read:

> W. H. Davidson, dispensing chemist. Poison, Tartar-emetic.
> Dose, $\frac{1}{16}$ th grain to $\frac{1}{4}$. To be taken with caution.
> 66 High Street, Hastings

Chapman was able to acquire the poison this time because he was well known in his community and had the proper connections. Davidson would later state, "I think he did have some other poisons, but they did not come under Schedule I."

In Davidson's poisons book Chapman was required to sign his name for his one ounce of death. He signed "G. Chapman" and indicated that the tartar emetic was for him to "take." But Chapman made sure that the word was hard to read. It would not be so with the signature, but then again, he was not really Chapman so that did not matter.

During this time Chapman was still seeing Alice Penfold, who he may have expected to replace Mrs. Spink. At one point Alice complained that she had a cold, at which time Chapman informed her that he had a medical background and would fix her up a little something to relieve her symptoms. He sent over some powders to her home, but the cautious Miss Penfold did not take the "cure," and simply disposed of the remedy. It is not known whether or not Chapman was trying to use Alice as his first test subject for the new poison, but it is a distinct possibility. He was, after all, being rejected by her and that may have been more than he could accept.

At their final meeting, Chapman took Alice to a public house at St. Leonards. He informed her that he intended to take a lease on the pub, and probably asked her to come with him. There must have been something in Chapman that somehow Alice could see that other women could not, for after that visit to the pub she never had anything to do with Chapman again. Even after their final outing, he wrote to her asking her to come to his new pub. But she completely ignored the man who would soon begin a series of murders with his deadly white powder.

With poison in hand it was time, once more, to move to a new lodgings and a new type of work. After only six months at his Hastings shop, and despite its financial success, Chapman sold it to a Mr. Robinson who owned a local furniture concern. A successful business was not the prime consideration of George Chapman. Chapman's whereabouts after leaving Hastings are unknown until the fall of 1897, when he resurfaces in London.

The Borough Poisoner Begins His Work

In the fall of 1897, 31-year-old George Chapman began his career as a publican, with the lease of the Prince of Wales public house in Bartholomew Square, just off City Road. He was back again in the killing fields of London, only a short ride from Whitechapel. Posing as an expatriate American, complete with upside down flag, he had changed his name, his country, his job, his address and his method of killing, before once again settling down in London. He was getting older now and it was time to try out a new way. This time be brought his victim with him in the guise of Mrs. Mary Isabella Spink, better known at the time as Mrs. Chapman. He knew that the knife must not take this one; the poison would have to do the trick.

It should be remembered that most Ripper victims had been drinking in public houses just before they were murdered. It is an interesting link to the past for the Ripper to have run a series of public houses in his later life.

In this later series of murders, Chapman would become a different kind of "collector." He photographed each and every victim, with himself, just before he killed them. Psychologically, this is the exact same thing as acquiring a trophy, such as a body part, like the Ripper did. Perhaps he no longer had a need for cutting—the readily available images of his victims was enough.

Chapman also began to see the need for a positive public image as a good cover. To this end, he began to go on cycling outings with the local police cycling club. He must have felt that these would deflect suspicion from him if there was a murder in his general area. It was all part of his overall plan to blend into the background of life, as he had done so well in the past. Chapman was a very long term planner.

It was not long after the Chapmans' arrival in London that Mary began to show signs of a serious illness. She had just received her final £300 from the trustees of her grandfather's will and there was no longer any reason for George to keep her around. She had been in good health for most of her life, but now she was confined to bed. She began to suffer major abdominal pains and severe vomiting, caused of course by her husband's dispensing of his little white powders.

The poison Chapman had chosen was a very good selection at the time since many doctors would not have recognized its effects. The deaths, for the most part, would have been attributed to natural causes. Tartar emetic was soluble in water, colorless, odorless and tasteless when mixed with juice or other drinks. It would have been undetectable when placed in soups or other foods. But the poison would have needed to have been dispensed by an expert, one who had a medical or chemist's background, as too large a dose would have resulted in the majority of the poison being vomited up by the intended victim. Death from this poison would have been slow and torturous. Something to be enjoyed over a long period of time by the sadistic Mr. Chapman.

As Mrs. Chapman's condition grew worse, George hired a neighbor, Mrs. Martha Doubleday, to take her place at the bar and to aid in his wife's recovery. It was not long before Mrs. Doubleday realized that a doctor's care was greatly needed, and soon, if Mary was to have any chance of recovery. Chapman reluctantly called in Dr. J.F. Rogers, who prescribed medications for an illness he thought she had. It was Chapman himself who would prepare and administer the good doctor's medications, or not. He was in full control of her slow and agonizing death.

Before long, the 41-year-old Mrs. Chapman began to slip away. For a few days, after her condition was pronounced hopeless, she wavered on the brink of lifelessness. Then, on Christmas day 1897, death, and with it release, finally came. It was a gift to the Borough Poisoner. Mrs. Elizabeth Waymark, a neighbor who had come to be with Mrs. Chapman in her last days, remembered the lack of interest shown by Chapman in his dying wife. Mrs. Waymark called down to him as he calmly prepared to open the pub. "At first he did not come up, and when he did she [Mary] said to him, 'Do kiss me.' She put her arms out for him to bend over to kiss her but he did not do so. The last time I sent for him just before she died he did not come up in time. I prepared the body for burial. It was a mere skeleton."

Time and time again in Chapman's relationships with women, as they became weaker he would become more abusive. Although he tried to appear caring to most people, at times it was hard for him to conceal his contempt for his "wives" as well as other women. It was at these times that he revealed his true feelings. As they died his contempt was fully on view.

Mrs. Doubleday was also at Mary's side when she died. She called to the husband, "Chapman, come up quickly! Your wife is dying!" As Mrs. Waymark said, he did not arrive in time. He then apparently went into the next room and shed a few tears before going downstairs to open the pub as usual for Christmas Day. Mrs. Doubleday would later testify that, "He went down and opened the house. She died at one o'clock. I said, 'You are never going to open the house today?' He said, 'Yes, I am.' I saw Mrs. Chapman's body after she was dead. It was in a very shocking condition; it was very much bruised."

As far as Doctor Rogers was concerned it was death by natural causes. On the death certificate, he ascribed the cause of death due to phthisis. He was misled by the emaciated condition of Mary, and had not even considered the possibility that Chapman had murdered her. The bruises meant nothing to him.

It would be a brief and not well-attended funeral. Mrs. Chapman was laid to rest, for the time being, in a common grave at Leytonstone, Essex, on December 30, 1897. Later, more than half a dozen other bodies would be placed on top of her coffin. All of these would have to be removed in order for the authorities to examine her remains for a trial, as yet, a few years down the road. For the time being, the death of his "wife" would leave George Chapman needing not only a new barmaid, but a new Mrs. Chapman.

The New Mrs. Chapman

It was not long before George Chapman felt it was safe to begin the hunt for his next victim. After a few months had passed he began to advertise for a barmaid to help him with his growing business at the Prince of Wales. Many women applied, but only one would get the job.

Her name was Elizabeth "Bessie" Taylor, a former domestic servant, who was looking for a new start in life. (Some sources place her former occupation as a restaurant manager.) She was the daughter of a cattle dealer and farmer named Thomas Parsonage Taylor from Warrington, Cheshire, near Liverpool. She had very little experience behind the bar, but Chapman was not really looking for a barmaid — what he wanted was a victim.

It would not be long before Bessie Taylor entered into a bogus marriage with the barber turned publican. They drove out together one Sunday for a reported wedding, allegedly at St. George's Cathedral, Southwark, but of course none occurred. The couple returned that evening, without a honeymoon, to open the bar as normal. After all, for Chapman, it was just business as usual. The new Mrs. Chapman would last a little less than three years before she succumbed to murder. But for the moment, the "happy couple" lived above the Prince of Wales public house.

In late 1898, Mr. and Mrs. Chapman gave up their lease on the Prince of Wales and moved to Bishops Stortford and took a lease on the Grapes public house. It was a good plan for Chapman as it would have been too much to expect the local residents to accept the untimely deaths of two of

Severin Klosowski (alias George Chapman) with poison victim Bessie Taylor. Photo was taken by George Chapman around 1900 and found at 213 Borough High Street by Inspector George Godley.

his wives from the very same condition. The move would allow him to take his time and enjoy his work without outside suspicions.

Just before Christmas, 1898, Bessie's friend from her days as a domestic servant, Elizabeth Ann Painter, came to visit at the Grapes for two weeks over the holidays. Even at that early stage of the relationship Bessie's health seems to have been affected, as her friend described her as having "lumps in her face, caused by her teeth." Not long after Painter's visit, Bessie needed to go to the hospital for an operation. It is not reported what the problem was but since her health had been good throughout the years before she met Chapman there is a strong possibility that the early signs of his abuse were starting to show. Four separate doctors had seen Bessie and yet none of them were able to correctly diagnose her condition. She was said to have had "cancer of the stomach, womb trouble, constipation or hysteria."

Elizabeth Painter would later report that, "He kissed me once or twice." She would also report that Chapman often threw things at Bessie and yelled at her, as a form of control. Perhaps Chapman was trying, once again, to have two women at one time living with him as he had done twice before. Painter seems not to have accepted his advances, perhaps out of loyalty to her friend Bessie, or possibly she saw Chapman for the thug he really was.

After Bessie came home from the hospital there was a marked difference in Chapman's treatment of her. She had been "cured" by her operation but she was still quite weak. It is possible that Chapman resented what the surgeons had done. After all, he was not a surgeon in England, and might even have been rejected for a medical position. Whatever the reason, he began to treat Bessie very cruelly, including threatening her with his loaded revolver. What is not part of the record is why Bessie, who was not actually married to this madman, would risk her life with him. Perhaps he had convinced her that she was nothing without him. It was not the first time, nor would it be the last, that someone was subjected to this kind of brainwashing which rendered them unwilling or unable to escape. Cult groups regularly use the method to capture weak minds.

In March 1899, Chapman, along with his wife Bessie, left the Grapes public house and returned to London. He leased the Monument Tavern on Union Street, Southwark, from the Bridge House Estates Committee. (It should be remembered that early in her life Martha Tabram lived on London Road, Southwark. Did Chapman remember reading this in the newspaper reports of her murder? Also, this area was just south of the River Thames and Whitechapel.) It would be within the confines of the Monument that Chapman's abuse of the now weakened and wasting Bessie would escalate. With her once strong constitution failing, due to the poisons being introduced into her body, Chapman felt strong enough to begin beating her whenever the mood possessed him. This was one killing he planned to enjoy as much and as long as possible.

Despite the abuse by Chapman no one seemed to suspect anything was amiss. Even a visit by Bessie's parents failed to uncover anything of note which would have placed suspicion on Chapman. In fact, he was able to hide his true feelings so well that Mrs. Taylor would later state that she "had never seen a better husband"! They were fully unaware, however, that a gift of £50 they had sent to their daughter had been intercepted by Chapman for his own uses.

Towards the end, Mrs. Painter visited her sick friend on most evenings. At one point, when she asked about Bessie's condition, Chapman showed the true callousness of his nature by telling her, "Your friend is dead." This proved to be a lie, though, at least for the present, as she found her friend very much alive in her bed upstairs.

It must have pained Chapman to see, despite his continued abuse, that Bessie was able to make quite a few friends during her stay on Union Street. She was much liked by both the nearby neighbors, and the pub's customers, for her kindness to them, as well as for the work she did for the poor. During Christmas 1900 she made sure to give out little hand made gifts of her own creation to many in the area. And she was well known for practicing her cycling back and forth on the nearby roads after the Monument closed for the evening.

Earlier in December 1900, Bessie's brother, William Taylor, made a brief visit. It would appear that Chapman made at least a passable act of being the dutiful husband. Bessie, for her part, never let on that she had entered into a fraudulent marriage with Mr. Chapman, and played the part of the obedient wife. And yet, by that time she was most certainly very ill.

Bessie's death was a long and painful one, moving ever closer during the early part of 1901. She had been attended by several doctors during 1900, but none of them could find a cure. Of course, no one was looking at poison as being a possible cause. Chapman's confidence in his use of poison grew as he increasingly found the doctors' abilities lacking. Her last doctor was Dr. James Morris Stoker, who had a practice at 221 New Kent Road, not far from the pub. He had been called into the case by a nurse who had been attending Mrs. Chapman. She had also been attended to by members of the All Hallow's Church on Pepper Street, along with two nuns.

Only days before Bessie's death she seemed to be making a recovery. She was apparently progressing so well that on February 7, 1901, Mrs. Painter, who was visiting her, felt she could put off her next visit for a week. Dr. Stoker found that she was playing the piano (possibly the same one used by Mrs. Spink for her musical shaves) and feeling better. Upon seeing his patient in such good spirits he rubbed his hands and exclaimed, "Capital!" This must have been far too much for Chapman to bear, so he set about to complete the work on his latest wife as soon as possible. Two days later, Bessie lay on her deathbed, much to the surprise of Dr. Stoker, who had sent the nurse home believing that her services would no longer be needed.

In the early morning hours of February 13, she died. According to a nurse who was present, Chapman said "Ah, she's gone!" At which point he put on a show of "crying bitterly." The surprised and greatly disappointed Dr. Stoker listed the cause of death on her certificate as "exhaustion from vomiting and diarrhoea." He offered no reason why a formally healthy 36-year-old woman would perish so quickly, or why she had been vomiting and had diarrhea in the first place. Bessie had died the month after the death of Queen Victoria who had been so vocal in her requests for action in the Ripper murders of 1888. Victoria had died, almost on cue, as a new century dawned. The Victorian age was over, but the killings, which had begun during her reign, would continue as long as George Chapman was free.

On the day after Bessie's death, Elizabeth Painter came to mourn her friend. She was surprised to find that the Monument was open for business as usual. Even though his wife had not been buried, he tried to kiss Mrs.

Painter. He was not about to change his ways no matter what had recently transpired. It is even more telling that Chapman thought women's attraction to him was so strong that he could toy with Mrs. Painter in the hour of his wife's death and still expect her to succumb to his advances.

To cover himself, Chapman thanked all those who had tried to help his wife. Bessie was buried only five miles from her village of birth, at Lynn in Cheshire. It was Chapman who would, as usual, have the last word on the matter. He placed a mourning card on the grave during the ceremony. It read:

> In loving memory of Bessie Chapman, wife of George Chapman, and the daughter of Thomas P. and Betsy Taylor, who died February 13, 1901, aged 36 years, and was interred at Lynn, February 15.

> Farewell, my friends, fond and dear,
> Weep not for me one single tear;
> For all that was and could be done,
> You plainly see my time was come.
> G. Chapman

Chapter Twelve

The Final Victim?

"I know nothing about it. I do not know how she got the poison."

George Chapman

It was not long before Chapman needed another woman to aid him in his business concerns, and to be his poisoning victim. A "respectable" six months had passed since Mrs. Chapman had died at the Monument and it was time for a replacement.

Eighteen-year-old Maud Marsh was living with her parents in Croydon in August 1901, when she advertised for a position as a barmaid. She had no idea that the man who would see her ad, and engage her, was one of the most notorious serial killers of all time. George Chapman contacted Maud through her advertisement. In doing so, he found his final victim in a series of murders which had gone on for at least 15 years without leaving a single clue for the authorities. Indeed, he had been so skilled that some of the murders had not even appeared to be murders. This time, however, he would make mistakes which would lead the police to his very door. And he himself would supply all the evidence they would ever need.

Before Maud could accept Chapman's offer of work, her parents decided that they should check out his business. To this end, Mrs. Marsh went with Maud to the Monument. During that preemployment visit, Chapman, as would be expected, lied to Mrs. Marsh, telling her that he was a bachelor. He did not reveal that he had previously been married and was a widower. He also told her that the upper section of the Monument building was occupied by a respectable family. Mrs. Marsh's acceptance of these falsehoods and omissions cleared the way for Maud to move into the

Monument and begin work as a barmaid. Mrs. Marsh would later recall, "My daughter had been out of a situation for two months before she became barmaid to the accused [Chapman]. I, as a mother, made all the inquires I could to satisfy myself that the place was respectable. From the very first the accused was attentive. My daughter was ill at the Monument for three days, but not sufficiently to keep her in bed."

It would not be long before Chapman began "paying her attentions," as Maud informed her mother. He gave her a gold watch and chain, and was pressing hard for her to stay with him. Indeed, in just a few weeks, he had already proposed marriage to Maud on several occasions. His attentions were beginning to worry Maud's parents, and this concern increased a great deal when Mrs. Marsh received a very strange letter from her daughter. It conveyed the type of pressure Chapman had been using to own another woman. It was a secret letter filled with tremendous anxiety.

> Monument, Borough, S. E.
> Dear Mother,
> Just a line to say on the QT. Mr. has gone out, so I now write this to you to say that George says if I do not let him have what he wants he will give me 35 lbs [£35] and send me home. What shall I do? It does worry me so; but still I am engaged, so it will not matter much, and if he does not marry me I can have a breach of promise, can't I? I must close, with love.
> Write soon. I remain your loving daughter,
> Maud.
> P. S. I have sent this without him knowing. Love to all.
> Let me know how Papa is.

Understandably, the letter shocked Mrs. Marsh, who wrote her daughter of her many concerns by the next day's post. Maud surely understood that Chapman only wanted his way with her and nothing else, and her mother fully understood this as well. She advised Maud to leave her position at once and come home. Mrs. Marsh knew that a serious problem was developing but felt she could do little about it. It was not long before Maud again wrote to her mother, but this time she said that all was well and promised she would visit on the following Sunday. It could very well be that Chapman intercepted Mrs. Marsh's return letter and dictated Maud's response. Nonetheless, Chapman knew that a new plan was now called for if he was to be successful in this venture. He would have to adapt.

That Sunday, Maud did make the visit home to Croydon to see her parents. And she went with Chapman. On this journey, Chapman declared once more that he wished to marry Maud. To aid in this particular fraud he produced a "will" which, in the event of his death, left £400 to "my wife."

It was witnessed by Mrs. Marsh and her son as Chapman signed the worthless document. He was, of course, already married and his name was not Chapman. Weeks later, Robert Marsh decided that he would check out the situation his daughter found herself in. He went to the Monument. It was not a very satisfying visit. He ended up having absolutely no trust in Chapman, who he felt had only dishonorable intentions. While he told Maud not to do anything secretive or underhanded, it would seem that he did not attempt to bring her home at that time. If he had "rescued" her, Maud would have lived.

Before long, Mr. Marsh became ill and had to be hospitalized. Although the circumstances of his illness are long lost, it is at least a possibility that Chapman poisoned him at the Monument. During his stay in the hospital, Maud visited him. It quickly became apparent that she had not followed her father's advice. He noticed that she was wearing a ring on her finger, and he asked her about it. She informed him that she had married Chapman in a ceremony in what she called the "Roman Catholic room in Bishopsgate Street." Once again, Chapman had been able to enter into a fraudulent marriage with a willing woman who knew she had no legal union with him.

It was on September 13, or possibly in October, that Chapman and Maud told friends and customers of the Monument that they were going off to be married, and made quite a show of leaving for the ceremony. Early in the day they drove away from the Monument in a carriage to become man and wife. Of course, they went to no particular place in town, but simply drove around to use up sufficient time in order to pull off the fraud. When they returned to the pub they received congratulations from the customers and were showered with confetti. They were now Mr. and Mrs. Chapman, of the Monument, Borough. Mr. and Mrs. Marsh were not amused, or ever fully confident about George Chapman. They were not even ever convinced of the validity of their daughter's marriage. It would be their suspicions which would eventually cause Chapman's downfall. That Chapman continued his poisoning activities is testimony to his overconfidence, no doubt brought on by his years of undetected crimes and the spectacular success he had achieved up until that time.

Upon hearing the news of the "marriage," Mr. Marsh demanded proof of the union from his daughter, in the form of a marriage certificate. It was proof she had no hope of providing. She could only lie to her father and tell him that the document was being held by her "husband." She further attempted to resolve his fears by telling him that all was as it should be. Maud's father came away with the definitive view that some sort of fraud had been perpetrated by the couple, yet he said nothing to the authorities.

For the moment, Chapman's luck would continue to hold. But time was running out for the Borough Poisoner!

The family would soon receive direct information about the relationship from Maud's sister, Louisa Sarah, who had visited her at the pub. She was married and was known as Mrs. Louisa Morris. The information came from an outing the sisters took which ran late. Maud burst into tears on realizing that they would not be back at the pub at the expected time. Louisa quickly learned that her sister was living in fear of Chapman's regular beatings, as her late trial testimony shows.

> MAUD: You don't know what he is.
> LOUISA: Well, has he hit you then?
> MAUD: Yes, more than once.
> LOUISA: How did he hit you?
> MAUD: He held my hair and banged my head.
> LOUISA: Didn't you pay him back?
> MAUD: Yes, I kicked him!

Yet, despite the fear and abuse at the hands of Chapman, Maud continued to live with this vicious individual and continued the fraudulent marriage. And if Maud knew Chapman's real identity, she never revealed it. At Chapman's trial, her sister, Mrs. Morris, told the court, "My sister told me he was an American. ... I never had any idea that [Chapman] was not his real name."

Other Crimes and Activities

With his luck so far holding in all his murders, Chapman decided to branch out into other areas. He needed a good deal of cash in the event of a hasty retreat so he tried his hand at arson. Just before the lease on the Monument public house was scheduled to expire, in late 1901, a fire broke out in the basement. It was an obvious attempt to defraud the insurance company of as much as possible. When the fire brigade arrived on the scene, they were surprised to find that the building had been nearly emptied of its furnishings and the tills fully cleaned out, but for a few coins. They also found the doors wide open. The place was deserted. After a great deal of effort, the blaze was brought under control, but serious damage had been inflicted on the property.

The *Morning Advertiser* reported the facts as they had been uncovered: that it was an arson fire and certainly not well thought out. The reporting caused Chapman to "issue a writ for libel" against the owners of the paper.

However, when he was shown the facts of the case by police authorities, backed up by the insurance company's investigation, he soon withdrew his libel action. He did, however, still have the nerve, even after his discussion with the police, to actually file an insurance claim. The claim was easily dismissed and his policy was cancelled. The fact that the police *did not* continue their investigation — which would have surely led to Chapman's arrest on charges of arson and insurance fraud — cannot be explained. Only after he was arrested for murder would the police properly investigate the fire, with the charge of arson to be used in the event he was found innocent of murder. If he had been arrested for the arson, Maud would not have been killed. And the many strange deaths surrounding Chapman may never have come to light.

This was by no means the only deviation from his murder spree. In June 1902, Chapman accused Alfred Clark and Matilda Gilmor (or perhaps Oxenford) of conspiring to acquire £700 from him under false pretenses. Unfortunately for Clark, he was a known criminal with a long record so his word in court did not amount to very much. At the time the case was filed Chapman had, officially at least, a spotless record.

Clark had met Gilmor while she was working as a domestic servant, and persuaded her to steal some stock certificates on the Caledonian Gold Mining Company, Limited, from her employer. She left her job, with the mostly worthless stocks, and travelled to London with Clark. There the pair went from pub to pub looking for, and failing to find, investors, until they came to the Crown, then in the hands of George Chapman. Gilmor had been a customer of Chapman's and this, as far as she was concerned, made the sale a much easier prospect. Chapman, being a complete fraud himself, could evidently smell the con a long way off and used the luckless pair for a plan of his own, which may have been to acquire the goldmining stock for himself.

During the trial Chapman took the stand and declared that he had given Clark and Gilmor £700 total, in two separate payments, for some of the certificates. There is no indication as to what Chapman actually expected to gain by this false charge. It has been suggested that he was hoping to "obtain" Gilmor after Clark was "sent up." But he could not be sure, by any means, that Gilmor would not herself go to prison, as she was the one who actually stole the certificates. However, he may have thought, if he failed to get Gilmor there were always more where she came from. When he was cross-examined by defense council, Chapman was asked to supply the numbers of the bank notes, which he readily did. This was a major error on Chapman's part: the authorities used these numbers to prove that Chapman had lied about the payments. But that would be later. For now the lie held. Indeed, Chapman even called to the stand Maud Marsh, or Mrs. Chapman, who was by that time more than willing to lie for her "husband." She corroborated his perjured testimony, even as he was slowly killing her.

In the end, the jury of 12 convicted Clark of conspiring to falsely obtain monies from Chapman, but acquitted Gilmor. Apparently the jury felt that she had been led astray by Clark and was therefore not responsible for what had happened. Clark received three years in prison and two years' probation for his part in the alleged crime. But he would not waste away that long in prison. Within months, Chapman would be arrested for murder, and the bank notes he testified he had given to Clark were subsequently found in Chapman's possession. With this evidence, Clark was freed from prison. At least this time he had not committed the crime for which he had been convicted. However, there was still the matter of the stolen mining stocks.

As far as international politics were concerned, Chapman liked to show that he was not sympathetic to British causes. Although he displayed an American flag in his pubs as part of his "American George Chapman" cover (one of Chapman's own photos shows Old Glory upside down next to an upside down British Naval Flag known as the "White Duster"), his support of the Boers in South Africa was decidedly European. Since 1899, the Boers (of Dutch origin, and the original white settlers) had been fighting the Second South African War, or Boer War against the British Imperial Forces. Upon each Boer victory, Chapman would toast their success, much to the displeasure of his mostly British customers. It would seem that he was, for a good while, a successful criminal, but a good public relations man he was not. As for the upside down hanging of the flags, it could very well be that Chapman viewed this as a sign of personal distress. Was this a glimpse into a mind split in two by the deaths he had caused and would continue to cause until he was finally caught?

A New Pub and a Turn for the Worst

After torching the Monument, Chapman and his ill wife moved not far away but to an area where he was not as well known. Despite the weak and transparent attempt to defraud the insurance company, Chapman was able to secure a lease on another pub, and in a place he knew very well. Just before Christmas 1901, he became the new proprietor of the Crown public house at 213 Borough High Street. Years later the building would serve as an office building. It was located just south of the Thames and only one mile, across London Bridge, from the heart of Whitechapel.

In the background of Chapman's other criminal activities the slow poisoning of Maud Marsh continued. Suffering almost continuously from diarrhea, abdominal pains and vomiting, she was finally admitted to the local Guy's Hospital, on July 28, 1902. For two weeks she could not be given a full examination due to the pain in her abdomen and her extreme tenderness. During that period she required a lot of pain killers in the form of opiates. She also had an average temperature of 103 and a rapid pulse.

At the hospital the doctors could not pinpoint the cause of her illness, and never considered poisoning. She was diagnosed as having cancer, acute dyspepsia and even internal rheumatism. One doctor felt that she suffered from peritonitis but later changed his mind and decided that tuberculosis was more in line with the symptoms. At one point she had a temperature of 104.6 before taking a turn for the better. Despite the false diagnoses of the doctors, Maud slowly showed signs of recovery after August 11, and was able to return home to her husband at the Crown. The doctors prescribed opiates to control her still terrible pains, along with light foods and brandy. Her improvement could only be ascribed to her distance from George Chapman and his "work." Maud's mother would later recall that Chapman "fetched her away from the hospital because she was going to be examined. ... Because he strongly objected to it. She [Maud] said, George said she was not to have an examination. When she wrote telling him she would have to be examined he took her away in a cab."

It was not long after her return that her illness reappeared, but this time there would be no visit to the hospital for a short recovery. George would not allow that to happen. He had other plans for Maud. And this time Chapman was in full control of her. He even allowed Dr. James Morris Stoker to attend her. This was the second Mrs. Chapman the doctor had seen with the same unknown illness, and yet he was completely unable to link the two women's suffering to anything Chapman was responsible for. The doctor treated Maud with many prescriptions, which Chapman may or may not have administered. He certainly gave her his "white powders." Despite the doctor's work, his patient steadily declined throughout the spring and summer of 1902. It was a slow and torturous murder conducted by a skilled and practiced poisoner.

In America there was finally freedom for Ameer Ben Ali, "Frenchy." On April 17, 1902, the Governor of New York, Benjamin Odell, granted him a full pardon in the Carrie Brown murder case. There had been grave doubts raised about his involvement and he could no longer be held. He would never know it, but within a few short months the real murderer of "Old Shakespeare" would be jailed for a different series of crimes and would pay the price. For Frenchy, his freedom must have been bittersweet as he reflected on his almost 11 years in prison for a crime committed not by him, but by Jack the Ripper.

In June 1902, while Chapman was busy framing Alfred Clark for a crime he had not committed, he found time to hire a new barmaid. This would once again place two women in his household at the same time. He would be literally killing one women off slowly while courting a second. Her name was Florence Rayner, and it would not take long for Chapman to make his intentions clear. Florence had been living at Peckham, working as a domestic servant near the Crown, and on occasion had taken her lunch at the local pub. She met Mr. and Mrs. Chapman and soon accepted the job with them at 5s. per week including, as Chapman always preferred, room and board. At his trial she recalled, "After I had been there about a fortnight [two weeks] the accused kissed me and asked me to be his sweetheart and go to America with him. I used to take my meals with him alone. When he asked me to go to America with him I said, 'You have got your wife downstairs; you don't want me!' He said, 'If I gave her that (snapping his fingers) she would be no more Mrs. Chapman.' I left because the accused came upstairs into my bedroom in the afternoon. He kissed me constantly when we were at meals together."

Rayner soon quit. She left Chapman's pub in July and took a new and, as history would show, safer position as a barmaid at the Foresters Tavern in Peckham. She had not, however, seen the last of the formidable Mr. Chapman. He visited her at the Foresters, still attempting to persuade her to go with him to America, without the "wife." "I can send you to America and can come on after you!" It was an offer that Miss Rayner might very well have accepted, had it not been for the untimely, at least for Chapman, arrest of her amorous pursuer.

The Final Torso

As Chapman was making plans to consolidate his funds for another quick move, and looking for a new woman to escape with to America, the final torso murder was uncovered in London. It was the fifth such murder in a series which had begun 15 years earlier. This last became known as the Salamanca Place Mystery.

Charles Whiting worked for Messrs. Doulton's Works, laboring the night shift with his friend, a Mr. Muntzer. It was a cool June Sunday morning, at around 4 a.m., and both men were walking across Broad Street parallel to the Albert Embankment near the River Thames in Lambeth. (It was at Lambeth Workhouse that Polly Nichols had labored before her murder; she had also stayed at Lambeth Infirmary.) As they spoke the men turned into Salamanca Place, and Whiting spotted the pile first. He grabbed

Muntzer by the arm and said, "Oh, what's that?" With a gasp Muntzer was able to see that piled up near the front gate of Doulton's Works were the remains of a human being. What had stopped the men, literally in mid-stride, was the sight of a head placed on top of the pile, with the dead eyes looking directly at them with a glassy, terrifying stare. They had found the final torso less than one and a half miles from Chapman's pub on Borough High Street. Once again it would seem that the bodies had followed Chapman's movements in time and space.

Gathering their wits, and their breaths, they both ran inside to inform the night watchman, John Cox, of their gruesome discovery. Cox had left his post in the lobby of the building at 3 a.m. that morning for a short walk in the cool night air, and was certain the remains had not been there at the time. His post was only 70 yards from where the remains were found, but he had heard and seen nothing. Cox went off in search of a policeman while Whiting and Muntzer guarded the mutilated remains. Just then, two young men described as "medical students" came upon the remains. After examining the pile of body parts one of them said, "Oh, it's a woman's head," and they calmly continued on their way, never to be seen again.

Cox soon located Police Constable Birton, near the Embankment, but was so excited that he was unable to give a clear account of what had happened. He was only able to say, "Come here, I want you." Seeing the obvious distress in the man, Birton quickly followed him to Salamanca Place. In the early morning light of the new day P.C. Birton saw a sight he would never forget. The arms and legs had been crudely ripped off with great force. The backbone had been sawn in half, roughly, evidently with no great skill. The head and other portions of the body had been boiled in water, or roasted in some type of oven. It was later felt, by the authorities, that this had been done to make a positive identification difficult or impossible, presumably because the victim could be easily linked to her killer. The head and face were in particularly bad shape, and badly disfigured. The "cooking" had shrunk much of the skin, so much so, that one ear appeared much smaller than the other. Several front teeth were missing and most of the scalp on top of the head was gone. However, there was enough hair remaining to show that the woman had been a brunette. The feet and hands had been crudely removed and were never found. Most likely they were deposited in the Thames River and simply floated out to sea. Was there a barmaid missing?

P.C. Birton soon called for more officers, and the police surgeon, to aid in the investigation. Birton reported that the local lamplighter had been in the area where the body was found, at 3:10 a.m., and that he had patrolled the very same street (no more than an alley in truth) himself at 3:30 a.m. He had not noticed anything unusual and had seen no one about. It would later be surmised, by the police, that the killer had probably meant to dump his murderous cargo into the Thames, but the presence of P.C. Birton on the Albert Embankment forced him to drop the remains in Salamanca Place. Once again, with silence and stealth, the killer had escaped into the early morning mist of a London long ago. Once again, the Ripper's name was spoken. But the authorities were not about to link this death to the killer who had bested them so many times in years past.

A later coroner's inquest would hear that the victim had been a woman from 25 to 30 years of age, with a slim muscular build, of about five feet in height. The cause of death had been suffocation based on a medical examination of the nose and mouth. Coroner, Dr. Michael Taylor, stated that the latest torso murder was "on all fours" with (the same type of murder as) that of Elizabeth Jackson in 1889, and by inference the rest of the torso murders. One man had killed all five of these women, as far as Dr. Taylor was concerned. Once again the final verdict would be "murder by person or persons unknown." It was this murder which would clearly prove the postulation that serial killers not only change methods of murder from time to time, but may also return to a preferred method after a long period.

Writing of the torso (or Thames dismemberment) series in *Great Thames Mysteries*, 1928, Elliott O'Donnell stated, "With the Salamanca Place murder, however, the Thames dismemberment cases seem to have come to an end. Possibly the fiend who was responsible for them (it is, I think, generally agreed that one person did them all) died in 1902 or about that time, but at all events, so far as we know, there have been no cases of the same description since that date."

Mr. O'Donnell was not too far off in his remarks. Chapman would soon be out of business one way or the other, and for good.

End Game for Maud

Despite Chapman's now reckless criminal and female pursuits, he continued to play the part of the dutiful and concerned husband, as Maud slipped closer to death. The act, however, was not enough to keep Maud's mother from coming to the Crown from her home in Croydon to care for her daughter. What she saw distressed her greatly, as Maud's condition had gone from bad to worse. Yet there is no record of Mrs. Marsh demanding her daughter be moved to a hospital. Up until that point no one had suspected that Maud's illness was a slow torturous murder for Chapman's personal gratification. Even the doctors failed to insist that she be taken to the hospital. The only record would be the photograph series taken by Chapman detailing the slow murder of Maud.

At one point during Maud's illness, as later testimony shows, Chapman betrayed himself to Mrs. Louisa Sarah Morris, who was visiting her very ill sister again at the Monument.

> LOUISA: Don't you think it is funny that Maud is like this?
> CHAPMAN: It is constipation.
> LOUISA: That is funny, because I saw her a short time before and she had diarrhoea.
> CHAPMAN: She should have done what I have told her, taken the medicine I gave her.
> LOUISA: Maud would never take medicine.
> CHAPMAN: If she comes out of this lot, she will do as I tell her.
> LOUISA: It seems very funny that the doctors cannot find out what is the matter with her.
> CHAPMAN: I could give her a bit like that, (making a gesture) and fifty doctors could not find out.
> LOUISA: What do you mean?

Chapman must have realized that his own bragging had just placed him at risk, and he did not answer Louisa. He had made a major error. Yet, even with this direct indication of Chapman's true feelings and actions, no one in the family was prepared to challenge his control and abuse of Maud. No one had the courage to save the girl's life.

Along with her mother, a second woman, Mrs. Jessie Toon of 23 Eltham Street, Borough, who had been a customer of the Crown, had now come to help with Maud's care. Nothing they did seemed to help. The cure which eluded them would have been to remove Maud from Chapman's "care." For his part, Chapman insisted he be the only one to prepare food and drink for Maud while she was sick. This would later be shown to be truly reckless behavior. With only Chapman giving food to Maud, he would be the only suspect in her death. Inspector Godley would state, "I may add that from inquiries I found that he [Chapman] was the only person who used to feed her, and would not allow any other person in the kitchen while he made the food. He has had three deaths in five years — two Mrs. Chapman's and Marsh." During Maud's last days, Chapman seems to have been completely reckless, even insane, in that he went about murdering her in full view of her family and friends and probably thought he could get away with it. After all, he had been getting away with murder for years. He must have really felt that he would never be caught. A passage in *The Trial of George Chapman* says: "It has been proved many times that multiple murderers become more daring and reckless with each successful crime, until at length they fail to observe even very ordinary precautions." Even the Ripper got careless in the end.

Any food or drink Maud was given gave her a violent reaction, until all she was able to ingest were small amounts of liquid and even that with great difficulty. It is in this context that an incident occurred which should have sent up red distress flags in the minds of those caring for Maud, yet no action was ever taken until it was far too late. The incident began with Chapman preparing a brandy-and-soda for Maud. As was becoming the norm she was unable to drink much of the liquid and the glass had been set aside. Later in the day, Mrs. Marsh and Mrs. Toon drank from that very same glass of brandy, which Chapman had left behind. It did not take long for both women to become ill with attacks of diarrhea and vomiting. Incredibly, despite the obvious source of their distress — the brandy — no one suspected it of being poisoned. Even Dr. Stoker continued to treat Maud for some unknown illness, in spite of the now overwhelming evidence before him. Interestingly, Dr. Stoker seemed to know that Maud had not married Chapman. "She was not actually Mrs. Chapman, but she passed as such," he later said.

Mrs. Marsh related, "I put a little iced water with it [the brandy] and drank it myself. ... I was taken very sick. About two hours, I was taken with sickness and diarrhoea very bad. I had to leave my daughter, and while I was away the accused was with her." Mrs. Toon would later ask Chapman if Maud was any better. She was not, but Chapman replied, "No, her mother is bad now. You had better go upstairs and tell her to get to bed [and] out of the way, the old cat."

Not long after the brandy incident Mr. Marsh arrived, along with Maud's sister, to help care for the dying girl. With five people now in attendance, including the doctor, Chapman continued his work on Maud. He also continued to show great outward concern for his wife, an indication of not only his ability to deceive those around him but of his great confidence in being able to do just about anything he wanted without being detected. But on that score, time was running very short for him.

Mrs. Toon would later testify that "On Sunday before she died she said her mouth and throat burned, and that they seemed to be on fire. On 20th October the accused [Chapman] brought a stethoscope into the room. He first felt the pulse of the girl Marsh, then pulled her eyelids up and examined her eyes, afterwards putting the stethoscope to her heart and listening for two minutes. I have never seen him use the stethoscope before, or examine her eyes." Chapman wanted to enjoy the slow murder of Maud from every aspect he could think of, and close up.

As she saw her daughter failing, Mrs. Marsh pleaded with Dr. Stoker for some type of medical treatment which would help Maud. Stoker replied, "I am at my wits end to know what to do with her; my means are exhausted."

Finally, Mrs. Marsh began to suspect that her daughter's illness was not natural, even in the disease ridden East End of London, but was somehow caused by George Chapman. She made her husband aware of her suspicions. Together they asked their local family doctor in Croydon, Dr. Francis Gasper Grapel, who lived on London Road, to come to south London and consult with Maud's doctor, Dr. Stoker. Dr. Grapel would not be looking for a natural cause of Maud's illness, which gave him a distinct advantage over Dr. Stoker. Dr. Grapel's entry into the case was of great concern to Chapman who was shocked that someone outside his control had been brought in. He found it difficult to control his resentment as he must have known that there was a good possibility that his plan would be uncovered. Chapman confronted Robert Marsh about the new doctor. He told Marsh, "If one doctor cannot cure her, fifty cannot." To which Mr. Marsh replied, "It is no good making a bother; I wished the doctor to come." This was the first practical engagement against Chapman's control over one of his victims but it would prove to be far too little, far too late.

Before long, Dr. Grapel had come to the correct conclusion, that Maud was being slowly poisoned. He was the first doctor to suspect that one of Chapman's wives was being murdered. He was the first to suspect a serial killer in their midst. As the Solicitor General, Edward Carson, later stated at Chapman's trial, "It is a most serious thing for a doctor to throw suspicion upon a household." Perhaps that is why Dr. Stoker held back as long as he did, but Dr. Grapel seemed to have no such concern. He acted with great speed. He could not, however, pinpoint the method of delivery or for that matter who the poisoner was, although Chapman was high on his very short list of suspects. As he returned to his home, Dr. Grapel came to the conclusion that arsenic was the agent being employed. Upon arriving there, he immediately telegraphed Dr. Stoker, who had stayed in London to attend to his now obviously dying patient. In the telegraph Dr. Grapel advised Dr. Stoker to look for arsenic poisoning as the cause of Maud's illness, but the warning arrived too late.

Robert Marsh, visiting Maud at the Crown, said to Chapman, "I think my daughter will pull through now, George." Chapman coldly replied, "She will never get up no more." He was right.

Maud Marsh died on October 22, 1902. She was the last victim of Severin Klosowski alias George Chapman alias Jack the Ripper. Chapman was there for the end when Maud said, "I am going." Emotionless, he replied, "Where are you going?" Her last words were, "Good-bye, George."

Chapman had reacted in a way he had never done before: he had panicked. With the physicians closing in, he had administered a much larger, and thus fatal, dose of poison. Although Maud's year long struggle was

East End, London

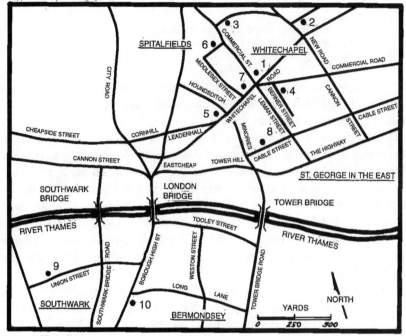

1 - Martha Tabram   2 - Polly Nichols   3 - Annie Chapman   4 - Elizabeth Stride   5 - Catherine Eddowes
6 - Mary Jane Kelly   7 - Alice Mc Kenzie   8 - Frances Coles   9 - Bessie Taylor   10 - Maud Marsh
R. Michael Gordon   1998

Locations of Ripper and Poison murders.

over, Chapman's was just about to begin. Dr. Stoker would later report, "I heard that the deceased had died at 12:30. When I went there the Crown was open for business; there was nothing to indicate there had been a death there. When I saw her on Tuesday I had no reason to anticipate she would die so soon."

With Dr. Grapel's telegraph and the quick death of Maud, Dr. Stoker refused to issue a death certificate, much to the surprise and anger of George Chapman. He demanded to know why the certificate was being held up, and confronted the doctor face to face. Chapman knew that he was losing control. The doctor told him that he did not know what had caused the vomiting and diarrhea and informed him that he would conduct a limited post-mortem examination. Chapman said: "I do not see the good of it."

> DR. STOKER: I shall have a post-mortem. I cannot give a death certificate.
> CHAPMAN: Why?

DR. STOKER: I cannot find what is the cause of death.
CHAPMAN: It was exhaustion caused by inflammation of the bowels.
DR. STOKER: What caused the inflammation?
CHAPMAN: Continual vomiting and diarrhoea.
DR. STOKER: And what caused the vomiting and diarrhoea?

To this final question Chapman of course could not give an honest answer. He had been trapped by his own work and a few late but accurately directed questions from the doctor.

The doctor would now move with speed to prove that his patient had been murdered by poison. He obtained permission from the clerk at the Old Vestry Hall, which held the Southwark Borough Council Medical Department, to remove the body from the Crown for the purpose of conducting a private post-mortem. The body was subsequently moved to a local mortuary located at the back of St. George's Church, Borough, without, it would seem, any objections being raised by Chapman. (The coroner was, interestingly enough, not notified of the private post-mortem until after the work had been completed.)

After the death of Maud Marsh, Chapman's old confidence returned and he once again appeared to feel superior to those around him. He wasted no time in moving on. His first priority was to take care of Maud's clothes. When Mrs. Toon recommended he "ought to have ... the clothes and dirty things washed ... because they smelt nasty," he replied, "I have destroyed them!"

The post-mortem was conducted by Dr. Stoker, with the assistance of Doctor P. G. Cotter of 57 Caledonian Road, Islington, and attended by doctors French and Poycott. The doctors, however, could not immediately determine the cause of death, which seemed to indicate it was not natural causes. They removed her stomach, along with other internal organs, and placed them in containers. The remains were then taken to the Chemical Research Association, located a short distance from the mortuary on Borough High Street. It was also not far from the Crown.

Even with all this medical investigation and probing going on in the background, Chapman was once again his old misogynist self. On the day after he had finally finished his work on Maud, October 23, he had tea with Mrs. Marsh and Maud's other sister, Alice May Marsh. He took the opportunity to invite Alice to live with him. He told her, "There is a chance for you as barmaid now. Will you come?" The record does not indicate how shocked Alice or her mother was at the offer so soon after Maud's death, but Alice's reply was definitive. "I said, no thanks, London does not suit me." She would later tell the court, "The accused had asked me (before) to go and live with him and my sister." Her reply must have been the same as the last time, but it again proves Chapman's need to be surrounded by women, and to have two or more living with him at one time. This was a continuing objective of his since at least 1889–90, during his old Ripper period.

Action at Long Last

The day after the post-mortem on Maud was completed, the results came in from the Chemical Research Association. The tests conducted by Richard Bodmer, a fellow of the Institute of Chemistry, showed that arsenic had been found in Maud's organs. Bodmer also found conclusive evidence of the presence of antimony. The arsenic was in trace amounts: it was not the main poison used by Chapman. It was the massive amounts of antimony which had actually killed Maud. With proof now in his hands, Dr. Stoker informed Dr. Wald, the area coroner, of the results. He also brought the police into the case.

When informed of the private post-mortem, Dr. Wald voiced his concerns about a possible loss of evidence in such an action. He later stated, "I lunched with the judge in the case at the Old Bailey, and he agreed with me that the post-mortem carried out by the medical attendant on Maud Marsh might have ended in the contents, etc. of the stomach being lost...." That was not to happen.

On Saturday morning, October 25, 1902, as Londoners watched the coronation parade of King Edward VII, George Chapman was arrested in the Crown public house. Death would no longer be the prerogative of Severin Klosowski. As of that day, it passed to the courts, and the judgment of the jury soon to be impaneled, in the "case of the Borough Poisoner." This case would be followed very closely, especially by the East End press and the ladies in the area.

Chapter Thirteen

Investigation of a Serial Killer

"I am innocent. Can you let me have bail?"

Severin Klosowski, a.k.a. George Chapman

On October 25, the crowds lined London's streets for the Coronation of Edward VII. Later that evening, the people would find their way to the many pubs dotted throughout the city. For the customers of the Crown the drinks would also flow, but the proprietor would not be there to greet them. Around noon, Detective Inspector George Godley of M Division, and Detective Sergeant Kemp, walked into the Crown. They had not come for refreshment. After identifying Chapman to his satisfaction, Inspector Godley identified himself: "I am an inspector of police for this district and I wish to speak to you quietly." Godley would later testify, "There was nobody in the parlor on the same floor, and he asked me to go in there." Moving then to the end of the billiard room, the inspector continued. "Maud Marsh, who has been living with you as your wife has been poisoned by arsenic, and from the surrounding circumstance I shall take you to the police station while I make inquires about the case." Chapman replied: "I know nothing about it, I do not know how she got the poison. She has been in Guy's Hospital for some sort of sickness."

It would appear from Godley's statement that the authorities already had a good idea that Chapman had not married Maud, as they never referred to her as "Mrs. Chapman." At the upcoming trial Godley would further elaborate on his investigation into the suspect's situation and his thorough search of the Crown. "I also found the little book in Polish, the papers in Russian, the will, an American revolver in a case, fully loaded (a rare find in England), a number of photographic chemicals, and bottles of various kinds; also a number of papers and documents, amongst them the photograph of Bessie Taylor. ... I left him, and again saw him at 10:15 (p.m.). I said; *I have made it now my duty to charge you with the wilful murder of Maud Marsh by poisoning* her with arsenic. He said, 'I am innocent; can I have bail?' I said, 'no!' ... In answer to the charge of murder he said, 'By what means, stabbing, shooting, or what?'"

Chapman of course knew that she had died of poisoning; everyone involved in the case knew it. Godley had said as much when he took Chapman into custody. Also, the other two known victims had been poisoned, or such was suspected at the time. So why did Chapman raise the question of stabbing? Was this a *major* slip of the tongue as he recalled the Ripper murders, or some other type of ploy? Whatever the reason it was clear that Chapman had lost control.

Detective Inspector Godley pressed Chapman on his true identity, and related Chapman's responses. "He said, 'Who is the other fellow?' I said, 'That is you; we call you Severin Klosowski, otherwise George Chapman.' He said, 'I do not know anything about the other name.'" At this point it is fascinating to note that the accused admitted to being Chapman, who was charged with murder, but he was not about to admit to being Severin Klosowski. Did he believe the authorities were looking for Klosowski as a Ripper suspect? He may have felt that he had a chance in the poison deaths, but he knew that anyone convicted of Jack the Ripper's murders would have no chance at all: they would be hanged for sure. Yet Chapman's own personal documents proved beyond a doubt that he was indeed Severin Klosowski. So was this denial some kind of hopeless attempt to distance himself from Klosowski? Or was it just possible that this individual had two separate personalities, neither admitting the existence of the other? One of course was Jack the Ripper, or Severin Klosowski, and the other the Borough Poisoner, or George Chapman. When Chapman claimed not to know "the other fellow," was he telling the truth?

A Search for Clues

The Ripper was a collector and so was George Chapman. Despite all he had done to cover up and remove his past, Klosowski could not bring himself to part with many of the documents which defined his life and detailed who he truly was. It can be only a matter of speculation now, how much evidence the police could have found linking him directly to the Ripper murders had they pushed their investigations past his most recent crimes. Perhaps they would have located jars which contained the body parts he had extracted from his victims and which they had searched in vain for 15 years earlier.

Inspector Godley was the officer who searched the quarters of Chapman in the Crown. What he found was a bonanza for the prosecution. He unearthed Chapman's medical books, including several on how to treat poison related illnesses, and he discovered drugs. And interestingly, there was a book written by "Hangman" Berry about his long career as an executioner for the Crown. When this was reported in the press Berry himself contacted Godley by letter asking that his book be kept out of the case. It seemed that Mr. Berry was no longer proud of his professional accomplishments. He had destroyed all his personal copies of the work, as well as all others he could find. His book would become a sideline, however. The court case was far too strong against Chapman-Klosowski to warrant any mention of "Hangman" Berry's memoir.

Upstairs, in a drawer, Godley located Klosowski's money: £143 10s in gold, £15 in silver, three £10 notes, and sixteen £5 notes, for a total of £268 10s. It was a large sum at the time (about $12,000 today), and would be used in the pretrial hearings to show how ready Klosowski was to flee at a moment's notice. He had done that many times before; this time, though, he had moved too slowly.

Nearby was located a bottle which had contained medicine prescribed for Maud by Dr. Stoker. However, it had been cleaned out and now contained a bit of "white powder" which would later prove to be poison. In one of Klosowski's medical books was found the little red label placed on the poison's original container. Klosowski was still a collector.

Godley had also located a file of documents (translations of which may be found at the end of Chapter One) in Russian and Polish, which clearly established the prisoner was Severin Klosowski and not the American George Chapman, and detailed his medical training. Along with these papers were found the undertaker's bills for Mary Spink (i.e., Mrs. Chapman I), and Bessie Taylor (i.e., Mrs. Chapman II) as well as memorial cards. These items led the authorities to the two murdered women's graves. There were also photos taken by Klosowski himself of his three victims posing with their killer. What Godley did not find was any physical evidence which would have pointed directly to Klosowski as the long sought Ripper. Perhaps that evidence went up in smoke during the Monument Tavern torching.

At the first proceeding, held at Southwark Police Court while

Klosowski was under arrest, his attorney requested all of the funds found in the "bank of Klosowski" be returned to his client. There was no objection from Inspector Godley to returning the gold and silver, but he requested that the bills be held for a while longer. The inspector thought he recognized some of the numbers from a past case, and wanted time to check to see if he could match them.

Inspector Godley's memory was excellent. He was soon able to prove that some of Klosowski's notes were those he testified in court that he had paid to Alfred Clark for the worthless mining certificates. With this new evidence in hand, Godley informed his superiors that an innocent man had been convicted on fraudulent testimony. Before long, the Home Office ordered the Governor of Portland Prison, where Alfred Clark was being held, to release the prisoner. On December 29, 1902, Clark walked free, but not with what he might have expected — a full pardon. He was, after all, a man with a long history of criminal activity. His release certificate read:

Portland Prison

I have this day discharged Alfred Clark absolutely
and unconditionally from His Majesty's Prison.
Conduct Good
Signed (J. E. Broome, Governor)
29th December, 1902

Alfred Clark was now a free man. As for his accusers: one was dead, Maud Marsh, and the other, Klosowski, would soon stand trial for her murder. Any irony felt by Mr. Clark, career criminal, is not part of the record.

As the Marsh investigation continued, the police sought to confirm the true identity of their prisoner and they were soon rewarded. Detective Sergeant Arthur Neil tracked down Klosowski's real wife, Lucy Klosowski, who easily picked him out of a lineup. Klosowski, however, gave no indication that he recognized his wife. He was not about to admit to being Severin Klosowski. "I don't know this woman." To this Lucy replied, "Ah, Severino, don't say that! You remember the time you nearly killed me in Jersey City!" Why was this the first thing to come to her mind?

Klosowski was also put in a lineup for Mr. William Davidson, the chemist who had sold him the poison, but he only knew the prisoner as George Chapman. It was left to his "real" wife's sister, Mrs. Rauch, to confirm the man in the dock was the Polish junior surgeon, Severin Klosowski. By the time Maud Marsh was laid to rest, the myth of the American George Chapman had evaporated.

A Final Funeral

As Klosowski stood before the police court he placed a few words on a card and signed his alias initials. The card read:

In Memorium
From a devoted friend, G. C.

It was the final lie in an almost endless list by a man who certainly murdered 15 women and probably more. The card was placed on a flower wreath made of camellias, pink chrysanthemums, tuber roses and lilies and held together with a violet ribbon.

It was a gesture which did not find a great deal of favor from at least one individual. Someone, possibly her father, had written to the newspapers promising that any wreath or card being from Klosowski would not reach her grave. In the end, though, the wreath, including the message, was slowly lowered into the grave with the Ripper's last victim, and buried with her. Klosowski's wreath would be allowed to rot underground. The rest of the flowers remained above and were distributed to Maud's friends and family.

Bizarrely, it was Klosowski himself who paid for the funeral near Maud's home in Croydon. The service was heavily attended, despite the driving rain which is so much a way of life in London. It was not reported whether the large crowds were due to the press coverage of the last murder of the Borough Poisoner, or because many expected someone to cause a scene at the funeral.

Police Court and a Coroner's Inquest

Klosowski stood before Mr. Paul Taylor at Southwark Police Court on Monday, October 27, 1902, accused of the "feloniously killing and slaying of Maud Marsh." It was entered into the court records that Klosowski was the 36-year-old "licensed victualler of the Crown public house," located at 213 Borough High Street, Southwark, London. Mr. Thomas Sydney was defending the man who would soon be known as the "Borough Poisoner." For his part, Klosowski would be cynical and disinterested in the police proceedings. During his trial he would present a whole new persona.

The general facts of the Maud Marsh murder were related to the court on the first day. Klosowski's arrest was detailed by Inspector Godley, as he recalled finding Klosowski attending bar at the Crown. It was noted that he had been pointed out to the officer, and that he had taken Klosowski aside to speak with him. The court was informed that a goodly sum of money had been found at the Crown and that "white powders" had also been located, but at that point in the procedures, it was not said what they were.

When Godley was asked if he had any medical evidence against the accused he replied, "Yes. I have seen the certificate of analysis, which states that arsenic was found. The doctor who attended Marsh also attended Mrs. Chapman, who died on 13 February, 1901, at the Monument public house, Union Street. The sickness was so identical that the doctor was suspicious, and he is now of opinion that the woman who died at the Monument public house was poisoned. [Inspector Godley was referring to the analysis of Maud Marsh's organs. The tests had shown that the stomach contained an "appreciable quantity of arsenic." It was thought at the time, before a more detailed test was performed, that arsenic had been the principal poison. It was soon discovered, though, that arsenic was only an impurity found within the antimony.] He has had three deaths in five years — two Mrs. Chapmans and Marsh."

At this point Klosowski was remanded for eight days, at which time more testimony would be expected from several witnesses. Mr. Sydney then requested bail for his client.

> MR. SYDNEY: There is really no evidence against the accused, except what has been stated by the Inspector. He is a licence-holder, and there has been an absolute denial of the charge on his part from the beginning.
> INSPECTOR GODLEY: I object to bail. There is nothing to stop this man from quitting the country. He came from America in 1893, and there is nothing whatever to keep him here. He has no banking account, but between £200 and £300 in notes and gold were found at his premises.
> MR. TAYLOR: I shall not grant bail.
> MR. SYDNEY: With regard to the money found in the house, of course, the police have no right to that.

Except for the notes that Godley had requested held for a check of the numbers, no objections were made by the authorities to returning the money.

> MR. TAYLOR: I consider that all the money ought to be handed over. In a charge of this kind it is essential that the man should have the money for the purposes of his own defense. It is not a question of robbery in this case.

With the money issue settled, the proceedings ended for the day with Klosowski being held until the next session which was to be convened on November 4. In the meantime, the coroner would start his work the next day, as the second line of official inquiry into the death of Maud Marsh began.

On Tuesday, October 28, 1902, at the mission hall in Collier's Rents, Long Lane, Bermondsey, Doctor Waldo opened the coroner's inquest into the death of the 20-year-old girl. He had conducted a post-mortem himself with Dr. Thomas Stevenson at the mortuary also located in Collier's Rents. The local press reported that 18 jurymen were called to duty and sworn in. Outside, a large group of mostly women gathered to hear the latest about the case. During the examination sections were extracted and placed in containers and taken to Guy's Hospital for chemical examination. Several days later the results showed conclusively that Maud had been purposely poisoned by antimony. There was little doubt as to what the jury would conclude. The first day of the inquest was to be a short one with only Inspector Godley called to give evidence. He stated that he had arrested Chapman on a murder charge and that the investigation was progressing. The inquest was then adjourned for a week.

Testimony, however, would be hard come by. At the time of Klosowski's arrest there was a good deal of debate as to how much evidence should be allowed in such cases due to the public nature of the inquest system. Police authorities were fighting hard to cut back on the amount of information released through the process. Coroner Waldo discussed the problem when he was interviewed after the trial. "I went into—as fully as I could with what evidence was available—the Chapman case. Dr. Stevenson was prevented from giving evidence before me until he had been before the magistrate [Police Court] and Mr. Bodkin [the Director of Public Prosecutions, Archibald Bodkin], for the Crown, although the police from Scotland Yard had agreed to produce him before me when wanted by me. Mr. Bodkin apparently did not like my having so full an inquiry—which was in Chapman's interest—and criticized me in the magistrate's court, which was reported in the *Times*. His feeling was then, as now, against the coroner and jury having a full inquiry into cases charged before a magistrate or bench of J.P.s."

He also protested the new legislation which he felt disadvantaged the accused. "I think the new Coroner's Act, clipping the wings of the coroner in cases in which there is a charge of a crime by the police, will be against the interests of the prisoner, especially before a legal coroner, as in London and in other big cities." Archibald Bodkin held a different view, as Hargrave Adam later wrote: "Bodkin, is a strong opponent of the premature holding of coroners' inquests in murder cases; he is of the opinion that they seriously impede the police in carrying out their difficult duties, and are detrimental to the true interests of law and justice and public security."

Despite the debate and unrest moving through the British legal system at the time, by the end of November the coroner's jury was able to investigate the murder of Maud Marsh and eventually came to the expected conclusion. This time there was no unknown assassin who would escape justice. The jury found that Klosowski, alias George Chapman, was responsible for the death of Maud Marsh and, as such, should stand trial for his life on the matter. In the meantime, the work of Police Court continued.

South London Observer— November 1, 1902
Southwark Poisoning Mystery
Publican Charged with Murder
Great interest has been manifested in the strange story which was opened at Southwark Police–court on Monday before Mr. Paul Taylor, when George Chapman, 36, licensed victualler, of the Crown public house ... was brought up in custody and charged with feloniously killing and slaying Maud Marsh, aged 20, who had been cohabiting with him....

Tuesday, November 4, found Klosowski once again at Southwark Police Court. It would be a short hearing. Paul Taylor, on vacation, had been replaced by Mr. Cecil Chapman. Inspector Godley requested a "formal remand" from Chief Clerk Nairn so that the police could continue to hold Klosowski while the investigation continued.

MR. NAIRN: Until what day?
INSPECTOR GODLEY: Any day that suits the court.
MR. NAIRN: Will tomorrow week do?
INSPECTOR GODLEY: Yes.

With that simple exchange Klosowski must have known that he had no chance of being released before his upcoming trial. And surely he must have known, with all the evidence then mounting against him, that he could not possibly win his case and thus the hangman's noose was but a few months away. Mr. Sydney would have his work cut out for him defending the Borough Poisoner.

On November 12, the hearings continued with Mr. Bodkin opening for the Crown. He was reluctant to have any evidence given because there was, as he stated, "another inquiry proceeding," and indeed he felt it was "unfortunate" that it was proceeding. He was of course referring to the ongoing coroner's inquest being conducted by Dr. Waldo. He informed the court that in his opinion the coroner's inquest should be finished up or continued after the Police Court had finished its work.

Nevertheless, Mr. Bodkin did call Maud's father, Robert Marsh, to testify since he had already given evidence in the matter the day before at the coroner's inquest. Marsh informed the court that he had visited Dr. Grapel of Croydon the day before Maud had died, and asked that Dr. Grapel examine her, which he did, on her deathbed at the Crown public house. Later, Marsh continued, he went himself to see Klosowski alias Chapman, at the Crown.

> MR. BODKIN: Did the accused say anything about Dr. Grapel's visit?
> MR. MARSH: He said, "If one doctor cannot cure her, fifty cannot." He said he did not like the idea of Dr. Grapel's calling.
> MR. CECIL CHAPMAN: What reply did you make?
> (Magistrate)
> MR. MARSH: I said, it is no good making a bother; I wished the doctor to come.
> MR. SYDNEY: From first to last, did your daughter and the accused live on the best of terms together?
> MR. MARSH: I have had no complaints.
> MR. SYDNEY: There was never any friction, so far as you saw?
> MR. MARSH: No!
> MR. SYDNEY: I think you made inquires about your daughter's health. Did he answer frankly?
> MR. MARSH: Yes.
> MR. SYDNEY: Did the accused appear upset on 21st October?
> MR. MARSH: No.

It would be a little more than two weeks before the next police court hearing, which opened on the morning of November 28. By that time the coroner's jury had made its decision. Mrs. Eliza Marsh, Maud's mother, was next called to give evidence. She testified that Maud had responded to an advertisement for a barmaid placed in the local paper by "Chapman" and spoke of her first visit to the pub. It was at this first meeting, Mrs. Marsh said, that she noticed a ring on Klosowski's finger. Klosowski informed her that he had been widowed. He did not, of course, inform her of the circumstances of his "wife's" death.

A bit later, Mrs. Marsh would visit her daughter now employed at Mr. Klosowski's establishment. It was during this visit that Klosowski asked permission to marry Maud. He was, as usual, moving with great speed; he was, as usual, driven to control women.

> COUNCIL: Did you agree to it there and then?
> MRS. MARSH: I said I would ask her father about it.

Mrs. Marsh went on to tell the court about her visit to the Crown pub on Sunday, September 13, 1901, when she arrived just after the "marriage" of her daughter and Klosowski. "Confetti was lying all over the place." Maud told her mother the marriage had taken place, and Klosowski invited his new "mother-in-law" to dinner.

The court then shifted to Maud's death and Klosowski's feeble attempt to blame her poisoning on a rabbit which had been eaten by everyone. (Afterward, he would shift to a noncommittal position on the matter.)

COUNCIL: Did your daughter make some statement as to what she attributed her illness to? Did she mention anything which she had taken?

MRS. MARSH: Yes; and I asked the accused if he thought the rabbit of which she had eaten part was the cause of the illness?

COUNCIL: What did he say?

MRS. MARSH: He said he could not tell, or he did not know. He also said they all had some of the rabbit. I stayed with my daughter all that night.

COUNCIL: The next day did you say anything to Dr. Stoker?

MRS. MARSH: I suggested calling in my own medical man, Dr. Grapel, of Croydon.

COUNCIL: And he agreed?

MRS. MARSH: Yes. I stayed all that day and night. The next morning I was suffering from sickness and diarrhoea myself. I noticed a change in my daughter's condition, and saw that she was dying.

COUNCIL: Did you tell the accused anything about a conversation you had with Dr. Grapel?

MRS. MARSH: I told him Dr. Grapel said she was poisoned.

COUNCIL: Did the accused say anything to that?

MRS. MARSH: He said he did not know, unless it was the rabbit.

COUNCIL: Did you make any reply?

MRS. MARSH: I said, "Dr. Grapel says you do not find arsenic in rabbit."

Next to give evidence were Maud's three sisters, Mrs. Louisa Sarah Morris, Alice May Marsh and Daisy Harriet Helen Marsh. Each in turn told the court of Klosowski's manipulation of Maud during her stay and illness at the Crown public house. And yet, none of them were able to state that they had suspected any foul play at the time. However, Alice did relate the story of her being asked by Klosowski to tend bar the day after her sister's death.

Finally, the session ended with Mrs. Jessie Toon taking the stand. She informed the court that she had been hired by Klosowski as a nurse for Maud. She painted a picture of Maud "frequently vomiting," and asking for water all of the time, but with Klosowski only giving her brandy. (It was the brandy, at that point, which held the poison.) She also stated that Klosowski, acting as "doctor," injected Maud with what he called a "beef, tea and milk" combination. As for the brandy, Mrs. Toon stated that when she tasted it, "It burnt my mouth and throat."

Even after both Mrs. Marsh and Mrs. Toon became ill just after drinking the brandy, neither seems to have suspected that the drink which burned their throats, and which had been served to Maud, was to blame for their sudden illnesses. At least, they did not suspect it at the time. Continuing on December 5, Mr. Sydney, Klosowski's attorney, attempted to bring the later conclusions about the brandy into question.

> Mr. Sydney: Were you in the habit of taking brandy?
> Mrs. Marsh: No.
> Mr. Sydney: Have you been told about Jessie Toon's statement with regard to some brandy?
> Mrs. Marsh: No. I know she tasted it.
> Mr. Sydney: It is only after you have had some conversation with Inspector Godley that you say the brandy caused the diarrhoea?
> Mrs. Marsh: I do not say it caused the diarrhoea.
> Mr. Sydney: But you suggested it?
> Mrs. Marsh: It followed it. I did not think at the time the brandy caused my illness.

The day's testimony ended with an examination of Dr. Francis Grapel by Mr. Bodkin. After informing the court that Klosowski was surprised to find that he was on the case he described how Maud's sudden and unexpected death prompted him to telegraph Dr. Stoker. He had concluded that she had been poisoned and had decided to examine Maud's body. Interestingly, Klosowski made no objection to the examination or to a private autopsy being conducted on her remains. Perhaps Klosowski felt that even an autopsy would not show the nature of his work. If so, it was a *fatal* error.

Dr. Stoker had told Klosowski that he only wanted to examine Maud's intestines at Southwark mortuary. He found that Maud's lungs, heart and liver were normal and healthy and further that a preliminary look at her stomach and intestines showed no obvious cause of death. "Finding nothing to account for death presented to my mind the possibilities of something." He further testified that he placed "certain parts of the intestines in glass bottles." When the results came in showing poison he informed the police that a murder had evidently been committed.

The coroner's inquest and police court inquires had done their work well, despite the territorial feuds. Klosowski would be held for trial in the old Central Criminal Court, conveniently located next to Newgate Prison.

Chapter Fourteen

The King's Justice

"Not Guilty, Sir."

Severin Klosowski, a.k.a. George Chapman

On Monday, March 16, 1903, 36-year-old serial killer Severin Klosowski, under his alias of George Chapman, went before Judge Sir William Grantham, in a trial for his life, for the wilful murder of Maud Marsh. By that time the bodies of Mary Spink (in November) and Bessie Taylor (in December 1902), had been exhumed. Due to the preserving effect of antimony, both corpses were easily identified. Taylor's body had been covered with mold but not enough to mask her features. Mary Spink's corpse was in amazing condition after having been buried for five years. On hand to view Mary's remains was her friend Elizabeth Waymark who had no trouble recognizing her. "She looks as if she had only been buried about nine months. The only difference was that her hair had grown a little longer on the forehead. The face was perfect."

Klosowski's attorney, George Elliott, submitted to the court that the prosecution was not entitled to try to prove his guilt in the deaths of Spink and Taylor. However, Judge Grantham ruled that evidence could be admitted for all three murders with which Klosowski was then charged. Klosowski, according to the *South London Press*, "...looked pale and careworn, [and] stepped quietly into the dock." He was asked to plead to the three charges of murder, and each time spoke in a soft voice:

"Not Guilty, Sir."

The judge then ordered the jury to hear evidence in the murder of Maud Marsh. Klosowski began to take notes. There would be time enough for a later trial on the other two murders if the need arose and Klosowski was, for some reason, found innocent in the death of Maud. It would be a much attended four day trial. But the name of Jack the Ripper would never be spoken. No one at the time, save a few detectives, truly believed that the Ripper had finally been brought before the bar.

The Court

It was called "Old Court Number One" and was in the Old Bailey of Newgate Prison. It was the Central Criminal Court for the city of London. The structure itself was so old that its foundations were ancient Roman stone. Described as looking more like a cellar than a courtroom, it was badly lit, with a large reflector to amplify the light from the single external window. A large wooden dungeon could be called to mind. In the center of the building, a wooden spiral staircase twisted up into the court itself providing access for officials. The main entrance, used by witnesses, was reached by a dark side passage which was never well lit even on the brightest days. There was a public gallery with limited seating just above the dock, and it was accessible by a short flight of wooden stairs. As witnesses entered through the side passage they would see the dock to the right and the jury box to the left. Between the judge and the jury was the witness box. Above the floor of the court was a small one man booth in which sat the court reporter. The Old Bailey was a thoroughly depressing room and completely appropriate for the trial of the Borough Poisoner.

Newgate Prison itself had a frightful reputation, well earned in years past. Many unspeakable atrocities were committed on those held within its walls. In 1904 the jail would be demolished, and along with it would vanish the screams of those tortured inside its cold stone walls.

During his trial, Klosowski was held in a small cell near the courtroom. From his cell he walked through a stone-paved passage designed as a conduit from cell to courtroom. It was a path known as "Dead Man's Walk" or "Birdcage Walk" for its cage like appearance. It was an ancient, fully enclosed hall with high, filthy walls, covered overhead with old rusted crossbar ironworks serving as a roof. On its stones were carvings centuries old. They were the marks of men long dead who had passed through the hall to their inevitable doom. As the prisoner shuffled down this path, he went over the prison graveyard just below. If a man was convicted of murder and the sentence was carried out at Newgate, he would literally be walking over his

future grave. The condemned man went from court to one of the two condemned cells to the in house scaffold. It was simple, fast, efficient and self-
contained. There was also a "black hole" cell for those men who were
uncooperative in their executions, or those who needed extra attention.

For this trial Under-Sheriff Langton, wearing full dress uniform with
sword on hip, would escort well-known visitors to their seats in the visitor's gallery. On hand were the Earl of Dysart, the Public Prosecutor and
Alderman Sir Joseph Savory. Tickets had been issued to a lucky handful.
Some of the guests had even brought food and drinks with them so as to
not loose their seats. Many even carried opera glasses to get a closer view
of the accused. Due to the continuous press coverage there was a good deal
of public interest in the trial among the general public, which manifested
itself in the large crowds which gathered outside hoping to get a seat or hear
the news. It would be quite a show. But few, perhaps none, would know
that it was Jack the Ripper on trial.

Judge Grantham entered the court through a heavy crimson colored
curtain located behind his seat. The curtain covered a door which allowed
a private entrance to the courtroom. On the wall, beneath the gallery, hung
a large discolored clock showing that it was almost 11 a.m. After years of
murder, and untold other crimes, Klosowski was about to face British justice for the very first time. It was not a prospect he had ever believed would
occur.

Moments after Grantham's arrival Klosowski walked along Dead Man's
Walk and through a door into the dock which was surrounded by guards.
No longer cynical, he appeared to be a broken man. He was pale, nervous
and unable to keep focused on any one area as he stared around the old
courtroom. Gradually he realized that he was the center of attention which
caused him great concern and embarrassment. After he quietly pled not
guilty the prosecution opened its case for the Crown.

The Prosecution

Presenting the King's evidence in prosecution would be the Solicitor
General Edward Carson with Mr. H. Sutton, Mr. Charles Matthews and
Mr. A. Bodkin assisting. Carson began describing the general facts of the
case as they had been gathered from the coroner's inquest and police court
proceedings. He informed the court that Klosowski had been living with
Maud at the Crown public house, and that she had died there on October
22, 1902, under his ever watchful eye. He further stated that the attending
physician refused to sign a certificate of death because he had suspected

some type of foul play. Continuing, he stated that a post-mortem had shown that Maud's body was "literally saturated with antimony," that further investigation had shown that a large dose had been administered to her just before she had died, and that she had been given poisons for a long time before she was finally murdered.

Carson went on, "I submit that no murder can be more determined and more malicious than that by poison. Certainly no murder could be more demonstrative of the cruelty of the person perpetrating it than that of a man standing by the bedside, day after day, of the person he professed to love, and seeing her suffering torture...."

Although accused under the alias of George Chapman, it was soon shown that the prisoner was indeed Severino Antonovich Klosowski, from Poland and not from the United States as he claimed. Documents submitted to the court showed that Klosowski had studied medicine in Russia and Poland, and that he had married Lucy Baderski in October of 1889. It could be shown that he had purchased, in 1895, a house on High Road, Tottenham, using his real name. In 1897, he had purchased a barber shop in Hastings, and lived there with Mary Spink as Mr. and Mrs. Chapman. This, the court was informed, was when he took up the alias of George Chapman.

Continuing, Mr. Carson told the court that the accused had purchased "at least" 146 grains of antimony from chemist William Davidson. It was with this poison that Klosowski slowly killed Mrs. Spink at the Prince of Wales public house in Bartholomew Square, finishing her off on December 25, 1897. It was later found that, even though her body had been in the ground for five years, it still contained 3.83 grains of antimony. Next on Klosowski's list was Bessie Taylor who would also live with the accused as "Mrs. Chapman." Moving to the Monument public house on Union Street, Borough, soon proved fatal to the second Mrs. Chapman, who died on February 13, 1901. Her body, when exhumed, was shown to contain an amazing 29.12 grains of antimony. Saturated was an understatement. That same year Maud Marsh met and "married" Klosowski and became the last victim of his poison.

Finally, Mr. Carson informed the court that Maud's body had contained 20.12 grains of the deadly powder and that the police had found a rinsed out bottle which had once contained a prescription for Maud but was found to have been filled later with antimony. Only Klosowski could have administered the poison, as he was the only person in constant contact with Maud. He was also the only person in the room when she was given food and water. And he was the only one with the medical training. According to Carson, he was the guilty party. "There is no reasonable hypothesis which can lead you to come to any other conclusion." It was Carson who would later state of Klosowski, "I have never seen such a villain. He looked like some evil wild beast. I almost expected him to leap over the dock and attack me." Stripped of all pretense, the true nature of this serial killer was finally shown to the people of London.

With the overview completed the prosecution began calling witnesses, concentrating on establishing Klosowski's background while in England, as well as his medical training before his arrival. The one individual who seemed to be at many of the same places as the defendant at the same times was Wolff Levisohn. He told the court of his many encounters with Klosowski. Levisohn had first met Klosowski in Poland. He had worked as a feldscher, or assistant surgeon and had seven years' training in the Russian Army and thus had a similar medical background to Klosowski. He had visited Klosowski at his hairdresser's shop in Whitechapel where he spoke to him in Yiddish. Levisohn testified that Klosowski used the name Ludwig Zagowski when he met him between 1888 and 1890. He confirmed that Klosowski had asked him to obtain "a certain medicine [poison] but I said no." Finally, he stated that Klosowski moved around quite a few times during 1894-95. Defense attorney Sydney was quick to point out Levisohn's enthusiasm at testifying. "You seem to have a lot of feeling in this matter." Levisohn replied, "Not at all, why, bless your heart, the moment I see the name Chapman I knew this is the man...." And yet, it is interesting that Klosowski never passed himself off as Chapman to Levisohn. It would also appear the Levisohn was unaware of Klosowski's move to America.

Despite knowing Klosowski by three different names and noting his many moves and suspicious activities, it seemed never to have crossed Levisohn's mind that he should contact the authorities about him. Perhaps the good Mr. Levisohn was more involved than history records. It has been suggested that he was a criminal as well but this is purely speculation at this late date. Even after he admitted knowing the man being held was Klosowski, he waited for the police to come to him. He never officially came forward of his own accord. It is also speculation but many researchers feel that the Ripper had help at times. Could this help have come from Levisohn?

Mrs. Ethel Radin, wife of Abraham Radin, was then called to testify about her early contact with Klosowski. While she was on the stand Klosowski fixed a hard look on her. Perhaps she knew something which could tie him to the Ripper murders. It was after he had left the Radin's employ that the Ripper series began. She informed the court of his working for them as an assistant hairdresser on West India Dock Road "around 1888." She had seen his medical documentation, but not being able to read Russian or Polish she had taken Klosowski's word for their meaning. She pointed him out in court but never looked directly at him during her time on the stand.

Stanislaus Baderski informed the court that the prisoner was "introduced to me as Severin Klosowski." Baderski stated that his sister, Lucy, met Klosowski at a Polish Club in Clerkenwell in 1889, and after four or five weeks, married him and moved into his barbershop on Cable Street, St. George-in-the-East. An older sister, Mrs. Rauch, then testified to meeting Klosowski and said that, "When I came to London my sister was living with him in Greenfield Street...." She confirmed that he was indeed Severin Klosowski and not George Chapman.

Another alias was confirmed when witness Alfred Wicken took the stand. He related that Klosowski had worked at Mr. Haddin's hairdresser's shop in South Tottenham, but the only name he ever heard him referred to as "Schloski." There is some doubt, however, as to whether this was indeed an alias or simply an inability of Klosowski's fellow workers to properly pronounce his name.

Due to the discovery of important documentation by the police in Polish and Russian languages it was necessary to call the man who had translated the documents to testify. Joseph Betrikowski stated that he had translated the documents from Polish to English, and that he lived locally at 30 New Street, Kennington Park Road. He was able to give the police a well documented history of the man in the dock fighting for his life.

Finally, the all important chemist, Mr. William Henry Davidson, was called. He had identified the prisoner as the man who had purchased "1 ounce of Tartar-emetic" from him in 1897. "I think he did have some other poisons...." He was also able to produce his poison book which clearly showed Klosowski's Chapman signature, next to the line of poison purchase. Had Klosowski admitted that he was himself, he may have been able to defend against this type of damning evidence. But even under the cloud of death he would not admit to being Severin Klosowski.

After the first day's testimony, the basic facts of Klosowski's background and general movements were well established. He was no longer an unknown quantity to the jury or those who were lucky enough to have taken one of the few seats in the gallery. To many who closely followed the case, there was little doubt as to the final outcome in the trial, even before the testimony directly linking him to Maud's murder was even given in the days ahead.

A collection of drawings from Chapman's trial. (Scotland Yard's Museum of Crime — The Black Museum.)

The Second Day

With the gallery once again fully packed, the second day of Klosowski's trial began on Tuesday, March 17, 1903. The day started with testimony from Mrs. Eliza Marsh, the mother of Maud. She related to the court how she had visited Klosowski at his business and how her daughter had faked a marriage before moving to the Crown. "Confetti was lying all over the place." Maud's last days, with her mother in attendance, were also recalled, as well as Mrs. Marsh's suspicions about the reason for her daughter's death. She informed a silent court that she had told her husband of her suspicions and how they had asked Dr. Grapel to examine Maud. Mrs. Marsh was also able to confirm that Klosowski was the only person who gave Maud any food or drink. "He came in every few minutes."

Next to be heard were two of Maud's sisters. Mrs. Louisa Sarah Morris testified that she did not know Klosowski's real name or that he was Polish. She had been deceived by her sister Maud and stated, "My sister told me he was an American." Clearly Maud must have known that Klosowski, crude as he was, could not have been an American, and yet, as with those before her, she went blindly along with the deception. Alice May Marsh then came before the court to relate the events which had occurred the day after Maud's death when she and her mother visited Klosowski. She told the court that a calm and relentless Klosowski had said, "There is a chance for you as barmaid now. Will you come?" Her answer was "No!" she added. The event clearly established for the jury that the heartless pursuit of women was always foremost in the prisoner's mind.

Florence Rayner was then called to show how Klosowski pursued one woman while his "wife" was systematically being poisoned under the same roof. She was also able to testify as to his plans to once again escape the hands of justice in England. "After I had been there about a fortnight the accused kissed me and asked me to be his sweetheart and go to America with him. ... I used to take my meals with him alone. ... He kissed me constantly when we were at meals together." If Klosowski had not moved so fast to capture Florence there was a very good possibility that she would have gone to America with him. That would of course have been *after* he had finished his work on Maud.

Near the end of that second day's testimony, Annie Chapman was called to establish a direct link between the man known as George Chapman and Severin Klosowski. (She was also a possible direct link to the Ripper, but the court did not know, and thus did not pursue, that line of inquiry at the time.) Annie informed the court that she had first met the prisoner at the end of 1893, and knew him as Severin Klosowski. According to her, he was working at the time as a hairdresser at Haddin's shop on West Green Road. Later, she recalled, they lived together as Mr. and Mrs. Klosowski from November 1893 to December 1894 when she felt he went back to *Whitechapel*. "When I told him I was going to have a baby he did not take much notice." With this link now fully established it is interesting to note that the only women to survive living with Klosowski, for any length of time, both bore him children. Was this the only reason he did not kill them? And if this was the reason, what is the psychological background behind this strange behavior?

The Third Day

The trial was moving with great speed. Counsel for the Crown continued to press their prosecution on the third day, Wednesday, March 18. It would be Dr. James M. Stoker's turn next, as he was called to the court to explain why he had suspected murder in the case of Maud Marsh's death. He stated that after he had been alerted by Dr. Grapel to the possibility of a poisoning, he had refused to sign the death certificate. "I heard that the deceased had died at 12:30. When I went there the Crown was open for business; there was nothing to indicate there had been a death there. When I saw her on Tuesday I had no reason to anticipate she would die so soon. ... I had never had a case in which poisoning had been deliberately administered until the case of Maud Marsh came before me."

Dr. Stoker went on to testify that he had performed a private autopsy of Maud focusing on the stomach and intestines. After he was unable to explain the death by a visible examination he told the court that he removed parts of Maud's body and placed them in jars to be examined later for poison. Dr. Stoker then submitted the samples to Mr. Richard Bodmer.

Mr. Bodmer was a chemist and public analyst for the Borough of Bermondsey and was next to testify. He stated that he had received the samples from Dr. Stoker and began his tests. "I subjected ... [Maud Marsh's] stomach to ... a test for arsenic and antimony. I discovered both present by that test, and also found that there was far more antimony present than arsenic." Science had now confirmed that Maud had indeed been poisoned, but it was left up to Dr. Stevenson to finalize the medical evidence.

Called to the stand, Dr. Thomas Stevenson was questioned as to his involvement in the case. He stated that he had conducted the post-mortem on Maud but could not find any natural cause of death. "I found no evidence of any natural disease which would account for her death. I suspected that she had died from some form of irritant poison, which had set up enteritis. [An inflammation of the intestines, usually the small intestine.] I came to the conclusion that death was caused by poisoning with antimony in a soluble form Tartar-emetic or metallic antimony." When he was cross-examined by defense council Dr. Stevenson was forced to admit that antimony was at times used to cure drunkenness. The *South London Press* reported "...on this point the Solicitor General immediately put Mrs. Marsh into the box again, and asked if her daughter had been addicted to drinking habits. Mrs. Marsh declared that the unhappy girl never drank too much." When called back to the stand to give evidence on the death of Mary Isabella Spink (Mrs. Chapman I) Dr. Stevenson stated, "The body was so fresh that it might have been buried that day." Kept intact by Klosowski's poison no doubt.

The prosecution then continued the very damaging testimony by calling a series of witnesses who could confirm Klosowski's use of his alias, George Chapman, and thus his need to hide his real identity. William Wenzel testified that he had advertised for an assistant for his hairdresser's shop in Leytonstone around 1896 and that he had hired the prisoner under the name George Chapman. He told the court that the man he hired worked for him for six or seven months. "I knew him as George Chapman." Joseph Smith Renton was then called, he being the cousin of Mary Spink. He testified, "I noticed my cousin was keeping company with the accused, whom I knew as Chapman, and he was employed at Wenzel's." John Ward then came forward to state that he had rented a room to George Chapman around October 1895 and that "He said he was a Polish Jew." And it was in those rooms that Klosowski lived with Mrs. Spink as Mr. and Mrs. Chapman.

Mrs. Harriet Greenway was then called. She had lived in Hastings when "A family named Chapman came to live in the same house about a month before I left." It was March 1897 when she met the Chapmans. But he had made a slip, she pointed out. He had confused his identities. "He went to a hairdresser's shop in George Street. ... He said he was a Russian Pole, and that he had been in America." It was a rare piece of honesty for Klosowski, but being a Russian Pole was not part of his George Chapman persona.

The last witness to testify about Chapman and Mrs. Spink was Martha Doubleday who knew them when Klosowski was leasing the Prince of Wales beer house in Bartholomew Square. The couple had moved there in the fall of 1897. After Mrs. Spink's death at Klosowski's hand, it was business as usual for the Borough Poisoner. "He went down and opened the house." Mrs. Doubleday was also able to tell the court how the prisoner had beaten his wife before she died, and her condition upon death. "I saw Mrs. Chapman's body after she was dead. It was in a very shocking condition; it was very much bruised."

To have testimony on Bessie Taylor's murder, the Crown called Mrs. Elizabeth Ann Painter, who had been a friend of Bessie's. She testified that Bessie had moved into the Prince of Wales around Easter 1898 and lived there as Mrs. Chapman. Later, she found them living at the Grapes pub in

Bishops Stortford. She visited them at the pub for two weeks just before
Christmas of 1898 when, as always, Klosowski attempted to bring another
woman into his home and under his control. "He kissed me once or twice."
The couple then went to the Monument pub where Bessie died on February 13, 1901. Visiting the next day, Mrs. Painter found the Monument open
for business, and Klosowski unaffected by his wife's death. For Klosowski
it was just another day and there were more women to be had.

The *London Times*—March 19, 1903
Central Criminal Court — March 18
The Southwark Poisoning Charge
The trial of Severino Klosowski, otherwise George Chapman 36, pub-
lican, for the wilful murder of Maud Marsh, otherwise called Maud
Chapman, was resumed.

Judgment Day

The fourth and final day of trial began on Thursday, March 19. The
South London Press reported, "On Thursday for the first time the prisoner
appeared to realize his terrible position, and abandoning his attitude of
passiveness, he displayed a keen, indeed a feverish, interest in the proceedings. When he entered the dock he was ghastly pale.... The restless
movements of the hands, the twitchings of the mouth, all betrayed the emotion which he would fain conceal."

On that day, the prosecution presented its last witnesses, closing with
the man who, 15 years earlier, had searched so desperately for Jack the Ripper. Detective Inspector George Godley had finally arrested the serial killer,
but after his second series of murders. Inspector Godley related in a calm
matter-a-fact manner to the court, his capture and arrest of the man he
had known as George Chapman. "At noon [October 25, 1902] I went to the
Crown and saw the accused. I said, 'Are you Mr. Chapman?' He said 'Yes.'
I said I wish to speak to you quietly. I did not say who I was. There was
nobody in the parlor on the same floor, and he asked me to go in there. I
said, 'I am inspector of police for this district; Maud Marsh ... has been
poisoned with arsenic, and from the surrounding circumstances I shall take
you to the police station....'" Inspector Godley then testified that after an
inspection of Klosowski's rooms he returned to the police station and again
faced the accused. "It is now my duty to charge you with the wilful murder of Maud Marsh by poisoning her with arsenic."

The case for the Crown was now complete, and the prosecution rested
its case. It would be now up to the defense to bring forth any evidence it

could muster on behalf of Klosowski. It would prove to be an impossible task. From the start of the police proceedings and on through the trial there had been very little the defense could use to try to establish Klosowski's innocence. The defense called no witnesses on behalf of the accused. Instead, Mr. George Elliott went into an adjoining room to confer with Klosowski and one of the doctors who had given testimony in the trial. Returning, Elliott faced the jury and said, "I am not here to prove the accused's innocence. I am here to refute the proofs of guilt put forward by the Crown."

Mr. Elliott went over all the prosecution's points in an attempt to show that, although Klosowski clearly had possession of the poison, others had access to Maud and could have administered it to her. He also pointed out that the accused gained nothing from the deaths in a monetary sense and that he had never, outwardly, abused anyone. Elliott also tried to bring up the "alien question" by stating that a foreigner could not expect to receive a fair trial in an English court. As he summed up, it was clear to one and all, save Klosowski, who had tears in his eyes, that his words had had no effect on anyone. Klosowski had burst into tears near the end of the summation and covered his face with a handkerchief as the guards moved closer to him in the event he collapsed. With the summation over, the defense rested its case. From the *South London Press*, it was reported that Klosowski took his eyes away from his attorney, "...to shoot a penetrating glance at the jury, trusting to detect some gleam of hope there, or some sign that the impassioned appeal of counsel was making an impression upon their minds. There was not a scrap of evidence directly favourable to the prisoner."

As a final rebuttal, the Solicitor General, Edward Carson, addressed the issue of what Klosowski had to gain in the deaths he had spent years orchestrating. "In this instance there was the most ample motive, for the prisoner's was a history of unbridled, heartless, and cruel lust. The prisoner's skills in medicine showed how far he could go. The attentions paid by the prisoner to these women were the *necessary mask for all that foul plot*." Upon hearing this, Klosowski slumped in his seat, head dropped to his chest, and cried.

Summing up the case, Judge Grantham told the packed courtroom, "It is unique from a legal and criminal point of view from the fact that, as far as I know, it is the first time in which the antecedents of the prisoner had been investigated. ... It is a very sad thing that a person who has up to now occupied only the position of a hairdresser, has been able to defy the doctors, and who for years, if the evidence is true, has been carrying on practices of the kind perfectly irrespective of the doctors and without the slightest fear of their being able to discover it."

And finally to the jury of twelve.

"Gentlemen, my task is over. I was going to say that your task begins, but the painful part of your duty will be to say what your verdict will be. Think over the evidence which has been given and come to a proper conclusion in the case, namely, a clear conclusion if you can, one way or the other, is the prisoner guilty or not? If there is any doubt in your minds, by all means give the prisoner the benefit of it. If you have no doubt about it, then, gentlemen, you have one duty, a painful one it must be, in the verdict you must find. Gentlemen will you consider your verdict?"

The jury members were then escorted to the jury room to consider the evidence they had heard over the previous four days. Klosowski, near physical collapse, was helped from the dock by two guards who took him into a nearby cell to await his fate. He would not have long. The jury, which had left the courtroom at 5 p.m., returned at 5:10 p.m. ready to render its verdict. There was silence as the Clerk of Arraigns asked the foreman, "Have you agreed upon your verdict?" From the foreman came the clear and decisive response.

"We have. We find the prisoner Guilty."

Klosowski was asked if he understood the verdict. But the terrified serial killer was unable to speak or move. It was left up to Judge Grantham to deliver the sentence that all who had witnessed the trial knew would surely come. Death!

"Severin Klosowski, for I decline to call you by the English name you have assumed, the only satisfactory feature in the case we have just completed is that I am able to address you as a foreigner and not as an Englishman. The jury have come to the only conclusion which I am sure everyone who has heard the case would have too. It is not necessary for me to go through the harrowing details of the case, or refer again to the frightful cruelty you have been guilty of in murdering year by year women on whom you have gratified your vile lust. I have but one duty to perform — and it is not necessary for me to say more — it is the duty of sentencing you to death." The sentence washed over Klosowski, and he turned ashen white with fear; near physical collapse, he began to tremble.

From his own words Judge Grantham appeared convinced that Klosowski was nothing more than a sexual serial killer of the most vicious kind. It can only be imagined what he would have said if he had suspected that he was sentencing Jack the Ripper to death. What he did not say was, "And may God have mercy on your soul."

Following the sentencing, a staggered Klosowski, half supported by guards, was taken from the court, placed in a police vehicle, and driven to Wandsworth prison and took his well earned place in the condemned cell.

The areas outside the courtroom, and in the streets, were crowded with people trying to get a look at the condemned man. As the police vehicle was driven away the crowd began hissing and yelling at the prisoner. There would be no pity for the Borough Poisoner. He had slowly murdered, for the pure pleasure of it, three "wives" whom he could easily have walked away from with no legal responsibility to care for them in any way. Now he would be required to pay the price, at least for this "work."

After Klosowski's conviction, retired Inspector Frederick Abberline sought out his old friend and colleague, Inspector George Godley, to congratulate him on his work. Then he told his fellow officer,

"I see you've got Jack the Ripper at last!

Chapter Fifteen

Aftermath

"Shall be now starting preparing for my deth as it is past four o'clock afternoon."

Severin Klosowski

Serial killer Severino Antonovich Klosowski, the convicted Borough Poisoner, was executed by hanging at Wandsworth Prison, on April 7, 1903. With him went the secrets of Jack the Ripper.

Before Klosowski went to the scaffold, he was held in a one man cell which had recently been occupied, and vacated, by fellow murderer Edgar Edwards. Edwards had killed an entire family in Camberwell. Upon hearing of Edwards' crimes Klosowski reportedly told a guard, "Edwards is a hot 'un!" While in that cell, he awaited the outcome of his appeal which his attorney had sent to the Home Secretary. As would be expected, in such a serial murder case as this, the appeal was rejected, and a suicide watch was put in place. It was implemented because Klosowski had become restless and the authorities did not want him to escape his final destiny.

His visitors were few. In fact, the only person he knew who tried to see him was his wife Lucy Klosowski. However, he refused to meet with her, claiming, to the end, that he did not know Severin Klosowski, and therefore did not know Lucy. He also refused to see his then ten-year-old daughter, Cecilia, whom he had not seen since her birth. Nothing would be allowed to stand in the way of his claim of being George Chapman — American! When he was asked if he wished any of his friends to visit he replied, "I have none." In fact, the only outside visitor to see him in his death cell was a Roman Catholic priest. What he confessed to this man was, of course, never recorded. But perhaps there was one man who finally knew the truth about Jack the Ripper during his lifetime. What a great burden that must have been to bear alone. Or did he "confess" to another priest?

Klosowski did, however, write several letters, of which parts were reproduced in *The Trial of George Chapman*.

> One thing whod I wish is this to be Remembered as I am an American orphend of good family and I left my foster father, against his wish, and I took to erning my own living at age of ten.
> And since that time I worked the best I could get, and although I never been so unlucky since I lost that poor Bessie Taylor and Therefore I regretted that day ever since I have stopped in this country.

One thing Klosowski never did learn was to tell the truth. He never admitted to being Severin Klosowski while in custody and he never admitted to being the Borough Poisoner or for that matter Jack the Ripper. But, he was most certainly all three men. In the end he protested his sentence by stating that he had never committed *any* crimes and that those who had testified against him had perjured themselves. He also claimed that the police had falsified evidence in his case. Naturally, neither claim was true. No one believed those shallow lies, at the time or since.

As George Chapman, he made out a will which interestingly enough included Mr. and Mrs. Marsh who had been instrumental in bringing him to justice and the gallows. It was of course a ploy. He left the Marshes some clothes and a ring, most probably owned by their daughter Maud. (Or was it a Ripper victim ring?) He also left around £140 worth of "property" to the relatives of Bessie Taylor. It is not known if this property included a certain black bag. It would seem that Mrs. Spink had by that time been forgotten, but he did have much on his mind. His will would be his final lie as George Chapman — American.

The *Daily Chronicle* — March 23, 1903
The police officers who have been engaged in tracing Klosowski's movements in connection with the three murders with which he was charged, are forming some rather startling theories as to the antecedent history of the criminal. These theories are connected with the Whitechapel murders which startled the world some fifteen years ago, and were attributed to "Jack the Ripper." The police have found that at the time of the first two murders Klosowski was undoubtedly occupying a lodging in George Yard, Whitechapel Road, where the first murder was committed.

Once again, the London papers felt the pull of Jack the Ripper, and began to seek out the men who had been connected with the Whitechapel murder investigations years earlier. The *Pall Mall Gazette* published a lengthy interview with then retired Chief Detective Inspector of Scotland Yard, Frederick George Abberline. Abberline did not hold back on his conviction that Klosowski was indeed Jack the Ripper, as he reviewed his old case notes with the reporter.

The *Pall Mall Gazette*— March 24, 1903
Should Klosowski, the wretched man now lying under a sentence of death for wife-poisoning, go to the scaffold without a "last dying speech of confession," a great mystery may forever remain unsolved, but the conviction that Chapman and Jack the Ripper were one and the same person will not in the least be weakened in the mind of the man who is, perhaps, better qualified than anyone else in this country to express an opinion in the matter. We allude to Mr. F. G. Abberline, formerly Chief Detective Inspector of Scotland Yard, the official who had full charge of the criminal investigations at the time of the terrible murders in Whitechapel.

When a representative of the *Pall Mall Gazette* called on Mr. Abberline yesterday (in the southern city of Bournemouth) and asked for his views on the startling theory set up by one of the morning papers, the retired detective said: "What an extraordinary thing it is that you should just have called upon me now. I had just commenced ... to write to the Assistant Commissioner of Police, Mr. Macnaghten, to say *how strongly I was impressed with the opinion that Chapman was also the author of the Whitechapel murders.*

"*I have been so struck with the remarkable coincidences in the two series of murders,*" he continued, "that I have not been able to think of anything else for several days past — not, in fact, since the Attorney-General [Carson] made his opening statement at the recent trial, and traced the antecedents of Chapman before he came to this country in 1888. Since then the idea has taken full possession of me, and everything fits in and dovetails so well that I cannot help feeling that this is the man we struggled so hard to capture fifteen years ago.

"As I say," went on the criminal expert, "*there are a score of things which make one believe that Chapman is the man*; and you must understand that we [the police] never believed all those stories about Jack the Ripper being dead, or that he was a lunatic, or anything of that kind. For instance, the date of the arrival in England coincides with the beginning of the series of murders in Whitechapel; there is a coincidence also in the fact that the murders ceased in London when Chapman went to America, while similar murders began to be perpetrated in America after landed there. The fact that he studied medicine and surgery in Russia before he came over here is well established, and it is curious to note that the first series of murders was the work of an expert surgeon, while the recent poisoning cases were proved to be done by a man with more than an elementary knowledge of medicine. The story told by Chapman's wife of the attempt to murder her with a long knife while in America is not to be ignored....

"There are many other things extremely remarkable. The fact that Klosowski when he came to reside in this country occupied a lodging in George Yard, Whitechapel Road, where the first murder was committed, is very curious, and the height of the man and the peaked cap he is said to have worn quite tallies with the descriptions I got of him. All agree, too, that he was a foreign-looking man, but that, of course, helped us little in a district so full of foreigners as Whitechapel."

The controversy as to whether or not Klosowski-Chapman was the elusive killer, Jack the Ripper, had begun. Most of the skepticism focused on the murder methods in both series of crimes. At the time many felt that a wife poisoner could not be a slasher of women because the methods were so different. It is a debate that has gone on for a century. But Abberline would forcefully address that issue in a second interview with the *Pall Mall Gazette*.

The *Pall Mall Gazette*—March 31, 1903
"As to the question of the dissimilarity of character in the crimes which one hears so much about," continued the expert [Abberline], "*I cannot see why one man should not have done both*, provided he had the professional knowledge, and this is admitted in Chapman's case. A man who could watch his wives being slowly tortured to death by poison, as he did, was capable of anything; and the fact that he should have attempted, in such a cold-blooded manner, to murder his first wife with a knife in New Jersey, makes one more inclined to believe in the theory that he was mixed up in the two series of crimes. ... Indeed, if the theory be accepted that a man who takes life on a wholesale scale never ceases his accused habit until he is either arrested or dies, there is much to be said for Chapman's consistency."

It must also be remembered that just because the police did not suspect Klosowski of any knife murders between the end of the Ripper series and when he was arrested for the poison deaths, does not mean that he did not murder anyone with a knife during that period. He may have done, and not been suspected. After all, he was never caught for the Ripper murders either. There was nothing to prevent him from murdering his wives *and* committing other atrocities. As evidenced by his arson and fraudulent activities, he was a very busy criminal. Surely, there were more crimes committed by this vicious and cowardly individual than we know about.

The authorities were never able to bring to light that one definitive piece of evidence which would conclusively point to Severin Klosowski, or

George Chapman, as being Jack the Ripper. However, as far as retired Inspector Abberline was concerned, even though the case could not be proven in a court of law, *there was no doubt* that the man, hung for the poison murders of his three "wives," had indeed been Jack the Ripper. Perhaps if he had been tried for the Ripper murders after the poison trial, history would have been satisfied, but sadly this was not the case. At the time, justice moved swiftly in meting out its sentences.

It is a mammoth historical loss that no police officer who felt that Severin Klosowski was Jack the Ripper ever showed a photo of Klosowski to some of the witnesses who had given descriptions of the Ripper. George Hutchinson, who had seen Mary Kelly's visitor, was still alive and living in London. Perhaps Elizabeth Long was still around, too: she described Annie Chapman's alleged killer. And what of Mary Miniter the assistant housekeeper in New Jersey who saw Carrie Brown's killer? These were all chances to close this morbidly fascinating case years ago, and all chances lost.

> The London *Times*—April 8, 1903
> Execution.—Severino Klosowski, otherwise George Chapman, 37, a Russian Pole, described as a licensed victualler of the Borough, was executed yesterday morning within the walls of Wandsworth Prison for the wilful murder of Maud Eliza Marsh by poisoning her with antimony in October last. Billington was the executioner, and death was instantaneous. At the inquest which was afterwards held by Mr. Troutbeck, Major Knox, the prison governor, said that the convict made no confession. The jury found that Chapman had been duly executed according to law, and a notice to this effect was afterwards posted outside the gaol.

A Strange Twist

In light of speculation that Klosowski-Chapman had somehow developed a split personality, it is necessary to look at a theory developed at the turn of the century. Dr. Thomas Dutton who lived at 130 Aldgate High Street at the time of the murders is reported to have written a book named *Chronicles of Crime*. *Chronicles of Crime* was an unpublished three volume work which had either been destroyed or lost upon his death in 1935. Other reports simply state that his family took the work and that there is a copy, as yet unrecovered, in some dark vault. No reason is given, however, as to why his family would hide this possibly critical work.

It has also been reported that the good doctor gave his work to a Miss Hermione Dudley. As detailed in an article published after the doctor's death she was interviewed by the Sunday Chronicle about Dr. Dutton's book. She said, "I knew the doctor when I was quite a young girl. ... By far the most interesting document he compiled was his *Chronicles of Crime*, three volumes of handwritten comments on all of the chief crimes of the past sixty years. My father was one of the few men to whom he showed this document and owing to my interest in it, Dr. Dutton gave it to me some time ago...."

Writer and researcher Donald McCormick has reported that he was given the chance to view this work in 1932 prior to Dutton's death and had the opportunity to take a few good notes. He has written that the work was "not a single narrative, but rather a collection of impressions and theories which he noted at various periods." McCormick, at least up to this point, is the only source of the information contained within the book, and as such, his story must be viewed with a careful eye. It is surely worth recounting, though, as some of it pertains to the best suspect to ever be brought forward in the case of the Ripper murders, and could bring valuable understanding to some of the events of the period. With Miss Dudley's confirmation of the existence of the *Chronicles of Crime*, there were then at least two people who affirmed the existence of the work.

McCormick reported that Dr. Dutton was a friend of Inspector Abberline and that the doctor would on occasion enjoy visits from the inspector during the period of the Ripper murders (and, it would be expected, others). The ongoing case would of course have been a topic of great interest to both men and Dr. Dutton would surely have voiced his opinions on it. In fact, writer Colin Wilson has reported that Klosowski "was actually under suspicion in 1888, the year of the Ripper murders," by none other than Inspector Abberline.

In 1903, Abberline congratulated Inspector Godley for his work in the notorious Borough poisoning case. According to Godley, the congratulation took the form of telling him that he had caught Jack the Ripper. McCormick, using his notes on Dutton's work, wrote that some 14 years later Inspector Abberline had revised his opinion in a very interesting way. McCormick writes, "What finally convinced Abberline that he had made a mistake in thinking Klosowski was the Ripper was his discovery that the Polish barber-surgeon had a double in London and that this double, a Russian and also a barber-surgeon, sometimes posed as Klosowski for reasons which were not apparent." The name of that "other" Klosowski was Alexander Pedachenko. But was he Klosowski's double, or was Pedachenko Klosowski himself working as a surgeon after perhaps being denied that chance under his own name? And, did Abberline change his mind in the later years of his life or during the Ripper investigation? The 1903 congratulations to Godley would suggest later.

Again we return to Dr. Dutton's work as reported by McCormick. He writes that Dr. Dutton had interviewed a Dr. John Frederick Williams who stated that he did have an assistant named Pedachenko who was, according to Dr. Williams, a Russian barber-surgeon who assisted him on an unpaid basis at St. Saviour's Infirmary, as well as working in other areas in the south London area "removing warts, and treating skin diseases." In point of fact both Dr. Williams and the infirmary did exist at the time of the Ripper murders, so at least part of the story does have a ring of truth to it. St. Saviour's Infirmary has been reported to have aided at least four Ripper victims — Tabram, Chapman, Nichols and Kelly — at one time or another. Dr. Dutton had also written that Pedachenko was working part time for a hairdresser named William Delhaye on Westmoreland Road, Walworth, as a barber-surgeon. That establishment existed, too, as did Mr. Delhaye. Author Tom Cullen writes, "When he [Chapman-Klosowski] emigrated to London, Whitechapel in June, 1887, he found work as a barbersurgeon, removing warts and performing simple operations."

It is at this point that we again run into the ever present Wolff Levisohn who, according to Dr. Dutton, was in contact with Inspector Abberline during the Ripper murders. Dutton reports Levisohn as telling Abberline that "he should look for a Russian who lived somewhere in Walworth, did a certain amount of illicit doctoring and attended barber's shops to cut out warts and moles." Levisohn also reported that he had seen Dr. Pedachenko on Commercial Street on September 29–30, 1888, in the center of the Ripper area: it was the night of the double event. This report of course places Levisohn there as well. Did this information mislead Abberline or was it in fact correct? Dr. Dutton is reported to have written that "Abberline for a long time thought that Pedachenko and Klosowski were one and the same person." If so, it would be a very good reason for Klosowski to change his name as well as his occupation. Perhaps he could ill afford to run into Wolff Levisohn again. It may also be why he could never admit to being Klosowski once he was arrested and why Abberline felt that at last the Ripper had indeed been captured.

Finally, Dr. Dutton wrote, "I have learned from a French doctor of a Russian junior surgeon, or feldscher, who was known to him in Paris about 1885–88. He was suspected of having killed and mutilated a grisette in Montmartre, but he left Paris before he could be arrested."

As for the man said to be named Alexander Pedachenko, there is no other information about this man in or around London after the Ripper murders. It was suggested that a similarly named individual went back to Russia, but the sources are equally mysterious.

Hard Evidence

Despite the fact that over 110 years have passed since the beginning of the Ripper series, there is much which can still be brought to light. Evidence could emerge of yet another victim living with Klosowski or being associated with him. There could of course still be a real Ripper diary, written in Polish, hidden in some long forgotten cubby hole or behind a wall in an old pub. Or perhaps a bundle of Ripper news articles with comments by the Ripper himself could still come out. Maybe the priest who took Klosowski's death cell confession wrote a few notes or a letter in which he left a clue to the murders.

However, the real, hard evidence would be the weapon's discovery, or the location of body parts in jars, in such a place or places as to render the identity of the Ripper beyond doubt. It may still be possible to knock down a wall in one of the pubs run by Klosowski, and find that hard evidence. He had to have concealed his parts somewhere, and his knife. DNA matching

SOUTHBANK - EAST END of LONDON

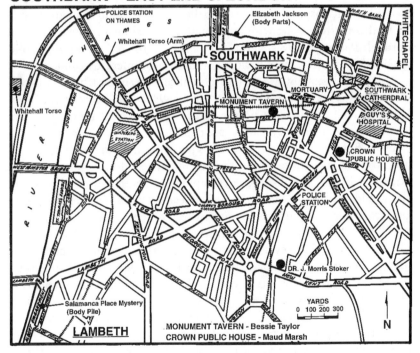

Locations of the victims of the Poison murders, and of body parts and torsos.

of body parts to descendants of the victims could be conclusive proof. But if body parts were found there would be little question as to who they belonged to. Blood on the letter from hell could also have been conclusive, had the original note not gone missing years ago. And, as mentioned before, a skull or two could be found on the property of 126 Cable Street, thus fully linking Klosowski with the Pinchin Street murder at the very least. It would also show that he was capable at the time of the Ripper murders of a vicious knife attack. And, the Crown public house building is still located at 213 Borough High Street. It still has its original basement!

Perhaps there is a Chapman or a Klosowski living today who has that old trunk once owned by their great grandfather many years ago. In it there may be surviving handwritten letters, penned by Klosowski while awaiting his execution, which could be compared with the letter "from hell" sent to George Lusk. Perhaps there is a piece of hair or other memento taken from one of the Ripper's victims. An interesting prospect to be sure, but would they want people to know that they were related to Jack the Ripper? Perhaps.

Real diaries of police officials may also come to light which could provide keys to the Ripper murders which, for some reason, were overlooked by the detectives themselves. Those of Inspector Abberline, who died at age 86 in 1929, and Inspector Godley, who died in 1941, would be of great interest in this matter, along with any notebooks used during the Ripper and Borough Poisoning investigations. Finding Klosowski's name in a police notebook from the Ripper period would be most interesting indeed.

As a final thought, we turn to ex–Police Superintendent Arthur Neil, who recorded his views on Klosowski in his 1932 work, *Forty Years of Man-Hunting*. Neil had worked on the Chapman case as an investigator and wrote: "We were never able to secure definite proof that Chapman was the 'Ripper.' But the strong theory remains just the same. No one, who had not been trained as a surgeon and medical man, could have committed the 'Ripper' crimes. As we discovered, Chapman had been a surgeon in Poland, and would, therefore, *be the only possible fiend capable of putting such trained knowledge into use against humanity*, instead of for it. 'Jack the Ripper' was a cold-blooded, inhuman monster, who killed for the sake of killing. The same could be said of Severino Klosowski, alias George Chapman, the Borough Poisoner. Why he took to poisoning his victims on his second visit to this country can only be ascribed to his diabolical cunning, or some insane idea or urge to satisfy his inordinate vanity. In any case, it is the most fitting and sensible solution to the possible identity of the murderer in one of the world's greatest crime mysteries. ... [As] every detective very quickly learns there are things you cannot prove in a court of law but of which you feel quite certain in your own mind. ... The only description ever given by an eye-witness of the Ripper tallied exactly with Chapman, even to the height, deep-sunk eyes, sallow complexion and thick black moustache."

It would seem that when all is said and done, the men who worked most closely on the Ripper and Borough Poisoning murders did indeed get their man, in both cases. The Ripper may not have officially paid for his first atrocities, but he most certainly paid the price for his last. In 1903, on the gallows of Wandsworth prison, Jack the Ripper was executed. And in the end, does it really matter what series of murders he was executed for, as long as justice was finally done?

> *"A man who could watch his wives being slowly tortured to death by poison, as he did, was capable of anything...."*
>
> Inspector Frederick George Abberline, 1903

Circumstantial — But More Than Enough to Convict

Is it conceivable that a convicted sexual serial killer, executed by hanging for three brutal murders, could be in all the same places at all the same times as the Ripper and not be the killer? Is it possible that Severin Klosowski was innocent, despite the fact that the murders began just when he came to London, and stopped just when he left? Would a demented man suddenly start murdering at the age of 31? Could it possibly be a coincidence that some of the victims were slaughtered practically in front of the houses he stayed in? The first death in the building he lived in cannot be a coincidence.

There is no smoking gun. There is no diary or written confession. But we do know who the mass murderer Jack the Ripper really was, beyond a reasonable doubt. No other suspect lived or worked closer to the victims, and none matched so perfectly the many descriptions given by eyewitnesses. Serial killers do not stop killing of their own accord. But they do change their techniques, and that is exactly what Klosowski did. The circumstantial evidence becomes overwhelming as it is constructed, piece by compelling piece.

A Review

EARLY BACKGROUND
• Grew up amid violence and uncertainty in his home in Poland
• Suspected of criminal activity at a young age

- Fully qualified as Surgeon's Assistant with "full knowledge of the subject"
- Evidence that he qualified as a Junior Surgeon; no evidence to the contrary (cut up bodies as he trained in Surgery)
- Torso murder in Paris, France, while he would have been travelling there, en route to England
- Paid hospital dues and then suddenly left his homeland
- Made no known contact with anyone in Poland after he left the country

TIME FRAME, MOVEMENTS AND LOCATIONS
- Arrived in London and, soon after, the Ripper attacks began
- Moved to Ripper area of Whitechapel just before Ripper murders began — left his job
- Lived near every single victim in the 1888 series, closer than any other suspect
- Worked in the central Ripper area throughout the Ripper murders
- Attempted to purchase poison just before Ripper murders
- Lived on the street and possibly in the very building where the first murder victim was found, putting him closer than any other suspect
- Torso murders began after he arrived in London's East End
- Lived and worked in the "great search area" but possibly moved during, or close to, the time of the search
- Ripper series ended when he left London for United States
- Torso murders were "suspended" when he left London for United States
- Late in the Ripper series his "wife" confirmed that he stayed out at night until three or four in the morning with no explanation
- Lived within yards of where Louis Diemschutz stabled his pony in George Yard (Stride murder)
- Moved around a great deal during the latter part of the Ripper series but was always near the Ripper murder sites; as he moved so did the murders
- Torso was located yards north of Klosowski's residence-workplace on Pinchin Street while body parts are found in River Thames just to the south
- October 1888 police believe the Ripper lived between Middlesex Street and Brick Lane — Klosowski lived *and* worked in that area
- Ripper style murder occurred in New York at about the time Klosowski was known to have moved there
- Ripper style murder occurred in New Jersey at the time Klosowski was known to have lived and worked there
- Klosowski had worked, and possibly lived, only five blocks from where Rose Mylett's body was found, fully two miles from Whitechapel

- Klosowski did not work at London Hospital, as he was hiding his surgical skills or had been prevented from working there
- Klosowski's "real wife" from Poland disappeared at about the time of Pinchin Street Torso murder
- Actions and movements of Ripper matched those of Klosowski in every single point including location of bodies, addresses of victims and timing of *all* events
- After Stride's murder the Ripper walked in direction of Klosowski's lodgings
- After Eddowes' murder the Ripper walked in direction of Klosowski's lodgings
- After Chapman's murder the Ripper walked in direction of Klosowski's lodgings
- Chapman continued to move around to avoid detection even after the Ripper series concluded
- Lived in George Yard Buildings, possibly at the same time as Mary Jane Kelly; a matching of victim to killer

SKILLS
- Spoke Yiddish, which allowed him to hide in Jewish area and pose as a Jew (Liz Stride spoke Yiddish)
- Ripper had surgical skills: Klosowski had them, too, whereas most East End residents did not
- Several murders required anatomical knowledge which Klosowski had
- Knew about poisons, and was trained in bloodletting and was complimented for his skills

GENERAL INFORMATION
- Convicted and executed serial murderer for three poison killings
- Methodical cold blooded killer — matched the psychological profile of Jack the Ripper exactly
- Used aliases to hide his identity several times
- Created a whole new identity after Ripper murders, upon his return to London
- Matched many witness descriptions of Ripper very closely, including composite drawing
- Matched witness descriptions of New York City killer very closely
- Matched witness description of New Jersey killer very closely
- Ripper had a regular job as did Klosowski
- Matched description *and* address of man seen at International Workingmen's Club before Stride murder

- Ripper is thought to have lived alone during 1888 series: Klosowski did
- Letter "from Hell" was crude and written by someone unfamiliar with the English language; Klosowski was unfamiliar with the English language
- Klosowski could have easily known Stride through her friend Charles Preston, a fellow local barber working only three blocks from Klosowski's lodgings
- Possibly lived with the daughter of Ripper victim, Chapman, taking her name as his own
- Attacked his wife with a knife identical to Ripper weapon
- Klosowski's clothes matched that of the Ripper; i.e., he was a good dresser
- Klosowski was a violent misogynist, as was the Ripper
- Only suspect who is known to have been violent continuously towards women
- Threatened to murder women several times
- Owned "secret black bag" which could have been carried on his murders
- Torso murders ended only after Klosowski was arrested and executed

Finally, there is *no known evidence* which excludes Klosowski in any way. Before he changed his name, his addresses, his identity, his marital status, his country, and his killing style, Severino Antonovich Klosowski was, Alias — Jack the Ripper!

Chronology of a
Serial Killer

Severin Klosowski, alias George Chapman,
alias the Borough Poisoner, alias Jack the Ripper

Poland

December 14, 1865 —   Severin Klosowski is born in the village of Nagornak,
                        Poland.

1880 —   Severin is apprenticed at the age of 14 to Moshko Rap-
                        paport and will serve his apprenticeship until 1885.
                        Rappaport is a Senior Surgeon in Zvolen, Poland.

1885 —   Klosowski moves to Warsaw, Poland, after completing
                        his apprenticeship. He carries a certificate signed by
                        Rappaport which states that he is "diligent, of exem-
                        plary conduct, and studied with zeal the science of
                        surgery."

October 1885 —   Klosowski attends a practical surgery course at the Praga
                        Hospital, Warsaw.

1885–1887 —   Klosowski works as an assistant-surgeon or feldscher in
                        Warsaw, Poland.

1887 —   Klosowski qualifies as Junior Surgeon, but no certificate
                        could be located in his files.

February 1887 —   Klosowski pays hospital fees, confirmed by receipt. Last
                        confirmed paper trail of Klosowski in Poland.

Poland/England

March–June 1887 —	Best guess period for immigration of Klosowski to London, England. He speaks little or no English, and moves to one of the most crowded and crime ridden areas of London. It would be easy for him to hide in this mostly Jewish area as he did speak Yiddish and was posing as a Jew. He was actually Roman Catholic.
May 1887 —	*The Rainham Murder*
Late 1887–early 88 —	Klosowski begins work as an assistant hairdresser in Abraham Radin's shop at 70 West India Dock Road, Poplar. He holds this job for around five months. It is during this period that he helps nurse Mrs. Radin's oldest son who is ill. A qualified surgeon is now working as a hairdresser.
February 25, 1888 —	*Annie Millwood* is attacked by a knife-wielding man. "The man was a stranger."
March 28, 1888 —	*Ada Wilson* is attacked by a man with a knife and stabbed twice in the neck. She survives the attack to report that the man was a stranger and describes her attacker.
1888–1890 —	Wolff Levisohn visits Klosowski at a hairdresser's shop in Whitechapel. They speak in Yiddish. Klosowski tries to buy "a certain medicine."
Summer 1888 —	Klosowski works at a barbershop in Whitechapel and lives in George Yard buildings. Confirmed by police to be living in a cheap lodging house, c. July 1888.
August 7, 1888 —	*Martha Tabram* is murdered in George Yard Buildings. She lived on George Street. First successful Ripper murder.
August 11, 1888 —	St. Judes Vigilance Committee is formed.
August 20, 1888 —	*Murder of woman* whose torso would be found on October 3.
August 31, 1888 —	*Mary Ann "Polly" Nichols* is murdered in Buck's Row. Lived on Flower and Dean Street.
September 1, 1888 —	Nichols inquest begins.
September 8, 1888 —	*Annie Chapman* is murdered in backyard of 29 Hanbury St. She lived on Dorset Street.
September 8, 1888 —	Inspector Abberline assumes street level command of Ripper investigation.
September 9, 1888 —	James Monro's secret department begins search for Ripper.
September 10, 1888 —	Mile End Vigilance Committee formed.
September 12, 1888 —	Chapman inquest begins.

September 16, 1888 —	Whitechapel Vigilance Committee requests that the Home Secretary increase the amount of money then being offered as reward for the Ripper's capture.
September 27, 1888 —	Central News Agency receives letter using the name "Jack the Ripper" for the first time.
September 30, 1888 —	*Elizabeth Stride* is murdered in Dutfield's yard off Berner Street. She had lived on Flower and Dean Street.
September 30, 1888 —	*Catherine Eddowes* is murdered in Mitre Square. She lived on Flower and Dean Street.
September 30, 1888 —	Whitechapel Vigilance Committee requests an official reward be offered by the Home Office for the Whitechapel killer.
October 1, 1888 —	Stride inquest begins.
October 1, 1888 —	Bloodstained knife with nine-inch blade is found in Whitechapel Road.
October 1, 1888 —	The Lord Mayor offers a £500 reward for the Whitechapel killer along with a £300 reward offered by the Financial News.
October 3, 1888 —	*Headless Torso* dumped on building site of New Scotland Yard.
October 4, 1888 —	Eddowes inquest begins.
October 7, 1888 —	George Lusk suggests a pardon be granted by the Home Office. Home Secretary Henry Matthews rejects suggestion.
October 13, 1888 —	House to house search operations begin.
October 16, 1888 —	George Lusk receives a package in the mail which contains the "letter from hell" and half a kidney thought to have come from the body of Catharine Eddowes.
November 9, 1888 —	*Mary Jane Kelly* is murdered in her room off Dorset Street.
November 12, 1888 —	Home Office offers pardon to "anyone other than the murderer."
November 12, 1888 —	Kelly inquest — one day.
December 20, 1888 —	*Rose Mylett* is strangled by cord.
January 2, 1889 —	Mylett inquest begins.
Late 1888–early 1889 —	Klosowski is now running a hairdresser's shop at 126 Cable Street.
c. June 2, 1889 —	*Elizabeth Jackson* is killed, parts of her body are found in the Thames June 2–25.
June–July 1889 —	Stanislaus Baderski meets Klosowski at a Polish Club.
July 17, 1889 —	*Alice McKenzie* is murdered in Castle Alley. She lived at 52–54 Gun Street.

July 17, 1889 —	McKenzie inquest begins.
July 25, 1889 —	Letter arrives at Scotland Yard signed "Jack the Ripper."
August 1889 —	Lucy Baderski moves in with Klosowski on Cable Street.
September 10, 1889 —	*Woman's headless torso* found on Pinchin Street across tracks from Klosowski's shop.
October 29, 1889 —	Klosowski marries Lucy Baderski. She reports that he stays out until 3 or 4 A.M.
September 1890 —	Klosowski lives with Lucy at barbershop at 89 Whitechapel High Street, under a pub.
February 13, 1891—	*Frances Coles* is murdered very near Klosowski's old shop on Cable Street.
February 15, 1891—	Coles inquest begins.
March 3, 1891—	Klosowski's son Wohystaw dies of pneumonia asthenia. Family was living at 2 Tewkesbury Buildings, Whitechapel.
April 5, 1891—	National census of 1891 shows Klosowski supposedly still living in Whitechapel.

England/United States

c. April 1891—	Klosowski and Lucy move to New York City only weeks after the last Ripper murder.
April 24–25, 1891—	*Carrie Brown* is murdered in New York City. Killing closely resembles the Ripper murders.
April–May 1891—	Klosowski and Lucy move to Jersey City and he works in a barbershop.
July 3, 1891—	Ameer Ben Ali falsely convicted of Carrie Brown's murder.
January 31, 1892 —	*Elizabeth Senior* is murdered in New Jersey. Killing closely resembles the Ripper murders.
February 1892 —	Klosowski's wife Lucy leaves him and returns to England after he threatens to cut off her head with knife she found under his pillow. Klosowski was "seeing" other women.
Summer 1892 —	Ripper case is inactive and is closed by Scotland Yard.

United States/England

May 15, 1892 —	Second child of Klosowski, Cecilia, is born in Whitechapel, East End, London.
c. June 1, 1892 —	Klosowski arrives back in London for a short reunion with his wife. May have lived at 26 Scarborough Street, Whitechapel.

1892–1893 —	Klosowski leaves no trace for half of 1892 and most of 1893.
End of 1893 —	Annie Chapman meets Klosowski. He is working at Haddin's hairdresser's shop at 5 West Green Road, South Tottenham.
November 1893– December 1894 —	Annie Chapman lives with Klosowski, possibly at Haddin's shop.
Fall 1894 —	Klosowski brings in a second woman to live with him and Annie Chapman.
December 1894 —	Annie Chapman leaves Klosowski, because of the second woman, and is pregnant.
Early 1895 —	Klosowski buys a house on High Road, Tottenham.
February 1895 —	Annie Chapman seeks support from Klosowski for his third child; he takes no notice.
Early 1895 —	Klosowski now takes on the alias of George Chapman; lives with Renton family.
Mid 1895– early 1896 —	Klosowski becomes assistant barber of shop at 7 Church Lane, Leytonstone owned by Wenzel. Works for six or seven months.
c. October 1895 —	Klosowski lodges at a house on Forest Road owned by John Ward.
October 27, 1895 —	Klosowski and Mrs. Spink report that they have been married. She hands over to Klosowski £250 from trustees.
c. March 1896 —	Klosowski uses Spink's money to lease a barbershop in Hastings.
February 1897 —	Klosowski and Spink move to 1 Coburg Place, Hastings.
c. February 1897 —	Klosowski buys a boat which capsizes and Spink almost drowns.
February 1897 —	A servant girl named Alice Penfold is courted by Klosowski. He informs her that he is single and that he is the manager of a pianoforte shop.
April 3, 1897 —	Klosowski purchases one ounce of tartar emetic poison at William Davidson's chemist shop at 66 High Street, Hastings.
Fall 1897 —	Klosowski returns to London and leases the Prince of Wales public house in Bartholomew Square off City Road.
Fall 1897 —	Balance of Spink's money is paid to "Mr. & Mrs. Chapman." Spink becomes ill from slow poisoning.
December 25, 1897 —	*Mary Spink* is murdered by poison. After she is dead Klosowski goes to open his pub.

April 1898 —	Klosowski advertises for a new barmaid. Bessie Taylor answers the ad and is hired.
c. June 1898 —	Klosowski and Bessie Taylor create a bogus marriage and are now "Mr. and Mrs. Chapman."
Late 1898 —	Klosowski and Taylor move to Bishops Stortford for a short stay. Klosowski gives up the Prince of Wales and leases the Grapes.
Before Christmas 1898 —	A friend of Bessie's visits, Elizabeth Painter. Later reports that Klosowski threatened Bessie with a revolver.
March 1899 —	Klosowski and Taylor move to the Monument public house on Union Street, Southwark, London.
December 1900 —	Bessie's brother William visits at Monument. Klosowski begins to beat Bessie.
February 13, 1901—	*Bessie Taylor* is murdered by poison.
August 1901—	Eighteen year old Maud Marsh is hired by Klosowski as new barmaid at the Monument.
September 13, 1901—	Klosowski again creates a bogus marriage with Marsh. Now living as "Mr. and Mrs. Chapman." Klosowski begins to beat Maud.
Late 1901—	Klosowski tries to burn down the Monument for insurance money.
Before December 25, 1901—	Klosowski moves into the Crown public house at 213 Borough High Street with Maud Marsh. He is one mile from Whitechapel.
April 17, 1902 —	Ameer Ben Ali is pardoned for the Carrie Brown murder.
June 1902 —	Klosowski hires Florence Rayner as a barmaid. He asks her to go to America with him. He is preparing to leave the country.
June 1902 —	Klosowski falsely accuses Alfred Clark and Matilda Gilmor of conspiracy to defraud him of £700. Clark is convicted but later released.
June 1902 —	*Salamanca Place Torso murder*
October 22, 1902 —	*Maud Marsh* is murdered by poison. The final murder.
October 23, 1902 —	Klosowski asks Maud's sister to be his new barmaid.
October 25, 1902 —	Klosowski is arrested by Inspector George Godley for Maud Marsh's murder.
March 16, 1903 —	Klosowski trial begins.
March 20, 1903 —	Klosowski is convicted of Maud Marsh's murder. Jury takes 11 minutes to convict.
April 7, 1903 —	*Severino Antonovich Klosowski* goes to the scaffold at Wandsworth Prison.

Appendix 2

Victims of a Serial Killer

c. May 1887	Unknown	First torso murder. Body parts found near River Thames
February 25, 1888	Annie Millwood (1850–1888)	Stab wounds on legs and lower torso with a clasp knife. (Survived the attack)
March 28, 1888	Ada Wilson (1849–)	At home when attacked by an unknown man. Stabbed twice in the throat. (Survived the attack)
August 7, 1888	Martha Tabram (1849–1888)	39 stab wounds: 5 in left lung, 2 in right lung, 1 in heart, 5 in liver, 2 in spleen, 6 in stomach
c. August 20, 1888	Unknown	Headless torso dumped at building site of New Scotland Yard
August 31, 1888	Mary Ann Nichols (1845–1888)	Throat cut down to the vertebrae, abdomen cut several times
September 8, 1888	Annie Chapman (1841–1888)	Strangled? Throat cut deeply, abdomen laid open, uterus, upper vagina and posterior two-thirds of bladder taken
September 30, 1888	Elizabeth Stride (1843–1888)	Throat cut deeply, not mutilated
September 30, 1888	Catherine Eddowes (1842–1888)	Throat cut deeply, face mutilated, body opened from breast bone to pubes, liver stabbed, kidney and womb taken
November 9, 1888	Mary Jane Kelly (1863–1888)	Attacked inside. Throat cut deeply, body and face greatly

323

		mutilated, parts removed, heart taken, most mutilated victim
December 20, 1888	Rose Mylett (1863–1888)	Strangled by cord
c. May 31, 1889	Elizabeth Jackson (–1889)	Headless torso, parts of her body were found in the Thames River from May 31–June 25, 1889
July 17, 1889	Alice McKenzie (1849–1889)	Stabbed twice in throat, cut on chest from left breast to navel
c. September 8, 1889	Unknown (Lydia Hart ?)	Headless torso found on Pinchin Street. Abdomen mutilated, missing womb
February 13, 1891	Frances Coles (1865–1891)	Throat cut. Alive when found, but died on stretcher
April 24, 1891	Carrie Brown (1829–1891)	USA. Strangled, mutilated with a knife similar to Kelly murder
January 31, 1892	Elizabeth Senior (1819–1892)	USA. Strangled, throat cut and stabbed 11 times
December 25, 1897	Mary Spink (1856–1897)	Poisoned by antimony
February 13, 1901	Bessie Taylor (1865–1901)	Poisoned by antimony
c. June, 1902	Unknown	Torso and body parts dumped at Salamanca Place, mutilated
October 22, 1902	Maud Marsh (1884–1902)	Poisoned by antimony

Descriptions of Jack the Ripper

Witness	*Description*
Annie Millwood:	The man was a stranger.
Ada Wilson:	He was a man of around 30 years of age with a sunburnt face, fair mustache, standing 5'6" in height.
Elizabeth Long: (from behind)	Dark complexion, and was wearing a brown deerstalker hat. He was a man over forty, as far as I can tell. He seemed a little taller than the deceased. He looked to me like a foreigner as well as I could make out. He looked what I should call shabby genteel.
Joseph Lawende:	30 years old, 5'7" in height, fair complexion and mustache, medium build, wearing a salt and pepper colored jacket fitting loosely, gray cloth cap with a peak of the same color. Reddish handkerchief knotted around his neck.
Matthew Parker:	Age 25 to 30 years old, 5'7" tall. Long black coat buttoned up, soft felt hawker hat, broad shoulders.
P. C. William Smith:	5'7" tall, hard dark felt deerstalker hat, dark clothes. Carried newspaper package 18" × 7". 28 years old, dark complexion, small dark mustache.
James Brown:	5'5" tall, age 30, dark complexion, small mustache, black diagonal coat, hard felt hat, collar and tie.
Israel Schwartz:	Age 30, 5'5" tall, dark haired, fair complexion, small brown mustache, full face, broad shoulders, dark jacket and trousers, black cap with peak.
George Hutchinson:	Age 34–35, 5'6". Pale complexion, dark hair, slight mustache curled at each end, long dark coat, collar cuffs of

	astrakhan, dark jacket underneath. Light waistcoat, thick gold chain with a red stone seal, dark trousers and button boots, gaiters, white buttons. White shirt, black tie fastened with a horseshoe pin. Dark hat, turned down in the middle. Red kerchief. Jewish and respectable in appearance.
Mary Miniter: (United States)	Around 32 years old, 5'8" tall, slim build, long sharp nose, heavy mustache of light color, foreign in appearance, possibly German. Dark brown cutaway coat, black trousers, old black derby hat w/dented crown. Speaks broken English.
Mr. Kelly: (United States)	About five feet nine inches in height, light complexion, long nose and light mustache, wore a shabby cutaway coat and a shabby old derby hat. He was smeared with blood. Pronounced German accent.

With Klosowski, who was not a tall man, living and working in the central Ripper area and matching several descriptions of the killer, it must be asked why he was never picked up as a suspect. He had to have been at least generally known in the area since he worked in a local barbershop. And he would have been noticed in any of the pubs in the general area. Also, with all of the enquires, he must have been questioned by the police face-to-face more than once. Why then was he not captured? There is a possible clue to be found in the reports of a mustache. The description of the mustache changes even as the general description of the man himself holds relatively steady. Most of the witnesses who saw part or all of his face describe the mustache. Could it be that the murderer never had a mustache and used false ones as part of a disguise? Any man in the general area with a real mustache would have been looked at with suspicion, but a man without a mustache could have easily walked among the people and the police and not have been suspected. With a change of clothes and different false mustaches he could have kept up the game for a very long time. It could have been a completely successful strategy.

Appendix 4

Report on
"The Whitechapel Murder"
(Facsimile)

Report by James Monro, Commissioner of Police, to J. S. Sandaes, private secretary to Home Secretary Henry Matthews. This report, filed September 16, 1889, was sealed until 1990.

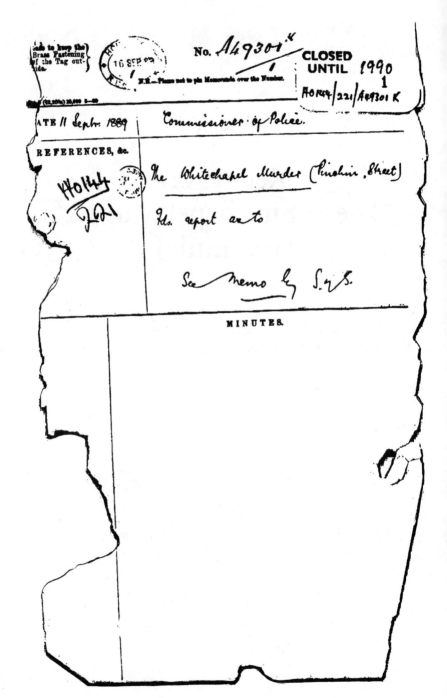

No. A49301 K

CLOSED
UNTIL 1990
1
HOR4/221/A49301 K

DATE 11 Septr. 1889   Commissioner of Police.

REFERENCES, &c.

HO144
221

The Whitechapel Murder (Pinchin Street)

Fds. report as to

See memo by S.q.S.

MINUTES.

Sep. 11. 89.

Mr. Sandars.

I communicated to you yesterday the finding of the trunk of a female, minus head legs in one of the railway arches in Pinchin Street.

This street is close to Berner Street which was the scene of one of the previous Whitechapel murders. It is not a very narrow street, but is lonely at night. & is patrolled every half hour by a constable on beat. The arch where the body was found abuts on the pavement —

The Constable discovered the body somewhat after 20 minutes past five on the morning of Tuesday. As was in consequence of the pressure for men in Whitechapel just now: working part of two beats in addition to his own, but been so he passed & he passed the spot every half hour. As is positive

3

That when he passed the spot about five the body was not there. I am inclined to accept his statement thoroughly, for from another circumstance which has come to my knowledge he evidently was on the alert that night. It may therefore be assumed that the body was placed where it was found some time between 5 & 5.30 a.m. of Tuesday the 11th.

Although the body was placed in the arch on Tuesday morning, the murder — (and altho' there is not as yet before me proof of the cause of death, I assume that there has been a murder) was not committed there nor then — There was almost no blood in the arch, and the state of the body itself showed that death took place abt 36 hours or more previously — This then enables us to say that the woman was made away with probably on Sunday night, the 8th September. This was the date on which one of the previous Whitechapel murders was committed —

4

The body then must have been concealed, where the murder was committed during Sunday night, Monday, or Tuesday up till dawn. This leads to the inference that it was so concealed in some place to which the murderer had access, over which he had control and from which he was anxious to remove the corpse. He may say then that the murder was committed probably in the house or lodging of the murderer, and that he conveyed the portion found to Pinchin Street to get rid of it from his lodging where the odour of decomposition would soon betray him —

Why did he take the trunk to Whitechapel and what does the finding of the body there show? If this is a fresh outrage by the Whitechapel murderer known by the horribly familiar nickname of Jack the Ripper the answer would not be difficult, aitho this murder, committed in the murderers house &c.

5

be a new departure from the system hitherto pursued by this ruffian. I am however inclined to believe that this case is not the work of the "Ripper". What has characterized the previous cases has been death caused by cutting the throat – b/ mutilation. c/ evisceration. d/ removal of certain parts of the body. e/. murder committed in the street, except in one instance in Dorset Street. In this last case there was evidence of a serious mania. The murderer, having plenty of time at his disposal slashed and cut the body in all directions, evidently under the influence of frenzy.

In the present case, so far as the medical evidence goes there is a/. nothing to show that death was caused by cutting the throat. b/. There is no mutilation as in previous cases, altho' there is dismemberment. c/ There is no evisceration. d/. There is no removal of any portion of the organs of generation or intestines. e/. The murder was indubitably committed neither

6

in the street, nor in the victims house, but probably in the lodging of the murderer. Here where there was as in the previous case of murder in a house, plenty of time at the disposal of the murderer, there is no sign of frenzied mutilation of the body - but of deliberate or skilful dismemberment with a view to removal. These are all very striking departures from the practice of the Whitechapel murderer, and if the body had been found elsewhere than in Whitechapel the supposition that death had been caused by the Ripper would probably not have been entertained.

But the body has been found in Whitechapel and there is a gash on the front part extending downwards to the organs of generation - and we have to account for these facts - I place little importance on the gash; it seems to me not to have been inflicted as in the previous cases - The inner coating of the bowel is hardly touched, and the termination of the cut towards the vagina looks almost as if he

knife had slipped, and that as of that portion
of the wound had been accidental. The whole of
the wound looks as if the murderer had intended
to make a cut preparatory to removing the
intestines in the process of dismemberment, & had then
changed his mind. Had this been the work of the
previous frenzied murderer we may be tolerably sure that he
would have continued his hideous work in the way which
he previously adopted. It may also be that the
gash was inflicted to give rise to the impression that
this case was the work of the Whitechapel murderer
& so divert attention from the real assassin.

As to how the body got to Whitechapel
this is a great difficulty unless it be supposed that
it was removed in some conveyance & placed where it
was found. & unless it be supposed that the murderer—
being other than the "Ripper" had good knowledge of

8
END

the locality. I may get some light on this point as the Case goes on — Meanwhile I am inclined to the belief that, taking one thing with another, this is not the work of the Whitechapel Murderer but of the hand which was concerned in the murders which are known as the Rainham mystery — the New Police buildings case — and the recent case in which portions of a female body (afterwards identified) were found in the Thames —

Sep. 11. 89 .   *[signature]*

Thank Mr [   ] for his Report.
H. M.
12 Sept. 89

Appendix 5

Letters from the
Jack the Ripper Files

The Dear Boss letter. First reference to "Jack the Ripper." No "Ripper" letter was ever written by the killer.

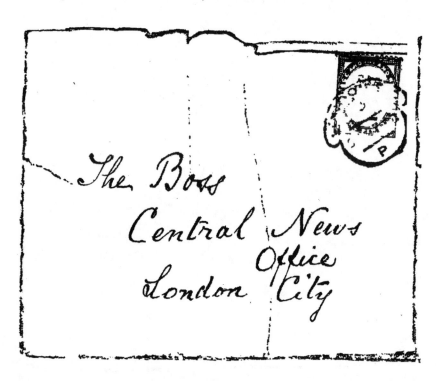

25. Sept 1888

Dear Boss

   I keep on hearing the police
have caught me but they wont fix
me just yet. I have laughed when
they look so clever and talk about
being on the right track. That joke
about Leather apron gave me real
fits. I am down on whores and
I shant quit ripping them till I
do get buckled. Grand work the last
job was. I gave the lady no time to
squeal. How can they catch me now
I love my work and want to start
again. you will soon hear of me
with my funny little games. I
saved some of the proper red stuff in
a ginger beer bottle over the last job
to write with but it went thick
like glue and I cant use it. Red
ink is fit enough I hope ha. ha.
The next job I do I shall clip
the ladys ears off and send to the

police officers just for jolly wouldnt
you . Keep this letter back till I
do a bit more work then give
it out straight. My knifes so nice
and sharp I want to get to work
right away if I get a chance.
Good luck .

               yours truly
                   Jack the Ripper

Dont mind me giving the trade name

Facsimile of the letter from Hell. The only letter ever written by the killer about his series of deaths.

Bibliography

The Press

The *Times* [London]
   August 10, 1888 — The Murder in Whitechapel
   August 24, 1888 — Inquests
   September 1, 1888 — Another Murder in Whitechapel
   September 3, 1888 — The Whitechapel Murder
   September 4, 1888 — The Whitechapel Murder
   September 10, 1888 — The Whitechapel Murders
   September 11, 1888 — The Whitechapel Murders
   September 15, 1888 — The Whitechapel Murders
   November 10, 1888 — Another Whitechapel Murder
   March 17, 1903
   March 18, 1903
   March 19, 1903
   March 20, 1903
   April 8, 1903 — Execution — Severino Klosowski

The *New York Times*
   September 1, 1888 — A Terribly Brutal Murder in Whitechapel
   September 9, 1888 — Whitechapel Startled by a Fourth Murder
   October 1, 1888 — Dismay in Whitechapel
   October 2, 1888 — London's Awful Mystery
   October 3, 1888 — London's Record of Crime
   October 5, 1888 — The Whitechapel Murder Mysteries
   October 7, 1888
   November 10, 1888 — Exciting London Events
   December 11, 1888 — Is This Jack the Ripper?
   July 18, 1889 — The Whitechapel Crime
   July 21, 1889 — Gossip of the Day Abroad

September 11, 1889 — Another London Murder
February 13, 1891 — Jack the Ripper Again
February 14, 1891 — The Whitechapel Mystery
April 28, 1891 — The Murderer Still at Large
April 25, 1891 — Choked, Then Mutilated
April 26, 1891 — Byrnes Says He Had a Clue
April 29, 1891 — Byrnes Quite Mystified
June 27, 1891 — Jury Ready for "Frenchy" No. 1
July 1, 1891 — "Frenchy's" Varied Stories
July 2, 1891 — Experts Against "Frenchy"
July 3, 1891 — "Frenchy's" Trial Nearly Over
July 4, 1891 — "Frenchy" Found Guilty
February 1, 1892 — A Brutal New Jersey Murder
February 4, 1892 — The Murder of Mrs. Senior
February 7, 1892 — The Senior Murder
February 18, 1892 — The Murder of Mrs. Senior
June 9, 1892
April 26, 1892 — An Elizabeth Officer's Encounter with an Unknown Man
April 17, 1902 — "Frenchy" Is Pardoned

The London *Evening News*
October 2, 1888

The *South London Observer*
November 1, 1902 — Southwark Poisoning Mystery
November 2, 1902 — Publican Charged with Murder

The *South London Press*
March 21, 1903 — Southwark Murder

The *East London Advertiser*
August 11, 1888
August 18, 1888
September 8, 1888

The *Los Angeles Times*
October 1, 1888 — London Alarmed — The Whitechapel Fiend Again at Work
November 10, 1888 — The Whitechapel Fiend
November 11, 1888 — Latest Device to Trap the Whitechapel Murderer

The *East End News*
October 5, 1888

The *Weekly Herald*
August 17, 1888 — A Mysterious Murder
September 7, 1888 — Horrible Murder of a Woman
September 14, 1888 — Another London Tragedy
September 28, 1888 — A Terrible Murder at Gateshead
October 5, 1888 — London's Horrors
October 26, 1888 — The "Ripper" Scare in Aberdeen

November 16, 1888 — A Woman Fiendishly Mutilated
December 7, 1888 — The Whitechapel Fiend

The *Eastern Post*
February 25, 1888

The *Police Gazette*
October 19, 1888

The *Echo*
August 20, 1888

The *Daily Telegraph*
October 4, 1888 — The Whitehall Murder
October 5, 1888 — Whitehall Tragedy
November 12, 1888

The *Illustrated Police News*
August 24, 1888
September 8, 1888 — The Murder in Whitechapel
November 17, 1888 — Intense Excitement in the East-End
November 24, 1888 — Is He the Murderer?

The London *Observer*
October 9, 1888

The *Star*
August 31, 1888 — A Revolting Murder
September 8, 1888 — Horror Upon Horror
October 19, 1888

The *Manchester Guardian*
November 10, 1888 — Another Whitechapel Murder

South London Observer
November 1, 1902 — Southwark Poisoning Mystery
November 2, 1902 — Publican Charged with Murder

The South London Press
March 21, 1903 — Southwark Murder

The *Pall Mall Gazette*
November 10, 1888
December 31, 1888
November 4, 1889
March 24, 1903
March 31, 1903

The *Daily Chronicle*
March 23, 1903

The *Police Chronicle*
October 6, 1888

The Writers and Researchers

Adam, Hargrave L., ed. *The Trial of George Chapman.* London: William Hodge & Company, April 1930.

_____, ed. *The Trial of George Chapman.* Toronto, Canada: Canada Law Book Company, 1930.

Altick, Richard D. *Victorian Studies in Scarlet.* New York: W. W. Norton, 1970.

Anderson, Robert. *The Lighter Side of My Official Life.* Hodder and Stoughton, 1910.

Begg, Paul. *Jack the Ripper — The Uncensored Facts.* London: Robson Books 1988.

_____, Martin Fido and Keith Skinner. *The Jack the Ripper A to Z.* London: Headline Book Publishing, 1994.

Borchard, Edwin M. *Convicting the Innocent.* Hamden, Connecticut: Archon Books, 1961 (1932).

Cullen, Tom A. *When London Walked in Terror.* Boston: Houghton Mifflin, 1965.

Dew, Walter. *I Caught Crippen.* London: Blackier & Son, 1938.

Fido, Martin. *The Crimes, Detection and Death of Jack the Ripper.* London: George Weidenfeld and Nicolson, 1987.

_____. *Murder Guide to London.* London: George Weidenfeld & Nicolson, 1986.

Fishman, W. J. *East End 1888 — Life in a London Borough Among the Laboring Poor.* Philadelphia: Temple University Press, 1988.

Hooper, W. Eden. *The History of Newgate and the Old Bailey.* London: Underwood Press, 1935.

Jones, Richard Glyn. *Unsolved Classic True Murder Cases.* New York: Peter Bedrick Books, 1987.

London, Jack. *The People of the Abyss.* Sonoma State University, California: Joseph Simon, 1980 (1903).

Nash, Jay Robert. *Almanac of World Crime.* Garden City, New York: Anchor Press/Doubleday, 1981.

O'Donnell, Elliott. *Great Thames Mysteries.* London: Selwyn and Blount, 1928.

Rumbelow, Donald. *Jack the Ripper — The Complete Casebook.* Chicago: Contemporary Books, 1988.

Smith, Henry Smith. *From Constable to Commissioner. The Story of Sixty Years, Most of Them Misspent.* Chatto and Windus, 1910.

Sugden, Philip. *The Complete History of Jack the Ripper.* New York: Carroll and Graf, 1995.

Tully, James. *Prisoner 1167 — The Madman Who Was Jack the Ripper.* New York: Carroll and Graf, 1997.

Wilson, Colin. *A Casebook of Murder.* New York: Cowles, 1969.

_____, and Patricia Pitman. *Encyclopaedia of Murder.* London & Sydney: Pan Books, 1961.

The Documents

Booth, Charles. *Descriptive Map of London Poverty.* 1889, Volume 1. Reprint, Stanford's Geography, London, 1969.

Macnaghten, Melville. Macnaghten's Memorandum. February 23, 1894.
Warren, Charles. Letter to the Under Secretary of State. November 6, 1888.

Personal Documents held by Severino Antonovich Klosowski
- Birth Certificate, December 15, 1865
- Primary School Report, December 7–19, 1880
- Society of Surgeons Receipt, October 23–November 5, 1882
- Magistrate's Conduct Certificate, November 16, 1882
- Surgical Pupil Registry Receipt, November 22–December 3, 1882
- Apprentice Certificate, June 1, 1885
- Instruction Certificate, April 29, 1886
- Employment Certificate, November 15, 1886
- Employment Certificate, November 24–December 6, 1886
- Klosowski Personal Biography, November 15, 1886
- Passport, November 24, 1886
- Junior Surgeon Degree Petition, December 1886
- Junior Surgeon Degree Acceptance, December 5, 1886
- Hospital Fees Receipt, February 28, 1887

The Official Files

Public Record Office, Kew

METROPOLITAN POLICE:
- MEPO 3/140 — Whitechapel Murder Files
- MEPO 3/142 — "Jack the Ripper" Letters
- MEPO 3/153 — Post-Mortem — Mary Kelly; "Dear Boss" Letter; Pinchin Street News Report; Murder Pardon — Kelly Murder
- MEPO 3/155 — Whitechapel Murder Victims — Photos

(This material in the Public Record Office is the copyright of the Metropolitan Police and is reproduced by permission of the Commissioner of Police of the Metropolis.)

HOME OFFICE:
- HO 144/221/A49301 F — Mary Kelly Murder
- HO 144/221/A49301 H — Rose Mylett Murder
- HO 144/221/A49301 I — Alice McKenzie Murder
- HO 144/221/A49301 K — Pinchin Street Torso Murder
- HO 144/680/101992 — George Chapman Poison Case

PUBLIC RECORD OFFICE, CHANCERY LANE
- CRIM 1/84 — George Chapman Poison Case, Depositions
- CRIM 4/1215 — George Chapman Poison Case, Indictments

The Internet

Casebook

HTTP://RIPPER.WILDNET.CO.UK/MAIN.HTM.

Index

Caunter, Eli 44
Chandler, Joseph 73, 74
Chapman, Annie 5, 64–74, 197, 218,
  248; burial 85; description 66
Chapman, Annie Georgina 66, 85, 248,
  249, 297
Chapman, George (alias of Severino
  Klosowski) 38, 39, 111, 249–280;
  abuse of partners 252, 257, 258, 259,
  272–4; arrest for murder 277, 279,
  300; arson 265–6; black bag 253; buys
  poison 253–4; convicted of murder
  302; fraud 266; residences 250, 251,
  252, 255, 257, 259; see also Kloskow-
  ski, Severino Antonovich
Chapman, John 66
Charles, Benjamin 38
Chronicles of Crime 14, 144, 184, 308–10
Clapp, George 108
Clark, Alfred 266, 267, 269, 282
Clark, Percy John 200
Clark's Yard 179, 180
"Clay Pipe" see McKenzie, Alice
Coles, Frances 206–13, 220; description
  206
Colimouski, Marianna 10
Collier, George 41, 43, 77
Collins, Albert 102
The Complete History of Jack the Ripper
  176–7
Connolly, Mary Ann "Pearly Poll" 36,
  44, 45
Conway, Thomas 103
Coram, Thomas 117
Cosgrove, [Detective] 243
Cotter, P.G. 276
Cowdry, Samuel and Sarah 48
Cox, John 270
Cox, Mary Ann 155, 156, 159
Crawford, Henry H. 129
Cross, Charles 51, 61
Crossingham's Lodging House 67, 68
Crown (pub) 267, 271, 272, 277, 283,
  286, 293–4, 298; search of 280–1
Crow, George 40
Cullen, Tom 144
Cutbush, Thomas 217–8

Danford, G. 22
Davidson, William Henry 253, 254,
  282, 293, 295

Davis, John 70, 71, 82
"Dear Boss" letters 91–2, 189
death certificates: Eddowes 126; Kelly
  171; Nichols 55
Descriptive Map of London Poverty 1889
  49
Dew, Thomas 47
Dew, Walter 21, 74, 131, 149, 160, 222; I
  Caught Crippen 131
Diemschutz, Louis 98–9, 100, 101, 102
Diemschutz, Mrs. 101
documents: Bond's medical report
  168–70; Home Office phone call
  report 163; Macnaghten's memoran-
  dum 201, 217–20; Monro's report 199,
  327–35; poison label 254; Swanson's
  marginalia 214–6; Warren's handwrit-
  ten murder pardon 167; Warren's
  report to the Home Office 138
Donovan, Timothy 68, 83
Doubleday, Martha 256
Drage, Joseph 117
Druitt, M.J. 6, 215, 219
Dunscombe, T. 132
Dushevitch, Mr. 11
Dutfield's Yard 97, 98, 102
Dutton, Thomas 14, 144, 184, 308–10

Eagle, Morris 97, 101
Eddowes, Catherine 5, 6, 102–9, 125–8,
  218; burial 132
Edwards, Edgar 304
Elliot, George [Attorney] 290, 301
Elliot, George [Constable Detective] 210
Encyclopedia of Murder 14
Evans, John 68, 83

Faircloth, John 185, 186
Farmer, Annie 177
Fido, Martin 38
Fisher, L.E. 187
Fitzgerald, Edward 228
Foresters Tavern 269
Fraser, James 118, 119
Freemasons 57, 89, 128, 129
"Frenchy" see Ali, Ameer Ben
Frying Pan 50

George Yard 38, 39, 48, 99
George Yard Buildings (George Yard
  Dwellings) 36, 37, 43, 65, 143